Innovative Technologies and Services for Smart Cities

Innovative Technologies and Services for Smart Cities

Special Issue Editors

Subhas Mukhopadhyay
Tarikul Islam

MDPI • Basel • Beijing • Wuhan • Barcelona • Belgrade

Special Issue Editors

Subhas Mukhopadhyay
Macquarie University
Australia

Tarikul Islam
Jamia Millia Islamia (Central University)
India

Editorial Office
MDPI
St. Alban-Anlage 66
4052 Basel, Switzerland

This is a reprint of articles from the Special Issue published online in the open access journal *Electronics* (ISSN 2079-9292) from 2017 to 2019 (available at: https://www.mdpi.com/journal/electronics/special_issues/smart_cities)

For citation purposes, cite each article independently as indicated on the article page online and as indicated below:

LastName, A.A.; LastName, B.B.; LastName, C.C. Article Title. *Journal Name* **Year**, *Article Number*, *Page Range*.

ISBN 978-3-03921-181-4 (Pbk)
ISBN 978-3-03921-182-1 (PDF)

Contents

About the Special Issue Editors

Subhas Mukhopadhyay holds a B.E.E. (gold medalist), M.E.E., Ph.D. (India), and Doctor of Engineering (Japan). He has over 30 years of teaching, industrial, and research experience. He is currently Professor of Mechanical/Electronics Engineering, Macquarie University, Australia, and is the Discipline Leader of the Mechatronics Engineering Degree Programme. Before joining Macquarie, he was Professor of Sensing Technology, Massey University, New Zealand. His fields of interest include smart sensors and sensing technology, instrumentation techniques, wireless sensors and network (WSN), Internet of Things (IoT), numerical field calculation, and electromagnetics. He has supervised over 40 postgraduate students and over 100 Honours students. He has examined over 50 postgraduate theses. He has published over 400 papers in different international journals and conference proceedings, written 7 books and 42 book chapters, and edited 17 conference proceedings. He has also edited 32 books with Springer-Verlag and 24 journal Special Issues. He has organized over 20 international conferences as either General Chairs/co-chairs or Technical Programme Chair. He has delivered 335 presentations including keynote, invited, tutorial, and special lectures. He is a Fellow of IEEE (USA), a Fellow of IET (UK), a Fellow of IETE (India). He is a Topical Editor of IEEE *Sensors* journal. He is also an associate editor of IEEE *Transactions on Instrumentation and Measurements*. He is a Distinguished Lecturer of the IEEE Sensors Council from 2017 to 2019. He chairs the IEEE IMS NSW chapter. More details are available at https://scholar.google.com.au/citations?user=8p-BvWIAAAAJ&hl=enhttps://orcid.org/0000-0002-8600-5907http://web.science.mq.edu.au/directory/listing/person.htm?id=smukhopa.

Tarikul Islam is Professor in Electrical Engineering. He received his M.Sc. Eng. Degree in instrumentation and control system from A. M. U. Aligarh, U.P. in 1997, and his Ph.D. (Eng.) degree from Jadavpur University, Kolkata, India, in 2007. He has over 20 years of teaching and research experience. He has authored/co-authored 4 book chapters, one edited book, 2 Indian patents, and more than 140 papers in peer-reviewed journals and conferences. He has received funding for his research projects from Indian Government Agencies of $US 214,000. His research interests include sensors and sensing technologies, and electronics instrumentation. He is a life member of IETE (India), ISTE (India). He is associated editor of the IEEE *Sensors Journal and International Journal of Smart Sensing and Intelligent Systems*. He is a co-editor of a Special Issue of an international journal.

Editorial

Innovative Technologies and Services for Smart Cities

Subhas Chandra Mukhopadhyay [1,*] and Tarikul Islam [2,*]

[1] School of Engineering, MQ Centre for Smart Green Cities, Macquarie University,
New South Wales, NSW 2109, Australia
[2] Department of Electrical Engineering, Faculty of Eng. & Technology, Jamia Millia Islamia (University),
New Delhi-110025, India
* Correspondence: subhas.mukhopadhyay@mq.edu.au (S.C.M.); tislam@jmi.ac.in (T.I.)

Received: 19 March 2019; Accepted: 22 March 2019; Published: 28 March 2019

---

1. Introduction

Smart cities represent a multidiscipline field continuously evolved by the advancement of sensor-based information technology and communication technology. Less budget, resource constraints, and continuous software upgradesare some of the few problems affecting the implementation of smart cities. However, it is to note that smart city is not only a technical issue but also smart governance as a complex process of institutional change and acknowledgement of the geopolitical nature of appealing visions of socio-technical governance [1,2]. The only solution to these problems is to develop smarter technologies and more efficient usage of available infrastructures in order to meet the needs of smart cities [3]. A combination of smart sensors, universal platform, information and communication technologies (ICT), Internet of Things (IoT), energy harvesting, cloud computing, and open source technologies, compatible with next generation networks (NGN), will help towards the actual achievement of a smart city [4,5]. It is now possible to develop significant technology platforms and IoT solutions for smart cities without a massive investment. However, IoT interoperability is still at a very early stage, and standardization is difficult to achieve as it is usually led by companies with strong market positions. There is a need for stand-alone development, where large companies will not dictate terms and conditions.

The aim of this special issue is to report on the design and development of smart sensors, a universal interfacing platform, along with the IoT framework, extending it to next-generation networks (4G, 5G, and future networks) for monitoring parameters of interest with the goal of achieving smart cities. Examples of this work include developing novel sensors for monitoring of environmental pollution and other parameters and making the data available to a wider community through remote access to cloud computing. The proposed universal interfacing platform with the IoT framework will solve many challenging issues, and it will significantly boost the growth of IoT-related applications, not just in the environmental monitoring domain, but in the other key areas, such as smart home, wearables, smart city with smart waste management, smart E-metering, smart water supply, intelligent traffic control, smart grid and remote health care applications, in any country [6]. The need is to develop a low-cost solution so that any country, without investing a massive amount of resources, can exploit the research outcomes.

2. The Present Issue

This special issue consists of twelve papers covering important topics in the field of innovative technologies and services for smart cities. The contents of these papers are introduced here.

In reference [7], a thin film metal oxide sensor to measure trace moisture from 3 to 100 ppm has been fabricated and its response characteristics are studied. Moisture measurement in ppm level is a challenging and costly affair. A simple method has been proposed to improve the sensitivity in ppm range and to prevent wastage of nanostructured materials. The response parameters of the sensor are compared with the commercial DEW point meter. The dew point is the temperature at which the water vapor present in air/gas condenses to liquid form. This sensor is useful for the condition monitoring of gas insulated substations (GISs), transformers, and circuit breakers in order to achieve an uninterrupted power supply in smart cities.

In [8], a smart prayer mat has been designed and tested for detecting human postures and counting posture cycles. This smart praying mat may be helpfulto help old and forgetful Muslims to perform their obligatory five times a day religious praying at regular prescribed times. Authors employ resistive force sensors placed at the prescribed locations in the mat, where forces are significant and consistent. Unique force patterns are observed according to the position of postures. This technology was successfully tested with 30 participants in the age group of 30 to 60 years.Recent trends are to develop a building-integrated photovoltaic system (BIPS) to generate low-cost environmentally friendly electrical energy. But the low-output efficiency and high costs are the challenges for the implementation of BIPS system. A low-cost solution with improved solar efficiency by using aluminum reflector has been proposed in [9]. A bi-reflector solar PV system (BRPVS) with thin film Al-foil reflector and an LLC converter for a BIPV system is proposed and experimented with a 400-W prototype. A cadmium–sulfide (CdS) photo-resistor sensor and an Arduino-based algorithm is developed to control the working of the reflectors. Experimental results show that there is an enhancement of 28% power efficiency with respect to the solar PV module.

A multiwalled carbon nanotube-based strain sensor is fabricated for structural health monitoring application [10]. The sensor is fabricated by mixing different amounts of MWCNT and epoxy resin (EpoThin®). The sensor works on resistive principle and is mounted on a metal specimen (beam). The impedance variation of the sensor is studied with the variation of tensile strength on the spavin with a controlled known force. The response of the sensor shows a significant change in impedance with a variation of tensile strength. An Internet of Things (IoT)-compatible smart trap detector for crawling insects and other arthropods in an urban environment has been developed in [11]. A box-shaped device attracts targeted insect pests, senses the presence of insects, and takes a picture of the internal space of the boxautomatically, and after a fixed time interval the picture is sent to an authorized person/stakeholder through a WiFi device. The device has detection efficiency in the range of 96% to 99%. Asemantic-based decision support system (DSS), depending on ontological models, to assist architects and interior designers in domestic environments' reconfiguration for independent living is discussed in [12]. The development process of the ontology is presented in detail together with the results deriving from reasoning processes. To ease the reconfiguration of domestic environments, a prototypical application taking advantage of the DSS is presented. A zero-power microwave sensor having two pairs of open-ended coaxial probes is used as a liquid sensor.One is inside a known pure reference water sample, and the other one is inside the water under test. The basestation propagates a single tone signal at the frequency of f0/2. At the sensing node, an antenna absorbs that signal and a passive frequency doubler makes its frequency twice, i.e., f0, which will be used as the carrier signal. At base station, the sensed signal is demodulated. The proposed system is tested for humic acid water at 2.5 GHz frequency [13].A wireless sensor network having four metal oxide gas sensors powered by a solar panel to discriminate four volatile compounds, such as benzene, toluene, ethylbenzene, and xylene (BTEX) has been proposed in [14]. Pattern recognition of data is carried out by a radial basis neural network and principal component analysis. ZigBee protocol is used to transmit data wirelessly to a self-developed data cloud. RoomFort, a smart comfort management system is developed to enhance the comfort of hotel room guests. It provides a set of domain ontologies to formalize comfort-related metrics and to exploit the automatic reasoning capabilities provided by Semantic Web technologies while gathering data through a network of sensors to ensure guests are provided with tailored comfort profiles during their stays in the hotel [15]. Automatic detection of unusual crowd dynamics using geotagged posts on location-based social networks (LBSNs) is proposed in [16]. Authors use Instagram API media/search endpoint to collect the location of the pictures posted by Instagram users in a given area periodically. Locations are summarized by their centroid. The entropy algorithm succeeds in finding abnormal events without the need for a training phase, being able to dynamically adapt to changes in crowd behavior. Cost-effective delivery of substantialdata content information is a big challenge facing modern mobile communication networks. In reference [17], authors propose an integrated, proactive content delivery scheme that jointly exploits the availability of multiple service tiers and multi-user behavior prediction. Three optimal algorithms and one heuristic algorithm are introduced to solve the cost-minimization problems of multi-user proactive content delivery under different modeling assumptions. In the traditional wireless sensor network (WSN), loading balancing technology is difficult to meet the requirements of adaptability and flexibility. In reference [18], the load balancing issue is addressed by software-defined WSN. This mechanism utilizes the advantages of a centralized control SDN (software-defined network) and flexible traffic scheduling. The simulation results show that the improved SDSNLB (software-defined sensor network load balancing) routing algorithm has better performance than LEACH (low-energy adaptive clustering hierarchy) protocol.

Author Contributions: S.C.M. and T.I. worked together in the whole editorial process of the special issue, 'Innovative Technologies and Services for Smart Cities", published by journal *Electronics*. T.I. drafted this editorial summary and S.C.M. reviewed, edited and finalized the manuscript.

Acknowledgments: First of all, we would like to thank all researchers who submitted articles to this special issue for their excellent contributions. We are also grateful to all reviewers who helped in the evaluation of the manuscripts and made very valuable suggestions to improve the quality of contributions. We would like to acknowledge the editorial board of *Electronics*, who invited us to guest edit this special issue. We are also grateful to the *Electronics* Editorial Office staff who worked thoroughly to maintain the rigorous peer-review schedule and timely publication.

Conflicts of Interest: The authors declare no conflict of interest.

References

1. Meijer, A.; Bolívar, M.P.R. Governing the smart city: A review of the literature on smart urban governance. *Int. Rev. Adm. Sci.* **2016**, *82*, 392–408. [CrossRef]
2. Angelidou, M. Smart cities: A conjuncture of four forces. *Cities* **2015**, *47*, 95–106. [CrossRef]
3. Mehmood, Y.; Ahmad, F.; Yaqoob, I.; Adnane, A.; Imran, M.; Guizani, S. Internet-of-things-based smart cities: Recent advances and challenges. *IEEE Commun. Mag.* **2017**, *55*, 17–23. [CrossRef]
4. Ghayvat, H.; Mukhopadhyay, S.C.; Liu, J.; Babu, A.; Elahi, E.; Gui, X. Internet of things for smart homes and buildings: Opportunities and challenges. *Austral. J. Telecommun. Digit. Econ.* **2015**, *3*, 33–47. [CrossRef]
5. Islam, T.; Mukhopadhyay, S.C.; Suryadevara, N.K. Smart sensors and internet of things: A postgraduate paper. *IEEE Sens. J.* **2017**, *17*, 577–588. [CrossRef]
6. Islam, T.; Mukhopadhyay, S.C. Wearable Sensors for Physiological Parameters Measurement: Physics, Characteristics, Design and Applications. In *Wearable Sensors: Applications, Design and Implementation*; Mukhopadhyay, S.C., Islam, T., Eds.; Institute of Physics (IOP): Bristol, UK, 2017; pp. 1–31, ISBN 978-0-7503-1503-6.
7. Kumar, L.; Islam, T.; Mukhopadhyay, S.C. Sensitivity enhancement of a PPM level capacitive moisture sensor. *Electronics* **2017**, *6*, 41. [CrossRef]
8. Kasman, K.; Moshnyaga, V.G. New technique for posture identification in smart prayer mat. *Electronics* **2017**, *6*, 61. [CrossRef]
9. Khan, M.A.; Zeb, K.; Uddin, W.; Sathishkumar, P.; Ali, M.U.; Hussain, S.; Ishfaq, M.; Himanshu; Subramanian, A.; Kim, H.-J. Design of a building-integrated photovoltaic system with a novel Bi-reflector PV System (BRPVS) and optimal control mechanism: An experimental study. *Electronics* **2018**, *7*, 119. [CrossRef]
10. Sam-Daliri, O.; Faller, L.; Farahani, M.; Roshanghias, A.; Oberlercher, H.; Mitterer, T.; Araee, A.; Zang, H. MWCNT-epoxy nanocomposite sensors for structural health monitoring. *Electronics* **2018**, *7*, 143. [CrossRef]
11. Eliopoulos, P.; Tatlas, N.; Rigakis, I.; Potamitis, I. A "smart" trap device for detection of crawling insects and other arthropods in urban environments. *Electronics* **2018**, *7*, 161. [CrossRef]
12. Spoladore, D.; Sacco, M. Semantic and dweller-based decision support system for the reconfiguration of domestic environments: RecAAL. *Electronics* **2018**, *7*, 179. [CrossRef]

13. Mirzavand, R.; Honari, M.M.; Laribi, B.; Khorshidi, B.; Sadrzadeh, M.; Mousavi, P. An unpowered sensor node for real-time water quality assessment (humic acid detection). *Electronics* **2018**, *7*, 231. [CrossRef]
14. Arroyo, P.; Lozano, J.; Suárez, J.I. Evolution of wireless sensor network for air quality measurements. *Electronics* **2018**, *7*, 342. [CrossRef]
15. Spoladore, D.; Arlati, S.; Carciotti, S.; Nolich, M.; Sacco, M. RoomFort: An ontology-based comfort management application for hotels. *Electronics* **2018**, *7*, 345. [CrossRef]
16. Garcia-Rubio, C.; Redondo, R.P.D.; Campo, C.; Vilas, A.F. Using entropy of social media location data for the detection of crowd dynamics anomalies. *Electronics* **2018**, *7*, 380. [CrossRef]
17. Hu, J.; Lai, Y.; Peng, A.; Hong, X.; Shi, J. Proactive content delivery with service-tier awareness and user demand prediction. *Electronics* **2019**, *8*, 50. [CrossRef]
18. Cui, X.; Huang, X.; Ma, Y.; Meng, Q. A load balancing routing mechanism based on SDWSN in smart city. *Electronics* **2019**, *8*, 273. [CrossRef]

 *electronics*

Article

Sensitivity Enhancement of a PPM Level Capacitive Moisture Sensor

Lokesh Kumar [1], Tarikul Islam [2,*] and Subhas Chandra Mukhopadhyay [3]

[1] Department of Physics & Astrophysics, University of Delhi, Delhi-110007, India; lok17@rediffmail.com

[2] Department of Electrical Engineering, Faculty of Engineering & Technology,
Jamia Millia Islamia (A Central University), Maulana Mohammed Ali JauharMarg,
New Delhi 110025, India

[3] Department of Mechanical/Electronics Engineering, Macquarie University, Sydney, NSW 2109, Australia;
subhas.mukhopadhyay@mq.edu.au

* Correspondence: tislam@jmi.ac.in; Tel.: +91-11-2698-1717 (ext.2355)

Academic Editor: Mostafa Bassiouni
Received: 21 March 2017; Accepted: 16 May 2017; Published: 20 May 2017

Abstract: Measurement of moisture at ppm or ppb level is very difficult and the fabrication of such sensors at low cost is always challenging. High sensitivity is an important parameter for trace level (ppm) humidity sensors. Anelectronic detection circuit for interfacing the humidity sensor with high sensitivity requires a simple hardware circuit with few active devices. The recent trends for increasing the sensitivity include fabricating nanoporous film with a very large surface area. In the present work, the sensitivity of a parallel plate capacitive type sensor with metal oxide sensing film has been significantly improved with an aim to detect moisture from 3 to 100 ppm in the industrial process gases used to fabricate semiconductors and other sensitive electronic devices. The sensitivity has been increased by (i) fabricating a nanoporous film of aluminum oxide using the sol-gel method and (ii) increasing the cross-sectional area of a parallel plate capacitor. A novel double sided capacitive structure has been proposed where two capacitors have been fabricated—one on the top and one on the bottom side of a flat alumina substrate—and then the capacitors are connected in parallel. The structure has twice the sensitivity of a single sensor in the same ppm range but the size of the structure remains unchanged. The important characteristics of the sensors such as the sensitivity ($S = \frac{\Delta C}{\Delta ppm} \times 100$), the response time ($t_r$), and the recovery time (t_c) are determined and compared with a commercial SHAW, UKdew point meter. The fabricated double sided sensor has comparable sensitivity ($S = 100\%$, t_r (s) = 28, t_c (s) = 40) with the commercial meter ($S = 100.5\%$, t_r (s) = 258) but has a faster response time. The proposed method of sensitivity enhancement is simple, and mass producible.

Keywords: porous alumina; sol-gel technique; capacitive sensor; sensitivity; dynamic range; ppm

1. Introduction

Humidity sensors are widely used in different industrial, agricultural, medical, food preservation, home ventilation and air-conditioning (HVAC), and respiratory monitoring applications for the development of smart cities. Moisture measurement at ppm level is essential for condition monitoring of gas insulated substations (GISs), transformers, and circuit breakers in orderto achieve uninterrupted power supply in smart cities. The trace moisture sensor is extremely useful in certain crucial applications, where it can withstand corrosive and contaminating gases. The sensor should be sensitive to sudden and drastic change of moisture and available at low cost with a relatively long calibration period. The dynamic range of humidity measurement, which extends from %RH to ppb level, is extremely large [1–5]. Capacitive sensors are widely used for the measurement of humidity over a wide range. The most widely used capacitive sensor in %RH is the interdigitated electrode structure. The interdigitated sensor, to the best of our knowledge, is only suitable for RH level humidity measurement [5]. Very recently, an attempt has been made by the authors to measure moisture at ppm level by a micro interdigitated capacitive sensor. However, the sensor does not show sensitivity less than 200 ppm [6]. A large number of research articles is published every year in different journals on the topic of %RH humidity measurement. However, the number of research papers for ppm level moisture detection is very low [5]. The cost of a commercial ppm level moisture sensor is at least fifty times higher than that of RH sensors [6,7].

Aluminum oxide may be suitable for trace level moisture measurement, since it is thermally stable, and chemically inert in a corrosive environment. Among the different methods of alumina film preparation, the sol-gel method is a simple, less expensive method to prepare a pure ceramic thin film of desired thickness. The film can be formed on the ceramic substrate by the dip coating, spin coating or spray coating method [1,2,6–10]. Incomparison to other ceramic materials, aluminum oxide (Al_2O_3) is highly hydrophilic and it is one of the most useful materials for moisture measurement in most industrial gases [4,10,11]. Several works have been reported in the recent past to measure moisture in the range of 0–100 ppm. However, enhancement of the sensitivity is still required to make a prototype system for the possibility of commercial applications. In addition, there is a need to increase the dynamic range below 10 ppm [8,9,12–23]. Continuous efforts are made by the researchers to fabricate highly porous nanostructures such as nanowire, nanotubes, and nanopores using different fabrication techniques. Such nanostructure films result in a very high surface area suitable for humidity sensing [23–29]. Efforts are also being made to explore new fabrication techniques and materials to achieve the goal of high sensitivity and selectivity [30]. The methods followed for the fabrication of nanostructures with desirable pore morphology are costly, time consuming and very often lead to failure. It is not necessary that the sensitivity will increase by increasing the surface area. It also requires tuning the pore morphology. Most recently, the sensitivity of a capacitive trace moisture sensor was enhanced by increasing the surface area of a pure alumina nanoporous film with the addition of polymer polyethylene glycol (PEG). The surface area of the alumina is increased two-fold but the sensitivity is increased by approximately 61%. It is found that with the increase in surface area, the size of the pores also increases [8].

In the present work, we have studied the sensitivity of a capacitive trace moisture sensor for measuring moisture in ppm. The sensitivity has been addressed by (i) selecting a suitable pore morphology nanostructured thin film of Al_2O_3; and (ii) increasing the cross-sectional area of the parallel plate electrode. To enhance sensitivity further, a unique structure with two identical parallel plate capacitors on each side of the alumina substrate has been fabricated. When these two capacitors are connected in parallel, the sensitivity is enhanced almost two-fold but the actual size remains unchanged. Also, this structure prevents the wastage of very useful dip-coated film on the opposite side of the substrate as reported previously in [7,9,14,16,17,21–23]. The proposed method of sensitivity enhancement is easy, simple, and less time consuming. The sensor can be utilized for condition monitoring of electrical equipment and moisture measurement in human respiration.

2. Experimental

2.1. Preparation of the Sol for the Al_2O_3 Sensing Film

Material aluminum hydroxide or Boehmite (AlO(OH)) sol was prepared by the addition of aluminum secondary butoxide ($C_{12}H_{27}AlO_3$) precursor into an excess amount of warm DI (Deionized) water [8,9,31,32]. The molar ratio of alumina precursor to water was fixed at approximately 1:100. The solution was initially hydrolyzed for nearly 1 h with continuous stirring on a magnetic hot plate stirrer at a constant temperature of 90 °C. The solution was then peptized by adding concentrated hydrochloric (HCl) acid drop wise with the molar ratio ~0.07 mol/mol. During peptization, the hydroxide molecules are positively charged ($Al(OH)_3^+$) and are dispersed uniformly in the colloidal solution. The dispersed ions form a net structure and after complete peptization, the sol becomes transparent. To remove the excess volatile organic impurities from the sol, the solution was refluxed for about 18 h at a constant temperature of 80 °C.Finally, the solution was stirred on a magnetic hot plate for nearly 24 h at a room temperature of 25 °C. To facilitate the adhesion of the film on the substrate, nearly 1% polyvinyl alcohol (molecular weight 125,000) was mixed in the sol solution.

2.2. Microstructures of the Porous Aluminum Oxide

Pore morphology of the γ-Al_2O_3 film was characterized by powder X-ray diffraction (PXRD), field emission electron microscope (FESEM) and Brunauer–Emmett–Teller (BET) surface area and a pore size analyzer respectively. X-ray diffraction and BET analysis were carried out using a powder sample of the ceramic. Powder ceramic samples were prepared from the fixed amount of sol solution. The solution was dried initially at 80 °C and then sintered for 1 h at different temperatures of 450 to 550 °C. XRD analysis was carried out with a Bruker D8 advance diffractometer using Ni filtered Cu-Kα radiation (λ = 1.54056 Å, 2θ = 20° to 80°) with a scanning rate of 0.05°/s. An XRD diffractogram of the sample sintered at 450 °C for 1 h is shown in Figure 1. The sample shows multiple XRD peaks showing the presence of γ-Al_2O_3 phase. However, the diffraction peaks were broad, indicating the small size of the crystals. The XRD peaks are almost identical to the peaks obtained from the sample sintered at the temperature of 450 °C for 6 h [9]. During sintering, aluminum hydroxide undergoes a number of polymorphic phase transformations. Finally, it is converted to highly stable α-alumina phase at around 1000 °C [9,31]. Debye–Scherrer's equation was used to calculate the average crystallite size from the strongest XRD peak, as shown in Figure 1.

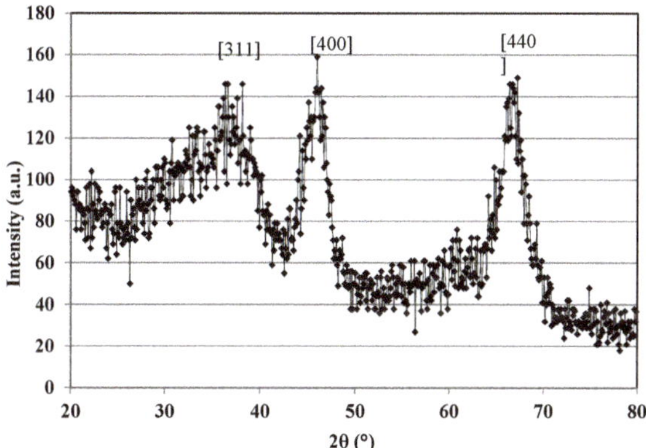

Figure 1. XRD results of the alumina powder prepared from the sol-gel method showing γ-Al_2O_3 (450 °C, 1 h).

The average size of the crystallite was found to be ~4 nm. The BET gas adsorption and desorption method was used to determine the surface area of the powder samples. The nitrogen gas adsorption isotherm of the sample is shown in Figure 2 [11,12].The isotherm was studied using a Nova 2000e (Quantachrome Instruments Limited, Boynton Beach, FL, USA) BET analyzer at liquid nitrogen temperature (77 K). The oxide sample in power form was placed in a sample cell and allowed to degas for nearly 2 h at 250 °C in vacuum. The degassed material was then exposed to a known concentration of N_2 gas at the constant temperature. The adsorption isotherm plotted between 1/[W((Po/P)-1)] and relative pressure P/P0 for γ-Al_2O_3 is shown in Figure 2.

The specific surface area, the average pore size and the micro-pore volume of the samples sintered at different conditions are shown in Table 1.

It is observed that with the increase in sintering time and temperature, the BET surface area reduces and the DA (Dubinin Astakhov) pore size increases. The roughness of the porous film deposited on an alumina substrate (α-phase) was determined by the atomic force micrograph (AFM). The microstructure of the alumina film deposited on the substrate was also studied using FESEM. The FESEM image of the top surface of the metal oxide film at 100 nm scale is shown in Figure 3. The surface contains a large number of voids (micropores) of different sizes. The average pore size of the voids is around 10 nm.

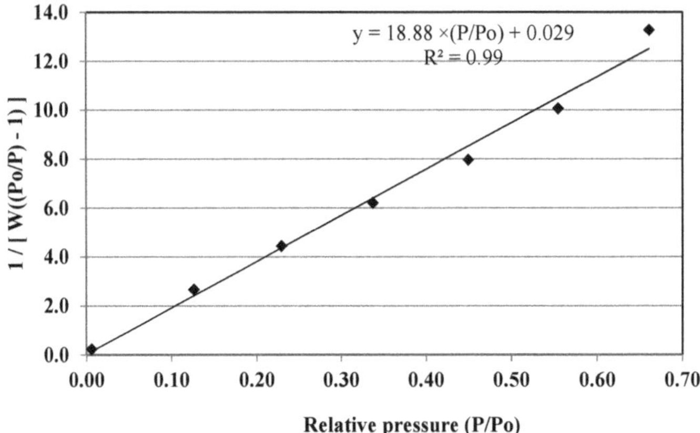

Figure 2. N_2 gas adsorption plot of the γ-Al_2O_3 film (450 °C, 1 h).

Table 1. Pore morphology of the film.

Sample	BET Surface Area (m^2/gm)	DA Pore Size (Å)	MicroporeVolume(cc/gm)
Alumina (450 °C, 1 h)	220	10.4	0.200
Alumina (450 °C, 6 h)	200.4	10.8	0.177
Alumina (900 °C, 1 h)	186	12.2	0.139

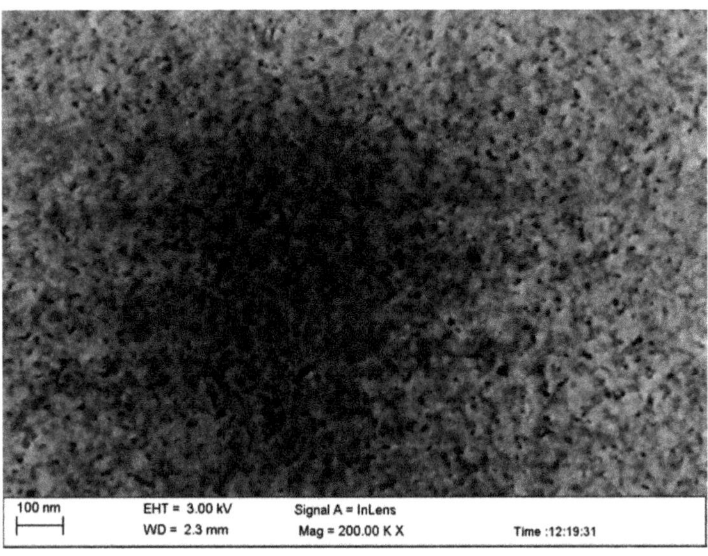

Figure 3. Scanningelectronmicrograph of the top surfaceofthe γ-Al_2O_3 film.

2.3. Fabrication of the Parallel Plate Capacitive Sensors

Capacitive sensors from four different sensing areas—C_{p1}, C_{p2}, C_{p3} and C_{p4}—were fabricated on the alumina substrates. The details of geometrical parameters and sintering temperature of each capacitor are shown in Table 2. The bottom gold electrode on each substrate was deposited by the screen printing method using a manual screen printer. Screen printing uses the stencil method to print the predefined electrode design on the screen. A screen of different electrode pattern was designed using PCB making software and the stencil of the screen printer with polyester fabric was made in the lab.

Table 2. Details of different types of the sensors fabricated.

Sample	C_{p1}	C_{p2}	C_{p3}	C_{p4}
Substrate size (mm)	$19 \times 19 \times 1$	$19 \times 19 \times 1$	$19 \times 19 \times 1$	$10 \times 10 \times 1$
Top electrode (mm)	11×10	9×8	6×6	3×2
Bottomelectrode	16×16	14×14	8×8	5×6
Electrode sintering	900 °C, 1 h	900 °C, 1 h	900 °C, 1 h	900 °C, 1 h
Sensing film	450 °C, 3 h	450 °C, 3 h	450 °C, 3 h	450 °C, 3 h
Sensing area (mm^2)	110	72	36	6
Film thickness (μm)	~6	~6	~6	~6

A thin film of binder mixed alumina sol was deposited on the gold printed alumina substrate by a desktop computer interfaced automatic Single Dip Coatinginstrument (Model: SDC-2007C, Apex Instruments Co. Pvt. Ltd., Kolkata, India). The substrate was dipped in the prepared sol at a dipping speed of 60 mm/m, wet time 30 s and then pulled out at a speed of 30 mm/m. The substrate was kept for 1 m in the solution before being pulled off. Deposited thin film was dried at 80 °C for nearly 5 min. The steps of film deposition over the substrates were repeated six times.

When the film was dried, a second gold electrode was screen printed on the sensing film. The top electrode is made macroporous with average pore size (~1–7 μm), which is much larger than the average pore size of the sensing film. The schematic of film deposition of γ-Al$_2$O$_3$ on gold plate by the sol-gel method is shown in Figure 4.

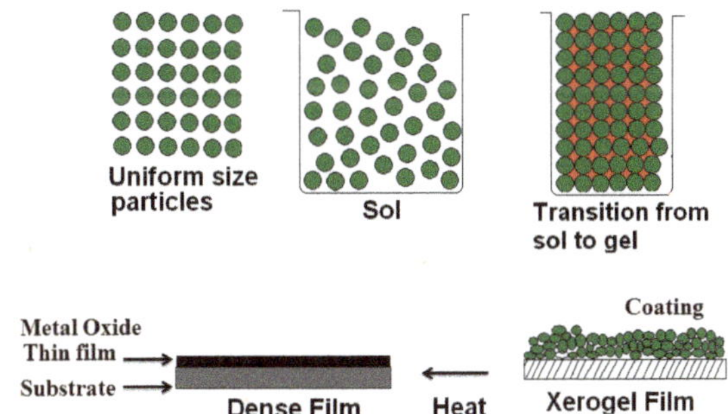

Figure 4. Schematic diagram of the film deposition on the gold electrode.

The red dots in the schematic indicate the formation of pores after sintering. Finally, two terminals are soldered at the top and the bottom electrodes for the electrical connection of the sensor. Precautions were taken to minimize the variation of the film thickness among sensors with the help of a software controlled automatic dipcoater. All the four sensors have almost identical dielectric films, except the electrode size. Figure 5a shows the schematic and Figure 5b shows the photograph of the sensors fabricated in the laboratory environment.

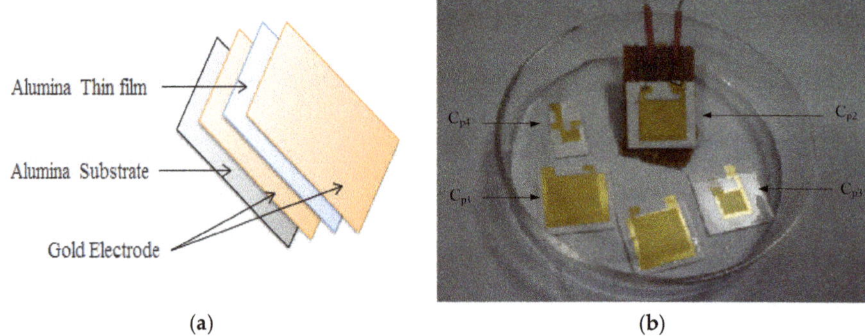

Figure 5. The capacitive sensor with different sensing area (**a**) schematic diagram of the sensor; (**b**) photograph.

3. Determination of the Response Characteristics of the Sensors

The electrical characteristics were determined by holding the sensors inside a rectangular steel chamber, which was made in a local workshop. The inner free space of the chamber is around 100 cc. The chamber has 0.25″ inlet and outlet gas pipelines and is connected in series with a reference SHAW dew point meter (model no SADP-TR, Westgate, Bradford, UK) [12]. The reference meter has ahyper thin film parallel electrode metal oxide sensor. The measurement range of the dew point meter is 0–1000 ppm with accuracy ±1 ppm (=0.1%). To refresh the sensor, the chamber was purged with dry N_2 gas at the flow rate of 4–6 L/m. Refreshing continues till the reference meter indicates an initial concentration of around 3 ppm moisture in the moist gas (moisture content of the dry gas cylinder). The desired moist gas concentration was achieved by mixing the commercial dry N_2 gas with water vapor at room temperature (25 °C). The concentration level of the moisture in the moist gas exposed to the sensors varied from 3 to 100 ppm. All the four sensors in the chamber were connected to the Impedance analyzer (4294 A) with a nearly 1 m long shielded wire. The wire was a Teflon insulated multiconductor with capacitance 79 pF/m. For proper shielding, the sensors were held in the grounded metallic chamber. The impedance analyzer was interfaced with a personal computer PC with the help of IEEE 488 interface bus. The input ac excitation for each sensor was of 500 mV (rms) and frequency 1 kHz. The observations of the capacitance values in the Cp-D mode of the impedance analyzer for C_{p1} and C_{p4} with moisture variation from 3 to 100 ppm are shown in Figure 6. The initial capacitance value of each sensor at dry humidity (3 ppm) is different. This difference of the base value is due to the fact that the effective cross-sectional area of each sensor is different. The pore morphology also influences the capacitance value but all the four sensors have identical morphology [1,2]. It is observed in Figure 6 that as the moisture concentration increases, the capacitance value increases but the change in capacitance for C_{P1} and C_{P4} for the same moisture range is significantly different. The highest (46.4%) and the minimum sensitivities (2.9%) are shown by C_{p1} and C_{p4} respectively. When a sensor is exposed to a certain moisture level, the water molecules in cluster form condense on the porous surface and then condense in the voids through capillary condensation in the micropores. As a result, the pores are filled up, causing an increase in the effective dielectric of the sensor. The size of water cluster depends on the moisture concentration. At saturation condition, when the pores are completely filled up, the capacitance value reaches the maximum. Since the sensor is exposed to a very low moisture concentration, the pores are partially filled and hence, the capacitance value continues to increase.

To determine the response (t_r) and the recovery time (t_c), the transient response curve of the sensor C_{p1} for the step change in moisture concentration from 3 to 100 ppm is shown in Figure 7. Such an instantaneous step change of moisture rarely occurs in practice but we have considered a worstcase scenarioin determining the transient response curve. The sensor takes a very short time, 29 s, to increase the capacitance value from 10 to 90% of its maximum value. During recovery, the sensor was refreshed by dry nitrogen gas to decrease the moisture concentration from 100 ppm to 3 ppm. The capacitance value of the sensor decreases with the decrease in moisture concentration as shown in Figure 7. The recovery time of the sensor is defined as the time taken by the sensor to decrease the capacitance value from maximum to 10% value and it is ~87 s. For the sensor C_{p2}, the response time is 28 s and the recovery time is 85 s. The response and the recovery time depend on the pore morphology, and the thickness of the sensing film. The humidity sensor which works on the adsorption and desorption principle, takes more time to desorb than to adsorb the moisture in the pores. It is observed that the output of the sensor is stable and recovers fully, when the sensor is refreshed by dry N_2 gas. Because of the small sensitivity of C_{p3} and C_{p4}, t_r and t_c of these sensors are not determined.

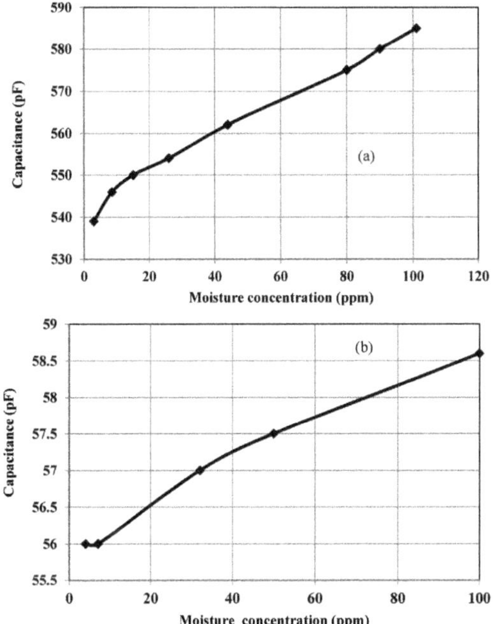

Figure 6. Capacitive response of the sensors (a) C_{p1}; (b) C_{p4}.

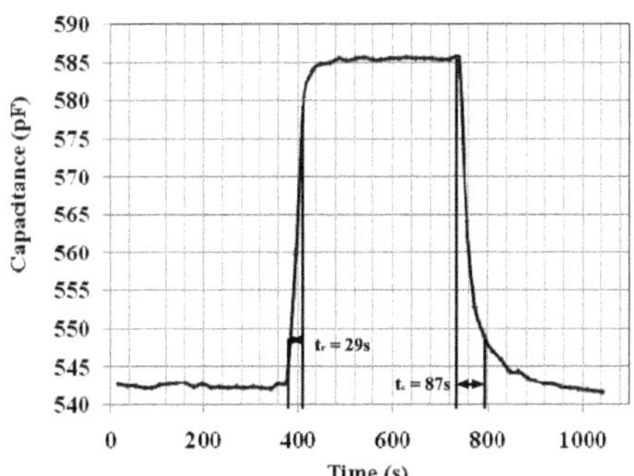

Figure 7. Transient response of the sensor C_{p1}.

4. Results and Discussion

For a parallel plate capacitive sensor, the effective capacitance in the presence of moisture can be represented by [8,22]

$$C_{eff} = \varepsilon_0 \varepsilon_{eff} \frac{A}{d} + C_f \tag{1}$$

where ε_0 is the permittivity of the free space, A is the area of the cross-section of the electrode, d is the thickness of the film, ε_{eff} is the relative dielectric constant of the moist dielectric film, and C_f is the capacitance due to fringing field. The fringing field capacitor will be negligible since the electrode size (A) is much larger than the gap between the electrodes (d) [8]. Therefore, the capacitance of the sensor can be approximately represented by

$$C_{eff} = \varepsilon_0 \varepsilon_{eff} \frac{A}{d} \tag{2}$$

The effective dielectric constant of the capacitor (γ-Al$_2$O$_3$) can be approximately given by Looyang's empirical equation as [5,6],

$$\varepsilon_{eff}^{1/3} = \gamma \left(\varepsilon_w^{1/3} - \varepsilon_a^{1/3} \right) + \varepsilon_a^{1/3} \tag{3}$$

where γ is the fractional volume of water adsorbed by the porous film, and ε_w is the dielectric constant of water. The fractional volume of water adsorbed in the porous film depends on the pore morphology. The well-known equation for the Kelvin radius gives us useful information about the desired pore morphology. It is reported that theoretically, the pore size as obtained from the Kelvin equation for sensing moisture in ppm should be below 10 Å [8,26]. The average pore size of the fabricated film as shown in Table 1 is 12.2 Å (γ-Al$_2$O$_3$ sintered initially at 450 °C and then at 900 °C for 1 h), which is close to the theoretical value.

The sensitivity (S) of a sensor can be defined as [1,2,20,27]

$$S = \frac{C_u - C_l}{C_l} \tag{4}$$

$$S = \frac{C_u - C_l}{RH_u - RH_l} \tag{5}$$

$$S = \frac{\frac{C_u - C_l}{C_l}}{RH_u - RH_l} \tag{6}$$

where C_u and C_l are the upper and the lower limit of the capacitance values of the sensor, RH_u and RH_l are the upper and the lower limit of humidity (%RH or ppm). The sensitivity represented by Equation (5) is more suitable in such a situation when the sensor has approximately linear response [20]. The output of the sensor is approximately linear ($R^2 = 0.95$, for perfect linear response $R^2 = 1$). Equation (5) is more usable to understand the performance of the sensor since it provides information about the input and the output parameters, but in Equation (4), the reader does not have an idea about the type of input parameter and its range.

The sensitivity parameters of four sensors have been determined using Equation (5). The sensitivity values of all the four sensors in the range 3–100 ppm are plotted with the variation of the cross-sectional area. It is observed in Figure 8 that the sensitivity increases almost linearly with the increase in effective area. When the effective cross-sectional area increases, more water molecules are adsorbed in the nanostructured porous film, resulting in an increase in effective dielectric constant.

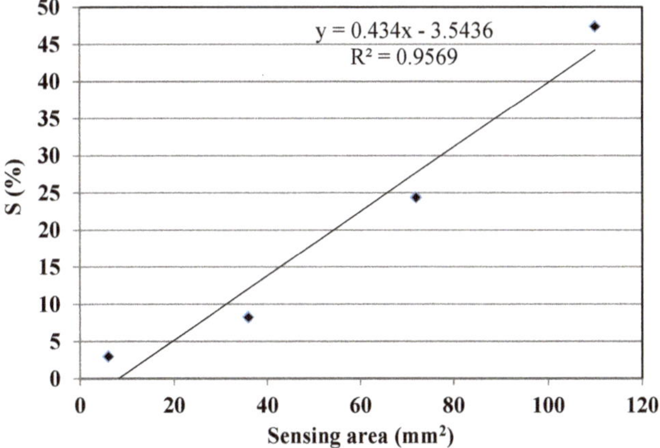

Figure 8. Variation of sensitivity with electrode area for 3–100 ppm moisture.

5. Sensitivity Enhancement by Connecting Two Capacitors in Parallel Fabricated on theSame Substrate

It has been investigated in the previous section that by keeping the pore morphology of the nanostructured film identical, the sensitivity can be increased by simply increasing the electrode area of the capacitor. However, if the electrode area increases, the size of the device will increase and it will create a problem to package the sensor in a small sample chamber. However, if we make two identical parallel plate capacitors on both sides of the alumina substrate, and connect them in parallel, the sensitivity becomes almost double. Additionally, the size of the device remains unchanged and the costly sensing film which is deposited on the opposite side can be effectively utilized. This is because, when thin film is deposited on the gold-plated electrode by the dip coating method, the film deposited on the opposite side of the alumina substrate remains unused [8,12–22]. This issue has not been addressed by previous reported work. Thus, a novel structure which consists of two identical capacitors on each side of the alumina substrate has been fabricated. In addition to this, if the sensitivity enhancement is not an issue for a particular sensor, the opposite capacitor can be used as a reference capacitor, which can be used to minimize the offset capacitance as well as any temperature error of the main sensor, provided the reference capacitor is covered by a hydrophobic film such as Teflon. If C1 is the parallel plate capacitor at one side of the substrate and C2 is another capacitor on the opposite side, then the equivalent capacitance, when both of them are connected in parallel, is C3 = C1 + C2. In comparison to the method of sensitivity enhancement by the preparation of nanostructure, this method is simple, less time consuming, less costly and mass producible.

Procedures to Fabricate the Device

The steps of the fabrication process remain the same as in the case of a single sided capacitive trace moisture sensor [6–8,12–22]. Two gold electrodes are deposited on each side of an alumina substrate (19 mm $\times$ 19 mm $\times$ 1 mm) by the screen printing method. The size of each electrode is 16 mm $\times$ 16 mm. The electrodes are sintered at 900 °C for 1 h in a furnace. Thin film of γ-Al_2O_3 is deposited on each electrode by the dip coating method under a similar deposition condition as discussed in Section 2.3. Film is deposited on both sides simultaneously. Finally, the top gold electrode is deposited on each side of the film. The dimension of the top electrode is 12 mm $\times$ 14 mm. However, due to manual fabrication, there may be minor variation of the electrode size of C1 and C2 respectively. Both the capacitances are connected in parallel. The response characteristics of C1, C2 and C3 are determined with the variation of moisture in the range of 3–108 ppm.The capacitive response curve of the sensor C2 with the variation of moisture is shown in Figure 9a. The capacitive response of C3 when both C1 and C2 are connected in parallel is shown in Figure 9b.

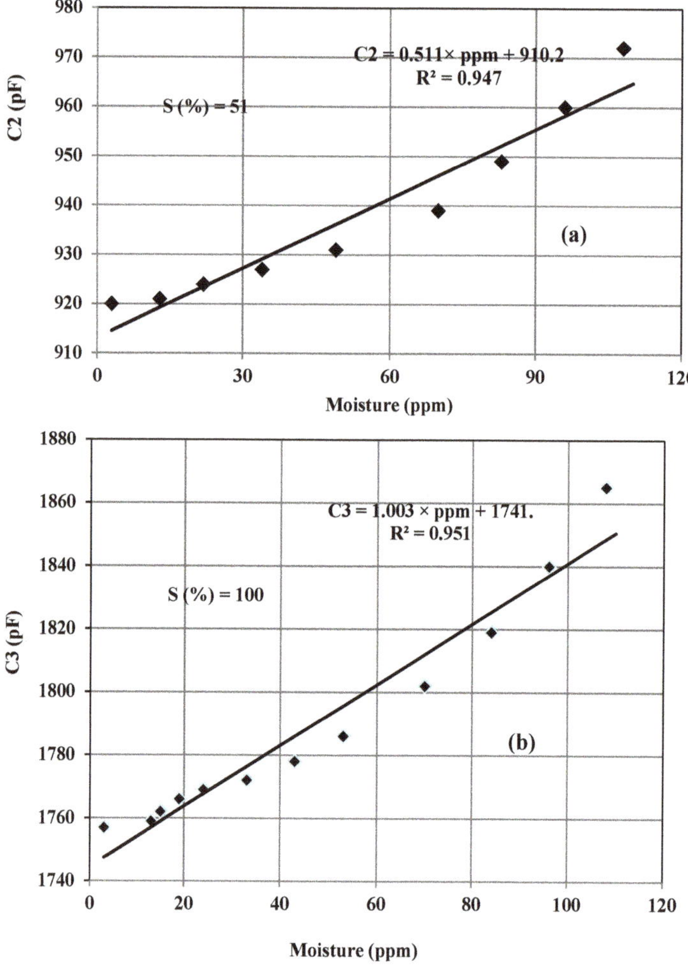

Figure 9. The response curve of the proposed sensor structure connected in parallel, (**a**) C2; the capacitor on the bottom side (**b**) C3 = C1 + C2.

It is observed that in the case of C3, the overall capacitance change for the same moisture range becomes almost double. This sensitivity enhancement is obtained by simply connecting the two capacitors in parallel without modifying the surface area or the thickness of the film. The correlation coefficient of the actual response curve from the linear fitted curve is 0.95, which is close to the desired value of 1. Linearity is always a desirable characteristic of a sensor for ease of calibration. For a linear response, only two calibration points are required to calibrate the reading. The conversion from a scale reading to the corresponding measured value of input moisture is most convenient if it is required to multiply a fixed constant rather than to refer to a nonlinear calibration curve or to compute from a nonlinear calibration equation.Hysteresis is another important parameter of a sensor. When a sensor is employed for moisture measurement in any application, the moisture level in the environment may increase or decrease. Ideally, the sensor should give the same capacitance at the same moisture level when approached in both directions. For a sensor withhysteresis error, different reading results for a particular moisture level are given, depending on whether the moisture level is applied from lower or higher values. The hysteresis plot for both increase and decrease in moisture from 13 to 108 ppm for C3 is shown in Figure 10. The maximum deviation of the capacitance value for the forward and reverse cycle of moisture is around 0.45%. The response and recovery times of C3 determined from the transient response curve for a 3–108 ppm step change in moisture are 28 s and 40 s respectively. The repeatability of the capacitive response of C3 for three similar step changes in moisture concentration is shown in Figure 11. The repeatability error is caused by the inability of the sensor to give the same capacitance under similar step change in moisture. The maximum repeatability error of the sensor output is ~0.2% and the standard deviation of the successive peaks is 0.7. Experiments were also performed to study the signal frequency effect on the capacitance values, by varying the frequency from 100 Hz to 100 kHz at fixed 80 ppm moisture. The rate of change of the capacitance value at lower frequency—below 20 kHz—is much higher than the frequency above 20 kHz. Therefore, the ac signal with frequency above 20 kHz is suitable to avoid the frequency dependency capacitance change. This is due to the fact that, when the sensor is interfaced with an electronic circuit for displaying the moisture value, the minor change in excitation frequency does not affect the reading of the meter. High capacitance change at lower frequency is due to the combined effect of dielectric adsorption capacitance and the double layer capacitance. At higher frequency, the effect of double layer capacitance is insignificant [33].

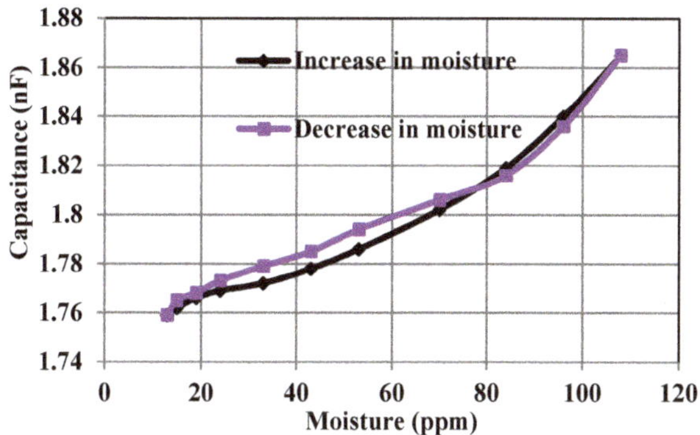

Figure 10. Hysteresis plot of the sensor C3.

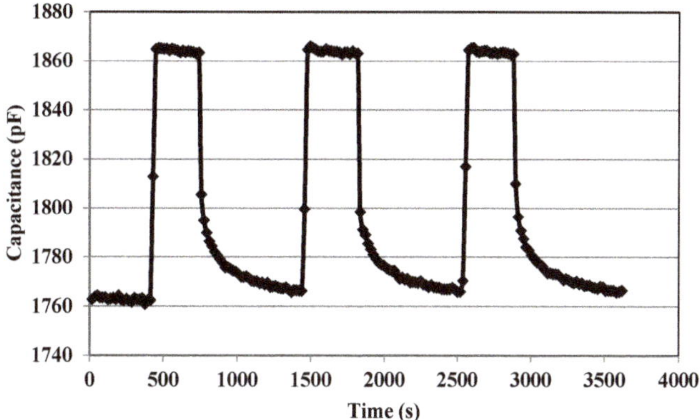

Figure 11. Repeatability of the sensor C3.

Investigation is needed to study the drift due to aging [2]. Our experience shows that if the sensor is kept in drying agent (molecular sieve) as practiced in a commercial dew point meter (SHAW), the reading will be stable for a long time [10,11]. However, if there is a drift in the output, it can be reduced by heating the sensor at a temperature of around 400 °C. Drift is caused due to deposition of residual impurity from the N_2 gas or due to gradual change in γ phase to γ-$Al_2O_3.H_2O$ (boehmite). This causes volume expansion of the oxide, resulting in a gradual decrease in surface area and porosity [2]. The sensor does not show any drift due to the change in working temperature [9,18,19,23]. Comparison of the characteristics of the single sided and double sided sensor with the reading of the commercial dew point meter is shown in Table 3.

Table 3. Comparison of the response characteristics of different sensors.

Sensor	Measurement Range (ppm)	S (%)	t_r (s)	t_c (s)
C_{p1}	3–100	46.4	29	87
C_{p2}	3–100	16.4	28	85
C3	3–100	100	28	40
SHAWdew point [19]	0–1000	100.5	258	-

6. Conclusions

The present work deals with the fabrication of capacitive porous alumina-based sensors with different sensing areas for sensing humidity in ppm. The pore morphology of the sensing layer of each sensor is identical. The characteristics of the moisture sensors were examined for 3 to 100 ppm moisture content in dry gas. We have found that a moisture sensor with a larger effective area has higher sensitivity in a lower range. Pore morphology, thickness of the film and the sensing area play an important role for the sensitive detection of humidity at trace level. The parallel plate sensor provides a better solution for trace moisture detection. In comparison to the conventional interdigitated sensor, the parallel plate sensor with very small size may sense humidity at the %RH level. We have also discussed another unique structure consisting of capacitors on each side of the substrate to enhance the sensitivity for trace level moisture detection. This double sided capacitor structure is easy to fabricate and it can enhance sensitivity greatly without affecting the overall size. It may be possible to obtain a measurementbelow 3 ppm, but due to the lack of a testing facility, an experiment was not conducted. Further work could test the sensor's ability to measure moisture in GIS or transformer oil.

Acknowledgments: Authors would like to thank the funding agency DRDO for providing the financial support.

Author Contributions: L.K. performed the experimental work under the supervision of T.I. S.C.M. gave the valuable suggestion to conduct experiments.

Conflicts of Interest: The authors declare no conflict of interest.

1. Fenner, R.; Zdankiewicz, E. Micromachined water vapor sensors: A review of sensing technologies. *IEEE Sens.* **2001**, *1*, 309–317. [CrossRef]
2. Feng, S.; Chen, X.; Chen, J.; Hu, J. A novel humidity sensor based on alumina nanowire films. *J. Phys. D Appl. Phys.* **2012**, *45*, 225305. [CrossRef]
3. Tetelin, A.; Pouget, V.; Lachaud, J.-L.; Pellet, C. Dynamic behavior of a chemical sensor for humidity level measurement in human breath. *IEEE Trans. Inst. Meas.* **2004**, *53*, 1262–1267. [CrossRef]
4. Fagan, J.G.; Amarakoon, V.R.W. Reliability and reproducibility of ceramic sensors, part III, humidity sensors. *Am. Ceram. Soc. Bull.* **1993**, *72*, 119–130.
5. McMillan, G.K.; Douglas, M. *Process/Industrial Instruments and Controls Handbook*, 5th ed.; Tata McGraw Hill Education Private Limited: Patel Nagar, New Delhi, India, 2009; pp. 4237–4247.
6. Blanka, T.A.; Eksperiandova, L.P.; Belikov, K.N. Recent trends of ceramic humidity sensors development: A review. *Sens. Actuators B* **2016**, *228*, 416–442. [CrossRef]

7. Islam, T.; Nimal, A.T.; Mittal, U.; Sharma, M.U. A micro interdigitated thin film metal oxide capacitive sensor for measuring moisture in the range of 175–625 ppm. *Sens. Actuators B* **2015**, *221*, 357–364. [CrossRef]

8. Mahboob, M.R.; Zargar, Z.H.; Islam, T. A sensitive and highly linear capacitive thin film sensor for trace 173 moisture measurement in gases. *Sens. Actuators B* **2016**, *228*, 658–664. [CrossRef]

9. Funke, H.H.; Grissom, B.L.; McGrew, C.E.; Raynor, M.W. Techniques for the measurement of trace moisture in high-purity electronic specialty gases. *Rev. Sci. Instrum.* **2003**, *74*, 3909–3933. [CrossRef]

10. Neumeier, S.; Echterhof, T.; Olling, R.; Pfeifer, H.; Simona, U. Zeolite based trace humidity sensor for high temperature applications in hydrogen atmosphere. *Sens. Actuators B* **2008**, *134*, 171–174. [CrossRef]

11. Islam, T.; Kumar, L.; Khan, S.A. A novel sol-gel thin film porous alumina based capacitive sensor for measuring trace moisture in the range of 2.5 to 25 ppm. *Sens. Actuators B* **2012**, *173*, 377–384. [CrossRef]

12. De Lange, M.F.; Vlugt, T.J.H.; Gascon, J.; Kapteijn, F. Adsorptive characterization of porous solids: Error analysis guides the way. *MicroporousMesoporous Mater.* **2014**, *200*, 199–215. [CrossRef]

13. Brinker, C.J.; Scherer, G.W. *Sol–Gel Science*; Academic Press: San Diego, CA, USA, 1990.

14. SHAW Moisture Meters (UK) Ltd. Westgate Bradford. BD13SQ. Available online: www.shawmeters.com (accessed on 15 March 2017).

15. General Electric. Moisture and Humidity Measurement. Available online: www.ge-mcs.com (accessed on 15 March 2017).

16. Hashiguchi, K.; Lisak, D.; Cygan, A.; Ciuryło, R.; Abea, H. Wavelength-meter controlled cavity ring-downspectroscopy: High-sensitivity detection of trace moisture in N_2 at sub-ppb levels. *Sens. Actuators A* **2016**, *241*, 152–160. [CrossRef]

17. Kapaa, P.; Pana, L.; Bandhanadhama, A.; Fanga, J.; Varahramyana, K.; Davis, W.; Ji, H.F. Moisture measurement using porous aluminum oxide coated microcantilevers. *Sens. Actuators B* **2008**, *134*, 390–395. [CrossRef]

18. Pandey, M.; Mishra, P.; Saha, D.; Sengupta, K.; Jain, K.; Islam, S.S. Nanoporous alumina (c- and a-phase) gel cast thick film for the development of trace moisture sensor. *J. Sol-Gel Sci. Technol.* **2013**, *68*, 317–323. [CrossRef]

19. Ohira, S.; Goto, K.; Toda, K.; Dasgupta, P.K. A capacitance sensor for water: Trace moisture measurement ingases and organic solvents. *Anal. Chem.* **2012**, *84*, 8891–8897. [CrossRef] [PubMed]

20. Doeblin, E.O. *Measurement Systems: Application and Design*, 4th ed.; Tata McGraw Hill: New Delhi, India, 2002; p. 198.

21. Basu, S.; Saha, M.; Chatterjee, S.; Mistry, K.; Bandyopadhay, S.; Sengupta, K. Porous ceramic sensor for measurement of gas moisture in the ppm range. *Mater. Lett.* **2001**, *49*, 29–33. [CrossRef]

22. Saha, D.; Sengupta, K. Trace moisture detection in oil filled transformer by ceramic sensor. *Mater. Sci. Eng.* **2015**, *73*, 012022. [CrossRef]

23. Chen, Z.; Jin, M.C. An Alpha-Alumina Moisture Sensor for Relative and Absolute Humidity Measurement. In Proceedings of the 1992 IEEE Industry Applications Society Annual Meeting, Houston, TX, USA, 4–9 October1992; Volume 2, pp. 1668–1675.

24. Islam, T.; Mahboob, R.; Khan, S.A. A simple MOX vapor sensor on polyimide substrate for measuring humidity in ppm Level. *IEEE Sens.* **2015**, *15*, 3004–3013. [CrossRef]

25. Kima, Y.; Junga, B.; Leea, H.; Kimb, H.; Leeb, K.; Park, H. Capacitive humidity sensor design based on anodic aluminum oxide. *Sens. Actuators B* **2009**, *141*, 441–446. [CrossRef]

26. Islam, T.; Khan, U.A.; Akhtar, J.A.; Rahman, M.Z.U. A digital hygrometer for trace moisture measurement. *IEEE Trans. Ind. Electr.* **2014**, *61*, 5599–5605. [CrossRef]

27. Bakhoum, E.G.; Cheng, M.H.M. High-accuracy miniature dew point sensor and instrument. *IEEE Sens. J.* **2015**, *15*, 1482–1488. [CrossRef]

28. Batumalay, M.; Harun, S.W.; Irawati, N.; Ahmad, H.; Arof, H. A study of relative humidity fiber-optic sensors. *IEEE Sens. J.* **2015**, *15*, 1945–1950. [CrossRef]

29. Babaei, F.H.; Rahbarpour, S. Alteration of pore size distribution by sol–gel impregnation for dynamic range and sensitivity adjustment in Kelvin condensation-based humidity sensors. *Sens. Actuators B* **2014**, *191*, 572–578. [CrossRef]

30. Lopez, F.M.; Briand, D.; Rooij, N.F. Decreasing the size of printed comb electrodes by the introduction of a dielectricinterlayer for capacitive gas sensors on polymeric foil: Modeling and fabrication. *Sens. Actuators B* **2013**, *189*, 89–96. [CrossRef]

31. Whelan, A.M. Sol-Gel Sensors. In *Sol-Gel Materials for Energy, Environment and Electronic Applications*; Springer: Berlin, Germany; pp. 121–153.

32. Yoldas, B.E. Design of sol-gel coating media for ink-jet printing. *J. Sol-Gel Sci. Technol.* **1998**, *13*, 147–152. [CrossRef]

33. Islam, T.; Rahman, Z.U. Investigation of the electrical characteristics on measurement frequency of a thin-film ceramic humidity sensor. *IEEE Trans. Instrum. Meas.* **2016**, *65*, 694–702. [CrossRef]

Article

New Technique for Posture Identification in Smart Prayer Mat

Kasman Kasman * and Vasily G. Moshnyaga

Graduate School of Engineering, Fukuoka University, Fukuoka 814-0180, Japan; vasily@fukuoka-u.ac.jp
* Correspondence: aasman2888@gmail.com; Tel.: +81-92-801-0833

Received: 26 July 2017; Accepted: 21 August 2017; Published: 23 August 2017

Abstract: Smart praying mats are essential to help old and forgetful Muslims perform their religious needs. Due to the binary representation of pressure sensors embedded into the mat for posture identification, existing smart praying systems either use large sensing arrays, thus becoming expensive and bulky, or utilize only a limited number of sensors, minimizing the cost of posture recognition accuracy. This article presents a new technique for detecting human postures and counting posture cycles by a smart mat. Unlike related solutions, the proposed technique identifies postures by voltage levels observed from five sensors only. The technique has been implemented in a prototype smart mat and experimentally evaluated by 30 Islam worshipers. The results show that it provides unobtrusive and robust (100%) recognition of all six postures of the Muslim praying cycle and reliable cycle counting. The implementation is inexpensive, easy to use and quite helpful for users.

Keywords: smart mat; pressure sensors; sensor systems and applications; assistive living

---

1. Introduction

Praying is a central pillar of the Muslim faith; a mandatory religious ritual performed five times a day at prescribed times. The ritual is quite challenging for elders whose attentive and cognitive capabilities are deteriorating with age. When praying, a worshiper has to perform a sequence of six postures (Figure 1) called Rakah (in singular) and Rakat (in plural). Because the sequence must be repeated a number of times while reciting passages from the Quran, elders frequently have difficulty remembering which cycle is being performed. Incomplete sequence, however, is not acceptable. Once forgotten, a worshiper must go back and fulfill an extra sequence to ensure that he has done the proper number of Rakat.

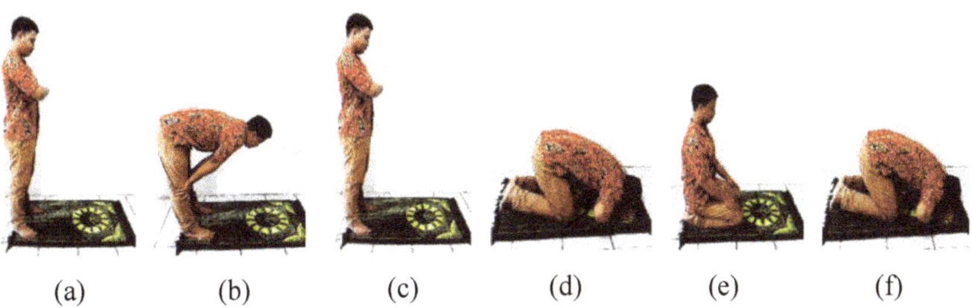

(a)   (b)   (c)   (d)   (e)   (f)

Figure 1. The sequence of postures to complete a single Rakah in a prayer: (**a**,**c**) standing (**b**) bowing; (**d**,**f**) prostration; (**e**) sitting.

Furthermore, the number of cycles, which must be repeated by a worshiper in a pray, varies according to the time of day as well as the day. For example, two Rakat must be performed at dawn prayer, four at each prayer at noon, afternoon and evening, and three at sunset prayer. Old and forgetful people have problems not only remembering how many ritual cycles have to be performed in a prayer but also losing track of the cycles that they have already completed [1]. Although Muslims with severe mental illness or intellectual disability are allowed to be exempted from praying, those with mild and moderate cognitive impairment are not. The options they currently have are quite limited: either to perform in a congregation following the leader or ask someone to inform them which Rakah is currently performed. Elders with cognitive impairment usually practice their rituals at home. They live independently and frequently do not have someone close to ask. At the same time, those who can usually hesitate being a burden to others and showing their cognitive problems, and may eventually lead to bad mood, depression, more extensive cognitive decay, and a stronger association with dementia [2]. Therefore, information and communication technologies capable of assisting forgetful Muslims in praying are important.

In this article, we present a new technique for automatic sensing and recognition of Rakat postures by using a smart mat.

2. Related Research

Over the years, various technologies have been proposed to help Muslims with prayers and Rakat counting. Google Play and Apple Store nowadays contain a number of software applications which can automatically count the number of Rakat on mobile devices (smartphones or tablet PC) with embedded accelerometers. In order to use the applications, a worshiper must possess a proper device in addition to a prayer mat (which is not always the case for old and forgetful people), and also be within the area of Global System for Mobile Communications (GSM) or Wifi coverage in order to access the application server. Therefore, research efforts have been concentrated on incorporating Rakat counting electronics into the prayer mat itself.

Khatri [3] proposed the use of a solar-powered electrical switch pad and liquid crystal display (LCD) operable by a forehead of a worshipper when he or she prostrates on the mat. Faouaz [4] also used LCD with a switch, built in the prayer mat, with the difference that the switch is turned on and off by the user. Abdelmohsen [5] advocated placing a so-called "pressurable plate" under an ordinary mat to detect a prostration posture anytime the user's forehead touches the mat, and incrementing the Rakat counter on display by every even prostration posture. Arrar [6] developed a portable cycle counter based on IR sensors embedded into the prayer rug. Kantarceken [7] presented a prayer assistance device with built-in camera, infra-red sensors, microphones, Bluetooth and acoustic transducers for detecting physical gestures and spoken words of a prayer. Ismail et al. [8] used pressure sensors embedded in the mat under the forehead area to detect the prostration posture. When a second prostration is recognized, the counter is incremented, and its value is displayed on an MP3 player and replayed as an audible cue.

Despite differences in implementation, all of these smart prayer mats have several features in common. Namely, they differentiate human postures by patterns of binary signals (0 and 1) generated from switches or pressure sensors embedded into the mat. The sensors operate locally while the postures span the entire area of the prayer mat. Therefore, the devices either employ a large number of sensors distributed over the mat, as shown in Figure 2a, in order to improve the detection accuracy on expense of cost (e.g., [6,8]), or use a few sensors placed under the forehead (see Figure 2b) to detect the prostration posture only (e.g., [4,5,7]). These cost-oriented solutions do not take into account the other postures of the Rakah sequence and thus might increment the counter when the user skips a posture or makes two prostrations consequently; which is unacceptable. Besides, to our knowledge, none of the existing prayer mats proposed so far can differentiate the standing posture from the bowing posture, thus impeding the correct posture recognition.

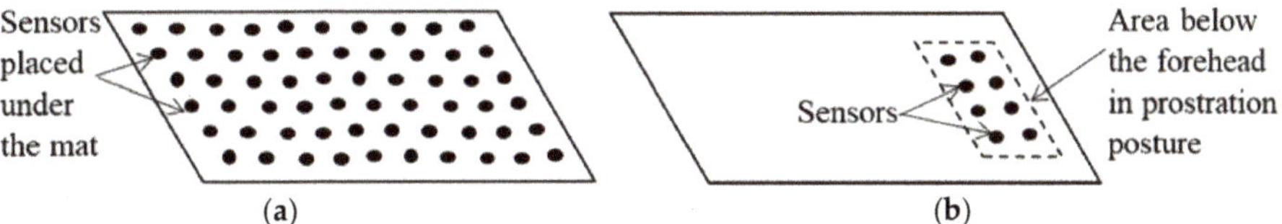

Figure 2. Distribution of pressure sensor in existing smart mats: (**a**) distributed over the mat area; (**b**) localized in the forehead area.

It should be noted that research on smart mats/carpets capable of recognizing human postures and analyzing the human gait has intensified recently, especially for health-care and medical applications. Middleton et al. [9] developed a gate-recognition "floor sensor" that had 1536 small sensing elements arranged in a 3×0.5 m^2 rectangular strip with an individual sensor area of 3 cm^2. Aud et al. [10] presented a fall-detecting smart carpet built from an array of signal-scavenging sensors that use energy available throughout the environment. Although this design does not have a power supply, the electronics put into the carpet make it thick and heavy. For example, a small mat of the carpet has four blocks of foil reading electronics parts, four AD convertors, one microcontroller, and one wireless transmitter. Miguel et al. [11] and Cheng et al. [12] advocated using arrays of pressure sensors made of electrostatic discharge protection foam mixed with carbon fiber to identify static activities on the carpet. Tanaka et al. [13] designed a smart carpet from an array of pressure-sensing tiles that can be easily assembled on a floor to monitor user position, motion and falls. Chaccour et al. [14] embedded a matrix of differential piezoresistive pressure sensors into a carpet for fall detection. Ho et al. [15] proposed a textile technology for making smart carpets from tension-sensitive electro-conductive yarns. The sensing yarn has an elastic core wound around by two tension-sensitive electro-conductive threads of polyester and stainless steel fibers separated by a non-conductive basal layer. The technology can detect light touch, tactile perception, and tensile forces, and seems to be promising though its application in smart mats has not been revealed yet.

In addition to the abovementioned research, a number of successful products have been already deployed. An example is a smart yoga mat [16] that employs over 21,000 built-in piezoresistive sensors to detect human poses and display them on a smartphone or tablet PC. The device provides robust identification of various yoga postures, thus allowing the user to improve his/her yoga practice. However, it is quite expensive (450 US$ retail price).

In this article, we propose a new technique for posture detection and identification by using smart mats. In contrast to related methods, the proposed technique differentiates postures based on voltage levels generated by mat sensors. According to experimental evaluation, it provides unobtrusive and robust detection of all six Rakah postures and reliable Rakat counting. Its implementation is simple and efficient, yet inexpensive.

The rest of the article is organized as follows. In the next section, we discuss the proposed technique. Section 4 describes the prototype's implementation in a smart mat and presents results of experimental evaluation. Section 5 summarizes our findings and outlines work for the future.

3. The Proposed Technique

3.1. An Overview

The key idea behind our method emanates from empirical analysis of output voltages produced by a pressure sensor of a single zone force-sensing resistor (FSR) family, which are largely used nowadays in automotive electronics, medical systems, and various industrial and robotics applications. A FSR is a two-wire device made from polymer thick film that "exhibits a decrease in resistance with increase in force applied to the surface of the sensor" [17]. As the force grows, the output voltage increases. When a person steps over the sensor, his weight causes the sensor to generate an output voltage proportional to the product of person's mass and the gravitational acceleration. For example, if a FSR sensor is tied to a measuring resistor R_M in a configuration shown in Figure 3a, the output voltage, V_{OUT}, increases with weight, as depicted in Figure 3b. Under a constant force, the output voltage remains constant. Note, the weight in the article is shown in terms of kilogram-force (1 kgf = 9.8 N).

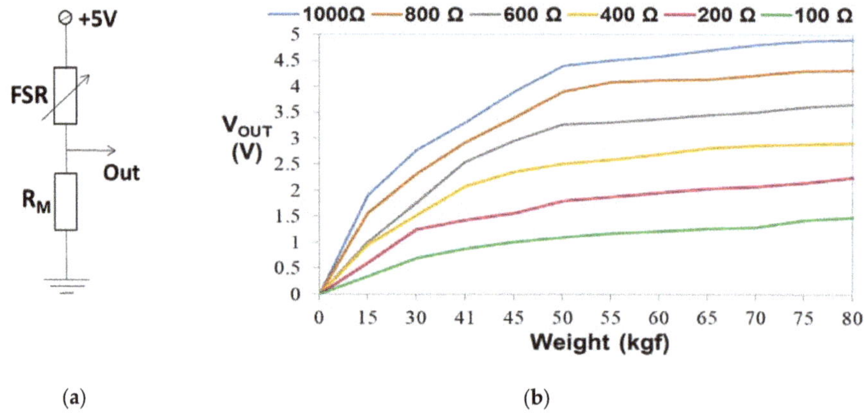

Figure 3. Results of force-sensing resistor (FSR) sensor testing: (**a**) a test circuit; (**b**) FSR voltage as a function of applied weight and output resistance R_M.

As a force, weight has both a magnitude and a direction associated with it. While the direction of the weight force always remains toward the center of the earth, the distribution of the weight over the body's center of gravity changes with human posture. For instance, when a person stands straight, his weight concentrates over his feet. So the weight force is maximal. When a person bows, sits or prostrates, his body's center of gravity shifts and so does the weight distribution. Because a posture affects the weight force applied to the sensor, it changes the voltage produced by the sensor.

Figure 4 depicts the FSR voltage variations with postures, accumulated (at $R_M = 600\ \Omega$) from a test in which 30 people of different weight were standing, sitting and prostrating while a FSR sensor was under their feet. As one can see, the postures induce distinguishable voltages though the levels of the voltages vary with the mass.

Our posture detection technique exploits this posture-voltage dependency. In contrast to existing approaches, which differentiate human postures by binary patterns of active sensors, the proposed technique identifies postures by voltage levels produced by the sensors. It assumes that the prayer mat contains an array of FSR strip-line sensors connected to an embedded microcontroller. The microcontroller reads the sensor voltages, and based on them, detects postures performed by the user.

3.2. Positioning of Sensors Inside a Mat

In order to determine sensor placement within the mat, we experimentally studied the mat usage in a prayer. The study involved 30 Muslims aged from 20 to 60 years old. The participants varied in height (140~178 cm), weight (40~72 kg), shape (slim, ordinary, fat), gender, and feet size (23~26 cm). In the study, each participant was asked to pray using same mat lined by squares of 5 cm × 5 cm in size.

We measured the positions of participants over the mat and recorded the squares touched by the participant's feet, knees, forehead or hands in different postures.

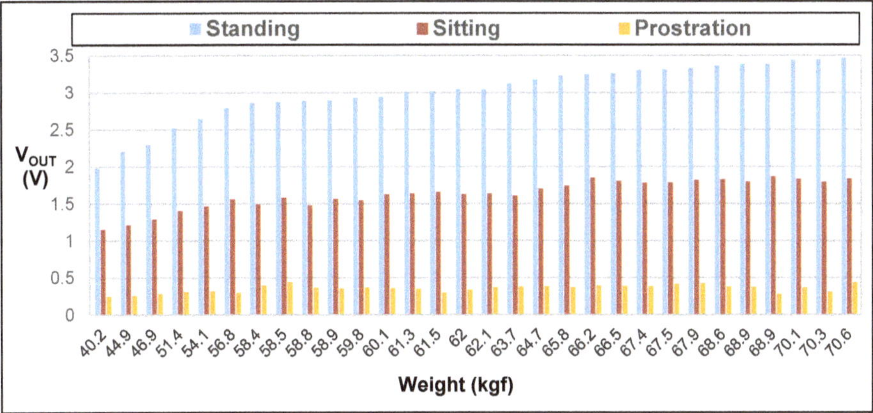

Figure 4. The FSR sensor voltage variation with the user's posture and weight.

The results revealed three distinguishable areas of the mat usage, associated with the user's feet (Area 1), knees, (Area 2) and head (Area 3), respectively, as shown in Figure 5. Without being asked, all participants used same area for feet, identified from a picture printed on the mat. Namely, the Area 1 was used in standing and bowing postures; Area 2 in sitting and prostrating postures; and Area 3 in the prostrating posture only.

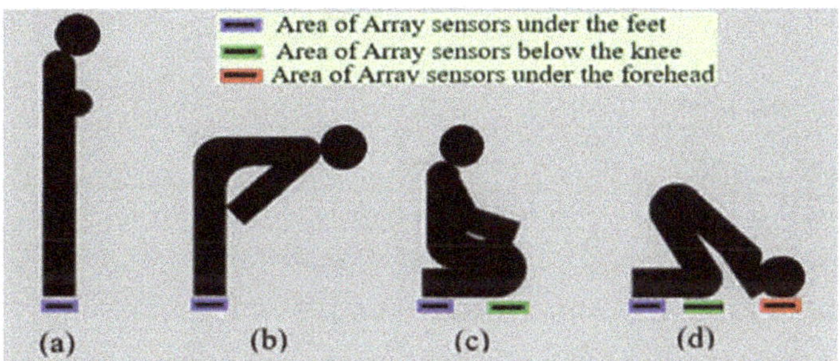

Figure 5. Sensing areas associated with praying postures: (**a**) standing, (**b**) bowing, (**c**) sitting, (**d**) prostration.

Figure 6 shows the details of mat area usage for each posture. In this figure, lines and columns determine the squares within the mat areas (see Figure 7); the vertical axis shows the square usage in terms of the number of participants that touched a particular square in a posture. The two visible peaks in the graphs, associated with Areas 1 and 2, correspond to the mat regions used by the left and the right legs, respectively; the graph at the bottom reflects the regions of Area 3 touched by head. As the results demonstrate, every participant in the test placed their feet over Line 3 of Area 1 in the standing posture, pressed Line 3 of Area 1 and Line 2 of Area 2 in the sitting posture, and in the prostration posture had their feet over Line 4 of Area 1, their knees over Line 4 of Area 2 and their forehead over Line 3 of Area 3. Thus, to detect all of the postures of the Rakah sequence, only five strip-type (Model 408) FSR sensors [16] are needed. A standard strip-type FSR-408 sensor is 622 mm long and 6.35 mm wide, and 1 mm thin. Because it responds to pressure applied from up to ±5 cm from its edge, we position the sensors on the mat as shown in Figure 7.

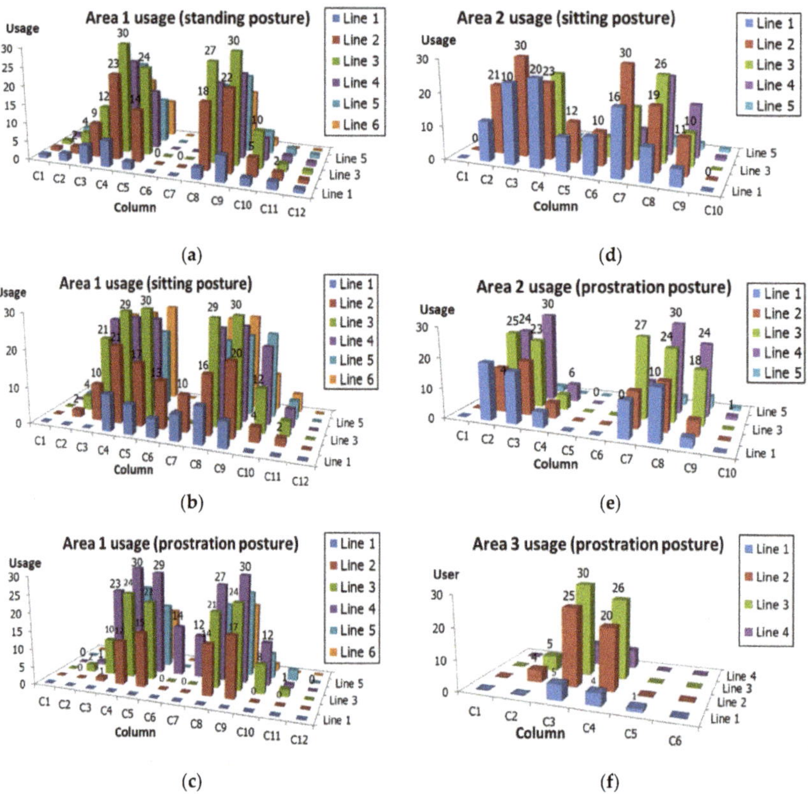

Figure 6. The mat area usage in different postures. (a) Area 1 usage at standing posture; (b) Area 1 usage at sitting posture; (c) Area 1 usage at prostration posture; (d) Area 2 usage at sitting posture; (e) Area 2 usage at prostration posture; (f) Area 3 usage at prostration posture.

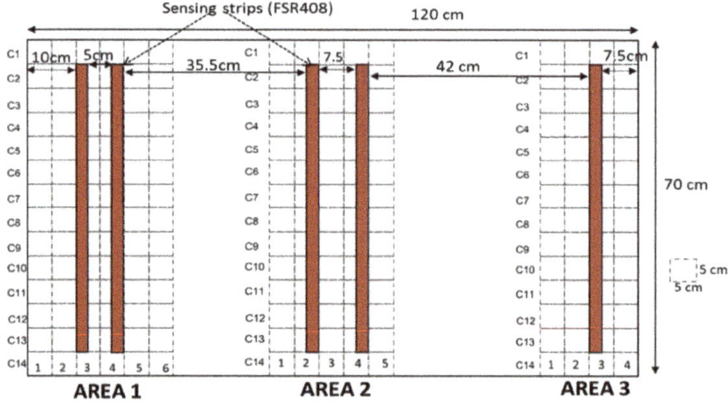

Figure 7. The FSR sensor voltage variation with the user's posture.

Now consider output voltages induced by these five FSR sensors when a mat user implements the Rakah postures. Table 1 presents an example observed for a 40 kg user ($R_M = 600\ \Omega$). The standing posture leads to the maximal voltage in comparison to the other voltages listed in the Table. This is because the user in this posture presses the mat by his entire weight. When the user bows, the Area 1 sensors generate voltages around 90–100% of the maximal level. The sitting posture causes only 80% of the maximal voltage on sensors in Area 1, and around 60% of the maximal level on sensors in Area 2. When the user takes the prostrating posture, the sensors of Areas 2 and 3 produce voltages in the range of 50–75% and 4–25% of the maximal level, respectively.

Table 1. Sensor readings (in volts) at different postures [1].

Posture	Area1		Area 2		Area 3
	Sensor 1	Sensor 2	Sensor 3	Sensor 4	Sensor 5
Standing	1.89	1.69	0	0	0
Bowing	1.79	1.72	0	0	0
Sitting	1.47	1.15	0.75	0.02	0
Prostration	0	0.98	0.04	1.21	0.2

[1] $R_M = 600\ \Omega$; 40 kg user.

To study the relationship between the user's posture, weight, and voltage ranges, we empirically measured the sensor outputs induced by 30 different users of the prayer mat. Figure 8 shows the results in terms of sensor voltages (V_{OUT}) normalized to the peak voltage levels (V_0) of the Area 1 sensors.

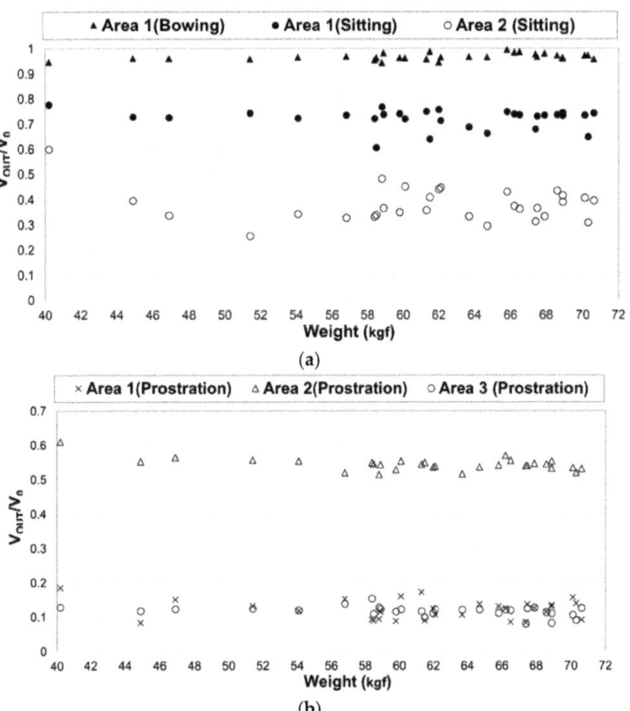

Figure 8. Normalized voltage variations observed on outputs of sensors in Area 1–3 when 30 users of different weight performed the bowing and sitting postures (**a**), and the prostration posture (**b**).

For the sake of simplicity, we depict only the maximal values of the normalized voltages generated by sensors in Areas 1 and 2 for the bowing, the sitting and the prostration postures. The absolute variation of peak voltage (V_0) with the weight is given in Figure 4. Interestingly, the voltage ranges associated with the postures are quite distinguishable and do not depend much on the user's weight. In the sequel, we exploit these voltage–posture correlation for posture detection.

3.3. The Posture Detection and Rakat Counting Technique

The proposed posture detection technique is based on identifying patterns of sensor readings associated with each posture of the Rakah sequence. In contrast to related techniques, which differentiate postures by logic patterns associated with positions of active sensors within the mat, it distinguishes patterns (and hence postures) by voltage levels produced by the sensors. At each time of prayer, the voltage levels of the sensor outputs are compared to the pre-defined thresholds. A posture is considered detected if and only if all of the sensors associated with the posture produce voltages within the specified range. If the completed sequence of postures matches the correct order of the Rakah sequence (Figure 1), the Rakat counter is incremented. Otherwise, it remains unchanged.

Figure 9 illustrates the proposed posture generation and Rakat counting technique in terms of state transition diagram. In this figure, circles represent postures; arrows show their execution order in Rakah sequence, the formulas above the arrows represent conditions at which the posture is considered detected i.e., the state transition occurs. The thresholds associated with the conditions have been obtained from an analysis of experimental data, of which a part is shown in Figure 8.

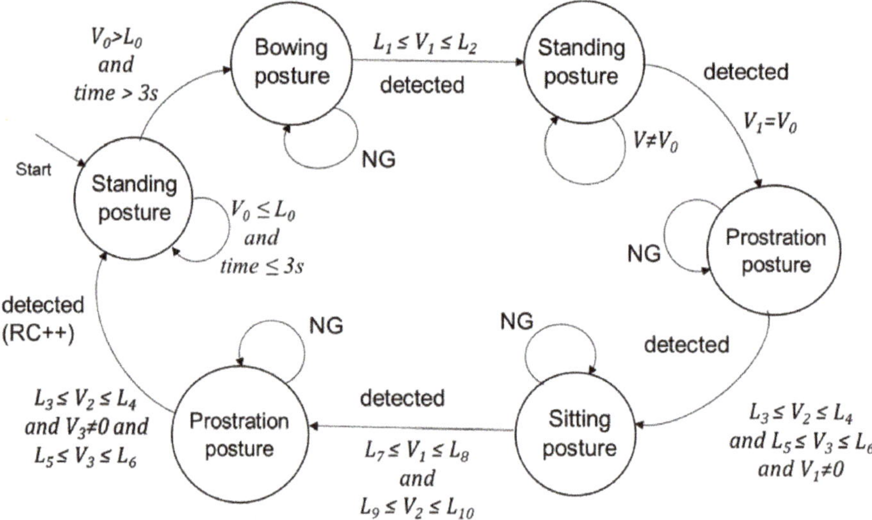

Figure 9. State diagram of the Rakat Counter.

The state machine works as follows. As the user activates the machine, it evaluates the outputs of sensors in Area 1 for 3 s in order to identify the peak voltage of the standing posture. If the voltage level is less than a given threshold (L_0), i.e., no pressure on sensors, the system remains in the initial stage. Otherwise, the calculated peak voltage is applied as a reference (V_0) for computing ten voltage thresholds (Li) of the detection conditions. Namely,

$$L_1 = 0.9 \times V_0, \tag{1}$$

$$L_2 = 1 \times V_0, \tag{2}$$

$$L_3 = 0.5 \times V_0, \tag{3}$$

$$L_4 = 0.65 \times V_0, \tag{4}$$

$$L_5 = 0.5 \times V_0, \tag{5}$$

$$L_6 = 0.12 \times V_0, \tag{6}$$

$$L_7 = 0.1 \times V_0, \tag{7}$$

$$L_8 = 0.8 \times V_0, \tag{8}$$

$$L_9 = 0.05 \times V_0, \tag{9}$$

$$L_{10} = 0.65 \times V_0, \tag{10}$$

For example, if the reference voltage $V_0 = 1.89$ V, the $L_1 = 1.7$ V, $L_2 = 1.89$ V, $L_3 = 0.945$ V, and so on. The bowing posture is detected when the output voltages of Area 1 sensors are within the range $L_1 \leq V_1 \leq L_2$. Otherwise, the system waits until the user implements the posture correctly i.e., the outputs of sensors 1 and 2 satisfy the specified condition. Note that even if the specified condition is satisfied but there is non-zero output from other sensors, the system will remain in the current state. To detect the prostration posture, we use Areas 2 and 3 sensors. If the outputs of the Area 2 sensors satisfy the condition: $L_3 \leq V_2 \leq L_4$, and the outputs of the Area 3 sensors satisfy the condition: $L_5 \leq V_3 \leq L_6$, then the system identifies the prostration posture. Otherwise, it continues waiting for the correct implementation of the required posture. To detect the sitting posture, we check whether the Area 1 voltages (V_1) and the Area 2 voltages (V_2) are within the ranges: $L_7 \leq V_1 \leq L_8$ and $L_9 \leq V_2 \leq L_{10}$. If either of these two conditions is unsatisfied, or there is a non-zero voltage output from the Area 3 sensors, the posture is rejected as incorrect. Thus, we proceed to the next state if the user correctly implements the postures. As the second prostration is identified, the system increments the Rakat Counter (RC) by 1 and repeats the cycle.

4. Implementation and Evaluation

4.1. Implementation

The proposed technique was implemented in a smart mat prototype [18] that additionally to Rakah counting also determined the start time of a next prayer and the direction to Mekkah (or Qibla). The praying mat was 120 cm $\times$ 70 cm in size, which is conventional for a medium height user. Figure 10 shows a block diagram of electronics embedded into the mat. The sensor array contained five force-sensing resistive strips (FSR 406) placed under Areas 1–3 of the mat, as shown in Figure 7. To reduce sensor displacement and eliminate undesirable effects of dirt, the sensors were fixed in special pockets made of cloth that were sewn to the backside of the praying mat. The processing unit (depicted by gray pattern in Figure 10) includes an 8-bit microcontroller (AVR ATmega32, from Atmel Crop., Chandler, AR, USA), a GPS receiver (Ublox NEO 6M, from Thalwil, Switzerland), a digital compass (CMPS10, from Robot Electroncs, Norfolk, UK), a real-time clock (RTC) unit, and an interface circuitry. The control panel contains a 128 $\times$ 64 graphical LCD display, a digital buzzer and a number of switches. By pushing a corresponding button on the control panel, the user can display on the screen either the ST (start time of the next prayer), QD (Qibla Direction), and RC (Rakah Counter). He or she can also reset RC, deactivate the buzzer (alarm off) or power off the smart mat if necessary.

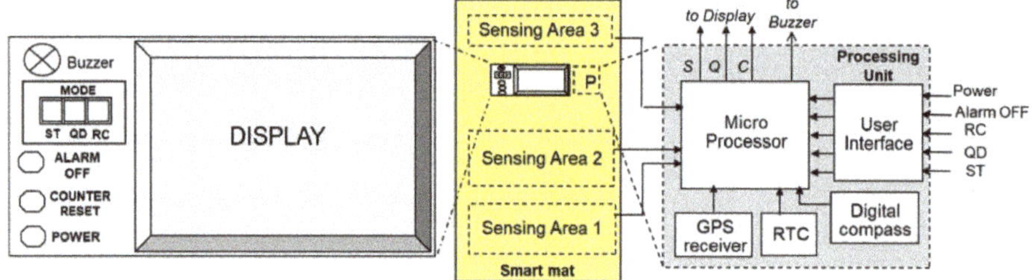

Figure 10. Block diagram of smart mat.

On the mat, the FSR sensing strips were attached to the backside of the mat, while the microcontroller and the control panel shared the board placed on the foreside of the mat. The proposed posture detection and Rakat counting technique was implemented in software.

Figure 11a,b shows photographs of the smart mat prototype and its usage in a prayer. The user activates the smart mat by pushing the power bottom on the control panel. By default, the RC is zero. When activated, the system displays the value of RC and the next posture to be taken by the user, thus guiding him or her through the Rakah sequence. If the system recognizes that the user completed a Rakah, it increments the RC value. Otherwise, the value of RC remains unchanged.

Figure 11c exemplifies data shown on the display as the user completed the sitting posture of the second Rakah sequence. At any time, the user can reset the counter or switch the power OFF if necessary.

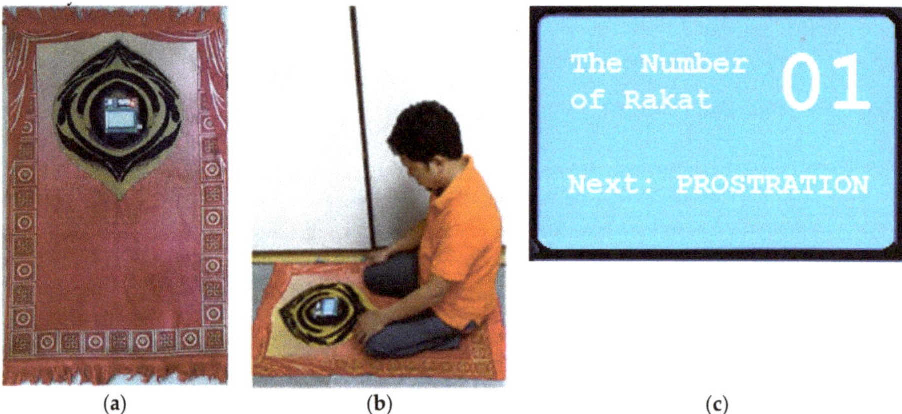

Figure 11. Photographs: (**a**) the smart mat prototype (**b**) the smart mat usage; (**c**) displayed data.

4.2. Evaluation and Results

To evaluate the quality of the proposed posture recognition and Rakat counting algorithm, we performed a number of tests, which involved 30 participants (of ages 10 to 60). The tests have been conducted in laboratory conditions with the smart mat placed on a flat, smooth, clean flooring. The temperature and humidity levels in the room were normal. The participants had different heights (from 128 cm to 180 cm), feet size (from 18 cm to 29 cm), and shapes (from 26 to 94 kg). During the tests, each participant was asked to perform the praying ritual with three Rakat correctly and then randomly skip or perform incorrectly (e.g., sitting instead bowing or vs. versa) one or several postures in a "faulty" Rakah sequence. These scenarios were repeated three times by each subject in a random order. In between the tests, the power was switched OFF. The tests totaled 120 simulated cycles of six postures each.

The evaluation revealed several results. First, when the system was switched ON and no pressure asserted to the mat, the voltage readings from the FSR sensors were almost 0, causing the system to remain in the initial state. The system operation started only when someone stepped over sensing Area 1, and when the level of voltage generated from the sensors of this area exceeds L_0. (Though we used $L_0 = 1$, the threshold level can be calibrated to reduce external noise if any. According to [17], the FSR sensors are no more prone to noise pickup than a passive resistor).

Second, the posture detection ratio of the proposed technique was 100%, even though the participants in the tests had different styles for sitting, standing, and prostration. Some of them inclined or moved forward/backward more than others; some used their hands to support their body when standing. Despite variations in posture style, the proposed method was able to effectively distinguish all six postures of the Rakah sequence and correctly count the Rakat. At the same time, we should notice that the posture detection and recognition might depend on the person's height. Namely, it might be possible that a mat designated for a person of an average height may fail to correctly identify postures of a very tall or a short person or vice versa. We assume that this issue will not pose a problem in reality, because worshippers usually use mats of sizes proportional to their height.

Finally, the tests showed that the sensors in the mat successfully detect gait characteristics and are not perceptible to the people as they stay, sit, or prostrate. Overall, all the participants of the evaluation experiments reported the proposed smart mat useful and quite helpful.

5. Limitations and Future Work

In this section, we discuss the limitations of our study. Recognizing human activity is a challenge for any cyber-physical system application, as it requires modeling the peculiarities of an application environment, as well as the complex behavioral, psychological, and physiological aspects of human beings. The level of modeling for each of these aspects depends on application requirements.

In the current work, we modeled the application environment through laboratory settings that resembled environmental conditions in a Mosque or at home (flat, smooth, dry, and clean surfaces), i.e., conditions typical to the majority of Muslims. In the future, we will consider other settings to cover praying outdoors. For example, people may pray in open air and place the mat on a bumpy, sandy and dusty surface. Though worshipers usually pray in dry and clean places outdoors and do not pray in the event of rain or snow, several external factors such as dirt, moisture, liquids, and trapped air bubbles can cause the FSR sensors to generate faulty signals. Also, proximity to high intensity radio frequency (RF) sources may require special measures to reduce electro-magnetic noise. To investigate these issues, we plan to conduct a larger study of outdoor mat use.

We should also acknowledge that the developed system prototype is just a testbed to evaluate the efficiency of the proposed method, as well as other techniques [18]. Though the strip-type sensors are flexible, neither the sensors nor the control panel can be folded, as this may cause shearing or breakup. We are now working on providing a foldable and portable solution of battery-operated smart-mat electronics which is reliable, easy to use and attach/detach whenever necessary.

Another limitation of the current work deals with the user modeling. The number of old and forgetful people involved in the study was very limited, and so it is hard to draw a statistically significant conclusion. Though all subjects considered in the study are real prayer mat users, some old people may implement postures differently than others or use assistive tools such as a cane to support their body. Also, people suffering from memory loss or cognitive impairment may also have different behavior. Extending the study to cover more elders and forgetful people will be performed in the near future.

Further, the current study assumed that the mat user is the only person who asserts force to the mat during a prayer. Moreover, the worshiper performs praying activities and takes postures within the mat area. Someone unfamiliar with Islam may argue that a mat user hypothetically might jump, step out of the mat during a prayer, go out, return back, and so on. Moreover, a prayer might be interrupted by a child, another person (e.g., caregiver), or a pet, for example, who might step over the mat and cause an error. While these events might happen hypothetically, they are far from reality. Religious people are very serious in their beliefs, obligations, and rituals. Preparations to pray are actually taken with a large care to prevent any external interruption. When a prayer starts, everyone in a Muslim family prays, including kids. During a prayer, each worshiper uses his own mat and is fully concentrated on the spiritual act of praying, i.e., communicating with God. So it is a realistic consideration that a Muslim will not be doing anything else other than praying if someone near them is also engaged in prayer. However, even if a hypothetical case takes place and a faulty action or posture is detected, the system will remain in its current state until the required posture is done correctly.

6. Conclusions

In this paper, we presented a new technique for unobtrusive human posture identification by a smart mat to assist Muslims in praying. As the experimental evaluation revealed, the proposed technique provides robust recognition of postures taken by a worshiper in a prayer and correct counting of the Rakat cycles in real time.

Finally, we would like to notice that the proposed voltage based posture identification technique is not limited to the smart prayer mat and Rakat counting, even though the paper has been focused on this specific application only. We think that it can be used in other applications as well. In healthcare, for example, the technique can be applied to identify the sleeping postures, or for monitoring the frequency of posture change of in-bed patients to decrease the development of ulcers. Similarly, it can be applied to detect sitting postures from sensors placed inside a chair. We are currently investigating further applications.

Acknowledgments: The authors thank colleagues from Tele-communication Laboratory of Moslem University of Makassar, Indonesia for assistance in accumulating experimental data and helpful discussions.

Author Contributions: All authors have contributed to the work presented in this article. Kasman Kasman conceived and designed the smart mat prototype, performed experiments and wrote the text; Vasily G. Moshnyaga directed the work, analyzed and interpreted the obtained results and revised the manuscript.

Conflicts of Interest: The authors declare no conflict of interest.

References

1. Ismail, J.; Noor, N.L.M.; Isa, W.A.R.W.M. Addressing cognitive impairment among elderly people: A techno-spiritual perspective. In Proceedings of the 5th International Conference on Information and Communication Technology for the Muslim World (ICT4M), Kuching, Malaisia, 17–18 November 2014; pp. 1–5.
2. Speck, C.E.; Kukull, W.A.; Brenner, D.E.; Bowen, J.D.; McCormick, W.C.; Teri, L.; Pfanschmidt, M.L.; Thompson, J.D.; Larson, E.B. History of depression as a risk factor for Alzheimer's disease. *Epidemiology* **1995**, *6*, 366–369. [CrossRef] [PubMed]
3. Khatri, A.E.S. Prayer Mat. UK Patent 2,263,003-A, 7 July 1993.
4. Faouaz, H. Muslim Prayer Counter. U.S. Patent 6,783,822, 31 August 2004.
5. Abdelmohsen, A.M.E. Prayer Carpet (for Muslims) Provided with a Number of Bowings (Rak'a) Digital Displayer Apparatus. WO Patent 2,007,104,321 A1, 20 September 2007.
6. Arrar, R.B.J. Portable Interactive Islamic Prayer Counter. U.S. Patent 7,508,316 B1, 24 March 2009.
7. Kantarceken, I. Prayer Assistance Device for Use As e.g. Personal Digital Assistant, Has Electronic Memory Unit Storing Program Flow that Acoustically Corrects Spoken Words and Physical Gestures of Prayer by Sound Transducer Unit. Patent DE 102,010,048,504 B3, 5 April 2012.
8. Ismail, J.; Noor, N.L.M.; Isa, W.A.R.W.M. Smart prayer mat: A textile-based pressure sensor to assist elderly with cognitive impairment in praying Activity. In Proceedings of the 5th International Conference on Computing & Informatics (ICOCI), Istanbul, Turkey, 11–13 August 2015; pp. 241–246.

9. Middleton, L.; Buss, A.A.; Nixon, M.S. A floor sensor system for gait recognition. In Proceedings of the 2005 4th IEEE Workshop on Automatic Identification Advanced Technologies, Buffalo, NY, USA, 17–18 October 2005; pp. 171–176.

10. Aud, M.A.; Abbott, C.C.; Tyrer, H.W.; Neelgund, R.V.; Shriniwar, U.G.; Mohammed, A.; Devarakonda, K.K. Smart Carpet: Developing a sensor system to detect falls and summon assistance. *J. Gerontol. Nurs.* **2010**, *36*, 8–12. [CrossRef] [PubMed]

11. Miguel, J.; Morgado, A.; Konig, A. Low-Power concept and prototype of distributed resistive pressure sensor array for smart floor and surfaces in intelligent environments. In Proceedings of the International Conference on Systems, Signals and Devices, Chemnitz, Germany, 20–23 March 2012; pp. 1–6.

12. Cheng, J.; Sandholm, M.; Zhou, B.; Kreil, M.; Lukowicz, P. Recognizing subtle user activities and person identity with cheap resistive pressure sensing carpet. In Proceedings of the International Conference on Intelligent Environments, Shanghai, China, 30 June–4 July 2014; pp. 148–153.

13. Tanaka, O.; Ryu, T.; Hayashida, A.; Moshnyaga, V.G.; Hashimoto, K. A Smart Carpet Design for Monitoring People with Dementia. In *Progress in System Engineering, Advances in Intelligent Systems and Computing*; Selvaraj, H., Zydek, D., Chmaj, G., Eds.; Springer: Berlin, Germany, 2015; pp. 653–659.

14. Chaccour, K.; Darazi, R.; El Hassani, A.H.; Andres, E. Smart carpet using differential piezoresistive pressure sensors for elderly fall detection. In Proceedings of the 2015 IEEE 11th International Conference on Wireless and Mobile Computing, Networking and Communications (WiMob), Abu Dhabi, United Arab Emirates, 19–21 October 2015; pp. 225–229.

15. Ho, V.A.; Imai, S.; Hirai, S. Multimodal flexible sensor for healthcare system. In Proceedings of the 2014 36th Annual International Conference of the IEEE on Engineering in Medicine and Biology Society (EMBS), Chicago, IL, USA, 26–30 August 2014; pp. 5976–5979.

16. The World's First Intelligent Yoga Mat. Available online: https://smartmat.com/ (accessed on 25 May 2017).

17. FSR 400 Series Data Sheet, Interlink Electronics. Available online: http://www.steadlands.com/data/interlink/fsrdatasheet.pdf (accessed on 25 May 2017).

18. Kasman, K.; Moshnyaga, V.G. A smart mat for assisting Muslims in praying. In Proceedings of the 2017 IEEE International Conference on Consumer Electronics (ICCE), Las Vegas, NV, USA, 8–10 January 2017; pp. 481–484.

 *electronics*

Article

Design of a Building-Integrated Photovoltaic System with a Novel Bi-Reflector PV System (BRPVS) and Optimal Control Mechanism: An Experimental Study

Muhammad Adil Khan [1], Kamran Zeb [1,2], Waqar Uddin [1], P. Sathishkumar [1], Muhammad Umair Ali [1], S. Hussain [1], M. Ishfaq [1], Himanshu [1], Archana Subramanian [1] and Hee-Je Kim [1,*]

[1] School of Electrical Engineering, Pusan National University, Busandaehak-ro 63beon-gil, Geumjeong-gu, Busan 46241, Korea; engradilee@gmail.com (M.A.K.); kami_zeb@yahoo.com (K.Z.); waqar_dir98@yahoo.com (W.U.); sathishnano2013@gmail.com (P.S.); umairali.m99@gmail.com (M.U.A.); sadamengr15@gmail.com (S.H.); engrishfaq1994@gmail.com (M.I.); himanshuhimanshu820@gmail.com (H.); er.ararchu@gmail.com (A.S.)
[2] School of Electrical Engineering and Computer Science, National University of Sciences and Technology, Islamabad 44000, Pakistan
* Correspondence: heeje@pusan.ac.kr; Tel.: +82-51-510-2364

Received: 29 June 2018; Accepted: 17 July 2018; Published: 18 July 2018

Abstract: Environment protection and energy saving are the most attractive trends in zero-carbon buildings. The most promising and environmentally friendly technique is building integrated photovoltaics (BIPV), which can also replace conventional buildings based on non-renewable energy. Despite the recent advances in technology, the cost of BIPV systems is still very high. Hence, reducing the cost is a major challenge. This paper examines and validates the effectiveness of low-cost aluminum (Al) foil as a reflector. The design and the performance of planer-reflector for BIPV systems are analyzed in detail. A Bi-reflector solar PV system (BRPVS) with thin film Al-foil reflector and an LLC converter for a BIPV system is proposed and experimented with a 400-W prototype. A cadmium–sulfide (CdS) photo-resistor sensor and an Arduino-based algorithm was developed to control the working of the reflectors. Furthermore, the effect of Al-foil reflectors on the temperature of PV module has been examined. The developed LLC converter confirmed stable output voltage despite large variation in input voltage proving its effectiveness for the proposed BRPVS. The experimental results of the proposed BRPVS with an Al-reflector of the same size as that of the solar PV module offered an enhancement of 28.47% in the output power.

Keywords: building integrated photovoltaics (BIPV); renewable energy; solar; LCC converter; half bridge; bi-reflector solar PV system (BRPVS)

---

1. Introduction

Recently, environmental pollution, global warming, and energy shortage have been generally seen as alarming global issues. The building sector consumes a major proportion of energy. For example, in the European Union, 30–40% of energy is consumed by the building sectors, that produce 32% of carbon dioxide emissions [1]. Attention has been given to zero energy buildings to develop future energy saving infrastructures. In this scenario, renewable energy is expected to play an important role. Photo–Voltaic (PV) systems are very attractive choices for production of electric power due to their noiseless and nonpolluting nature. Building Integrated Photo–Voltaic (BIPV) is a new version of the PV system, in which the building is used for installation of PV modules to reduce cost and improve the appearance [2]. In addition to the environmental influences of BIPV, they also reduce the long-term cost of the building sector. Compared to a standalone PV system, BIPV does not require any extra land for installation and the cost can be balanced by installing this on the rooftop of the building structure [3]. However, the lower efficiency and higher initial cost make BIPV less practical and difficult to commercialize. Dye-Sensitized Solar Cells (DSSCs) have attracted considerable attention in recent years because of their simple assembly, lightweight, flexibility, economical price of materials, satisfactory photocurrent transformation efficiency, precise energy return time, and tunable optical properties [4]. On the other hand, DSSCs have power conversion efficiency of more than 14% with a limited active area; the output power decreases with increasing cell effective area of the photoanode [5]. An alternate solution exists to increase the net output power from the PV module to reduce the cost of the system because the initial cost of the PV system is the main hurdle to the widespread use of this technology. The output power can be increased by increasing the incident light on the PV system [6]. The position of the Sun is not fixed to one place because it changes its position from dawn to dusk and also during the entire year, which means that a fixed PV system is inefficient. Therefore, the tracking of single- and dual-axis PV systems are suggested for this purpose [7,8]. On the other hand, such a system has two disadvantages, increase in initial cost and decreased lifetime of the mechanical parts of the PV system. Moreover, such a system also requires extra power supply and motors to move the solar system, which makes the system more complex and increases the size of the PV system, making it unrealistic for commercialization [8,9].

Another way is to reflect the light onto the PV module to increase the efficiency of BIPV systems. This system will increase the sunlight flux intensity per unit area on the BIPV, resulting in an amplified output power, which would allow a decrease in the size and cost of the PV module. With the help of the reflector with a planar shape, solar radiation will increase [10]. The advances in architecture and the artistic structure of buildings with narrow roof spaces has created a challenging situation for the installation of a BIPV system with reflectors and the crowded city has forced planning management to consider the roof and facade [11]. Despite this, installing such a system will make the architecture appear less attractive, which is a notable factor in new solar systems [12]. Moreover, the health concerns for BIPV can be a major disadvantage and a real challenge for BIPV systems. The study predicted a gain in annual output from amorphous Silicon (a-Si) PV modules of up to 25%, considering the latitude of 60° N and a specular reflector with a reflectivity of 0.8 [13]. Probst and Roecker reported the advantages of mixing solar collectors for developing a system [14]. The advantage of adding booster reflectors by placing the reflector at a 90° angle with a crystalline Silicon (c-Si) PV module and varying the inclination of the assembly was explored in [15]. Karlson and Wilson [16] designed the Maximum Reflector Collector (MaReCo) in 2000, which was then modified by Brogren and Karlson [17] from an edge reflector to a parabolic design, which boost the radiations falling on the PV module. On the other hand, not all the increasing radiation was converted to electrical power; some was reflected and some were converted to heat in BIPV module. From such studies, a small amount of heat was absorbed by the cell, which decreased the efficiency of the cell and module. The increase in temperature resulted in a 0.3–0.5% per K decrease in efficiency [18]. The increase in temperature in the BIPV system was overcome using a Building Integrated Photo-Voltaic Thermal system (BIPVT) [19]. Using such a system, the efficiency was increased to 30–40% and two separate collector quantities of space and material were minimized due to hybridization [20]. This choice was more substantial because of the low price and sufficient availability, and these two factors make it more practical. A Concentrated Photo-Voltaic (CPV) system, which applies an optical element, was used to focus the sunlight on the solar cell. Such type of intensified light increased the energy up to some extent [21,22]. Some studies suggested a horizontal arrangement of the reflector with the solar panel [23]. A model of ray tracing to calculate the irradiation rise was proposed [24]. Some used diffuse reflectors, which are a collective view factor and specular reflectance mode [25], whereas others use a 2-D specular reflectance model and experimental data [26]. The non-specular ridged booster reflector increased the output by 8% [27]. Although Mirror-Augmented Photo-Voltaic (MAPV) is low cost, it produces non-uniformity in irradiance, which is overcome by optimizing the system properly to maximize the annual power production. The uniformity in a PV system is the primary objective of the system, but the PV module is not ideal for MAPV because of its non-uniformity [28]. A different method was suggested by Van Dijk et al. for power conversion improvement. The solar module has a glass layer with a lens array on the top and a reflector on bottom side [29]. A reflector perpendicular to the PV panel with a width 2.7 times the panels obtains a result of 1.5 at solar noontime and was used keeping in view weather conditions of Tokyo, Japan [30]. Khan et. al. studied three different (i.e., flat mirror, spherical mirror and Al foil) reflector materials for studying high-performance materials and used a variety of cooling techniques to enhance the performance of existing PV systems [31].

Effective power conditioning for BIPV is crucial. In common practice, the boost DC-DC converter is used to increase the PV voltage and track the maximum point of the PV output power in real time. Considering that switching of semiconductor devices occurs at high currents, the efficiency of these converters is low at high frequencies because of the hard switching [32–36]. On the other hand, at low frequencies, the size and cost of the magnetic components and the capacitor would be high. Furthermore, the parasitic capacitance of the PV modules to the ground might cause leakage currents due to the lack of isolation in conventional power conversion topologies [37]. To handle these problems, a DC-DC LLC resonant converter was presented [38,39]. LLC converters have been utilized broadly in various DC converters as a result of their similar zero voltage Switching (ZVS) for the essential MOSFETs and zero current Switching (ZCS) for optional diodes, which enable them to achieve high proficiency and power thickness [40,41]. Typically, pulse width switching frequency modulation techniques is utilized as a part of LLC resonant converters to standardize the output current and voltage, yet the non-direct highlights of the input voltage make it difficult for ordinary linear control systems to accomplish the normal execution and a hybrid control scheme has been introduced for the purpose of switching [42,43].

Based on a literature survey and discrepancy available in existing solutions to enhance the PV module power for a BIPV system, this study evaluated the Al-foil sheet and LLC converter-based Bi-Reflector PV System (BRPVS). A reflector system was designed to enhance the output power, and a hybrid control scheme of a half-bridge LLC resonant converter is proposed for a wide input range application and medium power applications. The objective of this research is to design and briefly discuss a novel reflector system (BRPVS) its operation and possible outcomes. This study conducted real-time experiments to examine the performance of BRPVS and developed an algorithm to control the working of the BRPVS. Its effects on the output power were examined and its optimal control way of operation was defined. Moreover, an optical and thermal model was also evaluated. A detailed description of the system is provided in Section 2. The remainder of the manuscript is arranged as follows. Section 2 presents a detailed overview of the proposed system along with component required to design the BRPVS system. Experimental arrangements of the designed system are discussed in Section 3. Results for experimental study are discussed in Section 4 while Section 5 summarizes the conclusion of this study.

2. System Components and Development

2.1. An Overview of Proposed BRPVS

Figure 1 presents an overview of the proposed solution. The overall system was comprised of a Bi-reflector system (BRS), whose output is given to a half-bridge resonant LLC converter. Movement of the BRDF (Bidirectional Reflectance Function) system is achieved using an Arduino based automatic stepper motor and a CdS sensor arrangement, whose working was controlled by an algorithm developed in Section 2.2.2. The output power of the LLC converter was transferred to the energy storage system (ESS) to supply electric power to the building via an inverter and power distribution system. A detail description of the components of the system is provided in this section.

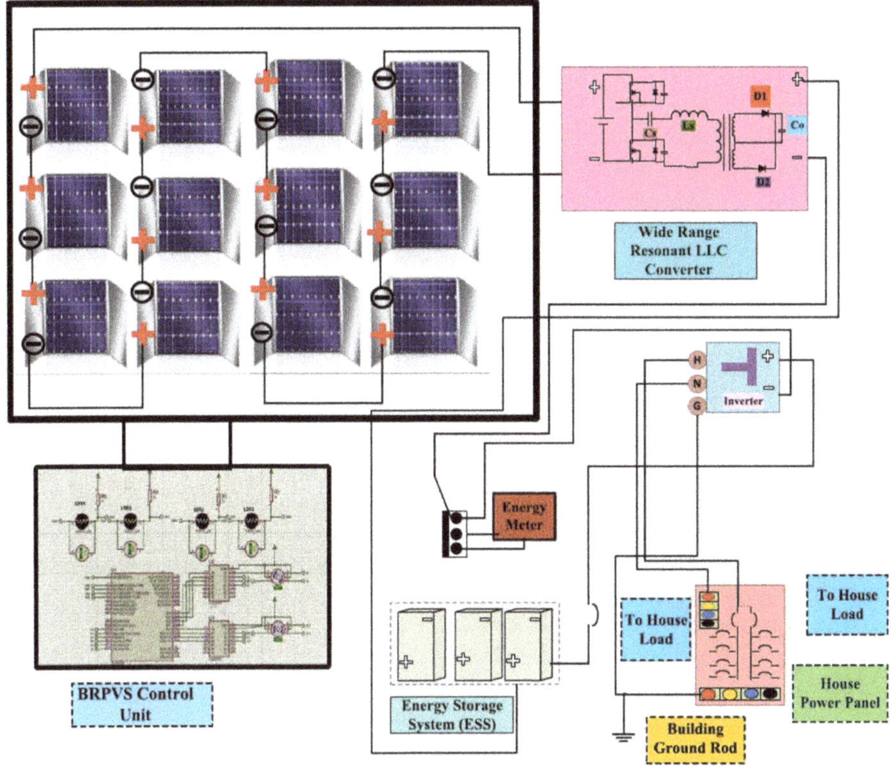

Figure 1. An overview Proposed BRPVS with its mandatory components (i.e., BRS, LLC converter, inverter, Energy storage system, distribution, and control unit).

2.2. Components of Designed BRPVS System for BIPV

A detailed overview of the components of the proposed system and their corresponding operating mechanisms is described below.

2.2.1. Wide Range Medium Power LLC Converter

Figure 2 shows the proposed topology of a wide range of LLC resonant converters designed for a wide range of input voltage variations. As the BIPV system undergoes voltage fluctuations, the design topology provides a fixed output voltage despite input voltage variations. The main structure of the LLC converter starts with a voltage divider, and in this design the load and resonant tank act as a voltage divider. The half-bridge LLC resonant converter topology is formed with the help of an input bridge. The resonant tank system is connected to the load, rectifier system, and filter network.

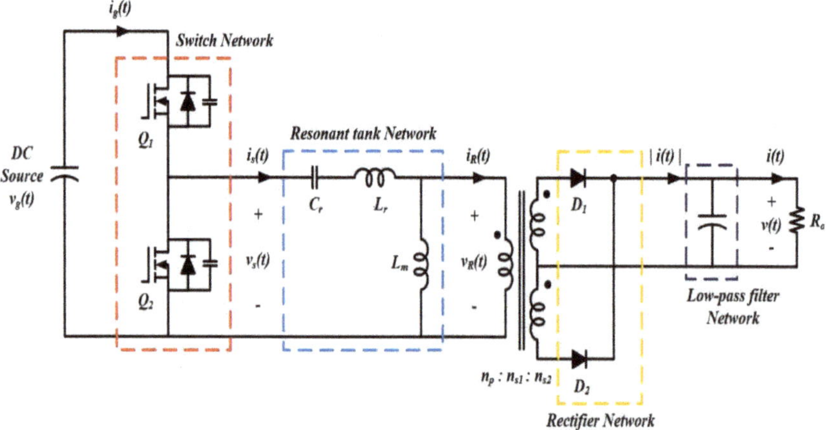

Figure 2. Half-bridge Converter Topology for BRPVS.

Figure 3 demonstrates that a square wave is produced by the switch network having frequency $f_s = \omega_s/2\pi$. With the resonant L-C network present in the topology of the converters, generates sinusoidal the current and voltage are using each frequency cycle and hence sinusoidal approximation is suitable to examine the characteristics and parameter determination of the converter.

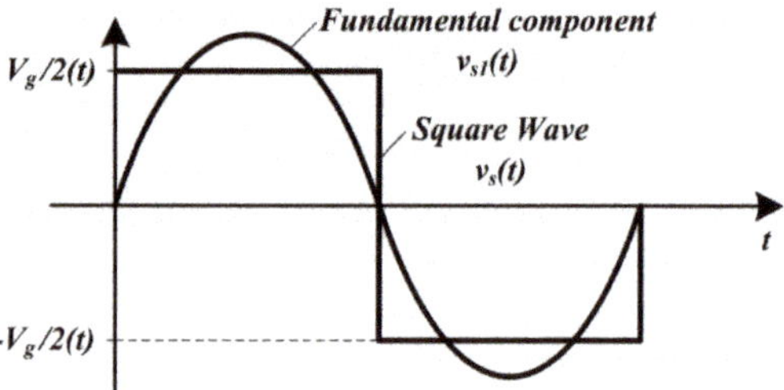

Figure 3. Output voltage of switch network along with its fundamental component.

The switching network, which produces a fundamental and odd harmonic of square wave voltage. Fundamental component $v_{S1}(t)$ can be calculated using Equation (1) [44].

$$v_{S1}(t) = \frac{2V_g}{\pi}\sin(\omega_s t) = v_{s1}\sin(\omega_s t) \tag{1}$$

where V_g shows amplitude of the input square wave. Resonant output current denoted by i_R is defined by Equation (2) a with peak amplitude (I_{R1}) and phase shift (θ_R)

$$i_R = I_{R1}\sin(\omega_s t - \theta_R) \tag{2}$$

The rectifier input voltage ($V_R(t)$) well be similar to its fundamental component (V_{R1}) and is given be below relation (i.e., Equation (3))

$$V_{R1} = \frac{4V}{\pi}\sin(\omega_s t - \theta_R) \tag{3}$$

As capacitor does not allow DC current to pass through it, steady-state load current i(t) and DC component (I) of rectifier input current are equal expressed by Equation (4).

$$I = \frac{2}{T_s} \int_0^{\frac{T_0}{2}} I_{R1} |\sin(\omega_s t - \theta_R| dt = \frac{2}{\pi} I_{R1} \tag{4}$$

The effective resistive load (R_e) of the RC-tank can be evaluated as ratio of $V_{R1}(t)$ and $I_{R1}(t)$ given by Equation (5).

$$R_e = \frac{V_{R1}(t)}{I_{R1}(t)} \tag{5}$$

The transfer function ($H(s)$) of the designed LLC converter is given utilizing Equation (6).

$$H(s) = \frac{sL_m \parallel R_e}{sL_r + \frac{1}{sC_r} + sL_m \parallel R_e} \tag{6}$$

The voltage gain (M) i.e., transfer function magnitude, is given by Equation (7).

$$M = \frac{\left(\frac{f}{f_r}\right)^2 (m-1)}{\sqrt{\left(\frac{f^2}{f_p^2} - 1\right)^2 + \left(\frac{f}{f_r}\left(\frac{f^2}{f_r^2} - 1\right)(m-1)\right)^2}} \tag{7}$$

where $L_p = L_m + L_r$, $m = \frac{L_p}{L_r}$, $Q = \frac{1}{R_e}\sqrt{\frac{L_r}{C_r}}$, $f_r = \frac{1}{2\pi\sqrt{L_r C_r}}$, $f_p = \frac{1}{2\pi\sqrt{L_p C_p}}$.

According to the mode of operation, the DC characteristics of the LLC resonant converter can be divided into three regions, as shown in Figure 4. In region 1, the converter works in a similar manner to SRC. In this region, L_m does not resonate with the resonant capacitor, C_r; it acts as a load of the series resonant tank when it is clamped by the output voltage. The LLC resonant converter can operate under the no load condition without the penalty of a very high switching frequency with a passive load. In addition, with a passive load, L_m, ZVS could be ensured for any load condition.

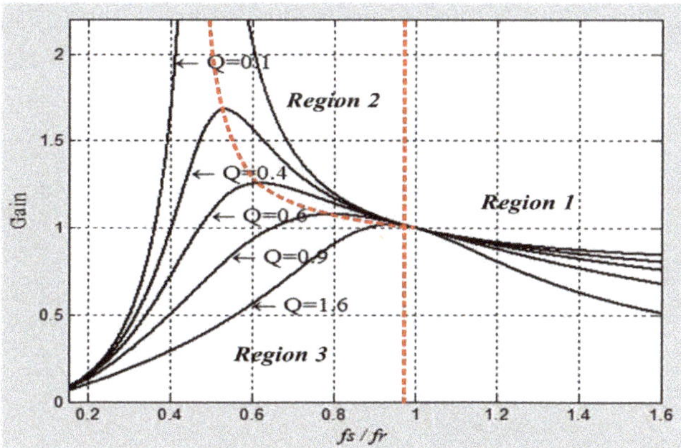

Figure 4. Operation regions for Half bridge LLC converter [43].

In region 2, the converter operation is more complicated. At the beginning L_r is resonant with C_r and L_m is clamped by the output voltage. As the L_r current reaches the same level as the L_m current, the L_r and C_r resonance is stopped, and L_m starts participating. As the LLC resonant converter acts as a multi-resonant converter, the resonant frequency is different in different intervals of time because of resonant process between $L_m + L_r$ with C_r. The designed operating region is region 2 and precautionary measure should be made to prevent the converter from entering region 3. For resonant converter output voltage control, controlling of switching frequency is used mostly to change the DC gain of the resonant tank. If the input voltage of the resonant converter changes or the load fluctuates, the resonant change impedance of the tank changes according to the switching frequency change of the control hybrid control system that adjusts the output voltage by changing the switching frequency. The net change in switching frequency is made according to the design of the resonant tank and consequently relates to the load conditions and the input voltage range.

2.2.2. Al-Foil Based Bi Reflector System (Al-BRS)

Aluminum foil, as an inexpensive reflective material, was used for economic and high output power solar PV systems, which is a very thin sheet of aluminum, ranging from approximately 0.006 mm to the upper ISO defined the limit of 0.2 mm (200 μm). For the protection of Al layer from oxidation aluminum oxide layer is placed on the top of it. As per requirement of thickness, aluminum foil is rolled with the help of beta radiation sensor. The common properties of Al foil are shown in Table 1.

Table 1. Properties of Al Foil sheets used for BRS [45].

Density	2.7 g/cm^3
Melting point	660 °C
Al foil specific weight	6.35 μm foil weighs 17.2 g/m^2
Melting point	660 °C
Electrical resistivity	26.5 nΩm
Electrical conductivity	64.94% IACS (IACS: International Annealed Copper Standard)
Thermal conductivity	235 W/m·K
Thickness	Foil is defined as measuring less than 0.2mm (<200 μm)

Figure 5 shows an overview of a BRS with an Al reflector with attached PV modules with detailed electrical and optical models given below.

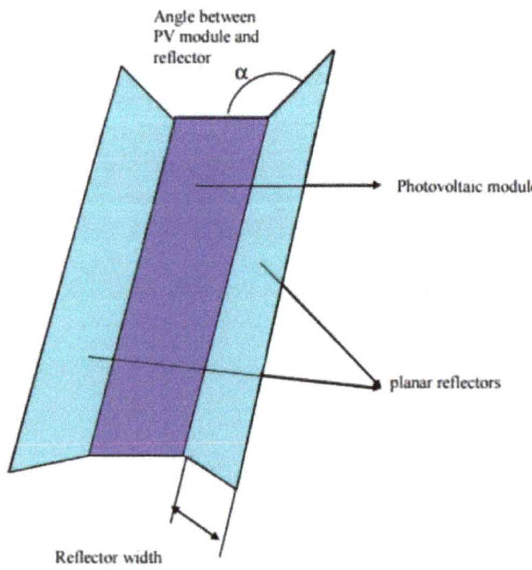

Figure 5. An overview of Al- foil based Bi reflector system (Al-BRS).

Electrical Modeling

For modeling of BRS, an equivalent electric circuit is developed, as depicted in Figure 6. The equivalent model consists of a current source for a solar cell with a photocurrent (I_L) with a pn junction diode, a parallel resistor (R_{sh}) and a series resistor (R_s).

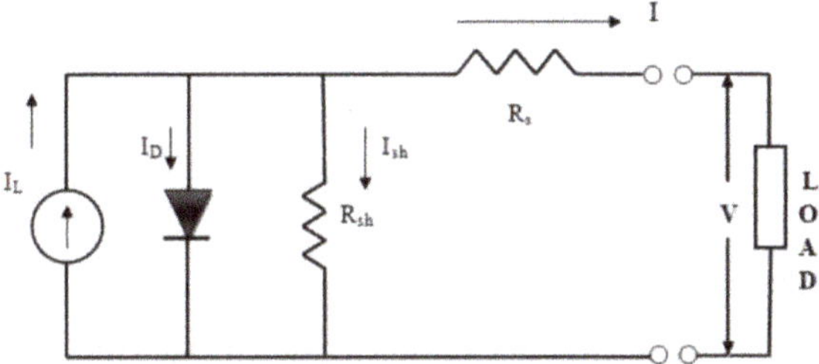

Figure 6. Equivalent circuit for an Al-BRS.

Solar irradiance and constant temperature and solar irradiance, the V-I characteristics of the model which has been proposed can be given using the Equation (8):

$$I = I_L - I_o \left[\exp\left(\frac{V + R_s}{a} \right) - 1 \right] - \frac{V + R_s}{R_{sh}} \tag{8}$$

Important parameters ($I_{L,ref}$, $I_{o,ref}$, $R_{s,ref}$, $R_{sh,ref}$ and a_{ref}) for modeling PV module with BRPVS can be estimated by using conditions in Table 2 [46].

Table 2. BRS electrical modeling, conditions used to evaluate important parameters.

At short circuit	$[dI/dV]_{sc} = -1/R_{sh,ref}$
At open circuit voltage	$I = 0, V = V_{oc,ref}$
At short circuit current	$I = I_{sc,ref}, V = 0$
At the maximum power point	$I = I_{mp,ref}, V = V_{mp,ref}$
At the maximum power point	$[dI/dV]_{sc} = 0$

Applying the condition defined in Table 2 to Equation (8), Equations (9)–(13) are derived [3]:

$$I_{L,ref} = I_{o,ref} \left[\exp\left(\frac{V_{oc,ref}}{a_{ref}} \right) - 1 \right] - \frac{V_{oc,ref}}{R_{sh,ref}} \tag{9}$$

$$I_{sc,ref} = I_{L,ref} - I_{o,ref} \left[\exp\left(\frac{I_{sc,ref}R_{s,ref}}{a_{ref}} \right) - 1 \right] - \frac{I_{sc,ref}R_{s,ref}}{R_{sh,ref}} \tag{10}$$

$$I_{m,ref} = I_{L,ref} - I_{o,ref} \left[\exp\left(\frac{V_{mp,ref} + I_{mp,ref}R_{s,ref}}{a_{ref}} \right) - 1 \right] - \frac{V_{mp,ref} + I_{mp,ref}R_{s,ref}}{R_{sh,ref}} \tag{11}$$

$$\left[\frac{dI}{dV} \right]_{sc} \cong - \frac{1}{R_{sh,ref}} \tag{12}$$

$$\frac{I_{m,ref}}{V_{mp,ref}} = \frac{\left(\frac{I_{o,ref}}{a_{ref}} \right) \exp\left(\frac{V_{mp,ref} + I_{mp,ref}R_{s,ref}}{a_{ref}} \right) + \frac{1}{R_{sh,ref}}}{1 + \left(\frac{I_{o,ref}R_{s,ref}}{a_{ref}} \right) \exp\left(\frac{V_{mp,ref} + I_{mp,ref}R_{s,ref}}{a_{ref}} \right) + \frac{R_{s,ref}}{R_{sh,ref}}} \tag{13}$$

Maximum power output (MPP), current (I_{mp}) and voltage (V_{mp}) are related using below listed equation:

$$P_{mp} = I_{mp}V_{mp} \tag{14}$$

Temperature dependency of maximum power point efficiency is a very important aspect when we are dealing with performance of PV module written in below equation:

$$\eta_{mp} = \frac{I_{mp}V_{mp}}{G_T A_m} \tag{15}$$

Optical Modeling

Using the traditional approach of optical geometry, the total irradiance (S_{tot}) absorbed into the BRPVS system can be easily predicted. Total solar radiation (S_{tot}) is the sum of the direct solar radiation (S_d) on the solar panel, the ground reflected radiations (S_g), the sky diffusion radiations (S_{SK}), the right reflector radiation (S_{reflR}) to the surface of the PV panel with a tilted plane angle, $\alpha 1$, and radiation reflected from the left reflector (S_{reflL}) to the PV panel with a tilted plane angle $\alpha 2$ [47]:

$$S_{tot} = S_d + S_g + S_{sk} + S_{reflR} + S_{reflL} \tag{16}$$

We used a reflector for PV system to model the solar system for BRDF [29]. The analysis method of integrative in which irradiation to point differential for PV module represented by (dx) from each differential scattering element on the reflector in (dy) to direction of dx has been presented [30]. So, in two dimension that is x and y-axis, integration is performed to show the solar irradiation on module surface. The module in which energy incident (E_r^i) is impacting plane reflector at point dx as shown in Equation (17).

$$E_r^i = E_p \cos(\theta') dy dz \tag{17}$$

Through the differential angle (E_{ref}), reflected radiant intensity per unit depth and radiant intensity per unit depth that strikes the surface of the module (E_m) as shown in Equations (18) and (19) respectively [48].

$$E_{ref} = E_r^i BDRF(\theta, \theta') \rho \tag{18}$$

$$E_m = E_{ref} d\theta \tag{19}$$

Equation (20) shows the angle of incidence (θ) of the differential ray onto the surface of the module and the distance that the ray has travelled.

$$d\theta = \frac{dy \cos(\beta)}{r} \tag{20}$$

$$BDRF(\theta, \theta') = \frac{D(\theta, \theta')}{\int_{-\frac{\pi}{2}}^{\frac{\pi}{2}} D(\theta, \theta') d\theta} \tag{21}$$

Equation (22) can be obtained from Equations (17)–(21) and integrated with characteristic dimensions, and multiplied by the depth of the module (A_{module}) and the irradiance (W/m^2) that is on the surface of the module due to reflection (G_m^i) can be calculated using Equation (22):

$$G_m^i = \frac{G_p \rho}{A_m} \int_0^{L_{sect}} \int_{L_{m,min}}^{L_{m,max}} BDRF(\theta, \theta') \cos(\theta') \frac{\cos(\beta)}{r} dx dy \tag{22}$$

where ρ is surface reflectivity, A_m module area, and θ' is the angle between the incoming ray and reflector surface

Control Mechanism

A motorized BRPVS system can be designed by studies done on the bases of the experiment in Section 4. This is an optional control mechanism to obtain greater efficiency. The system was designed with Arduino, Stepper motor, Stepper motor driver, reflectors, Cds/sensors, and power supply. Connecting the Stepper motor with Arduino requires a proper connection and wiring pattern using the driver circuits. Figure 7 gives an overview of a motorized BRPVS.

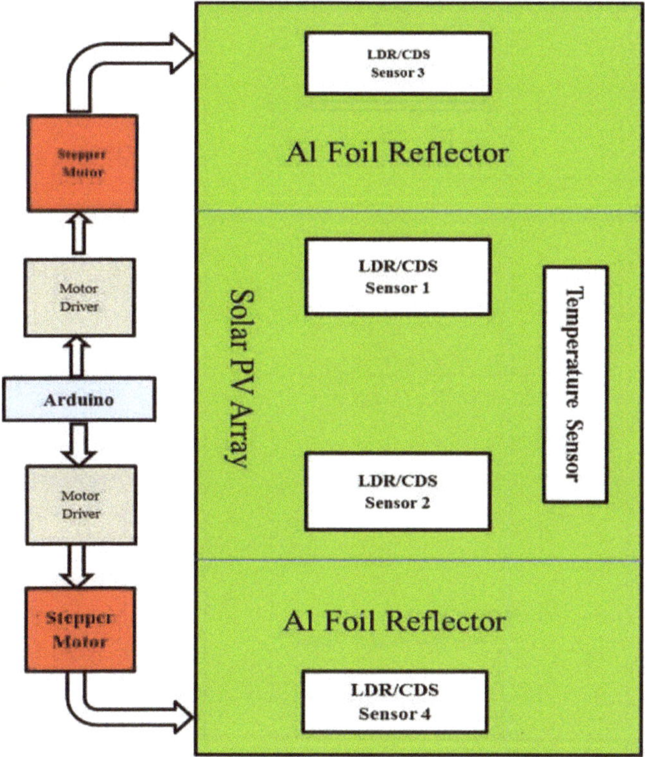

Figure 7. Scheme for control and hardware implementation of Al-BRS.

Figure 8. shows a controlled algorithm for movement of BRPVS. The movement of the reflector is controlled by the CdS sensors placed on the reflectors and solar panel using the controlled algorithm shown in Figure 8. This system is designed with four light-dependent resistors. The resistance of the LDR /CDS sensor varies with light. In the morning, when the amount of light on the right reflector is greater than the left reflector resistance, and the resistance LDR/CDS of the right reflector ($R_{CdS(R)}$) is less than the left ($R_{CdS(L)}$), the Arduino program compares these values and moves the stepper motor of the right reflector at the given optimal angle or tilt (θ_{TL}) when there is shade on the solar panel, i.e., the LDR placed on the right side of the panel resistance ($R_{CdS(PVR)}$) is no more than the normal bright light operating range (R_{th}). In the afternoon, the resistances of the LDR/CDS right and left sensor are equal and the stepper motor of both reflectors moves focusing light on the solar panel. In the evening, when the amount of light on the left reflector is more than that on the right reflector resistance of the LDR/CDS of the right reflector, the again Arduino program compares these values and moves the stepper motor of the left reflector at the given optimal angle or tilt when there is shade on the solar panel, i.e., the LDR placed on the left side of the panel ($R_{CdS(PVL)}$) is no greater than the normal bright light operating range. Compared to conventional tracing, which requires continuous tracking and movement of the entire Solar PV solar series and parallel array structure, the proposed BRPVS needs to adjust the movement of the reflector only three times per day, i.e., morning, afternoon, and evening. Moreover, this movement of reflectors is an optional feature to enhance the efficiency to a large extent.

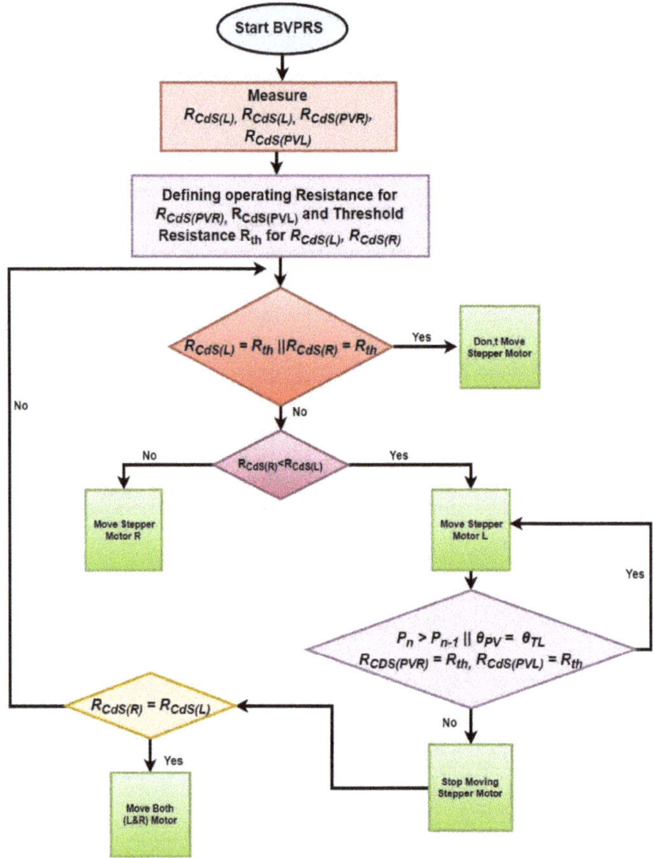

Figure 8. Flowchart explaining control algorithm for operating BRS.

2.2.3. Inverter (Full-Bridge)

Half and full bridge are common inverter topologies. The full-bridge (FB) of the inverter is comprised of two legs; switching of the switches makes it possible to prevent a short circuit at the DC input. Switching is carried out in such a way that the upper leg is complementary to the lower leg of the same bridge. In addition, a dead time is introduced between switching to ensure the protection of switches from a short circuit.

Unlike the half-bridge (HB), the output voltage is double that of FB having the same input voltage. Therefore, the current will be half in the FB inverter compared to that of HB inverter having the same power rating. Figure 9 shows the FB inverter of single-phase switching states.

The carrier-based modulation technique of the PWM controller is the most widely used and effective method. In this type of method, the carrier signal is modulated with the reference signal, and a mostly triangular shape wave is used as the carrier and sinusoidal signal for the reference signal. This technique is quite simple and provides an effective response for inverters.

Figure 9 presents a circuit with an inductor and capacitor along with parameters as a LC lowpass filter.

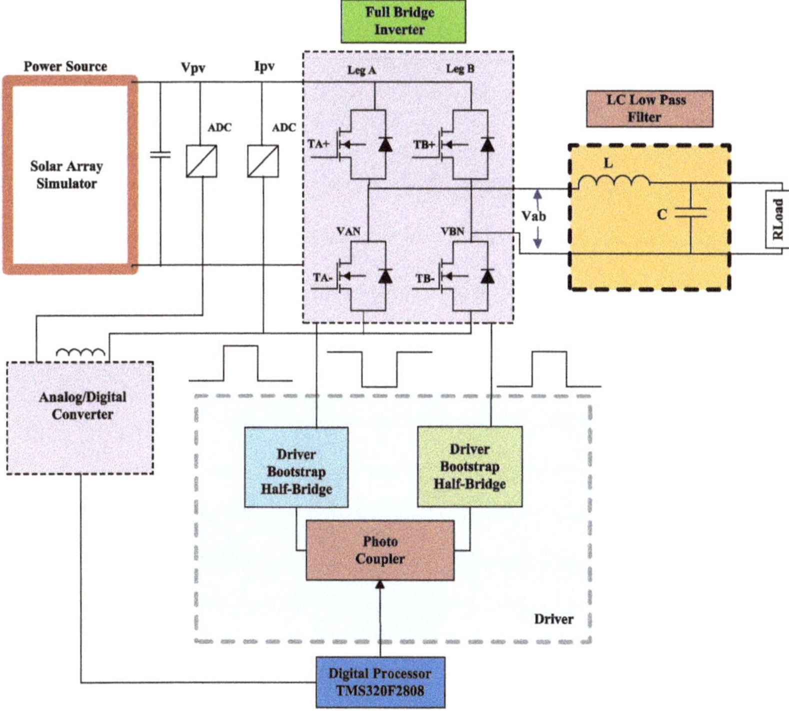

Figure 9. A full bridge inverter scheme with low pass filter and DSP controller for BRPVS.

The current swell is cut off to utilize the inductor. The value of the inductor is given by the following equations:

$$L = V \times di/dt \tag{23}$$

$$L = 2 \times Vdc \times Dmax\ \Delta Imax \times fs \tag{24}$$

where Vdc is the input DC voltage; fs is the switching frequency; L is the output filter inductor; ΔImax is the permissible ripple current and Dmax is the duty cycle maximum.

The capacitor depends on the inverter peak value and ripple voltage measurements of the output. Inductor current ripple is retained in the capacitor output. This can be shown in the following equation:

$$\Delta Vout = \Delta Vc \tag{25}$$

$$\Delta Vc \cong \Delta I_{Lc} \times fs + rESR \times \Delta IL \tag{26}$$

where ΔVout is the output voltage ripple; ΔI_{Lc} is the ripple current of the inductor and rESR is the capacitor equivalent series resistance.

2.2.4. Energy Storage System (ESS)

The variability and intermittency of the renewable energy sources within the renewable energy harnessing system can be mitigated to some extent while being integrated with the power grid. Residential dwellings and commercial buildings have a significant impact on the small-scale integration of renewable energy because of ESS. The storage technologies are not only for improving the levels of consumption from renewable energy sources, but also providing momentary benefit.

The implementation of future intelligent grid technology, smart pricing, demand-side management, peak load, smart grid, demand-side management, smart metering, peak load curtailment, might deliver the goals of the regulator and policymakers but may also create uncertainty for consumers regarding the price of power. Power consumption control will be experienced by consumers when they purchase power and assess how much they consume during power shortages [7]. Therefore, a storage system is needed to save some energy when there is insufficient solar power available to run a specific load. During the charging process, the ESS available capacity at time, "t" can be described as:

$$E_{ESS}(t) = E_{ESS}(t-1) - E_{CC-OUT}(t) \times \eta_{CHG} \tag{27}$$

The available ESS capacity during the discharging time can be given by Equation (28) [49].

$$ESS(t) = E_{ESS}(t-1) - E_{Needed}(t) \tag{28}$$

The depth of discharge (DoD) is a measure of how much energy has been withdrawn from a storage device, and is expressed as a percentage of the full capacity according to Equation (29).

$$DOD = (1 - d) \times 100 \tag{29}$$

The effective method of an energy management system that comprises storage elements allows consumers to shift their electricity purchases during peak hours to decrease the electricity demand

3. Experimental Setup

Figure 10 presents the experimental setup for a BRPVS system. To determine the effects of Al-BRS on temperature and power output, an experimental setup was developed, as shown in Figure 10a. The experiment was carried out near the Mechatronic Engineering Building 107 and the Laser and Sensor Laboratory, Pusan National University, having latitude 31.4861303° E. The optimal tilt angle of 30° was selected. A 20 watt PV module was used to determine the effects of reflector on the performance with the given latitude. A MASTECH MS827 millimeter for measuring current and voltage with different irradiance and reflector conditions. A FLUKE VT04A visual IR thermometer was utilized for thermal images at a specific time. An EL-USB-3 voltage and temperature data logger were used to measure the voltage and temperature of the PV module to recode the data.

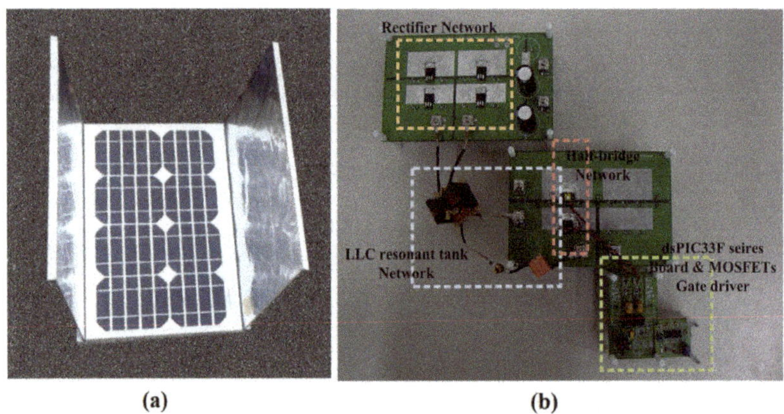

Figure 10. Experimental arrangements for (**a**) Al-foil based BRS; (**b**) Hardware implementation of 400 W Half bridge LLC converter prototype.

A 0.5-mm of thick aluminum foil sheet was wrapped on a paperboard of rectangular shape to make the structure firm. In the first experiment, aluminum foil was used as the equaling size as that of the solar cell. In the installation of the real-time BIPV system, the exact south (180 N) is not always available present so two different positions, south-east 150 N (diverted toward the east from south of 30°) and south-west 210 N (toward west diverted 30°), were used.

A 400-W prototype LLC converter was developed as shown in Figure 10b having an input voltage ranging 200–400 V and a fixed output voltage of 48 V. A MASTECH MS8217 millimeter to get voltage and current value under various point. The LLC resonant converter control scheme has two different input voltage ranges according to the control scheme that depends upon PFM control scheme having input voltage from 200 to 300 V and by the asymmetric PWM at the input voltage range from 300 to 400 V. The LLC resonant tank has 1.68 voltage gain with an input voltage 200 V and 1.12 voltage gain at input voltage 300 V, where switching frequency varied from 50 kHz to 112 kHz. Table 3 shows the LLC resonant converter design parameters. For the desired switching, the proposed hybrid switching scheme was used on a Microchip dsPIC33F16GS502.

Table 3. Specification of designed LCC converter for BRPVS.

Parameter	Value
Maximum Power (f_{max})	400 W
Switching Frequency (f_s)	60–112 kHz
Input voltage range (V_s)	200–400 V
Series Resonant Capacitance (C_r)	66 nF
Output voltage (V_o)	48 V
Series Resonant Inductance (L_r)	30.56 µH
Parallel Resonant Inductance (L_m)	103.44 µH
Turn Ratio of Transformer ($N_p : N_s$)	24:7
Input Capacitance (C_{in})	450 V/330 µF
Output Capacitance (C_o)	200 V/220 µF

4. Results and Discussion

Outdoor testing of the BRPVS was performed at Busan (35°10′0″ N, 129°4′0″ E), South Korea. The Korean Metrological Agency (KMA) was used as a source of authentic data for expected Busan weather conditions, to investigate the effect of BRPVS on the efficiency of PV system of solar PV module. The data of the solar insolation were provided in MJ/m^2, which was then converted for compatibility and simplicity to kW/m^2. Solar insolation for twelve days randomly selected days was considered, exactly one day for each month having sunny weather from morning to evening, as shown in Figure 11. The data showed that the solar irradiance was very low in cold weather: smaller than 1 kW/m^2 from morning 7:00 to 1:00 (Figure 11a) and evening from 3:00 pm to 6:00 pm (Figure 11c). During December, January, and February, and maximum solar insulation was 0.63 kW/m^2 at the afternoon from 11:00 to 2:00 pm (Figure 11b). The maximum solar irradiance from March to May was 0.70 kWh/m^2. Compared to the STC (1 kW/m^2) for the solar panel, this is still very low. Value incremented to 0.95 kWh/m^2 in summer but it could not generate electricity at full capacity because of the increase in temperature of the solar panels. The variation of irradiance throughout the year from morning and evening shown in Figure 11 was much lower than the STC. The data in Figure 11 supports the importance of the reflector system because output power will increase as the amount of incident light increases in the solar panel.

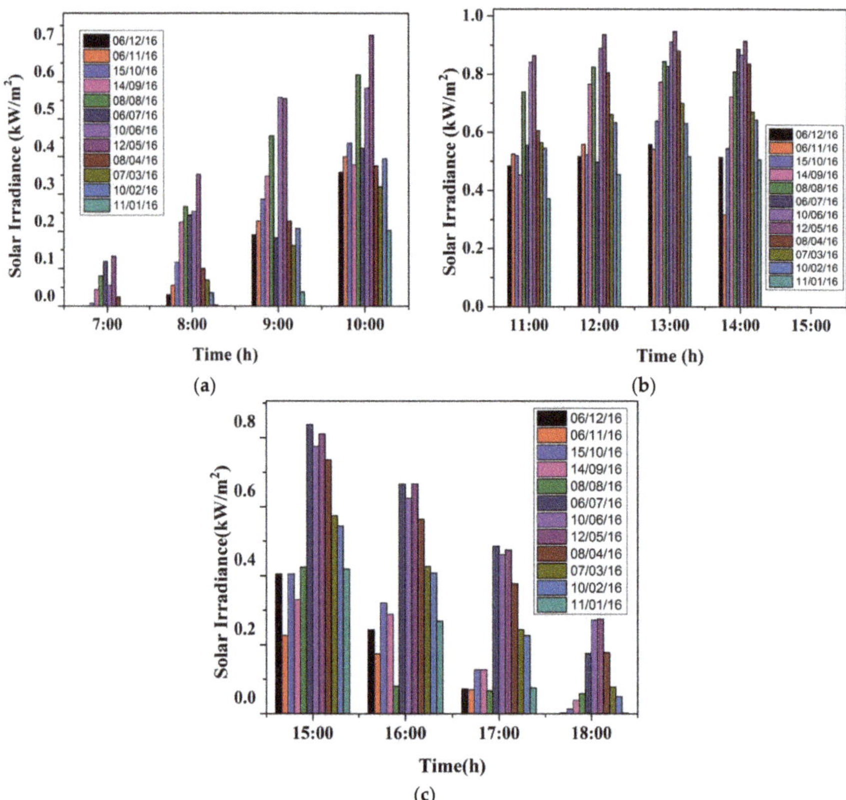

Figure 11. Solar irradiance of Busan (35°10′0″ N, 129°4′0″ E): (**a**) Morning (7:00 to 10:00); (**b**) Afternoon (11:00 to 14:00); (**c**) Evening (15:00 to 18:00).

4.1. Investigating Effectiveness of BRPVS

Effect of BRPVS with an Al-foil sheet on the output power of the solar PV module having a 20-W capacity, placed at 0° south was noticed. The data was examined for a time period from 8:30 to 16:30. Figure 12 show voltage of the open circuit (V_{oc}), short circuit current (I_{sh}) and output power. Figure 12a indicates that from 8:30 am to 4:00 pm, the V_{oc} was maintained on specific value but when the intensity of sunlight decreased, there was a sudden dip in voltage of the open circuit. On the other hand, the current varies with time, i.e., it increases, specifically from 0.67 A to 1.2 A for some time from 8:30 to 16:30 and decreases slowly from 12:00 to 16:30.

The performance comparison was made by comparing the output power of the Al-foil sheet reflector with a panel without a reflector. Significant improvement in the result was obtained while using the reflector. Using Al-Foil BRS produces an output of 20.31 W, while without a reflector, it is only 16.84 W.

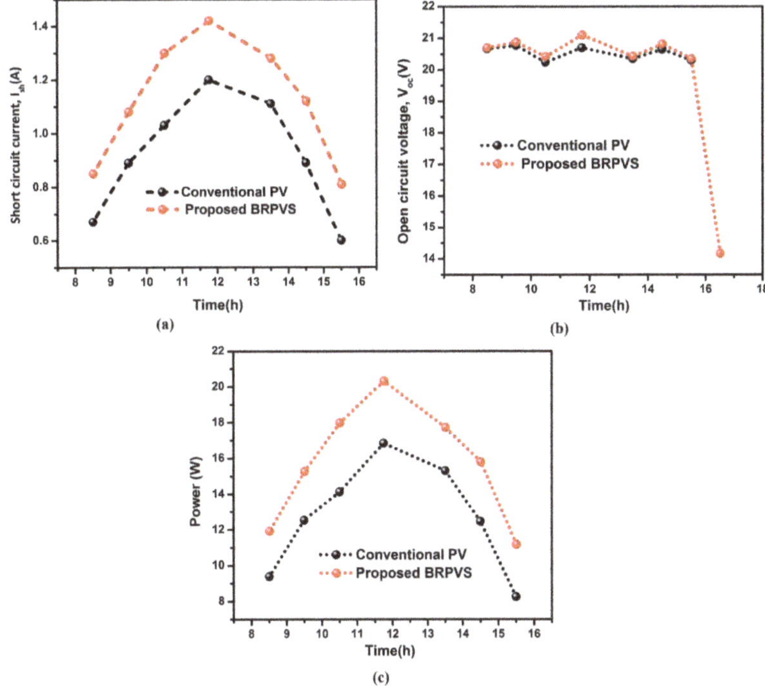

Figure 12. Comparative analysis of the (a) Short circuit current (Ish); (b) Open circuit voltage (V_{oc}); (c) Output power of BIPV system with and without Al foil based BRPVS.

The use of Al-foil reflector does not too much increase the cost of the PV system but improves its effectiveness. The temperature effect on Al-BRS was then monitored. During the experiment, the thermal images were photographed for the PV module with the BRPVS system.

In Figure 13, the thermal image showed a temperature hotspot at 11:30, 12:30, and 13:30 with no reflectors at 42.1 °C, 42.3 °C, and 43 °C, respectively. Conversely, at 11:30, 12:30, and 13:30 using the Al-Foil reflector, the hotspot temperatures for the solar power system were 38.9 °C, 39.4 °C and 40.5 °C, respectively. The above statistics show that using a reflector ensures that the PV system is safe and does not significantly increase the temperature of the BIPV system.

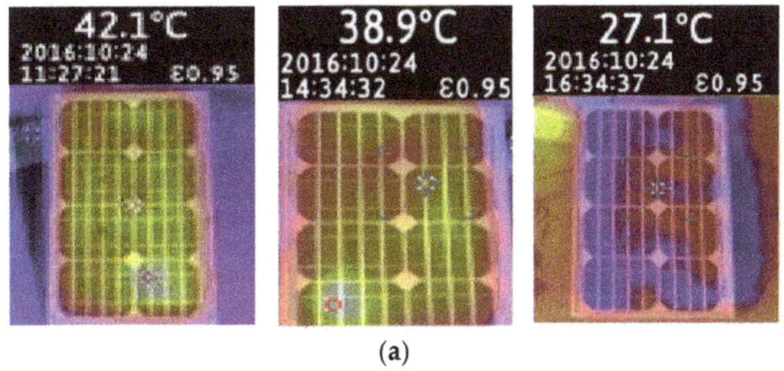

(a)

Figure 13. *Cont.*

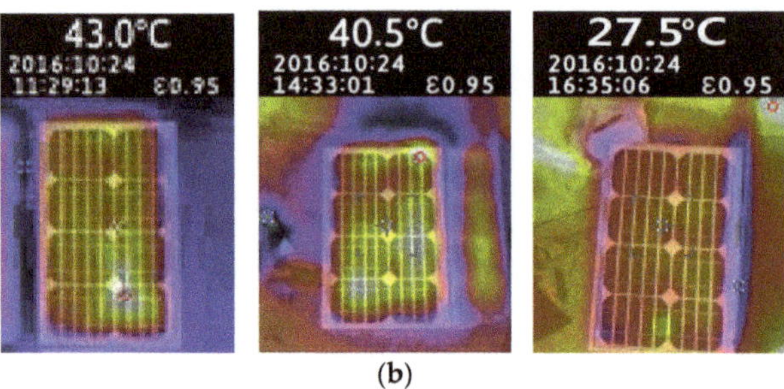

(b)

Figure 13. Studying effect on temperature of PV module (**a**) Without BRS; (**b**) Al foil BRS.

4.2. Al-Foil Reflector Optimal Size and Position for BRPVS

Al-foil has significant effects on the PV system output power. Moreover, it is quite inexpensive. The efficiency depends mostly on the size of the aluminum foil reflector. Different experiments were conducted with different sizes of Al foil as a reflector to determine the optimal size of the Al foil (Figure 14). The positions of the PV system in the solar panel were placed at South 0° (North 180°) with a tilt angle of 30°. Three different sizes of Al foil were selected: 1/3 (length = 54 cm width = 12 cm), 2/3 (54 cm width = 24 cm), and equal to the size of the solar panel. The output power of the solar PV module increased from 7.62% to 9.11% when the Al foil size was one-third of the solar panel (Figure 14a,b). The output power improved 16.05–17.57% when Al foil 2/3 of the solar panel size was used. The output power was increased 25.92–28.47% when the size of reflector was equal to the size of the panel. This shows that the output power increases with increasing size of the reflector.

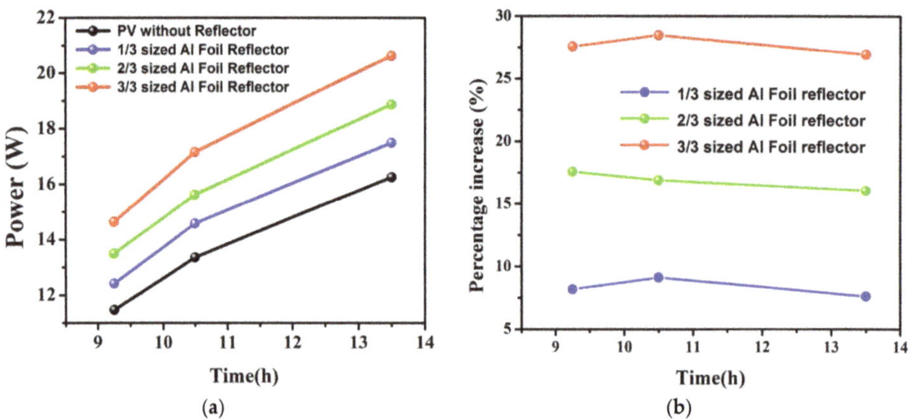

Figure 14. Finding optimal size of reflector: (**a**) Output power; (**b**)Percentage increase.

The next task was to find the optimal angle for BRPVS that gives the highest output power. Perfect south is difficult to achieve for every BIPV system. Hence, three different positions were selected: south 0°, south-east (30° from south towards east), and south west (30° from south towards west).

Figure 15 shows the output power of the solar module while using the Al-Foil BRS with the above-mentioned angles. The optical angle of BRS differs depending on position and time. The optimal BRS angles for the south, south-east, and south-west locations from 9:00 am to 11:00 am were 80°, 75° and 90°, respectively (Figure 15a–c). During the afternoon time i.e., 11:00 am to 2:00 pm keeping both reflectors at 90° delivers maximum output power. In the evening from 3:00 pm to 5:00 pm, the best angle for the south, south-east, and south-west position was 80°, 90°, and 75°, respectively. These results show as panel move for south the optimal angle for BRS changes however with little adjustment in the reflector angle can help to yield more power from the same module without reflector

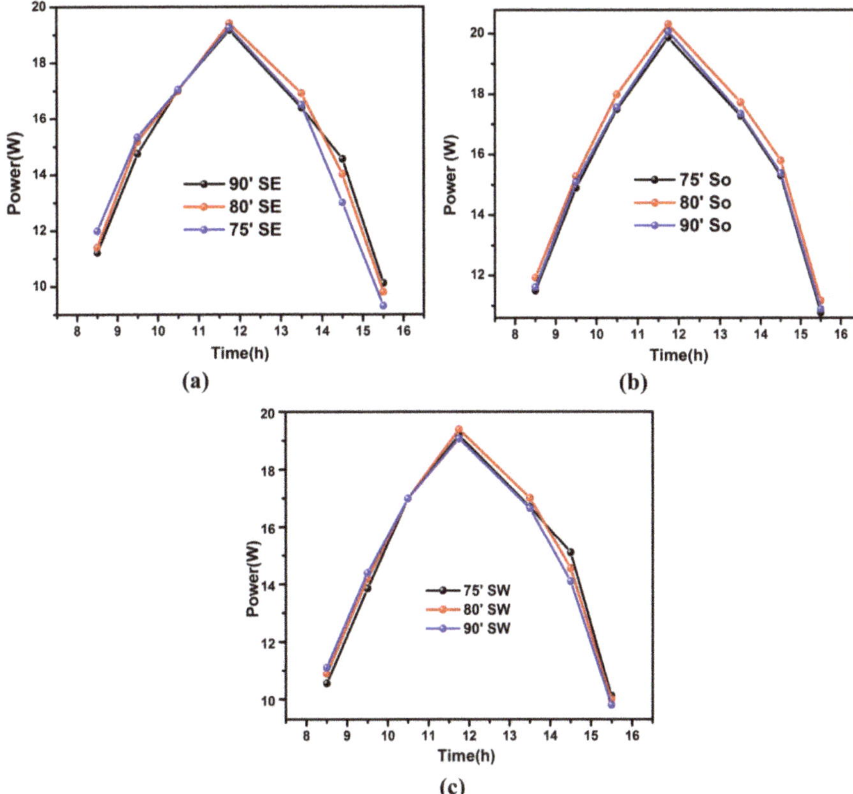

Figure 15. Output power of PV (**a**) south 0°; (**b**) south-east (30° from south towards east);(**c**) south-west (30° from south towards west).

4.3. Performance Evaluation of Designed Half Bridge LLC Converter

The 400-W LLC converter for wide range voltage variations was designed as discussed in Section 2.2.1, and the experimental setup was developed based on the parameters discussed in Section 3. Figure 16 shows the waveform of a half-bridge LLC resonant converter for the desired experimental study. Variable input voltages of 200–400 V with variable switching frequencies were considered for the analysis. The switching was performed at high frequencies ranging from 90.23 kHz to 110 kHz to reduce the size of the transformer. Figure 16 shows waveform for 200 V input with switching frequency 74.67 kHz. Figure 13a,b shows the waveforms for voltage 200 V, 230 V while Figure 13c,d represents 300 V and 400 V, respectively.

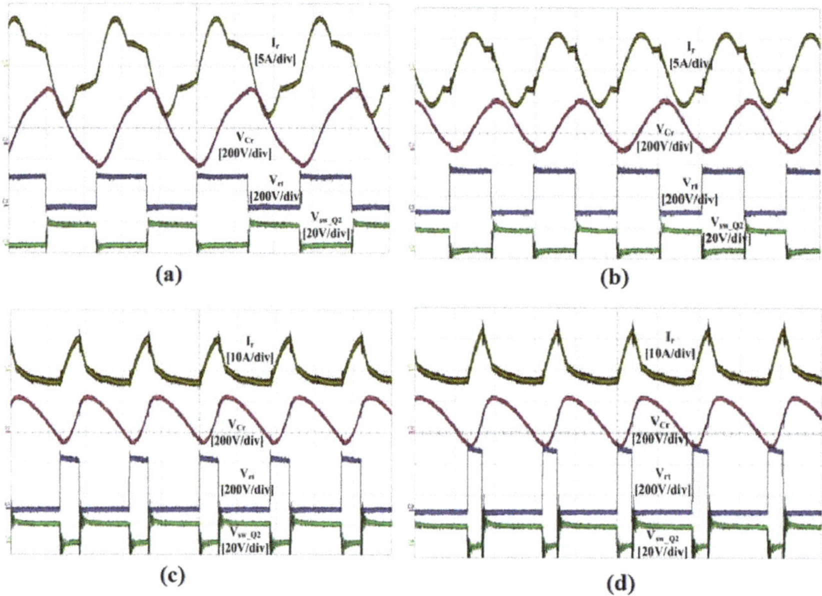

Figure 16. Testing operation of designed converter for wide range variable input voltage. (a) V_{in} = 200 V, f_s = 74.67 kHz; (b) V_{in} = 230 V, f_s = 82.31 kHz; (c) V_{in} = 300 V, f_s = 109.23 kHz; (d) V_{in} = 400V, f_s = 109.23 kHz.

Figure 16a shows the current of the resonant inductor (I_r), resonant voltage (V_r), and input voltage (V_{in}) of the LLC resonant tank and switching signal of Q2 at an input voltage of 200 V. The red line in the graph presents the output voltage while the blue line shows the input voltage. Similarly, the yellow and green input voltage (V_{in}) and switching signal of Q2 are shown. The output voltage was controlled and kept constant at 48 V. The results clearly show that the switching frequency increased with increasing input voltage in order to regulate the output voltage in the PFM operation region. In addition, resonance current peak value enlarged due to the increase in amount of current circulating in the resonant tank.

5. Conclusions

The power generation performance of the BIPV is influenced by the amount the of available solar radiation. The output power given by photovoltaic systems increases in proportion to the solar radiation. This study confirmed the effect of BRPVS on the performance of BIPV module through real-time outdoor experiments. Half-bridge LLC resonant converters for wide input range voltage fluctuations (200–400 V) and medium power applications have been proposed and tested by experiments using a 400-W prototype. Experimental results show that using a low-cost Al foil reflector in a BRPVS system can improve the output power by more than 28.47% depending on the time, size of the reflector, and location of the solar panel. Movement of BRPVS was controlled by the algorithm developed and discussed in this paper. A hardware implementation of the algorithm was performed using an Arduino-controlled CdS sensor and a stepper motor array. A BRPVS solar system was found to be a cost-effective solution for BIPV with conventional amorphous and crystalline solar panels and can be applied easily for future zero carbon green energy buildings, particularly in countries with lower annual solar radiation than the standard test condition defined for a solar PV system or building where it is difficult to face the PV panels completely towards south or the Sun. Future research should evaluate efficient reflector materials and effective control system operating mechanisms.

Author Contributions: H.-J.K. and M.A.K. conceptualize the idea of this research work. H.-J.K developed the proposal to the funding body. M.A.K. designed the experimental setup and procured the equipment and the material required for the experimental work. The fabrication and integration of the experimental setup was mostly carried out by the M.A.K. and S.H. under the supervision of H.-J.K., P.S., A.S., S.H. and H. helped in experimental work and fabrication of power conversion circuit. Results were analyzed by K.Z., M.U.A., W.U. and M.I. The paper was written by all the authors with different degrees of contribution.

Acknowledgments: This research was supported by Basic Research Laboratory through the National Research Foundations of Korea funded by the Ministry of Science, ICT and Future Planning (NRF-2015R1A4A1041584).

Conflicts of Interest: The authors declare no conflict of interest.

References

1. Liu, X.; Wu, Y.; Hou, X.; Liu, H. Investigation of the Optical Performance of a Novel Planar Static PV Concentrator with Lambertian Rear Reflectors. *Buildings* **2017**, *7*, 88. [CrossRef]
2. Tahir, S.; Wang, J.; Baloch, M.H.; Kaloi, G.S. Digital Control Techniques Based on Voltage Source Inverters in Renewable Energy Applications: A Review. *Electronics* **2018**, *7*, 18. [CrossRef]
3. Norton, B.; Eames, P.C.; Mallick, T.K.; Huang, M.J.; McCormack, S.J.; Mondol, J.D.; Yohanis, Y.G. Enhancing the performance of building integrated photovoltaics. *Sol. Energy* **2011**, *85*, 1629–1664. [CrossRef]
4. Öztürk, S.; Canver, M.; Çadırcı, I.; Ermiş, M. All SiC Grid-Connected PV Supply with HF Link MPPT Converter: System Design Methodology and Development of a 20 kHz, 25 kVA Prototype. *Electronics* **2018**, *7*, 85. [CrossRef]
5. Tian, H.; Yu, X.; Zhang, J.; Duan, W.; Tian, F.; Yu, T. The influence of environmental factors on DSSCs for BIPV. *Int. J. Electrochem. Sci.* **2012**, *7*, 4686–4691.
6. Mousazadeh, H.; Keyhani, A.; Javadi, A.; Mobli, H.; Abrinia, K.; Sharifi, A. A review of principle and sun-tracking methods for maximizing solar systems output. *Renew. Sustain. Energy Rev.* **2009**, *13*, 1800–1818. [CrossRef]
7. Yaden, M.F.; Melhaoui, M.; Gaamouche, R.; Hirech, K.; Baghaz, E.; Kassmi, K. Photovoltaic System Equipped with Digital Command Control and Acquisition. *Electronics* **2013**, *2*, 192–211. [CrossRef]
8. Hafez, A.Z.; Yousef, A.M.; Harag, N.M. Solar tracking systems: Technologies and trackers drive types—A review. *Renew. Sustain. Energy Rev.* **2018**, *91*, 754–782. [CrossRef]
9. Vračar, L.; Prijić, A.; Nešić, D.; Dević, S.; Prijić, Z. Photovoltaic Energy Harvesting Wireless Sensor Node for Telemetry Applications Optimized for Low Illumination Levels. *Electronics* **2016**, *5*, 26. [CrossRef]
10. Khan, M.A.; Zeb, K.; Sathishkumar, P.; Ali, M.U.; Uddin, W.; Hussain, S.; Ishfaq, M.; Khan, I.; Cho, H.-G.; Kim, H.-J. A Novel Supercapacitor/Lithium-Ion Hybrid Energy System with a Fuzzy Logic-Controlled Fast Charging and Intelligent Energy Management System. *Electronics* **2018**, *7*, 63. [CrossRef]
11. Chemisana, D. Building integrated concentrating photovoltaics: A review. *Renew. Sustain. Energy Rev.* **2011**, *15*, 603–611. [CrossRef]
12. Yoon, S.; Tak, S.; Kim, J.; Jun, Y.; Kang, K.; Park, J. Application of transparent dye-sensitized solar cells to building integrated photovoltaic systems. *Build. Environ.* **2011**, *46*, 1899–1904. [CrossRef]
13. French, R.H.; Murray, M.P.; Lin, W.C.; Shell, K.A.; Brown, S.A.; Schuetz, M.A.; Davis, R.J. Solar radiation durability of materials components and systems for low concentration photovoltaic systems. In Proceedings of the IEEE Energytech, Cleveland, OH, USA, 25–26 May 2011; pp. 1–5.
14. Probst, M.M.; Roecker, C. Towards an improved architectural quality of building integrated solar thermal systems (BIST). *Sol. Energy* **2007**, *81*, 1104–1116. [CrossRef]
15. Augustin, D.; Chacko, R.; Jacob, J. Canal top solar PV with reflectors. In Proceedings of the 2016 IEEE International Conference on Power Electronics, Drives and Energy Systems (PEDES), Trivandrum, India, 14–17 December 2016; pp. 1–5.
16. Karlsson, B.; Wilson, G. MaReCo design for horizontal, vertical or tilted installation. In Proceedings of the EuroSun, Copenhagen, Denmark, 19–22 June 2000.
17. Brogren, M.; Karlsson, B. Low-concentrating water-cooled PV thermal hybrid systems for high latitudes. In Proceedings of the Conference Record of the Twenty-Ninth IEEE Photovoltaic Specialists Conference, New Orleans, LA, USA, 19–24 May 2002; pp. 1733–1736.
18. Dubey, S.; Tiwari, G.N. Thermal modeling of a combined system of photovoltaic thermal (PV/T) solar water heater. *Sol. Energy* **2008**, *82*, 602–612. [CrossRef]

19. Anderson, T.N.; Duke, M.; Morrison, G.L.; Carson, J.K. Performance of a building integrated photovoltaic/thermal (BIPVT) solar collector. *Sol. Energy* **2009**, *83*, 445–455. [CrossRef]

20. Baitule, A.S.; Sudhakar, K. Solar powered green campus: a simulation study. *Int. J. Low-Carbon Technol.* **2017**, *12*, 400–410. [CrossRef]

21. Tien, N.X.; Shin, S. A Novel Concentrator Photovoltaic (CPV) System with the Improvement of Irradiance Uniformity and the Capturing of Diffuse Solar Radiation. *Appl. Sci.* **2016**, *6*, 251. [CrossRef]

22. Pérez-Higueras, P.; Muñoz, E.; Almonacid, G.; Vidal, P.G. High concentrator photovoltaics efficiencies: Present status and forecast. *Renew. Sustain. Energy Rev.* **2011**, *15*, 1810–1815. [CrossRef]

23. Kosti, L.T.; Pavlovi, Z.T. Optimal position of flat plate reflectors of solar thermal collector. *Energy Build.* **2012**, *45*, 161–168. [CrossRef]

24. Pucar, M.D.J.; Despic, A.R. The enhancement of energy gain of solar collectors and photovoltaic panels by the reflection of solar beams. *Energy* **2002**, *27*, 205–223. [CrossRef]

25. Hall, M.; Roos, A.; Karlsson, B. Reflector materials for two-dimensional low-concentrating photovoltaic systems: The effect of specular versus diffuse reflectance on the module efficiency. *Prog. Photovolt. Res. Appl.* **2005**, *13*, 217–233. [CrossRef]

26. Grassie, S.L.; Sheridan, N.R. The use of planar reflectors for increasing the energy yield of flat-plate collectors. *Sol. Energy* **1977**, *19*, 663–668. [CrossRef]

27. Tina, G.M.; Ventura, C. Energy assessment of enhanced fixed low concentration photovoltaic systems. *Sol. Energy* **2015**, *119*, 68–82. [CrossRef]

28. Lin, W.C.; Hollingshead, D.; French, R.H.; Shell, K.A.; Schuetz, M.; Karas, J. Non-tracked mirror-augmented photovoltaic design and performance. In Proceedings of the 38th IEEE Photovoltaic Specialists Conference (PVSC), Austin, TX, USA, 3–8 June 2012; pp. 2076–2081.

29. Van Dijk, L.; van de Groep, J.; Veldhuizen, L.W.; Di Vece, M.; Schropp, R.E.I. Concepts for external light trapping and its utilization in colored and image displaying photovoltaic modules. *Prog. Photovolt. Res. Appl.* **2017**, *25*, 553–568. [CrossRef]

30. Matsushima, T.; Setaka, T.; Muroyama, S. Concentrating solar module with horizontal reflectors. *Sol. Energy Mater. Sol. Cells* **2003**, *75*, 603–612. [CrossRef]

31. Khan, M.A.; Ko, B.; Alois Nyari, E.; Park, S.E.; Kim, H.-J. Performance Evaluation of Photovoltaic Solar System with Different Cooling Methods and a Bi-Reflector PV System (BRPVS): An Experimental Study and Comparative Analysis. *Energies* **2017**, *10*, 826. [CrossRef]

32. Filippini, M.; Molinas, M.; Oregi, E.O. A Flexible Power Electronics Configuration for Coupling Renewable Energy Sources. *Electronics* **2015**, *4*, 283–302. [CrossRef]

33. Sathishkumar, P.; Krishna, T.N.V.; Himanshu; Khan, M.A.; Zeb, K.; Kim, H.-J. Digital Soft Start Implementation for Minimizing Start Up Transients in High Power DAB-IBDC Converter. *Energies* **2018**, *11*, 956. [CrossRef]

34. Khan, M.A.; Krishna, T.N.V.; Sathishkumar, P.; Sarat, G.; Kim, H.-J. A hybrid power supply with fuzzy controlled fast charging strategy for mobile robots. In Proceedings of the International Conference on Information and Communication Technology Robotics (ICT-ROBOT 2016), Busan, Korea, 7–9 September 2016.

35. Khan, M.A.; Badshah, S. Design and analysis of cross flow turbine for micro hydro power application using sewerage water. *RJASET* **2014**, *8*, 821–828. [CrossRef]

36. Popavath, L.N.; Kaliannan, P. Photovoltaic-STATCOM with Low Voltage Ride through Strategy and Power Quality Enhancement in a Grid Integrated Wind-PV System. *Electronics* **2018**, *7*, 51. [CrossRef]

37. Moonem, M.A.; Pechacek, C.L.; Hernandez, R.; Krishnaswami, H. Analysis of a Multilevel Dual Active Bridge (ML-DAB) DC-DC Converter Using Symmetric Modulation. *Electronics* **2015**, *4*, 239–260. [CrossRef]

38. Buccella, C.; Cecati, C.; Latafat, H.; Razi, K. A grid-connected PV system with LLC resonant DC-DC converter. In Proceedings of the International Conference on Clean Electrical Power (ICCEP), Alghero, Italy, 11–13 June 2013.

39. Beiranvand, R.; Rashidian, B.; Zolghadri, M.R.; Alavi, S.M.H. Using LLC resonant converter for designing wide-range voltage source. *IEEE Trans. Ind. Electron.* **2011**, *58*, 1746–1756. [CrossRef]

40. Chang, C.H.; Chang, E.C.; Cheng, H.L. A high-efficiency solar array simulator implemented by an LLC resonant DC–DC converter. *IEEE Trans. Ind. Electron.* **2013**, *28*, 3039–3046. [CrossRef]

41. Mishima, T.; Nakaoka, M. A novel high-frequency transformer-linked soft-switching half-bridge DC–DC converter with constant-frequency asymmetrical PWM scheme. *IEEE Trans. Ind. Electron.* **2009**, *56*, 2961–2969. [CrossRef]

42. Jang, J.; Pidaparthy, S.K.; Choi, B. Current Mode Control for LLC Series Resonant DC-to-DC Converters. *Energies* **2015**, *8*, 6098–6113. [CrossRef]

43. Shin, D.; Lee, K.J.; Lee, J.P.; Kim, H.J. Hybrid Control Scheme for a Half-Bridge LLC Resonant Converter with a Wide Input Range. In Proceedings of the International Conference on Intelligent Robotics and Applications, Busan, Korea, 25–28 September 2013; pp. 345–352.

44. Feng, W.; Lee, F.C.; Mattavelli, P. A hybrid strategy with simplified optimal trajectory control for LLC resonant converters. In Proceedings of the Twenty-Seventh Annual IEEE Applied Power Electronics Conference and Exposition (APEC), Orlando, FL, USA, 5–9 February 2012; pp. 1096–1103.

45. The Facets about Aluminum. Available online: http://www.alufoil.org/facts.html (accessed on 24 July 2017).

46. Stutenbaeumer, U.; Mesfin, B. Equivalent model of monocrystalline, polycrystalline and amorphous silicon solar cells. *Renew. Energy* **1999**, *18*, 501–512. [CrossRef]

47. Bahaidarah, H.M.; Tanweer, B.; Gandhidasan, P.; Rehman, S. A Combined optical, thermal and electrical performance study of a V-trough PV System—Experimental and analytical investigations. *Energies* **2015**, *8*, 2803–2827. [CrossRef]

48. Andrews, R.W.; Pollard, A.; Pearce, J.P. Photovoltaic system performance enhancement with nontracking planar concentrators: Experimental results and bidirectional reflectance function (BDRF)-based modeling. In Proceedings of the IEEE 39th Photovoltaic Specialists Conference (PVSC), Tampa, FL, USA, 16–21 June 2013; pp. 229–234.

49. Khan, M.A.; Zeb, K.; Sathishkumar, P.; Himanshu; Rao, S.S.; Gopi, C.V.V.M.; Kim, H.-J. A Novel Off-Grid Optimal Hybrid Energy System for Rural Electrification of Tanzania Using a Closed Loop Cooled Solar System. *Energies* **2018**, *11*, 905. [CrossRef]

 *electronics*

Article

MWCNT–Epoxy Nanocomposite Sensors for Structural Health Monitoring

Omid Sam-Daliri [1,2], Lisa-Marie Faller [2,*], Mohammadreza Farahani [1], Ali Roshanghias [3], Hannes Oberlercher [4], Tobias Mitterer [2], Alireza Araee [1] and Hubert Zangl [2]

[1] School of Mechanical Engineering, College of Engineering, University of Tehran, Tehran 1417466191, Iran; Omid_sam@ut.ac.ir (O.S.-D.); mrfarahani@ut.ac.ir (M.F.); alaraee@ut.ac.ir (A.A.)

[2] Institute of Smart Systems Technologies, Alpen-Adria-Universität Klagenfurt, 9020 Klagenfurt, Austria; Tobias.Mitterer@aau.at (T.M.); Hubert.Zangl@aau.at (H.Z.)

[3] CTR Carinthian Tech Research AG, 9524 Villach, Austria; Ali.Roshanghias@ctr.at

[4] Mechanical Engineering Department, Carinthian University of Applied Sciences, 9524 Villach, Austria; H.Oberlercher@fh-kaernten.at

* Correspondence: Lisa-Marie.Faller@aau.at; Tel.: +43-463-2700-3563

Received: 22 July 2018; Accepted: 7 August 2018; Published: 9 August 2018

Abstract: We address multi-walled carbon nanotubes (MWCNTs) for structural health monitoring in adhesive bonds, such as in building structures. MWCNT-loaded composites are employed to sense strain changes under tension load using an AC impedance measurement setup. Different weight percentages of 1, 1.5, 2 and 3 wt % MWCNTs are added to the base epoxy resin using different dispersion times, i.e., 5, 10, and 15 min. The equivalent parallel resistance of the specimens is first measured by applying an alternating voltage at different frequencies. To determine the mechanical as well as sensory properties, the specimens are then subjected to a tensile test with concurrent impedance measurement at a fixed pre-chosen frequency. Using alternating voltage, a higher sensitivity of the impedance reading can be achieved. Employing these sensors in buildings and combining the readings of a network of such devices can significantly improve the buildings' safety. Additionally, networks of such sensors can be used to identify necessary maintenance actions and locations.

Keywords: carbon nanotubes; nanocomposite sensor; tensile testing; impedance measurement

---

1. Introduction

The aim to fabricate smart composite structures to improve safety and to monitor structures as part of our living environment has resulted in a major research effort regarding the composition and performance of composites based on advanced materials. Advanced materials are used to fabricate smart sensors based on carbon particles, such as carbon fibers, carbon blocks, graphite [1,2], and also multi-walled carbon nanotubes (MWCNTs). MWCNTs have distinctive mechanical and electrical properties. They provide a unique potential to improve the mechanical [3–5] as well as electrical properties [6–10] of polymer–matrix composites. MWCNT–epoxy adhesives are used for applications such as electronic devices, smart adhesive joints in buildings and bus structures [11–13], and gas sensors [14]. In [3], the authors study the tensile behavior of carbon nanotubes (CNT)-loaded epoxy nanocomposite films, and report that, by adding CNTs to the polymer matrix, the tensile modulus, yield strength, and ultimate strength of the final polymer films can be increased. In [7], the electrical properties of CNT–epoxy nanocomposites were improved by surface treatment of the CNT specimens. A comparison of the electrical and mechanical properties of various carbon-loaded composites with a focus on their piezo-resistive properties is presented in [15].

The changes in the electrical resistance result from deformations and failures within the polymer matrix when the composites are subjected to mechanical loading [16–18]. The two predominant factors governing the resulting resistance are as follows [19]: first, the contact between two adjacent carbon nanotubes, which might be broken; second, the change in the tunneling resistance between two adjacent carbon nanotubes due to variation of the distance between them. A detailed elaboration of the mechanisms governing the change of the electrical resistance of MWCNT–epoxy nanocomposites under mechanical stress is given in [20]. Based on these changes in electrical resistance, MWCNT thin films have been employed for damage sensing [21–23], and CNT-loaded composites were suggested as strain sensors in the industrial sector for health monitoring [24–26].

It has further been shown that the morphological properties of carbon nanoparticles influence the response of the respective nanocomposite sensors [27]. The nanocomposite sensors are comprised of conductive networks or agglomerates distributed within the polymer matrix, where MWCNT form 1-D structures. The network conductivity is further affected by the weight percentage of the nanoparticles, mutual interactions between them, and their state of dispersion in the polymer matrix [28,29], which strongly depend on the preparation and activation process.

In this work, we present a study which investigates the influence of weight percentage of MWCNT and its dispersion time on the alternating current (AC) impedance. This AC impedance measurement can provide higher sensitivity by considering, also, the electrostatic properties of the material. Considering also such frequency dependent parameters, the sensing functionality of MWCNT–epoxy composites can thus be exploited or even improved, investing less energy. This presents a novelty compared to aforementioned studies, where direct current (DC) measurement is employed to determine the electrical properties of the considered specimens.

Low necessary energy facilitates the design of autarkic sensor systems [30] to monitor building structures. Using technologies such as transducer electronic data sheets (TEDS) [31], these devices can additionally be integrated into modern building automation facilities. There, a network of such sensors can provide information on the health state of a building and indicate necessary maintenance.

In Section 2, the material and equipment needed for the preparation method, as well as the mechanical and electrical testing of the nanocomposites, is presented. First, the preparation method, which consists of only basic steps, such as mixing and deagglomeration, is introduced. Then, the tensile testing machine and the electrical impedance measurement for, first, the percolation threshold, and secondly, during the tensile testing, are described. In Section 3, the results of the percolation threshold measurements and tensile testing are described, then the microstructure of the nanocomposites is presented based on scanning electron microscopy (SEM) images. Finally, in Section 4, concluding remarks on the presented study are given.

2. Materials and Methods

2.1. Materials

The base of the prepared nanocomposites is epoxy as matrix, and MWCNTs as the conductive nanofiller. The used epoxy resin is EpoThin® (Buehler, Braunschweig, Germany), a free-flowing, low viscosity, low shrinkage epoxy resin which allows the nanofiller to easily distribute in the EpoThin matrix. It has a typical cure time of nine hours at 27 °C, according to the manufacturer datasheet. MWCNT conductive nanoparticles by Cheaptube (Grafton, VT, USA) were used. The outer diameter of the considered MWCNT is 30 to 50 nm. The length of the used MWCNT is between 10 to 20 µm, with a purity of more than 95%.

2.2. Preparation of Specimens

Due to the exploitation of the conduction, as well as electrostatic effect occurring in the specimen, the fabrication process can be kept less sophisticated than those reported in previous work [32,33] without significant loss of sensory properties.

Weighed amounts of epoxy resin and carbon nanotubes (measured by a digital scale with accuracy equal to 0.1 mg) were mechanically stirred for 5 min in a beaker. The mixture was then placed in a shear mixer (IKA T18 digital ULTRA TURRAX, IKA, Staufen, Germany), at 1000 rpm for 15 min. Then, the dispersion of the MWCNT in the epoxy resin was further accomplished using an ultrasonic bath (see Figure 1a). Effective means of deagglomerating and dispersing are needed to overcome the bonding forces after wettening the powders. Therefore, an ultrasonic bath with high frequency (35–60 kHz) was used to disperse the MWCNTs in the epoxy resin appropriately, and break agglomerated particles. The time was set accordingly to the considered respective time of dispersion (see Table 1), and the environmental temperature was kept constant at 25 °C. Thus, CNTs with weight percentages of 1, 1.5, 2, and 3 wt % were dispersed in the epoxy matrix at different dispersion times. The resin was then combined with hardener in the ratio of 2:1 for 15 min on the stirrer, and was immediately poured into the dog-bone molds. After 24 h, the dog-bone shape samples, for tensile testing, were extracted from the mold. The curing temperature affects the electrical properties and strength of the nanocomposites. Therefore, it is preferred to use room temperature (25 °C) for a duration of one day to cure the specimens. The mold was designed according to the ASTM D638 standard. In this process, we avoid commonly employed, often complex, activation procedures.

Table 1. Processing conditions of carbon nanotube (CNT)–epoxy sensor.

Amount of CNT	Dispersion Time
1; 1.5; 2; 3	5; 10; 15

To facilitate the electrical measurement of the samples, two metallic wires were applied close to the necking end parts at a specific distance of 7.5 cm. The wires are fixed using conductive silver adhesive. The surface-ring contact was used to minimize electrical contact resistance (see Figure 1b).

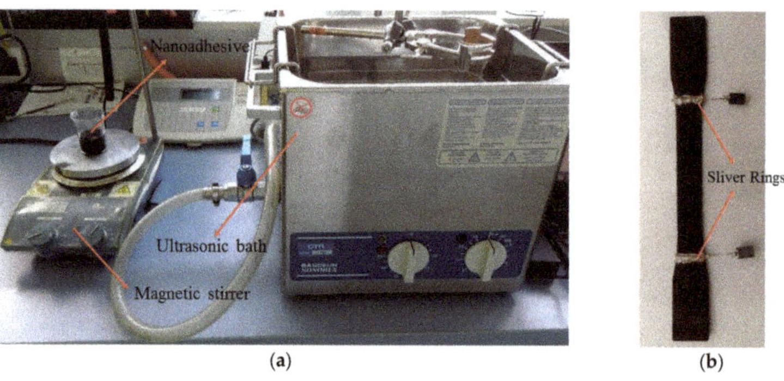

Figure 1. (**a**) Magnetic stirrer and ultrasonic bath (**b**) nanocomposite specimen.

2.3. Mechanical and Electrical Acquisition System

Three specimens were prepared under equivalent conditions for each test case of this study, and the effect of the dispersion time and various filler contents were investigated on the initial equivalent parallel resistance. Then, the specimens were subjected to a longitudinal loading until fracture using a Zwick/Roell Z020 (Zwick, Ulm, Germany) universal testing machine (see Figure 2 upper right). A crosshead displacement rate of 1 mm/min was applied according to the standard for polymer testing. The tensile force, longitudinal displacement, and voltage changes were measured simultaneously versus time.

Electrical measurements were conducted in two steps. The first step was to determine the frequency-dependent initial equivalent parallel resistance R_p of the specimens using an LCR measurement bridge by Extech Instruments. This instrument determines the equivalent parallel resistance at different frequency settings. The shape of the resulting measurement curves can be analyzed to determine the respective percolation threshold of the samples; for non-conducting materials, the resistance will decrease with increasing frequency. This is due to the predominant capacitive effect that can be observed here. Above the percolation threshold, the resistive behavior will dominate, and the impedance of the samples stays constant over frequency.

The second step is the impedance measurement at a fixed frequency during the tensile test. The frequency is chosen in order to optimally exploit the range of the input amplifier. These measurements are done using a high-speed, high-resolution measurement platform [34,35]. It is based on an FPGA system with a customized analog front-end to enable high-speed, high-resolution measurements. For series production, the components can be integrated into a system which, in terms of size and costs, is well suited for the application of commercial structural health monitoring in buildings.

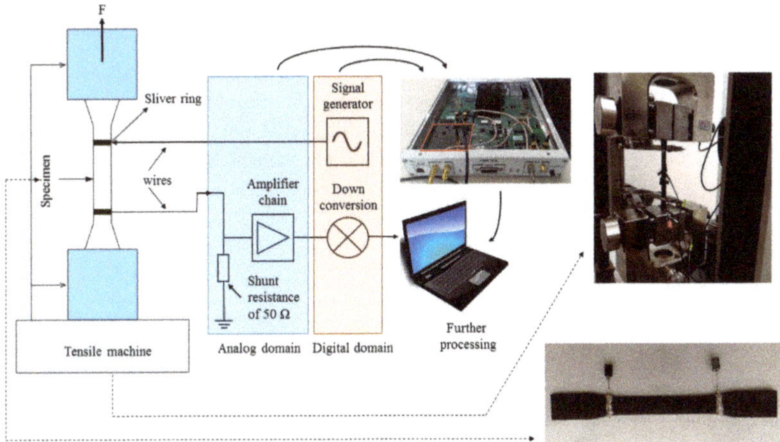

Figure 2. Illustration of the impedance measurement setup during the tensile test.

The measurement setup is illustrated in Figure 2: Left is the nanocomposite specimen which, on one side, is connected to the input analog amplifier chain as part of the impedance measurement hardware. The other side is connected to the output, which supplies a digitally generated sine signal. In the digital domain, the measurement platform also supplies the algorithms necessary for signal processing, e.g. down-conversion of the acquired signal. Down-conversion is done to transfer the measurement signal from a higher measurement frequency to a lower frequency, together with a reduction of the necessary number of samples. The results can then be used for further processing, such as analysis and visualization.

A higher measurement frequency can, in the first place, be beneficial to avoid or reduce the influence of other electrical equipment present near the sensors. This is important when these nanocomposite sensors are to be employed in buildings which commonly suffer from high electric emissions due to the used machinery and other equipment. Secondly, in this application, we assume that improved impedance readings are achieved also for samples below the percolation threshold through the application of a high frequency measurement signal. Thus, also samples with less attractive electrical properties, but prepared using a simplified and less time-consuming fabrication process, might as well be used for sensing.

Through preliminary analysis done in the initial impedance measurements described in Section 3.1, the measurement frequency for the tensile testing (Section 3.3) is chosen to be 100 kHz with an excitation voltage of 1 V (signal generator in Figure 2) to optimally exploit the input range of the equipment.

Via the shunt resistance of 50 Ω, which incorporates a voltage divider with the measurement impedance (see Figure 2), a voltage reading is recorded, which is proportional to the resistance of the sample. For a resistance change, the voltage signal also changes accordingly. To determine the impedance as illustrated in the result diagrams, first a calibration measurement using a known resistance is done. Using this calibration measurement, and a proportionality factor (to relate the voltage at the measurement impedance to the voltage at the shunt resistance), the recorded voltage reading can be corrected to give the equivalent impedance.

3. Results and Discussions

3.1. Achieved Impedance Without Mechanical Loading

The equivalent parallel resistance of the nanocomposite specimens changes significantly when measured at different frequencies. The results of this initial equivalent parallel resistance measurements are illustrated for dispersion times of 10 and 15 min in Figures 3 and 4, respectively. In all of these diagrams, the equivalent parallel resistance R_p decreases with increasing frequency. It can be seen from the Figure 3 that, when the filler content of MWCNTs increases up to 3 wt %, R_p decreases from 180 MΩ to less than 6 MΩ, given the same dispersion time. The equivalent parallel resistance clearly shows a flat curve shape at 3 wt %. At this point, the transition from the insulating to the conductive phase, called percolation threshold, is observed. The experimental method for the determination of the respective percolation threshold measurement was in compliance with the method used in [36]. Due to simplifications in the preparation process of the samples, the percolation threshold was achieved with samples containing a higher weight percent of CNTs.

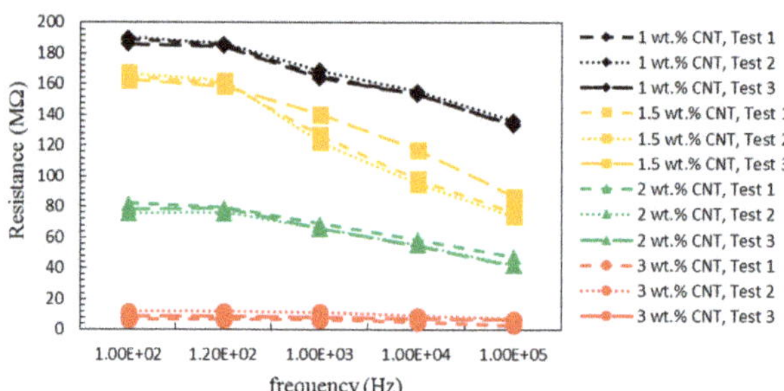

Figure 3. Equivalent parallel resistance of the nanocomposite sensors with a dispersion time equal to 10 min.

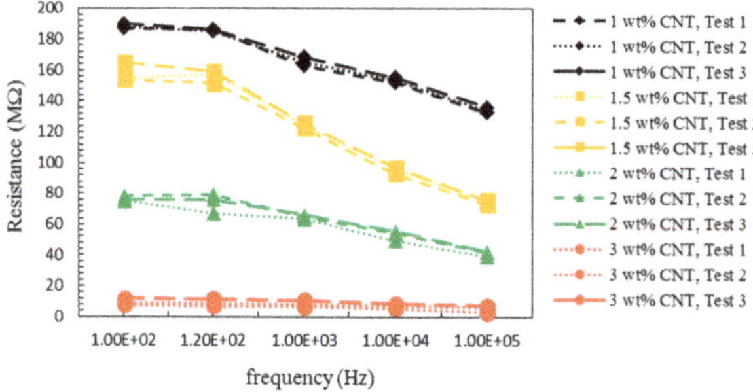

Figure 4. Equivalent parallel resistance of nanocomposite sensors with a dispersion time equal to 15 min.

Conductive networks formed in the epoxy matrix as conductive fillers are distributed appropriately within the epoxy matrix [37]. As a result, the initial resistance changes with the employed dispersion time.

Based on the equivalent parallel resistance value, the effect of dispersion time was investigated using statistical analysis in Minitab (see Figure 5a,b). Since the resistance does not change significantly for an increase of the dispersion time above 10 min, this value could be identified as sufficient with respect to the given process settings. Additionally, this analysis shows that the effect of the dispersion time is higher at a low weight percent of MWCNTs.

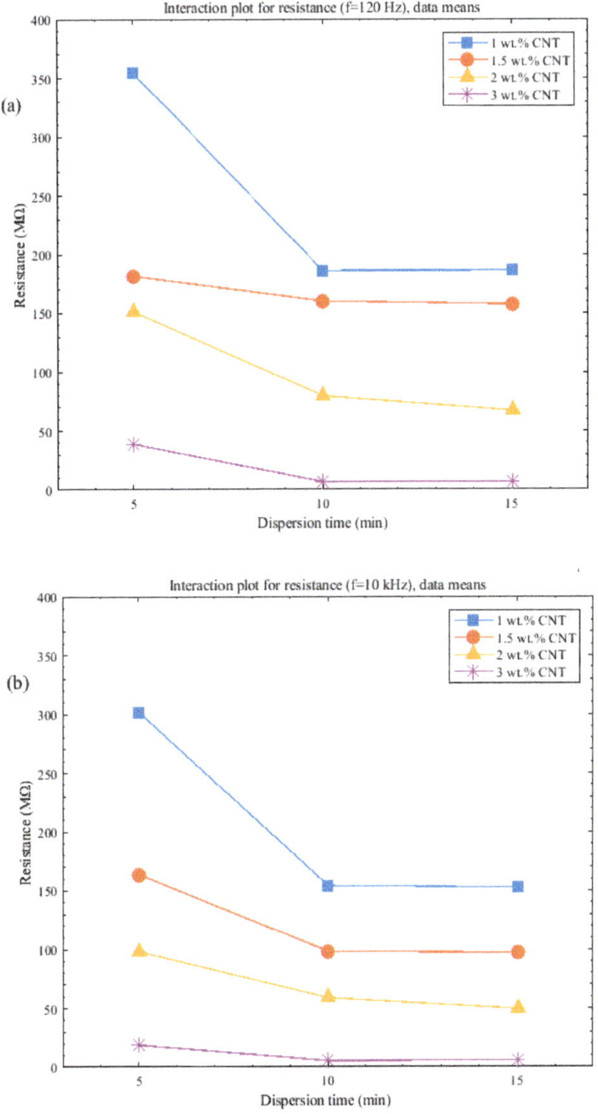

Figure 5. Interaction plots of the weight percent and dispersion time for R_p at different frequencies (**a**) 120 Hz (**b**) 10 kHz.

3.2. Morphology

The dispersion of MWCNTs in the epoxy resin was validated using SEM images. SEM pictures of the fracture surface of the nanocomposite specimens were taken after the tensile test. In Figure 6a,b, SEM images of nanocomposites containing 2 wt % MWCNTs at lower and higher magnifications with 5 min dispersion time are given. The highlighted circles in Figure 6a,b mark agglomerated zones of MWCNTs in the epoxy matrix. When compared to the scale given at the lower right corner of the images, it can be seen that the size of the highlighted zones is between 10 and 20 µm (see Figure 6b). However, high degrees of agglomeration have to be avoided when preparing MWCNT composites, agglomeration zones of diameters larger than 10 µm are required to achieve a sufficient conductivity. Additionally, we observed a nearly uniform distribution of MWCNTs in the epoxy matrix with increasing dispersion time and weight percent (see Figure 6c).

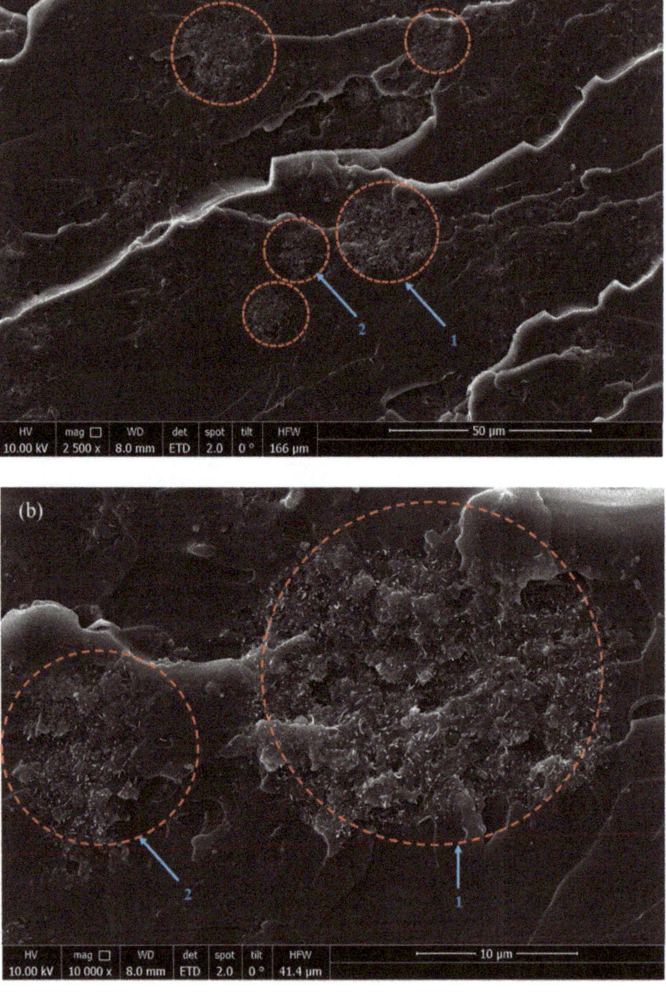

Figure 6. *Cont.*

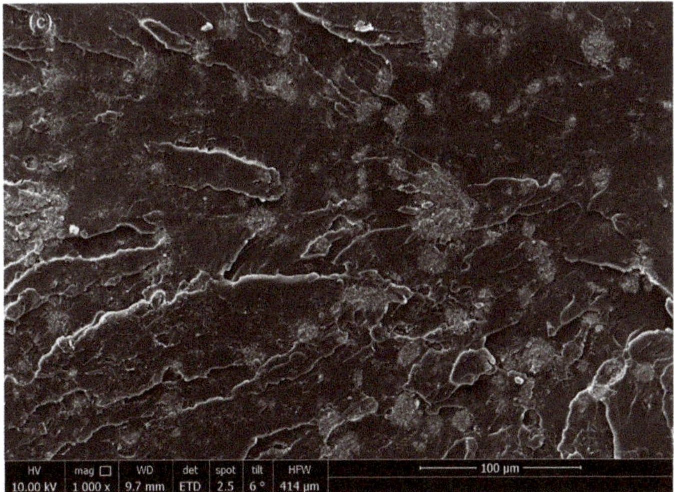

Figure 6. Fracture surface images of MWCNT–epoxy nanocomposite with (**a**) 2 wt % MWCNTs with magnification of 2500× at 5 min dispersion time and (**b**) 2 wt % MWCNTs with magnification of 10,000× at 5 min dispersion time, and (**c**) 3 wt % MWCNTs at 10 min dispersion time with magnification of 1000×.

3.3. Sensing Capabilities during Mechanical Loading

The majority of previous studies used the two-probe method to measure the electrical resistance changes during the tensile test [38–40], which may provide disadvantages for the DC measurements. Here, we use an AC measurement setup at an intermediate frequency, therefore, the two-probe method is sufficient, and the cumbersome preparation of two additional connections per specimen can be avoided. The sensitivity of the specimen is proportional to the normalized resistance change $\Delta R/R_0$, where ΔR is the resistance increment and R_0 is the equivalent parallel resistance value at the chosen measurement frequency (here 100 kHz). For every specimen, R_0 is constant, so that the sensitivity of the specimen can be related to the impedance changes ΔR [41]. In the following Figures, we consequently report the absolute impedance change ΔR. The axes giving the impedance changes are plotted at different scales in the following result graphs. This is done because the impedance changes are at different ranges.

According to the diagrams in Figure 7, for specimens with a filler content of 2 wt % MWCNTs and the lowest dispersion time of 5 min, a non-constant and non-uniform change of the electrical impedance was observed (see Figure 7a). The steep curve segments result from deferments of large agglomeration zones of CNTs in the epoxy matrix present due to the low dispersion time. The uniformity of the electrical impedance change curves improves for dispersion times of 10 and 15 min, separately, as depicted in Figure 7b,c. The curve observed for 3 wt % MWCNTs shows a nearly constant increase without additional peaks, and thus qualifies the fabricated nanocomposites for continuous sensing of damage and damage progression. Figure 8 shows the resistance change for a nanocomposite specimen including 3 wt % MWCNTs with a dispersion time value of 5 min. Nanocomposite specimens with higher percentage of carbon nanotubes generally exhibit a steeper slope in the electrical resistance change (see Figure 9). Although an impedance increase cannot be seen for the specimens with 1, 1.5, 2 wt % CNTs for a displacement lower than 3 mm, it is seen for 3 wt % MWCNTs and a displacement of at least 0.8 mm. In this region where there is no impedance change, we see the elastic behavior of the fabricated nanocomposite material. Up to the point where the impedance starts to change, the material is structurally able to compensate for the applied force.

Consequently, the specimen with 3 wt % with 10 min dispersion time is more sensitive than the others (see Figure 9) given the chosen measurement setup. These results are also further consistent with the SEM image of the nanocomposite with 3 wt % MWCNT at 10 min dispersion time (see Figure 6c). This filler amount is also determined to be the percolation threshold as elaborated in Section 3.1. In comparison to the specimens including 1 and 2 wt % MWCNT, the slope of the resistance changes diagram for the specimens with 3 wt % MWCNTs also exhibits a smoother shape. Georgousis et al. [36] reported that the highest sensitivity can be achieved close to the percolation threshold. In the present study, we confirm these results showing that the smoothest curves are achieved above the percolation threshold. Obviously, the samples below the percolation threshold (1, 1.5, and 2 wt %) can be used for sensing by applying an AC impedance measurement setup and a suitable read-out strategy to correct for the non-smooth curve shape. The employment of specimen with different filler content and dispersion times may be adapted to the application and the sensitivity requirements at certain force and displacement regions.

Based on the max forces of the specimens using different dispersion time, the max strength was obtained for every weight percent (Table 2). The maximum strength is the ultimate strength of the nanocomposite (the apex point of the force-displacement diagram). This is different from the failure stress, which occurs after this maximum point. A significant difference could be observed between the maximum forces achieved for specimens containing different percentages of MWCNTs. The specimens including 3 wt % MWCNTs could withstand less longitudinal force. It can further be seen from Table 2 that when increasing the filler amount from 1 to 3 wt %, the maximum strength decreases from 68.36 MPa to 50.19 MPa. In general, the strength of nanocomposites obtained from tensile tests were improved by adding MWCNT to the epoxy matrix. As reported in Table 2, the maximum strength of the nanocomposites increased with respect to pure epoxy. However, the maximum strength decreased by adding more than 1 wt % MWCNTs, which is similar to what was reported in [42].

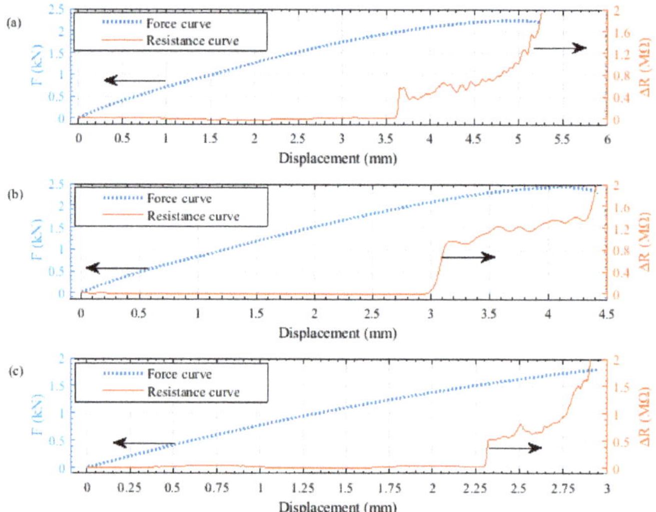

Figure 7. Force and impedance changes for the nanocomposite sensor with 2 wt % MWCNTs for the different dispersion times of (**a**) 5 min, (**b**) 10 min, and (**c**) 15 min. The arrows indicate the axis belonging to the respective curve. Note: the scaling on the righthand axis and displacement are not uniform throughout the illustrated results.

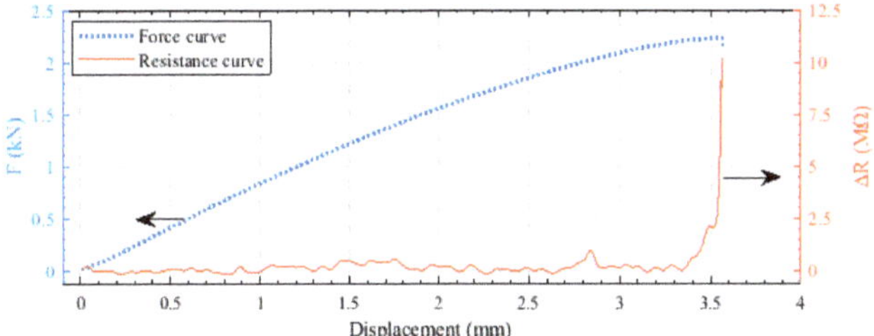

Figure 8. Force and impedance changes for the nanocomposite sensor with 3 wt % MWCNTs at 5 min dispersion time. The arrows indicate the axis belonging to the respective curve. Note: the scaling on the righthand axis and displacement below are not uniform throughout the illustrated results.

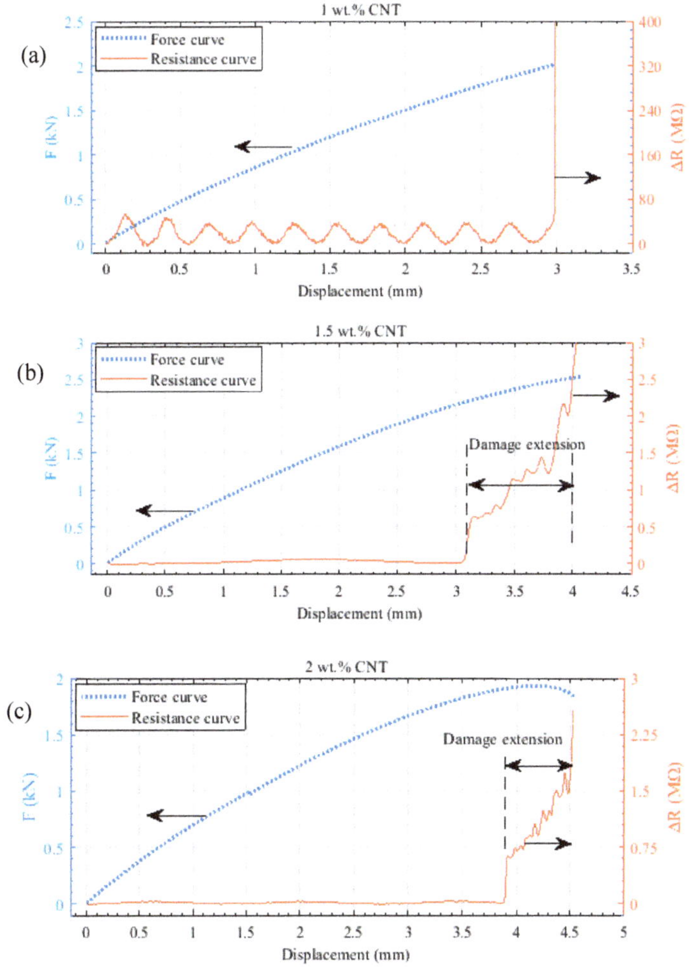

Figure 9. *Cont.*

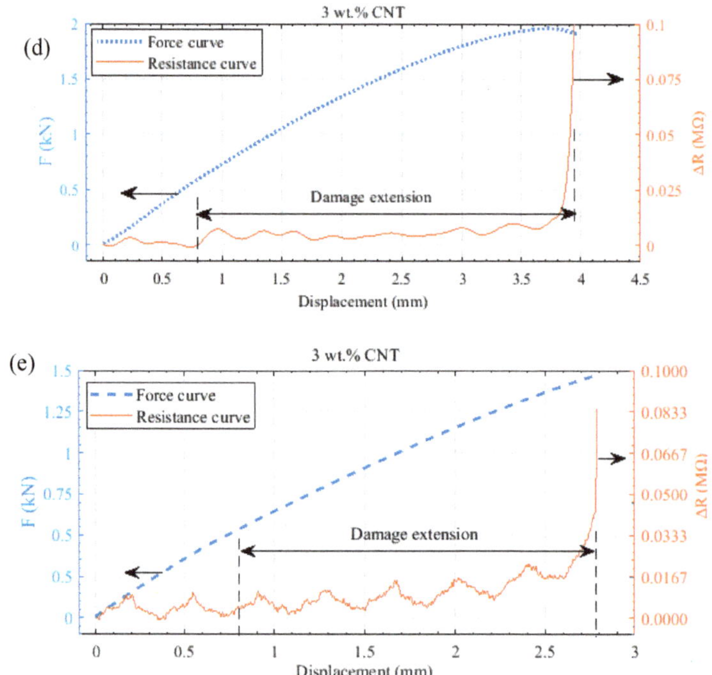

Figure 9. Force and impedance changes as a function of displacement for nanocomposites with different weight percent prepared at 10 min dispersion time and (**a**) 1 wt % CNT; (**b**) 1.5 wt % CNT; (**c**) 2 wt % CN; (**d**) and (**e**) 3 wt % CNT. The arrows indicate the axis belonging to the respective curve. Note: the scaling on the righthand axis and displacement below are not uniform throughout the illustrated results.

Table 2. Mechanical properties of the nanocomposites.

Specimen	Young's Modulus (GPa)	Max Strength (MPa)
Pure epoxy	3.533 ± 0.04	47.19 ± 1.05
1 wt % CNT–epoxy	3.045 ± 0.03	68.36 ± 2.74
1.5 wt % CNT–epoxy	3.109 ± 0.04	64.89 ± 1.33
2 wt % CNT–epoxy	2.932 ± 0.05	62.26 ± 1.40
3 wt % CNT–epoxy	2.008 ± 0.02	50.19 ± 1.65

The slopes of the electrical impedance diagrams show that a filler amount equal to 3 wt % MWCNTs, and at least 10 min dispersion time, provided the highest sensitivity with respect to displacement and applied force using the suggested measurement setup. However, the mechanical strength decreased to 50.19 MPa.

4. Conclusions

In this work, we introduce a measurement technique for condition monitoring of damage in composites for structures and buildings by conductive nano-adhesive. The conductive nano-adhesive was prepared with various MWCNT contents and different dispersion times. Then, the capability of the prepared MWCNT–epoxy composites as nanocomposite sensors was studied by determining their electrical impedance changes during longitudinal loading. It was observed that dispersion times longer than 10 min provide no significant improvement in the equivalent parallel resistance of the nanocomposite. Although the maximum tolerated forces of these nanocomposite sensors were achieved with 1 wt % MWCNT content, the nanocomposite sensors fabricated with 3 wt % MWCNTs and a dispersion time of 10 minutes showed better self-damage sensing capabilities in the considered setup, while still achieving a mechanical strength higher than that of pure epoxy.

Author Contributions: O.S.-D. prepared the specimens, contributed to electrical and mechanical testing and drafted the paper. L.-M.F. contributed to the electrical and mechanical measurements, did the analysis in MATLAB and edited the paper. M.F. gave suggestions on how to modify the paper and provided supervision. A.R. aided in preparation of the specimen and contributed the SEM analyses. H.O. contributed in the tensile testing, and T.M. worked on the suitable signal processing for the electrical measurements. A.A. is supervisor. H.Z. organized the financing and collaborations, L.-M.F. and H.Z. reviewed the paper and provided supervision.

Funding: This research received no external funding.

Acknowledgments: This study was financially supported by the Alpen-Adria-Universität. The preparation of specimens was conducted in the chemistry lab of the Carinthian Tech Research (CTR) AG and mechanical testing equipment was supplied by the Carinthian University of Applied Sciences (FH Kärnten) in Villach.

Conflicts of Interest: The authors declare no conflict of interest.

References

1. Lu, J.; Chen, X.; Lu, W.; Chen, G. The piezoresistive behaviors of polyethylene/foliated graphite nanocomposites. *Eur. Polym. J.* **2006**, *42*, 1015–1021. [CrossRef]
2. Le, J.-L.; Du, H.; Dai Pang, S. Use of 2d graphene nanoplatelets (gnp) in cement composites for structural health evaluation. *Compos. Part B* **2014**, *67*, 555–563. [CrossRef]
3. Thostenson, E.T.; Chou, T.-W. Aligned multi-walled carbon nanotube-reinforced composites: Processing and mechanical characterization. *J. Phys. D Appl. Phys.* **2002**, *35*, L77–L80. [CrossRef]
4. Suhr, J.; Koratkar, N.; Keblinski, P.; Ajayan, P. Viscoelasticity in carbon nanotube composites. *Nat. Mater.* **2005**, *4*, 134–137. [CrossRef] [PubMed]
5. Cha, J.; Jun, G.H.; Park, J.K.; Kim, J.C.; Ryu, H.J.; Hong, S.H. Improvement of modulus, strength and fracture toughness of cnt/epoxy nanocomposites through the functionalization of carbon nanotubes. *Compos. Part B* **2017**, *129*, 169–179. [CrossRef]
6. Wang, L.; Dang, Z.-M. Carbon nanotube composites with high dielectric constant at low percolation threshold. *Appl. Phys. Lett.* **2005**, *87*, 042903. [CrossRef]
7. Li, J.; Zhang, G.; Zhang, H.; Fan, X.; Zhou, L.; Shang, Z.; Shi, X. Electrical conductivity and electromagnetic interference shielding of epoxy nanocomposite foams containing functionalized multi-wall carbon nanotubes. *Appl. Surf. Sci.* **2018**, *428*, 7–16. [CrossRef]
8. Guadagno, L.; Raimondo, M.; Vertuccio, L.; Naddeo, C.; Barra, G.; Longo, P.; Lamberti, P.; Spinelli, G.; Nobile, M. Morphological, rheological and electrical properties of composites filled with carbon nanotubes functionalized with 1-pyrenebutyric acid. *Compos. Part B* **2018**, *147*, 12–21. [CrossRef]
9. Gardea, F.; Lagoudas, D.C. Characterization of electrical and thermal properties of carbon nanotube/epoxy composites. *Compos. Part B* **2014**, *56*, 611–620. [CrossRef]
10. Krainoi, A.; Kummerlöwe, C.; Nakaramontri, Y.; Vennemann, N.; Pichaiyut, S.; Wisunthorn, S.; Nakason, C. Influence of critical carbon nanotube loading on mechanical and electrical properties of epoxidized natural rubber nanocomposites. *Polym. Test.* **2018**, *66*, 122–136. [CrossRef]
11. Galvez, P.; Quesada, A.; Martinez, M.A.; Abenojar, J.; Boada, M.J.L.; Diaz, V. Study of the behaviour of adhesive joints of steel with cfrp for its application in bus structures. *Compos. Part B* **2017**, *129*, 41–46. [CrossRef]
12. Vajtai, R.; Wei, B.; Zhang, Z.; Jung, Y.; Ramanath, G.; Ajayan, P. Building carbon nanotubes and their smart architectures. *Smart Mater. Struct.* **2002**, *11*, 691–698. [CrossRef]
13. Koo, Y.; Shanov, V.N.; Yun, Y. Carbon nanotube paper-based electroanalytical devices. *Micromachines* **2016**, *7*, 72. [CrossRef]
14. Lee, J.; Lim, S.-H. CNT foam-embedded micro gas pre-concentrator for low-concentration ethane measurements. *Sensors* **2018**, *18*, 1547. [CrossRef] [PubMed]
15. Avilés, F.; May-Pat, A.; López-Manchado, M.; Verdejo, R.; Bachmatiuk, A.; Rümmeli, M. A comparative study on the mechanical, electrical and piezoresistive properties of polymer composites using carbon nanostructures of different topology. *Eur. Polym. J.* **2018**, *99*, 394–402. [CrossRef]

16. Nofar, M.; Hoa, S.; Pugh, M. Failure detection and monitoring in polymer matrix composites subjected to static and dynamic loads using carbon nanotube networks. *Compos. Sci. Technol.* **2009**, *69*, 1599–1606. [CrossRef]

17. Wang, Y.; Wang, S.; Li, M.; Gu, Y.; Zhang, Z. Piezoresistive response of carbon nanotube composite film under laterally compressive strain. *Sens. Actuators A* **2018**, *273*, 140–146. [CrossRef]

18. Kim, H.; Kim, Y. High performance flexible piezoelectric pressure sensor based on cnts-doped 0–3 ceramic-epoxy nanocomposites. *Mater. Des.* **2018**, *151*, 133–140. [CrossRef]

19. Hu, N.; Fukunaga, H.; Atobe, S.; Liu, Y.; Li, J. Piezoresistive strain sensors made from carbon nanotubes based polymer nanocomposites. *Sensors* **2011**, *11*, 10691–10723.

20. Prudencio, E.; Bauman, P.; Williams, S.; Faghihi, D.; Ravi-Chandar, K.; Oden, J. Real-time inference of stochastic damage in composite materials. *Compos. Part B* **2014**, *67*, 209–219. [CrossRef]

21. Kwon, D.-J.; Wang, Z.-J.; Choi, J.-Y.; Shin, P.-S.; DeVries, K.L.; Park, J.-M. Damage sensing and fracture detection of cnt paste using electrical resistance measurements. *Compos. Part B* **2016**, *90*, 386–391. [CrossRef]

22. Mishra, S.; Kumaran, K.; Sivakumaran, R.; Pandian, S.P.; Kundu, S. Synthesis of PVDF/CNT and their functionalized composites for studying their electrical properties to analyze their applicability in actuation & sensing. *Colloids Surf. A* **2016**, *509*, 684–696.

23. Na, W.-J.; Byun, J.-H.; Lee, M.-G.; Yu, W.-R. In-situ damage sensing of woven composites using carbon nanotube conductive networks. *Compos. Part A* **2015**, *77*, 229–236. [CrossRef]

24. Li, C.; Thostenson, E.T.; Chou, T.-W. Sensors and actuators based on carbon nanotubes and their composites: A review. *Compos. Sci. Technol.* **2008**, *68*, 1227–1249. [CrossRef]

25. Lee, B.M.; Gupta, S.; Loh, K.J.; Nagarajaiah, S. Strain sensing and structural health monitoring using nanofilms and nanocomposites. In *Innovative Developments of Advanced Multifunctional Nanocomposites in Civil and Structural Engineering*; Loh, K., Nagarajaiah, S., Eds.; Elsevier: Cambridge, UK, 2016; pp. 303–326.

26. Kang, I.; Schulz, M.J.; Kim, J.H.; Shanov, V.; Shi, D. A carbon nanotube strain sensor for structural health monitoring. *Smart Mater. Struct.* **2006**, *15*, 737–748. [CrossRef]

27. Meeuw, H.; Viets, C.; Liebig, W.; Schulte, K.; Fiedler, B. Morphological influence of carbon nanofillers on the piezoresistive response of carbon nanoparticle/epoxy composites under mechanical load. *Eur. Polym. J.* **2016**, *85*, 198–210. [CrossRef]

28. Alig, I.; Pötschke, P.; Lellinger, D.; Skipa, T.; Pegel, S.; Kasaliwal, G.R.; Villmow, T. Establishment, morphology and properties of carbon nanotube networks in polymer melts. *Polymer* **2012**, *53*, 4–28. [CrossRef]

29. Pal, G.; Kumar, S. Multiscale modeling of effective electrical conductivity of short carbon fiber-carbon nanotube-polymer matrix hybrid composites. *Mater. Des.* **2016**, *89*, 129–136. [CrossRef]

30. Zangl, H.; Muehlbacher-Karrer, S.; Hamid, R. Interfaces for autarkic wireless sensors and actuators in the internet of things. In *Advanced Interfacing Techniques for Sensors*; Springer: New York, NY, USA, 2017; pp. 167–189.

31. Zangl, H.; Zine-Zine, M.; Mühlbacher-Karrer, S. Teds extensions toward energy management of wireless transducers. *IEEE Sens. J.* **2015**, *15*, 2587–2594. [CrossRef]

32. Seyhan, A.T.; Tanoğlu, M.; Schulte, K. Tensile mechanical behavior and fracture toughness of MWCNT and DWCNT modified vinyl-ester/polyester hybrid nanocomposites produced by 3-roll milling. *Mater. Sci. Eng. A* **2009**, *523*, 85–92. [CrossRef]

33. Kueseng, P.; Sae-oui, P.; Rattanasom, N. Mechanical and electrical properties of natural rubber and nitrile rubber blends filled with multi-wall carbon nanotube: Effect of preparation methods. *Polym. Test.* **2013**, *32*, 731–738. [CrossRef]

34. Faller, L.-M.; Mitterer, T.; Leitzke, J.P.; Zangl, H. Design and evaluation of a fast, high-resolution sensor evaluation platform applied to mems position sensing. *IEEE Trans. Instrum. Meas.* **2017**, *67*, 1014–1027. [CrossRef]

35. Faller, L.-M.; Leitzke, J.; Zangl, H. Design of a fast, high-resolution sensor evaluation platform applied to a capacitive position sensor for a micromirror. In Proceedings of the 2017 IEEE International Instrumentation and Measurement Technology Conference (I2MTC), Turin, Italy, 22–25 May 2017; pp. 1–6.

36. Georgousis, G.; Pandis, C.; Kalamiotis, A.; Georgiopoulos, P.; Kyritsis, A.; Kontou, E.; Pissis, P.; Micusik, M.; Czanikova, K.; Kulicek, J. Strain sensing in polymer/carbon nanotube composites by electrical resistance measurement. *Compos. Part B* **2015**, *68*, 162–169. [CrossRef]

37. Pircheraghi, G.; Powell, T.; Solouki Bonab, V.; Manas-Zloczower, I. Effect of carbon nanotube dispersion and network formation on thermal conductivity of thermoplastic polyurethane/carbon nanotube nanocomposites. *Polym. Eng. Sci.* **2016**, *56*, 394–407. [CrossRef]

38. Ferrreira, A.; Rocha, J.; Ansón-Casaos, A.; Martínez, M.; Vaz, F.; Lanceros-Mendez, S. Electromechanical performance of poly (vinylidene fluoride)/carbon nanotube composites for strain sensor applications. *Sens. Actuators A* **2012**, *178*, 10–16. [CrossRef]

39. Ku-Herrera, J.; Aviles, F. Cyclic tension and compression piezoresistivity of carbon nanotube/vinyl ester composites in the elastic and plastic regimes. *Carbon* **2012**, *50*, 2592–2598. [CrossRef]

40. Grammatikos, S.; Paipetis, A. On the electrical properties of multi scale reinforced composites for damage accumulation monitoring. *Compos. Part B* **2012**, *43*, 2687–2696. [CrossRef]

41. Lim, A.S.; An, Q.; Chou, T.-W.; Thostenson, E.T. Mechanical and electrical response of carbon nanotube-based fabric composites to hopkinson bar loading. *Compos. Sci. Technol.* **2011**, *71*, 616–621. [CrossRef]

42. Yu, S.; Tong, M.N.; Critchlow, G. Wedge test of carbon-nanotube-reinforced epoxy adhesive joints. *J. Appl. Polym. Sci.* **2009**, *111*, 2957–2962. [CrossRef]

 *electronics*

Article

A "Smart" Trap Device for Detection of Crawling Insects and Other Arthropods in Urban Environments

Panagiotis Eliopoulos [1], Nikolaos-Alexandros Tatlas [2], Iraklis Rigakis [3] and Ilyas Potamitis [4,*]

[1] Department of Agriculture Technologists, Technological Educational Institute of Thessaly, 41110 Larissa, Greece; eliopoulos@teilar.gr

[2] Department of Electronics Engineering, Piraeus University of Applied Sciences, 12244 Athens, Greece; ntatlas@puas.gr

[3] Department of Electronics, Technological Educational Institute of Crete, 73133 Chania, Greece; rigakis@chania.teicrete.gr

[4] Department of Music Technology & Acoustics, Technological Educational Institute of Crete, 74133 Rethymno, Greece

* Correspondence: potamitis@staff.teicrete.gr; Tel.: +30-28310-21900; Fax: +30-28310-21913

Received: 23 July 2018; Accepted: 21 August 2018; Published: 24 August 2018

Abstract: We introduce a device for the automatic detecting and reporting of crawling insects in urban environments. It is a monitoring device for urban pests that complies with the context of smart homes and smart cities, and is compatible with the emerging discipline of the Internet of Things (IoT). We believe it can find its place in every room of a hotel, hospital, military camp, and residence. This box-shaped device attracts targeted insect pests, senses the entering insect, and takes automatically a picture of the internal space of the box. The e-trap includes strong attractants (pheromone and/or food) to increase capture efficiency and traps the insect on its sticky floor. The device carries the necessary optoelectronic sensors to monitor all entrances of the trap. As the insect enters it interrupts the infrared light source. This triggers a detection event; a picture is taken, and a time-stamp is set before delivering the picture through the Wi-Fi to an authorized person/stakeholder. The device can be integrated seamlessly in urban environments and operates unobtrusively to human activities. We report results on various insect pests and depending on the insect species, can reach a detection accuracy ranging from 96 to 99%.

Keywords: smart traps; insect surveillance; cockroaches; IoT

---

1. Introduction

The quality of life for most people in the future will be represented in the cities' quality of life index. The European Commission has, in recent years, been increasing its focus on urban issues, as a response to the fact that by 2020 it is estimated that almost 80% of EU citizens will be living in cities [1]. Cities provide development and growth, and generally better life benefits than in rural areas. Apart from quality of living, houses, buildings, roads, schools, hospitals, markets, and other structures that characterize the urban environment, cities also provide habitats for a special group of insects and other arthropods, some of which have attained pest status, the so-called "urban insects" [2–4].

Contrarily to agroecosystems, pest status in the urban environment may not be based on a measurable feature. The damage and the control treatments costs cannot always be determined. Structural damage (e.g., termites, wood boring beetles), sanitary problems (e.g., cockroaches), health threats (e.g., bed bugs), or simple annoyance only by the insect presence (e.g., insects in houses, stinging insects), have been developed to common cases in urban environments. A decision to apply control measures may be based on potential damage or personal injury, or solely or in part on emotion. Arthropods in the urban environment are completely unacceptable, whether their populations are low or high. Pest management and control strategies are based on early detection and pest identification before applying chemical and nonchemical control treatments.

Early pest detection is crucial for an effective and affordable control in urban environments. For this purpose, various trap types (mainly sticky) are frequently used by homeowners, pest management professionals, and urban entomologist researchers for detecting infestations of crawling insects like ants, termites, bedbugs, cockroaches, earwigs, beetles, moth larvae, etc., as well as other crawling arthropods such as spiders, millipedes, centipedes, etc. [2,5,6]. These devices provide consistent estimates not only of insects' presence (detection) and relative abundance (monitoring), but they are also useful for evaluating insecticide treatment efficacy (post-treatment analysis) and control purposes (population reduction) [7–9].

As a detection tool, sticky traps provide information on distribution and population density, thereby assisting in properly targeting insecticide applications. Because of their safety, ease of use, and non-toxicity, sticky traps are considered to be a valuable tool in integrated pest management (IPM) programs especially in urban environments.

For the purposes of this study, trapping tests were performed for the detection of three very common crawling insects in urban environments.

A. Cockroaches (Order: Blattodea): They are cosmopolitan insects, occurring nearly all over the world. Although, most of the approximately 4000 described species live in small populations in forest habitats, their association with decaying organic matter and humid conditions maintains some species (nearly 30) in the urban environment. They may become very serious pests given that they can passively transport pathogenic microbes on their body surfaces. Particularly, in environments such as hospitals [10,11], they are often linked with allergic reactions in humans [12] and asthma [13]. These allergens are heat-stable and persistent in the living space. Approximately 20–50% of homes with no visible sign of cockroaches have detectable cockroach allergens in dust [14].

B. Ants (Hymenoptera: Formicidae): The pest status of ants is based on their nesting and foraging habits. The urban environment provides a variety of soil types and conditions, suitable for a large number of ant species [2,15]. Nesting along building foundations can result in damage to structural members of buildings, and to exterior faces. Ants usually enter the buildings to find food, demonstrating remarkable persistence foraging inside and establishing satellite nests indoors. The habit of foraging ants to visit a variety of food sources increases their potential to acquire pathogenic and food decay microbes. A large number of pathogens have been recorded from ant species, including bacteria (*Burkholderia*, *Clostridium*, *Enterobacter*, *Salmonella*, etc.) and fungi (*Aspergillus*, *Penicillium*, etc.), [2,15,16]. Pest ants in the urban environment have a significant economic impact both on the pest control industry and the general public. Many times, ants have been ranked as the number one pest problem of households, even surpassing cockroaches [17]. Most important and well-studied species are the fire ants (*Solenopsis* sp.), because of their medical and agricultural impact [18]; the Pharaoh ants (*Monomorium pharaonis*), which are major household pests and can act as disease vectors in hospitals [19]; and carpenter ants (*Camponotus* spp.), which are important wood-destroying organisms [20].

C. Beetle pests of stored food (Order: Coleoptera): Beetle pests are often recorded in urban environments searching for food (e.g., cereals, grains, packaged food, flour, etc.). Their presence may become a serious problem in certain cases like in residences, markets, hospitals, bakeries, restaurants etc. There is a plethora of beetle species (*Sitophilus*, *Rhyzoperta*, *Tribolium*, *Cryptolestes*, *Oryzaephilus*, *Stegobium*, *Lasioderma*, etc.) invading abovementioned urban environments searching for food [21,22].

Recently, we observe an upsurge of interest in shifting sophisticated, high-tech procedures to insect sensing that are typically encountered in other research fields (see the LIDAR applications on insect fauna [23], Perles in optical sensing of termites [24], Potamitis for electronic e-traps for flying insects [25–28], and Zhong on applying deep learning to insects trapped on sticky traps [29]). This study belongs to this general trend but is different to its aim and cause. Our study aims to introduce a novel "intelligent" trap that can be hidden conveniently under a bed or fixed to the wall that can become a useful tool for the automated early detection of crawling insects and other arthropods in urban environments. Though we have tested three widely encountered cases the applicability can be directly extended to other cases as well, namely: The presence mainly of Bed Bugs (Hemiptera: Cimicidae) and Cloth Moths that feed on stored fabrics (Lepidoptera: Tineidae) can be devastating for the reputation and prospect of a hotel or hospital in the era of TripAdvisor, Instagram, and Facebook. The proposed device will curtail the cost of Integrated Pest Management (IPM) applied to hotels as it will limit the application of IPM from a prescheduled basis (i.e., once a year) to an on-time, localized (i.e., per room) application of IPM. More on, it allows the hotel to advertise that it takes best action to protect its customers and their children by applying surveillance control on insects.

2. Materials and Methods

2.1. Trap Design and Function

This box-shaped device with dimensions of 21 cm × 11 cm × 7.5 cm, including the plastic box and the attached electronic kit (Figure 1) attracts insect pests, senses the entering insect and takes automatically a picture of the internal space of the box. The picture is communicated through the Wi-Fi commonly found in such establishments to an authorized person/stakeholder receiving the picture to take proper action. In this way, continuous, accurate and verifiable, real-time detection is achieved, without the need for human intervention. It is a monitoring device for urban pests in the context of smart homes and smart cities, and is compatible with the emerging discipline of the Internet of Things (IoT) (see Figure 2 for the way we envision its application).

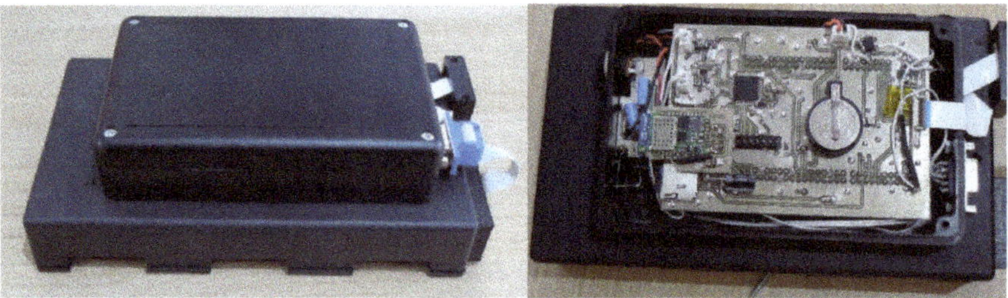

Figure 1. (**Left**) A prototype of the smart trap. (**Right**) The electronics are mounted on top of a plastic trap.

Our smart trap functions like a classic floor trap. Traps may differ greatly in design features (shape, size, surface material, etc.) and the presence of attractants (food, pheromone). All these factors along with placement method influence dramatically the trap efficacy [30].

The box includes a strong attractant to attract the insects and maximize captures. The insect is trapped on a sticky surface that is inside the device, basically a cardboard coated with special insect glue (Tangle-Trap® Sticky Coatings, Tanglefoot, Marysville, Washington, DC, USA) that lasts (remains sticky) for 4–6 months. The sticky floor provides the means for immediate verification of reported results. Captured insects frequently release additional pheromone by themselves and increase the attractiveness. The presence of multiple attractants targeting different insect species simultaneously is also possible and recommended.

The concept presented in this work does not depend on a specific trap configuration and many types are compatible with it. In this work, we modified a well-known trap for crawling insects (TRAPPER Pest Monitor®, Bell Labs, Murray Hill, NJ, USA) on which we added the electronic components (see Figure 1-Right). This trap has multiple entrances that are all monitored simultaneously by a single laser beam (infrared laser PN: 980MD-30-1230-CAB/NANMA). Any entering pest will interrupt the laser's beam, and this triggers a time counter. The wavelength of the laser is at 980 nm and its power at 30 mW.

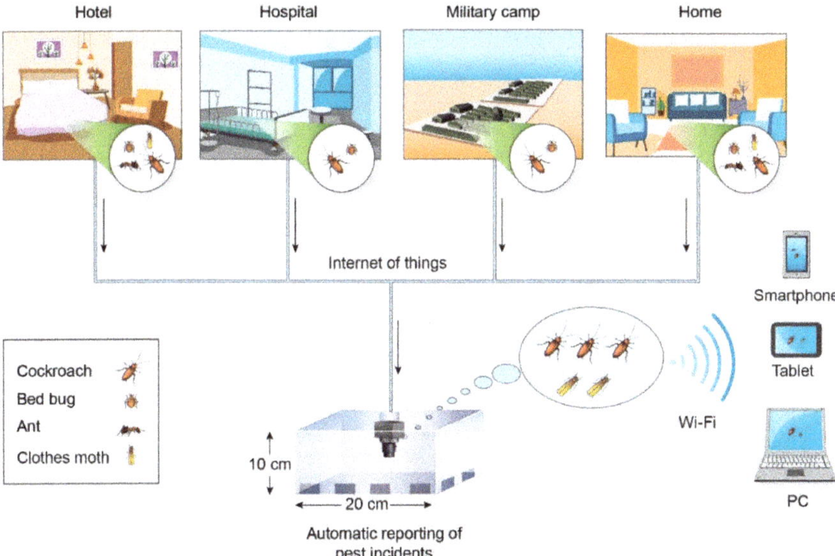

Figure 2. Surveillance of urban, crawling insects in the context of smart-cities. Residential accounts, food processing plants, military camps, underground stations, and hospitals are some of the main locations that can be monitored independently or as part of a regional/country network in the context of the Internet of Things (IoT).

After 20 s a photograph (Camera OV2640, cmos sensor camera module, Omnivision, Santa Clara, CA, USA) of the internal volume of the trap is taken (Figure 3), time-stamped and delivered to pre-stored mail addresses while a copy of the picture is stored internally in the SD card of the device. The time delay ensures that is given enough time to the insect that follows the chemical signals of the bait to crawl inside. The crossing of the laser beam by an insect effects a voltage drop in the receiver's amplifier. The drop is analogous to the size of the insect. A minimum and maximum threshold is set during monitoring of the voltage drop based on inactive, targeted pests. For example, when we need to monitor cockroaches we do not want the system to be triggered by the accidental entrance of an ant. Note that a random entrance is uncommon as targeted insects enter the trap because the follow their corresponding pheromones. Similarly, we monitor the time delay of the entering event based on marking the onset and the end of an entering event. A long delay is atypical for an insect movement and this initiates a possible malfunction notice sent through the Wi-Fi (e.g., an insect blocking the entrance). The speed of the entering pest is also calculated, and atypical speeds are rejected as false alarms.

The processor that handles all tasks is a STM32F767 ARM Microcontroller (see Figure 1-Right).

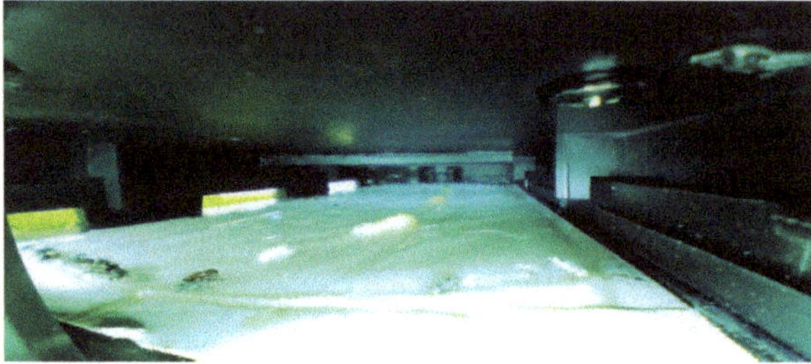

Figure 3. Photograph from the internal of the trap, automatically taken 20 s after insect's entrance.

A diagram of the system summarizing its modules and their interconnection is depicted in the block diagram of Figure 4.

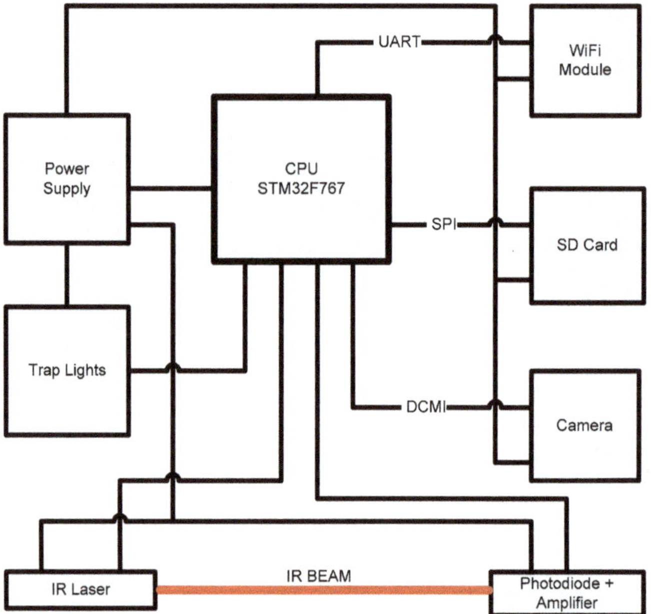

Figure 4. System diagram of the functionality of the suggested device.

The STM32F767 processors has all the communication buses that are required for the task. The laser sends 200 Hz pulses of 12 μs duration. The pulses are received by the photodiode and are amplified. The amplifier's output is driven to analogue input of the processor. The processor runs an algorithm that reads the amplitude of the signal and detects if the beam of light has been interrupted. If so, then, after 20 s a light illuminates the trap and the camera takes a picture. The jpeg picture is transferred through the 8-BIT DCMI interface to the memory of the processor and stored in the SD card. The communication of the processor with the SD is done through the 4-BIT SPI interface. Subsequently, the photograph is sent via the Wi-Fi functionality to predefined e-mails. The e-mails as well as other parameters are stored in a settings file stored in the SD card of the system. The software is written in C language using the IAR Embedded workbench. The programming of the flash memory has been done using the ST-Link V2 programmer. The code initialization was done using the STM32CubeMX of

ST. For programming the peripheral sub-components such as the SD and the camera, ADC and the Wi-Fi interface we made use of the STM32 HAL Drivers.

2.2. Evaluation

For the purposes of our study, a prototype of this trap was tested under real conditions in three cases. Our trap was placed:

(a) in an old food warehouse with an increased presence of cockroaches in Agrinio, Central Greece. Trap placement lasted from early to mid-May 2018.

(b) in a livestock unit with large ant populations in Larissa, Central Greece. Trap placement lasted from early to mid-April 2018.

(c) in an old-style granary (horizontal type) with a heavy insect infestation in stored wheat mass in Farsala, Central Greece. Trap placement lasted from early to mid-March 2018.

Trap placement lasted about two weeks in all cases. The trap was visually checked by a qualified entomologist on a daily basis, and the number of captured insect individuals was recorded. These manual records were compared with the data that were automatically recorded by the trap and sent wirelessly. Non-target insects or other arthropods that may enter the trap accidentally were not included in the results but in our experiments, these were rare cases. During each manual inspection the sticky surface with captured insects was removed for examination in the lab (Figure 5) and replaced by an identical one clean sticky cardboard surface. In all cases the proper attractant was placed in the center of sticky surface in order to make sure that insects would enter the trap. Baits applied for each target were: pure wheat germ oil (HealthAid, Harrow, London, UK) for stored food beetles, 25% sugar solution for ants, and Trapper roach attractant (Bell Labs, Murray Hill, NJ, USA) for cockroaches.

Figure 5. Evaluation of reported results. Sticky surface inside the trap after 2 days of placement in (**Left**) a cereal grain storage facility with serious insect infestations, (**Right**) in an old food warehouse with an increased presence of cockroaches.

3. Results and Discussion

Results from the evaluation of the prototype trap are presented in Figure 6 where the result of a linear regression analysis of the manual records and the automatic counts from our system. The slope of the regression line indicates the association between manual and system counting, and r represents the fraction of the total variance of system counting that is explained by the variation in manual records. The analysis result shows that the counting numbers of insects obtained by manual observation and automatic counting system are greatly related (96–99%).

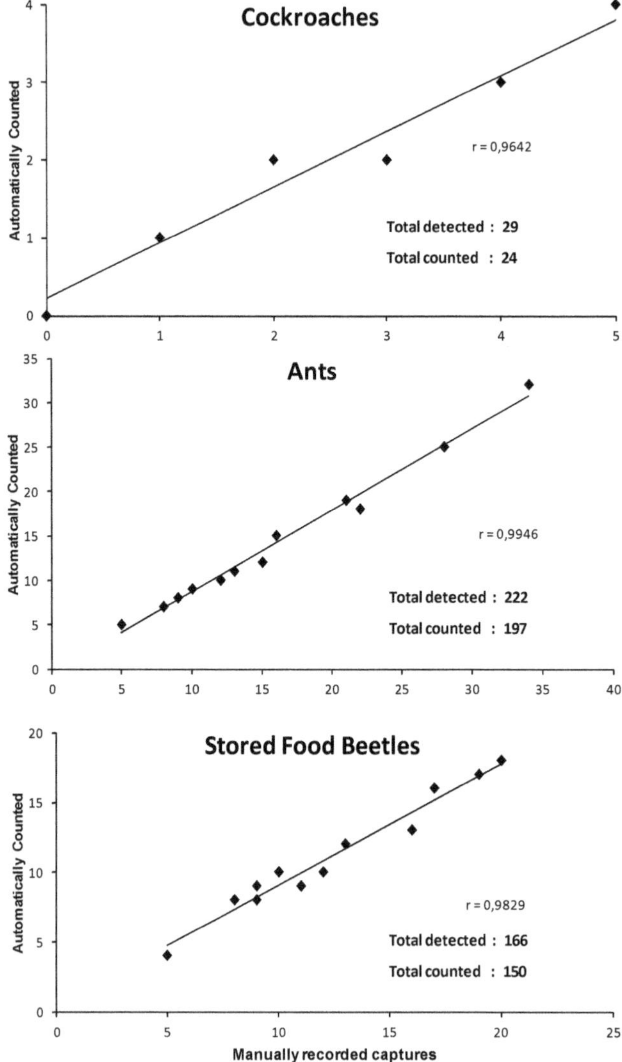

Figure 6. Accuracy of the automatic counting in comparison with actual detection, each species target insect. The values of the correlation coefficient *r* prove that our system is > 96% accurate (when detected and counted values are the same then *r* equals to 1).

In order to evaluate the accuracy of the proposed system, the numbers of the captures measured by the system were compared to those counted manually. The inaccuracy of the system is based on the error between manual counting and system counting. Equation (1), which represents the accuracy of the system, is shown as follows:

$$a = 1 - \frac{|Mc - Ac|}{Mc}.$$ (1)

where α is the counting accuracy of the system, Mc is the number of the captures by manual counting, and Ac is the number of the automatically counted captures. The results are shown in Table 1.

As it is clearly presented, our smart trap is very accurate, achieving about 90% accuracy on automatic counts compared with manually counted numbers of captured insects. The accuracy of our system in detecting insect presence is also shown by the very high correlation ($r > 0.96$ in all cases) between the generated signals and actual numbers of insects caught in the trap.

To the best of our knowledge, it is the first time that an automated remote system is evaluated under real conditions in detecting insect pests in urban environments. Lab studies have been carried out on the development of automated detection of insects [31–33] but in a totally different context from ours (e.g., probes inserted in the grain mass).

Our study aims to introduce a novel trap-device that we believe it can find its place to every urban environment such as houses, hotel rooms, hospitals, underground stations and trains, military camps, airports, food markets and storages. Such a device will also curtail the cost of Integrated Pest Management (IPM) as it will limit the application of IPM from a prescheduled basis (i.e., once a year) to an on-time, localized (i.e., per room) application of IPM.

Table 1. The counting accuracy of the proposed "smart" trap.

	Manually Recorded	Automatically Counted	% Accuracy (*a*)	Mean Accuracy
Cockroaches	3	2	66.7%	89.6%
	2	2	100.0%	
	0	0	100.0%	
	3	2	66.7%	
	5	4	80.0%	
	0	0	100.0%	
	2	2	100.0%	
	4	3	75.0%	
	3	2	66.7%	
	1	1	100.0%	
	2	2	100.0%	
	1	1	100.0%	
	2	2	100.0%	
	1	1	100.0%	
Ants	10	9	90.0%	88.7%
	12	10	83.3%	
	8	7	87.5%	
	21	19	90.5%	
	9	8	88.9%	
	5	5	100.0%	
	15	12	80.0%	
	16	15	93.8%	
	28	25	89.3%	
	13	11	84.6%	
	34	32	94.1%	
	8	7	87.5%	
	21	19	90.5%	
	22	18	81.8%	
Stored Food Beetles	8	8	100.0%	90.7%
	9	8	88.9%	
	5	4	80.0%	
	12	10	83.3%	
	9	8	88.9%	
	17	16	94.1%	
	19	17	89.5%	
	9	9	100.0%	
	11	9	81.8%	
	8	8	100.0%	
	16	13	81.3%	
	20	18	90.0%	
	10	10	100.0%	
	13	12	92.3%	

It has been well documented that insects may act as a "pathogen reservoir", which especially in a hospital environment, may cause serious health hazards [34–36]. Insect problems can be detrimental for the financial prospect of a private hospital establishment or for the managemental capability of the head of the hotel and finally of the Ministry of Health [37].

Again, the presence of ants, cockroaches, bed bugs or stored food insects in home residencies, schools or even in military camps may become a serious problem with unforeseen consequences [2,38]. With a cost of materials roughly 30 Euros (as per 13 August 2018) the device has also the prospect to be widely accepted by typical residencies at least to one device per house.

Finally, the suggested product conforms with the concept of the smart house and through the emerging trend of IoT it can connect the concept of a smart house to a smart city that keeps an eye-watch on the insects at larger spatial scales.

4. Conclusions

With the recent advancements in wireless communications, networks, and integrated sensors, the ability to use wireless sensor networks (WSNs) to cover large areas with a network of IoT nodes that collectively transmit information to a central server in real-time has become available. Wireless sensor networks have been demonstrated to exhibit the potential of being used in massive scale for environmental parameter monitoring. While they are constantly evolving to the point of a widely used technology, the requirements for an automated trap, including autonomous operation pose practical limitations to the use of off-the-shelf solutions, thus leading to the design and development of custom hardware. This is due to the type of sensor (imaging and presence), the application field, the need for low power operation, adaptable size to match the trap, robustness to environmental conditions, the need for spatial coverage and the existence of isolated or remote monitoring spots. The main concept is to hide a small, affordable device for insect surveillance of urban crawling insects and forget its existence until the user receives a picture in his/her mobile.

The smart trap presented in this work was developed following the above requirements, for fully-automated operation. The cost and size will allow multiple traps to be installed in possibly concealed locations such as under beds, as instructed by the IPM strategy with a sole technical requirement of sufficient Wi-Fi coverage, which is nowadays taken for granted in most indoor environments.

As the events are relayed via wireless networking, following the IoT architecture, these traps may be integrated to any smart-building infrastructure. This may allow the establishment of applications ranging from end-user notification/alerting in order to take appropriate measures, to condition-based insect management depending on set business rules. Moreover, as insect infestation may not be localized on a building basis but be widespread, by centralizing the server infrastructure and providing geolocational information for each smart trap, an interactive infestation map may be created, adding the system to the smart city concept. Future work relates detection of urban insects and deep learning classification algorithms that have become a standard in visual-based applications of artificial intelligence as in the paradigm of Zhong [29], where the device automatically counts the insects and reports their identity and as in Sadegh et al. [39] where the identity of wild animals is automatically inferred based on their picture.

Author Contributions: Conceptualization, I.P.; Methodology, P.E.; Software, I.R.; Validation, P.E., N.T.; Writing-Review & Editing, P.E., I.P., N.T.

Funding: This work was supported by the GSRT-Greece matching funds associated to No. 605073, FP7 Project ENTOMATIC.

Conflicts of Interest: The authors declare no conflicts of interest.

References

1.	European Commission. *Making Our Cities Attractive and Sustainable: How the EU Contributes to Improving the Urban Environment*; Publications Office of the European Union: Luxembourg, 2010.

2.   Robinson, W.H. *Urban Insects and Arachnids: A Handbook of Urban Entomology*; Cambridge University Press: Cambridge, UK, 2005.

3.   McIntyre, N.E. Ecology of urban arthropods: A review and a call to action. *Ann. Entomol. Soc. Am.* **2000**, *93*, 825–835. [CrossRef]

4.   Bonnefoy, X.; Kampen, H.; Sweeney, K. *Public Health Significance of Urban Pests*; World Health Organization: Geneva, Switzerland, 2008.

5.   Dhang, P. *Urban Pest Management: An Environmental Perspective*; CABI: Oxfordshire, UK, 2011.

6.   Dhang, P. *Urban Insect Pests: Sustainable Management Strategies*; CABI: Oxfordshire, UK, 2014.

7.   Owens, J.M.; Bennett, G.W. Comparative study of German cockroach (Dictyoptera: Blattellidae) population sampling techniques. *Environ. Entomol.* **1983**, *12*, 1040–1046. [CrossRef]

8.   Kaakeh, W.; Bennett, G.W. Evaluation of trapping and vacuuming compared with low-impact insecticide tactics for managing German cockroaches in residences. *J. Econ. Entomol.* **1997**, *90*, 976–982. [CrossRef]

9.   Ballard, J.B.; Gold, R.E. Field evaluation of two trap designs used for control of German cockroach populations. *J. Kansas Entomol. Soc.* **1983**, *56*, 506–510.

10.   Rivault, C.; Cloarec, A.; Le Guyader, A. Bacterial load of cockroaches in relation to urban environment. *Epidemiol. Infect.* **1993**, *110*, 317–325. [CrossRef] [PubMed]

11.   Elgderi, R.M.; Ghenghesh, K.S.; Berbash, N. Carriage by the German cockroach (Blattella germanica) of multiple-antibiotic-resistant bacteria that are potentially pathogenic to humans, in hospitals and households in Tripoli, Libya. *Ann. Trop. Med. Parasitol.* **2006**, *100*, 55–62. [CrossRef] [PubMed]

12.   Kutrup, B. Cockroach infestation in some hospitals in Trabzon, Turkey. *Turk. J. Zool.* **2003**, *27*, 73–77.

13.   Kang, B.; Vellody, D.; Homburger, H.; Yunginger, J.W. Cockroach cause of allergic asthma: Its specificity and immunologic profile. *J. Allergy Clin. Immunol.* **1979**, *63*, 80–86. [CrossRef]

14.   Eggleston, P.A.; Arruda, L.K. Ecology and elimination of cockroaches and allergens in the home. *J. Allergy Clin. Immunol.* **2001**, *107*, S422–S429. [CrossRef] [PubMed]

15.   Rust, M.K.; Su, N.Y. Managing social insects of urban importance. *Annu. Rev. Entomol.* **2012**, *57*, 355–375. [CrossRef] [PubMed]

16.   Máximo, H.J.; Felizatti, H.L.; Ceccato, M.; Cintra-Socolowski, P.; Beretta, A.L. Ants as vectors of pathogenic microorganisms in a hospital in São Paulo county, Brazil. *BMC Res. Notes* **2014**, *7*. [CrossRef] [PubMed]

17.   Whitmore, R.W.; Kelly, J.E.; Reading, P.L. *National Home and Garden Pesticide Use Survey, Final Report. Volume I: Executive Summary, Results, and Recommendations*; USEPA: Washington, DC, USA, 1992.

18.   Jemal, A.; Hugh-Jones, M. A review of the red imported fire ant (Solenopsis invicta Buren) and its impacts on plant, animal, and human health. *Prev. Vet. Med.* **1993**, *17*, 19–32. [CrossRef]

19.   Wetterer, J.K. Worldwide spread of the pharaoh ant, Monomorium pharaonis (Hymenoptera: For-micidae). *Myrmecol. News* **2010**, *13*, 115–129.

20.   Hansen, L.D.; Akre, R.D.; Wildey, K.; Robinson, W. Urban pest management of carpenter ants. In Proceedings of the First International Conference on Urban Pests, Cambridge, UK; 1993; pp. 271–279.

21.   Rees, D.P. *Insects of Stored Products*; Csiro Publishing: Clayton, Australia, 2004.

22.   Subramanyam, B. *Integrated Management of Insects in Stored Products*; CRC Press: Boca Raton, FL, USA, 1995.

23.   Jansson, S.; Brydegaard, M. Passive kHz lidar for the quantification of insect activity and dispersal. *Anim. Biotelem.* **2018**, *6*. [CrossRef]

24.   Perles, A.; Mercado, R.; Capella, J.V.; Serrano, J.J. Ultra-Low power optical sensor for xylophagous insect detection in wood. *Sensors* **2016**, *16*, 1977. [CrossRef] [PubMed]

25.   Potamitis, I.; Rigakis, I.; Fysarakis, K. Insect biometrics: Otoacoustic signal processing and its applications to remote monitoring of McPhail type traps. *PLoS ONE* **2015**, *10*. [CrossRef] [PubMed]

26.   Potamitis, I.; Rigakis, I.; Tatlas, N.-A. Automated surveillance of fruit flies. *Sensors* **2017**, *17*, 110. [CrossRef] [PubMed]

27.   Potamitis, I.; Rigakis, I. Large aperture optoelectronic devices to record and time-stamp insects' wingbeats. *IEEE Sensors J.* **2016**, *16*, 6053–6061. [CrossRef]

28.   Potamitis, I.; Eliopoulos, P.; Rigakis, I. Automated Remote Insect Surveillance at a Global Scale and the Internet of Things. *Robotics* **2017**, *6*, 19. [CrossRef]

29.   Zhong, Y.; Gao, J.; Lei, Q.; Zhou, Y. A vision-based counting and recognition system for flying insects in intelligent agriculture. *Sensors* **2018**, *18*, 1489. [CrossRef] [PubMed]

30. Wang, C.; Bennett, G.W. Comparative study of integrated pest management and baiting for German cockroach management in public housing. *J. Econ. Entomol.* **2006**, *99*, 879–885. [CrossRef] [PubMed]

31. Mankin, R.W.; Hodges, R.D.; Nagle, H.T.; Schal, C.; Pereira, R.M.; Koehler, P.G. Acoustic indicators for targeted detection of stored product and urban insect pests by inexpensive infrared, acoustic, and vibrational detection of movement. *J. Econ. Entomol.* **2010**, *103*, 1636–1646. [CrossRef] [PubMed]

32. Oliver-Villanueva, J.V.; Abián-Pérez, M.A. Advanced wireless sensors for termite detection in wood constructions. *Wood Sci. Technol.* **2013**, *47*, 269–280. [CrossRef]

33. Shuman, D.; Weaver, D.K.; Larson, R.G. Performance of an analytical, dual infrared-beam, stored-product insect monitoring system. *J. Econ. Entomol.* **2005**, *98*, 1723–1732. [CrossRef] [PubMed]

34. Fakoorziba, M.R.; Eghbal, F.; Hassanzadeh, J.; Moemenbellah-Fard, M.D. Cockroaches (Periplaneta americana and Blattella germanica) as potential vectors of the pathogenic bacteria found in nosocomial infections. *Ann. Trop. Med. Parasitol.* **2010**, *104*, 521–528. [CrossRef] [PubMed]

35. Feizhaddad, M.H.; Kassiri, H.; Sepand, M.R.; Ghasemi, F. Bacteriological survey of American cockroaches in hospitals. *Middle East J. Sci. Res.* **2012**, *12*, 985–989. [CrossRef]

36. Garcia, F.R.M.; Lise, F. Ants associated with pathogenic microorganisms in brazilian hospitals: Attention to a silent vector. *Acta Scientiarum. Health Sci.* **2013**, *35*. [CrossRef]

37. Owens, K.; Pesticides, B. Healthy hospitals controlling pests without harmful pesticides. In *Healthy Hospitals Controlling Pests without Harmful Pesticides*; HCWH: Washington, DC, USA, 2003.

38. Daar, S.; Drlik, T.; Olkowski, H.; Olkowski, W. *IPM for Schools: A How-to Manual*; USEPA: Washington, DC, USA, 1997.

39. Norouzzadeh, M.S.; Nguyen, A.; Kosmala, M.; Swanson, A.; Palmer, M.S.; Packer, C.; Clune, J. Automatically identifying, counting, and describing wild animals in camera-trap images with deep learning. *Proc. Natl. Acad. Sci. USA* **2018**. [CrossRef] [PubMed]

 *electronics*

Article

Semantic and Dweller-Based Decision Support System for the Reconfiguration of Domestic Environments: RecAAL

Daniele Spoladore * and Marco Sacco

Institute of Intelligent Industrial Technologies and Systems for Advanced Manufacturing (STIIMA),
National Research Council of Italy (CNR), 23900 Lecco, Italy; marco.sacco@stiima.cnr.it
* Correspondence: daniele.spoladore@stiima.cnr.it; Tel.: +39-0341-2350202

Received: 8 August 2018; Accepted: 4 September 2018; Published: 7 September 2018

Abstract: Researches in the field of ambient assisted living (AAL) have increased in the last ten years, and the paradigms of the smart home have widely spread. Smart homes must consider the health-related issues and the real needs deriving from the ageing of their dwellers. In the smart home, appliances are expected to provide support to the residents, especially when they are characterized by disabilities and/or impairments related to ageing. While most of the AAL solutions presented in literature rely on complex systems and architectures, residents affected by mild or moderate disabilities can take advantage of just a simpler reconfiguration of living environments, i.e., the replacement of certain appliances with others that are able to help them in coping with their limitations. This paper proposes a semantic-based decision support system (DSS), which relies on ontological models, to assist designers in domestic environments' reconfiguration. The ontology leverages semantic representations of dwellers and domestic environments' domains of knowledge to foster the adoption of appliances able to help the residents to live independently. The development process of the ontology is presented in detail together with the results deriving from reasoning processes. To ease the reconfiguration of domestic environments, a prototypical application taking advantage of the DSS is presented.

Keywords: decision support system; ambient assisted living; domestic environment reconfiguration; ontology

---

1. Introduction

The research in the fields of smart home, ambient assisted living (AAL) and domestic healthcare has strongly increased during the last ten years. One of the reasons of this attention lies in the remarkable increase of the ageing population (aged 65 or more), who is expected to reach the 30% of the European population over the forthcoming decades [1]. This segment of population is often characterized by a loss of independence in several activities of daily living (due to functional limitations or to the onset of disabilities), and by a diminishing sense of safety—which could potentially lead to injuries while performing activities inside the house [2]. In this context, the smart home is expected to deliver to its inhabitants tailored services able to assist the dwellers for a better, healthier and safer life in their everyday living environment. Therefore, the smart home has been widely addressed as a set of technologies with the potential to help ageing population in living independently, monitoring their safety and well-being, and preventing injuries and accidents in the domestic environments [3].

However, it has been highlighted how the possibility to rely on the set of technologies deployed in a smart home may raise some concerns in the ageing population. For instance, the user-friendliness of the devices and the need for training dedicate to older residents in the use and management of the smart home are two remarkable barriers that can jeopardize the real adoption of AAL solutions [4].

Besides, unfamiliarity with the devices and residents' concerns regarding stigmatization have also been reported as non-negligible issues for older residents [5]. Finally, privacy concerns can represent an obstacle for the adoption of monitoring devices in a smart home [6].

A solution for the problems raised by ageing population can therefore rely on a simple reconfiguration of a standard home with a set of appliances that can support the residents in coping with their impairments while performing activities of daily living [7]. This kind of reconfiguration appears promising to balance the support provided to the elderly inhabitants, and their concerns related to the unfamiliarity with the devices and to their privacy. Works related to the reconfiguration of living environments are mainly focused on ubiquitous computing and context-aware systems—distributed systems have been discussed as a promising tool to support the reconfiguration of domestic devices [8,9]. The possibility to have residents programming their own pervasive computing environments has also been investigated with the purpose of helping dwellers to be involved in the reconfiguration of their own domestic environments [10]. Another area where research is focused regards the possibility to provide adaptation over the time (reconfiguration) of the services provided by an intelligent environment [11,12]. Nonetheless, to the best of authors' knowledge, no work in literature faces the problem of providing ageing population with a set of existing and familiar tools (such as everyday appliances) designed to (or presenting some features that) help them to cope with their limitations.

The "Design For All" (D4All) [13] and "Future Home for Future Community" (FHfFC) [14] projects tackle the issue of easing the reconfiguration of existing domestic environments with familiar appliances by relying on semantic web technologies. These technologies (in particular ontology) are connected with decision-making processes, since they provide a formal (logic-based) and sharable interpretation of knowledge. Semantic models are exploited in DSSs' development since they can foster information integration; moreover, ontologies can support automatic reasoning processes, thus allowing to infer new information starting from the knowledge stated in the model [15].

Through the exploitation of a semantic knowledge base, a Decision Support System (DSS) aimed at helping architects and smart home designers to provide the inhabitants with a set of appliances that can help them in everyday-life activities is deployed. Through the use of the DSS, dwellers (especially those characterized by mild or moderate impairments and elderlies) can rely on familiar appliances that facilitate them in the execution of some activities. The DSS is designed starting from the characterization of the dwellers, i.e., the end-users of the AAL solutions and appliances, and relies on a standard and holistic framework for the description of their health conditions. The developed DSS is then exploited in an application designed to support designers and smart home architects during the reconfiguration process.

The remainder of this paper is organized as follows: Section 2 presents the existing works in the field of semantic-based DSSs, with a focus on AAL and user-oriented solutions. In Section 3, the methodology exploited for the creation of two use cases and the framework for health conditions description are introduced, as well as the key factors that led to the identification of the domains of interest for the ontology. Section 4 deepens into the application ontology description, illustrating the different solutions adopted for its development. The result of the development process constitutes the main component of the DSS, which takes advantage of semantic web-leveraged reasoning process to deliver sets of appliances suitable for each of the dwellers identified in the use cases. Section 5 describes an application using the DSS (RecAAL), and discusses the results obtained from reasoning process, while Section 6 provides the results of a preliminary testing conducted on RecAAL. Section 7 analyses the limits and future perspective of the DSS. Finally, the Conclusions summarize the main outcomes and sketch the future steps that need to be implemented to enhance the DSS.

2. Related Works

The topic of modeling the health-data is one of the main issues when tackling the interoperability among various data sources. Data integration is not a trivial task: The possibility to link different health-data is complicated by the heterogeneity of data formats and different naming conventions. The major importance of this topic gave birth to the Semantic Web for Health Care and Life Sciences Interest Group [16], whose mission is to advocate, support and develop the adoption of semantic web technologies across clinical research, healthcare and life sciences. In Reference [17], the authors relied on ontologies to integrate electronic health records to foster integrated care. In this work, ontology-based case-finding algorithms are exploited to enhance the accuracy of the diagnosis of Type 2 Diabetes and to foster the integration of different health-related data to improve the quality of care. A unified data model provided by ontology is the backbone of the method for accessing health data in Reference [18]; in the context of emergency medical services, the method allows IoT devices to access distributed and heterogeneous data. In Reference [19], the authors described an adaptive mediation system (ARIEN) leveraging ontologies to provide an accurate and seamless integration of heterogeneous medical data, enhancing data interoperability. To tackle the issues of the health-related concepts measured with differential accuracy from diverse data sources, the authors of Reference [20] designed a semantic-based application (PopHR), that was able to automates the integration and extraction of health-related data; the application uses an ontological framework to describe data relevant to chronic diseases. Ontologies are also exploited to normalize and integrate structured and unstructured data from multiple sources. In Reference [21], a semantic annotation lightweight model for healthcare data is presented; this model is intended to provide interoperability among diverse IoT devices monitoring patients' health, and adopts Resource Description Framework (RDF) [22] as modelling language, and SPARQL (SPARQL Protocol and RDF Query Language) [23] for health-records extraction. A framework for the management and reuse of clinical archetypes and data is described in Reference [24]; the framework allows to semantically annotate and transform health data in order to make them interoperable. With regard to the context of mobile health, Reference [25] illustrated a patient monitoring system for the IoT; the architecture of the system relies on an ontology that enables the monitoring of patients' health status. Inferences provided by the ontology are used to recommend workout routines and improving eating habits of patients. Datta et al. [26] presented an IoT architecture to provide personalized and connected healthcare services; part of this architecture leverages ontologies to manage and gather health-related knowledge, while semantic rules are exploited to combine cross-domain knowledge.

In the field of AAL solutions, some interesting examples of semantic-based DSS can be traced in the literature. The possibility of enabling reasoning processes and inferring new knowledge on context, dwellers' activities and comfort metrics gathers a great deal of interest [27]. Osman et al. [28] conceived a DSS for supporting independent living for people suffering from dementia is described. This DSS leverages the semantic representation of context information and semantic rules (modelled with Semantic Web Rule Language(SWRL) [29]), in order to build a knowledge base able to capture changes in the situational conditions and the inferred information are provided to clinical personnel to help them in their decisions. Zentek et al. [30] proposed an interesting use of ontologies to provide flexible management of AAL environments configuration. The framework takes into account two key factors of AAL solutions: the heterogeneity of settings and home environments, and the changing over the time of the user's needs. Zhang et al. [31] developed a sharable clinical DSS system providing clinical personnel with patient-based recommendations support clinical-decision process. The knowledge-base of the system takes advantage of both ontologies and SWRL rules to provide automatic suggestions.

Ontology-based technologies are a key factor in many works related to Internet of Things (IoT) and AAL solutions, since they allow to provide a formal description of many domains of knowledge involved. Energy efficiency and consumption is a relevant topic in smart homes and ambient intelligence, where semantic web technologies can play an important role. Fotopoulou et al. [32] presented an energy-aware IT ecosystem that leverages ontologies to provide recommendations related to energy consumption to the residents. The architecture collects energy, environmental and behavioral-related data and combines them to generate recommendations tailored on the residents' lifestyles. Fensel et' al. [33] described the OpenFridge platform, which leverages ontologies to transform into triples users' collected measurements of their refrigerators and analyzes the resulting semantic data with SPARQL. OpenFridge exploits specialized ontologies for representing and linking refrigerators' data in RDF format, with the ultimate aim of contributing to appliances' energy efficiency. Madrazo et al. [34] implemented a semantic-based energy information system, connecting several and various data sources exploiting ontologies; semantic models are used to integrate the information regarding energy certificates, building descriptions, energy monitoring in buildings and climate data. Bonino et al. [35] developed an ontology-based model for describing electrical energy consumption in a smart home; this ontology (PowerOnt) provides the means to support energy efficiency measures in residential homes.

Ontologies cover a pivotal role also in describing the interactions between the residents and the smart home (its services, devices, locations, etc.). Huang et al. [36] presented a dialog system for residents, who can inquire the smart home system for information related to appliances using their voice. The system adopts a semantic approach to manage residents' vocal inputs and transforming them into service requests. In Ni et al. [37], ontologies are exploited as a mean to represent human activity within the smart home, thus allowing the detection of residents' behaviors. The proposed semantic model is built as a network of ontologies describing the resident, the environmental context and the activities.

Contrary to the main trend in AAL, the DSS presented in this work is not dedicated to support the deployment of context-aware or ubiquitous systems: The DSS fosters the reconfiguration of domestic environments using everyday appliances, which are more familiar to the residents. In RecAAL's DSS the dwellers' health status and its formalization assume a central role.

3. Use Case Definition: A Dweller-Centered Approach

Traditional design is usually oriented toward "standard individuals", a generalized abstraction of real end-users, which often lacks an adequate comprehension of users' needs [38]. In fact, this kind of approach does not consider many variables regarding the users, such as their skills, limitations and knowledge. Furthermore, the under-representation of resident's needs and the general scarceness of residents-related studies are among the factors that hinder the widespread adoption of AAL solutions [3].

To overcome the limits of a generalized abstraction of residents, a new and holistic design paradigm has started to stand out: The "Universal Design". This paradigm aims at taking into consideration the different features characterizing human users; it focuses on proposing solutions able to adjust according to the needs of specific categories of users. The main principles of this discipline can be applied also in the field of AAL too. In this context, D4All and FHfFC projects aim at applying the guidelines of Universal Design into domotic and inclusive domestic environment. The design of this kind of environments for elderlies, people with disabilities or families requires a set of heterogeneous tools during its whole lifecycle process (e.g., design, utilization, control and monitoring). The outcome of the projects works to provide different categories of users with a set of tools able to help them coping with the limitations they have, and to grant them the possibility to perform autonomously several activities of daily living that would otherwise be precluded, dangerous or strenuous.

The development of the DSS and its underlying semantic knowledge-base starts from the definition of the dwellers—the end-users of the results generated by the DSS. Considering that a smart home must be able to provide tailored services to its residents, by anticipating their desires and helping them in coping with their impairments, the possibility to describe the dwellers and their health conditions in a holistic way is a topic of a paramount importance. Health conditions' description must define the appropriate level of detail for the physical and physiological status of an individual over time, such as their abilities in the environments where they live, and the eventual cognitive decline occurring with ageing. In order to cover these crucial aspects of dweller-related knowledge, the ontology relies on the International Classification of Functioning, Disability and Health (ICF) [39].

ICF is used to describe potential residents (Section 3.2); designers can then exploit this piece of information as an input of the DSS to provide a suitable reconfiguration of the set of domestic appliances (Section 3.3) to the dweller characterized with ICF.

3.1. The International Classification of Functioning, Disability and Health

The International Classification of Functioning, Disability and Health (ICF) is a standard World Health Organization-endorsed framework, aimed at providing a tool for the description of an individual's health and its related statuses. It conceptualizes the functioning of an individual as a "dynamic interaction between a person's health condition, environmental factors and personal factors" [39]. ICF is a tool able to ease the communication among the health-stakeholders (therapists, clinicians) providing a standard and worldwide comparable description of the functional experiences of the individuals. Due to its vocabulary, which is easily interpretable also by non-clinical personnel, ICF can also be used in a variety of health-related domains, such as AAL, as a common means to support and facilitate the collaboration and the exchange of information among different actors. Indeed, ICF has found interesting applications in several fields outside the strictly clinical field (but still related to individual's health and its description), such as work reintegration [40,41], home- and age-care [42] and disability management [43]. Therefore, the exploitation of ICF, leveraging on a common framework for disability and health description, can represent a solid base for the development of practical instruments aimed at assessing health conditions and functioning of people with disabilities.

The Classification is organized in two main parts, each of which is further categorized into components: The first part, "Functioning and Disability", provides a description of the components "Body Functions", "Body Structures", and "Activities and Participation"; and the second part, "Contextual Factors", provides the means to describe the impact of the components "Environmental Factors", and "Personal Factors". Each component (with the exception of Personal Factors) is further explained and categorized into Chapters, which identify the addressed domain of functioning. As a result of this framework, a person's functioning is described through the interaction between their health condition, and the context where they act.

Each of the four components is identified by a letter ("b" for Body functions, "s" for Body structures, "e" for Environmental factors, "d" for Activities and Participation) and can be detailed by adding digits. According to the number of digits following the letter, it is possible to get a code (up to five digits), whose length indicates the level of granularity. The lesser the number of digits following the letter is, the more general the health related-concept is described; contrariwise, the higher the number of digits is, the more extensively and thoroughly a health-related concept is represented. The following Figure 1 shows an excerpt of the whole classification representing some of the problems related to visual and hearing functions:

b "Body functions"	Component	
b2 "Sensory functions and pain"	Chapter	
b210 "Seeing functions"	*b230* "Hearing functions"	Second level item
b2102 "Quality of vision"	*b2300* "Sound detection"	Third level item
b21020 "Colour vision"	- - -	Fourth level item

Figure 1. An excerpt of the International Classification of Functioning, Disability and Health (ICF) classification illustrating the deepening of a component into two different health-related functions.

Figure 1 shows how under the same chapter both visual and hearing-related functions can be listed; to address properly the problems related to the "Quality of Vision", another level must be enabled—the fourth level item, characterized by a five-digits code.

The complete classification encompasses more than 1400 domains, organized according to the abovementioned hierarchy of concepts. Specifically, "Body Functions" component's domains aim at providing categories for the description of the functioning of human body systems, while "Body Structures" domains identify the anatomical parts of such systems. "Activity and Participation" domains describe the execution of tasks and actions in every-day situations, while the "Environmental Factors" domains provide the means to assess the social and physical impact of the environment on the individual, together with the possibility to describe the existence of physical barriers or facilitators in the environments where the individuals usually perform tasks.

The functioning or disability of an individual can be assessed selecting the suitable category and its corresponding code and then adding one or more qualifiers. A qualifier records the presence and assesses the severity of a problem in specific domains of functioning, personal or societal level. A generic qualifier can be added at the end of the domain code and serves as an indicator of the level of severity characterizing the domain; this generic qualifier can acquire a set of integer values:

- cXXX.0—indicates the absence of impairments or a negligible problem in a domain;
- cXXX.1—indicates a mild impairment in a domain;
- cXXX.2—indicates a moderate impairment in a domain;
- cXXX.3—indicates a severe impairment in a domain;
- cXXX.4—indicates a complete impairment in a domain;
- cXXX.8—indicates that the qualifier is not specified;
- cXXX.9—indicates that the qualifier is not applicable.

The value 8 is used when the information gathered to decide the qualifier are not enough, while 9 is used when no specification can be given about a specific domain (for instance, when coding b650 "Menstruation Functions" for a male person). The generic qualifier assumes the meaning of descriptor of barriers (defined as physical, social and attitudinal factors that could force an individual to perform below their capacities), or facilitators (factors that can ease or enhance the performance of the individual) for the specification of the Environmental Factors domains. The simple qualifier represents the impact of a barrier (e410.1 a mild barrier/negative impact in the "Individual attitudes of immediate family members"), while a qualifier presenting the "+" sign indicates a facilitator (e410.+2 a moderate facilitation/positive impact in the "Individual attitudes of immediate family members").

Each component can make use of other qualifiers (following the generic one) according to the qualifiers structure [39], reported in Figure 2.

ICF Component	First qualifier	Second qualifier	Third qualifier	Fourth qualifier
Body Functions	Generic qualifier	–	–	–
Body Structures	Generic qualifier	A qualifier to indicate the nature of the change in a specific body structure	A qualifier to indicate the location of the impairment in the body	–
Activity and Participation	Performance qualifier describing what a person does in his/her current environment (with assistance devices and or/personal assistance whether used by the individual)	Capacity qualifier describing an individual's ability to perform a task or action in a standardized environment (measured without assistance)	Capacity measured with assistance devices and/or personal assistance (*optional*)	Performance measured without assistance (*optional*)
Contextual Factors	Generic qualifier with negative and positive scale to denote extent of barriers and facilitators respectively	–	–	–

Figure 2. A description of all the possible qualifiers applicable for each ICF component and their meanings (according to References [39,44]).

ICF's component "Personal Factors" is yet to be completed, therefore the classification can rely on the remaining four components—enough to provide a sound and complete description of health-related issues, since "Personal Factors" are the particular background of an individual's life and living [45]. Although ICF presents many advantages, it has to be underlined that this framework is characterized by some shortcomings, such as problems regarding incongruent classification of some concepts, a lack of clarity between activities and their qualities, incorrect parent-child relationships of concepts and an overemphasis on subsumption [46–48]. The ICF has also been modelled into an ontology [49], which can be used as a reference model for other domain ontologies and that inherits all the flaws belonging to the classification.

For the purpose of the DSS, the developed ontology relies on the generic qualifiers and adopts the whole "Body Functions", "Body Structures", and "Activity and Participation" components (up to fourth level items).

3.2. Identification of the Personae

To identify prototypical residents, for which the DSS can provide a helpful set of appliances, the methodology described by Cooper [50] was adopted. The first phase of this methodology concerns the identification of the proper personae, fictional characters created to represent the users' types who benefits from the work of designers and architects using the DSS. Personae have been sketched also to facilitate communication between the different partners composing the projects stakeholders [51]. The five personae identified correspond to the target residents, and are defined as follow:

1. Elderly characterized by frailty—a persona that comprises men or women of 65 or more years old, characterized by unstable health condition and by one (or more) of these four criteria: (1) Involuntary loss of weight of 4.5 kg in the last year; (2) asthenia or sense of fatigue for at least three days in a week; (3) limited physical activity and sedentary life style; (4) limited walking speed, with a time required to cover 4 m greater than 6 s [52].
2. User with visual impairments—people with a visual impairment that compromises (totally or partially) their social and working activity.
3. User with hearing impairments—this persona includes people characterized by a partial or total hearing loss.

4. User with cognitive impairments—a persona comprising people affected by alterations or dysfunctions of fundamental cognitive functions, such as memory, language, visuospatial abilities and executive functions [53]; severe mental conditions and illnesses are excluded from this category.

5. User with motor impairments—a persona collecting people affected by a specific neuro-motor deficit; this persona comprises all the people affected by pathologies comprising the neuro-motor system.

The sketched personae are drafted together with the clinical partners of the two projects and reflect the range of possible dwellers. Each of them is a wide collection of specific cases that needs to be further explored and specified with the use of ICF framework.

Persona 1: Silvia is a 72-year-old woman living alone in her house. Although she is independent, she has started suffering from asthenia, loss of weight, weariness in the last two years. Her muscular weakness makes her strenuous using her arms in many activities, thus reducing her mobility. Silvia's health condition described with ICF reports the following domain as afflicted by some limitations (the generic qualifiers indicate the magnitude of the limitations):

- b4200.1—Increased blood pressure
- b4202.1—Maintenance of blood pressure
- b4550.2—General physical endurance
- b4552.2—Fatigability
- b530.2—Weight maintenance functions
- b7102.1—Mobility of joints generalized
- b7300.1—Power of isolated muscles and muscle groups
- b7356.2—Tone of all muscles of the body
- d4102.2—Kneeling
- d4105.2—Bending
- d4300.2—Lifting
- d4305.1—Putting down objects
- d630.1—Preparing meals
- s73002.183—Muscles of upper arm (indicating an unspecified change in the structure of both arms)

Persona 2: Giovanni is a 69-year-old widowed man living alone in his house. Starting from the age of 67, Giovanni has suffered some vision-related issues, and even if he wears his glasses the problems do not seem to be solved. This makes several activities difficult for him, such as reading a book or a newspaper, understanding icons and writings on appliance and food's packages, using text-based devices (such as mobile phone). Giovanni's health condition described with ICF reports the following domains and qualifiers:

- b21000.2—Binocular acuity of distant vision
- b21001.2—Monocular acuity of distant vision
- b21002.1—Binocular acuity of near vision
- b21002.1—Monocular acuity of near vision
- b220.1—Sensations associated with the eye and adjoining structures
- d110.1—Watching
- d360.1—Using communication devices and techniques
- d166.2—Reading
- d325.2—Communicating with/receiving written messages
- d345.2—Writing messages
- d630.2—Preparing meals
- (No alterations in the structures of the eyes are registered).

Clinical personnel involved in the projects tried to refer to the minimum amount of ICF domains to provide a proper description of the two personae's health conditions; for the codes involving Activity and participation domains, the qualifier choice was limited to the first (indicating how a person performs activities inside their environments and with devices such as glasses, cane, etc.). In Silvia's last code the full set of Body Structures qualifiers was used to represent that fact that the problem affects both of her arms. It is here intended that domains not specified in the above lists are not interested by any form of impairment.

3.3. Definition of the Use Case

In the second phase of Cooper's methodology, the identified personae were portrayed in use cases, in which they became the subject of a designer's activity of kitchen reconfiguration. The design of a use case consists in the allocation of different tasks and functions to the actors, and encompasses the narration of what happens during the interactions among the actors as expected outcome.

The use case scenario is focused on the possibility to configure a specific room of the smart home for two of the abovementioned personae with the help of a designer. In this scenario, a designer sets up a kitchen for specific categories of dwellers providing it with appliances suitable to cope with its impairments. The kitchen has been chosen as one of the most relevant domestic environments considering that:

- It is the room that can benefit most from AAL tailored solutions [54];
- It is the place where older people suffer from most domestic injuries [55];
- It is where one of the Instrumental Activities of Daily Living takes place (meal preparation) [7].

The following is the description of the use case related to the reconfiguration of the kitchen.

In the use case a designer is required to design the kitchens using a Decision Support System able to select the most suitable appliances for the two end-users, who are specifically:

- A 72 year-old woman characterized by frailty (Silvia);
- A 69 year-old man characterized by a visual impairment due to ageing (Giovanni);

Both users are characterized by moderate impairments that could jeopardize their safety and make their activities strenuous in the kitchen. The designer acquires the user's kitchens blueprints and the users' health conditions, via an application; users' sensible data (address, health conditions) cannot be seen directly by the designer, who can only see an aggregate information, such as a string reporting "user with moderate visual impairment" or "user characterized by mild frailty"; the designer elaborates virtual models of the two kitchens. In these models, the individual can place the most suitable appliances to cope with the users' impairment(s), such as an oven, refrigerator, cooktop, dishwasher and useful sensors (e.g., air quality detection, user's presence detection, luminance measurement), choosing them from a list. This list is the result of the activities of the DSS (an ontology-based reasoning process), which (according to the users' health conditions) automatically selects from the catalogues of appliances only those options that are suitable to improve end-users' autonomy. At the end of the design phase, the designer can save the kitchens' reconfiguration projects. During the reconfiguration the designer meets the users for who the reconfiguration projects are designed; the individual can discuss with them the choices of appliances and (according to their feedbacks) modify such choices. Then the designer can save again the project and export it in a construction drawing format.

In this use case the designer selects the most suitable appliance options together with the end-users of the reconfigured environment, so that dwellers' desires in terms of appliances' functionalities, interaction modalities and aesthetical characteristics (color, shape, etc.) can be met.

4. The Ontology-Based DSS

In this section the application ontology underlying the DSS is described, starting from its specifications and the methodology followed for the development. An application ontology is an explicit specification of a conceptualization engineered for a specific use or application focus and whose scope is specified through testable use cases [56,57]. The application ontology refers to canonical ontologies to construct ontological classes and relationships between classes and is used when modelling cross-domain concepts.

The application ontology at the base of the DSS is divided in two modules, each of which describes some specific concepts of domains of knowledge.

4.1. Specification and Methodology

The use case depicted in the previous paragraph allows highlighting the key points that the application ontology must include. Following a bottom-up approach (from the most concrete to the most abstract) [58], the key points are used to identify some of the concepts, which will be deepened through the NeOn methodology's [59] steps and through the compiling of the Ontology Requirements Specification Document (ORSD) [60]. This activity considerably simplifies the identification of the knowledge to represent in the form of an ontology, also providing useful indications about the foreseeable granularity of the model and its extent.

The compiling of the ORSD also allows to answer several other questions regarding the model. Referring to the NeOn methodology, it is possible to identify reusable ontological resources and therefore proceed to the development of the whole application ontology.

4.1.1. DSS's Ontology Requirements Specification Document

The ORSD is a tool that describes what a semantic model supports, the domain of application of the ontology, the intended users and uses for the model. It is useful to provide support to ontology engineers while evaluating the inclusion or exclusion of concepts in a model, as well as to guide the choice of reuse of existing knowledge sources [61]. The compiling of this document has been carried out according to the list of task provided in Reference [62], where an accurate methodology to compile the ORSD is specified. The tasks for the compiling of the ORSD start with the identification of the purpose for which the semantic model is developed, the scope of the ontology and the definition of the implementation language. The *purpose* of the ontology is to provide a holistic description of different kinds of users, which has to be realized with a language understandable by clinicians, caregivers and rehabilitation therapists. The model must also be able to provide a description of the different smart objects located in the user's home. Hence why the *scope* of the ontology must focus on the diverse extents: The description of the users' health condition; the description of the appliances and their features. Resource Description Framework (RDF) [22], and Ontology Web Language (OWL-DL) [63] are the selected *implementation languages* (with the use of Semantic Web Rule Language (SWRL) [29]), and the open-source ontology editor, Protégé, is the tool chosen to develop the semantic model. These languages are endorsed by the W3C consortium and therefore widely used.

The successive tasks foresee the identification of the *intended end-users and uses* of the ontology. End-users of the model are clinicians, caregivers and rehabilitation therapists, who access to the users' health condition data; the designers who have to configure the users' smart kitchens can access the aggregate data regarding the type of impairments characterizing the users; they can also access the appliances list and taxonomy to complete the domestic environment configuration.

Regarding the acquisition of a set of requirements that the ontology must satisfy, as *non-functional requirements*, one of the characteristics already emerged from the discussion of the use case regards the possibility to represent the users' health conditions using the ICF standard. The same consideration is valid for the possibility to express the appliances features in a standardized way, including the ones deriving from the sensors of the first use case.

The output of the *functional requirements* tasks are Competency Questions (CQs—a list of the questions that an ontology should be able to answer [64]), which can be grouped into categories. An excerpt of the outcome of this task is represented in Table 1, where different CQs are grouped into three categories and where the provided answers to the questions are used in the ontology.

Table 1. The list of Competency Questions (CQs).

Competency Questions—Group 1: Users and Their Health Condition
CQ1 —Who are the human end-users and beneficiaries of the DSS? The designer, Silvia and Giovanni —two users characterized by impairments.
CQ2—Which are the dwellers who need to be modelled into the ontology? Silvia and Giovanni.
CQ3—How are the dwellers identified? Through identity records for each resident.
CQ4—Which are the identity records for the dwellers? Name, Surname, Address, telephone number, email, birthplace, Tax Identification number.
CQ5—How is classified a dweller's health condition? Using the domains and qualifiers from the International Classification of Functioning, Disability and Health (ICF).

Competency Questions—Group 2: Appliances of the House
CQ6—Which are the appliances involved in the use case? Environmental thermometer, air quality sensor, presence sensor, air quality sensor, luminance measurement sensor, oven, dishwasher, cooktop, refrigerator, microwave oven, washer.
CQ7—How are the appliances identified? For each appliance the following information are compiled: Hardware version, mac address, software version, textual description of the appliance, name of the manufacturer, model of the smart object; in addition to these features, for each appliance a list of its programs is provided.
CQ8—How are the appliances assessed to be suitable to cope with the impairments of specific types of users? Each appliance is categorized by a team of architect, designer and bioengineer on the basis of its features and programs into specific categories.

The final task foresees the extraction of the terminology from the CQs and their answers to form a pre-glossary of terms. These terms were later formally represented into the ontology, in the form of concepts, instances and relationships. The terms with a higher frequencies highlight the domains for which an activity of research of existing or reusable knowledge sources must be conducted.

4.1.2. Development of Ontology with the NeOn Methodology

Following the NeOn methodology, the efforts focused on the development of a set of interconnected modules (smaller ontologies focusing on specific aspects of the domains of interest), characterized by domain-dependent relationships. This methodology is based on a set of scenarios that may occur during the development of an ontology [59]. These scenarios encompass a variety of situations, from the development of semantic model from scratch to the reuse of existing models. The NeOn methodology includes nine scenarios, which are: (1) Development of an ontology from scratch—this scenario starts with the development of an ORSD and lead to the development of a new semantic model. (2) Reuse and reengineering of non-ontological resources—taxonomies, thesauri, schemes and other knowledge resources existing in a non-ontological form and covering the domain of interest can be transformed into ontologies or contribute to the development of a semantic model. (3) Reuse of ontological resources—it is a possible scenario when the developers find ontological resources reusable as they are. (4) Reuse and reengineering of ontological resources—similar to the previous scenario, in this case the found ontological resources can be reengineered to serve the intended aim. (5) Reuse and merging of ontological resources—this scenario applies when a variety of ontological resources for the same domain are found and are eligible for reuse. These resources can be merged into a new model or mapped or aligned. (6) Reusing, merging and reengineering of ontological resources—in this scenario the outcomes of the previous scenarios can be reengineered into a model suitable for the aims. (7) Reusing design patterns—this scenario takes place in the conceptualization phase of the ontology engineering process and suggests reusing ontology design patterns [65]. (8) Restructuring ontological resources—in this scenario, the outcomes deriving from the other scenarios that must be integrated into a new ontology must be reworked somehow (modularizing, pruning, extending or specializing one or more parts). (9) Localizing ontological resources—in this scenario the terms of the ontology are translated in different natural languages.

The development process of the ontology underlying the DSS considered the scenario (1) and the scenario (4), developing new ontologies from scratch and adapting already existing models to the project's needs. In the following paragraphs, the chosen approaches are specified for each module. The ontology was developed in English. The reusable ontologies identified following this methodology was one: The ICF Ontology [49].

4.2. Dwellers and Their Health Condition Module

This module describes the users and their health conditions. This application ontology is composed of two main sub-modules: The "Dweller's Registry Records and classification" and the "Health Condition", which provides an ICF-based description of the health conditions of the residents.

4.2.1. Dwellers' Registry Records and Classification

Each of the residents is identified through a list of identity records, which constitute a sort of ID-card of the dweller describing static data about the resident. This module is composed of a T-Box containing a single class, "Dweller" an object property "hasHealthCondition" that links a dweller to their Health Condition and the datatype properties useful to assert facts about a resident. With these properties, it is possible to assert the resident address (street, city and country), their date of birth, their age (expressed in years), their email address, the first name(s) and the surname, telephone number(s), the Tax Identification Number. The domain of these properties is the class "Dweller". In the ABox it is possible to assert a list of residents, describing their identity records through these ten datatype properties. The class "Dweller" also presents another subclass, "Dweller with impairment", which gathers the "Vision Impaired Dweller", the "Motor Impaired Dweller", the "Cognitive Impaired Dweller", the "Hearing Impaired Dweller"; these subclasses are then deepened, classifying the resident according to their grade of impairment.

4.2.2. Health Condition

Resident's Health Condition consists of their ICF-based assessed health status. The modeling of the ICF-based Health Condition required the recourse to the information modeled in the ICF Ontology. Considering the scope of the projects and its ontology, a partial pruning and reengineering process was conducted on this model. The result is a simplified TBox containing the ICF's components "Body functions", "Body Structure", "Activity and Participation" under the class "ICF Category". Each Chapter making up the components is further detailed by modeling the sub-classes for the second-level, third-level and fourth level items. A datatype property allows to specify the generic qualifier for each ICF domain (the list of acceptable integer numbers are 0, 1, 2, 3, 4, 8, and 9, and represent the generic ICF qualifier denoting the severity of an impairment, or the performance for Activity and Participation domains).

A resident's health condition can then be described by specifying the ICF categories interested by an impairment and the magnitude of the disability by using a descriptor, an individual that gathers one ICF domain and its qualifier. An example of health condition description for a resident is given in Figure 3.

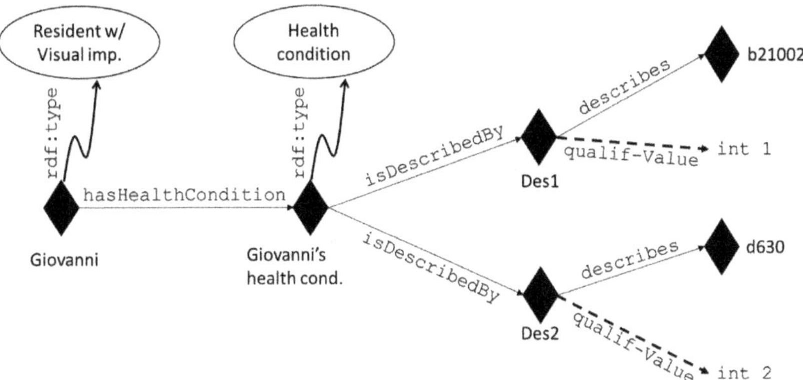

Figure 3. An excerpt of the modelling of Giovanni's health condition; individuals are represented with diamonds, concepts are represented with circles, and roles are represented with arrows (dashed arrows indicate datatype properties, full-line arrows represent object properties). The type of an individual is stated with a curved arrow.

The TBox provides a description of the user's "Health Condition", allowing to distinguish them among "Vision Impaired Health Condition", "Motor Impaired Health Condition", "Hearing Impaired Health Condition", and "Cognitive Impaired Health Condition". For each of these subclasses, a further sub-classification regarding the grade of impairment is provided according to ICF qualifiers, as shown in Figure 4.

A dweller is linked to the individual's health condition through the object property "hasHealthCondition" and each health condition is associated with a dateTime Stamp value through the datatype property "isAssessedOnDate"; in this way it is possible to keep track of the evolution of a dweller's physical and physiological status over time.

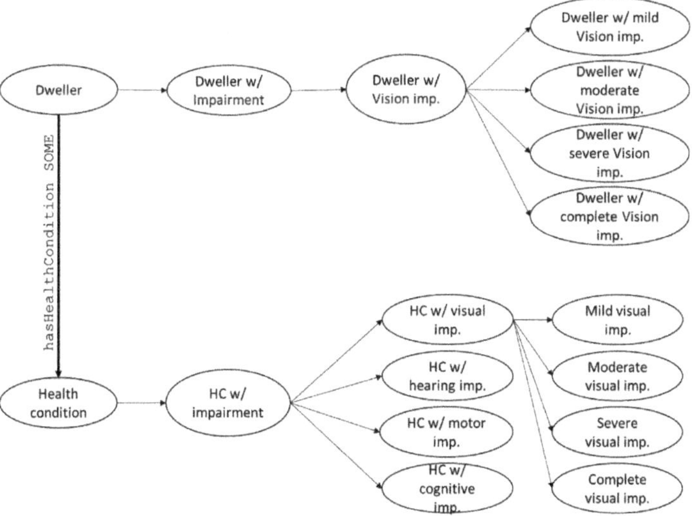

Figure 4. An excerpt of the classification of dwellers and their health conditions (concepts are represented with circles). HC, health condition; w/, with; imp., impairment.

4.3. Appliances and Sensors

The main goal of this module of the ontology is to provide a description of appliances and the sensors that populate the DSS. This module is composed of two sub-modules: The "Appliance and sensors" module, which collects the list of appliances and sensors and provide a description for each of them; the "Programs descriptor" module, which describe the programs used by each appliance; the "Reconfiguration project" module, which describes the reconfiguration projects performed by a designer.

4.3.1. Appliances and Sensors Classification

This module is composed of a TBox and an ABox and collects the appliances that can be placed in the resident's home. For each appliance, it is possible to specify several information using specific datatype properties: Application and physical protocol, hardware and software version, mac-address, manufacturer and model. An object property "hasProgram" links the appliances with their programs. It is also possible to sub-classify each appliance according to its typology (with the classes "Cooktop", "Dishwasher", "Oven", "Refrigerator", "Washer", "Microwave") and also environmental sensors can be detailed in the same way ("Air quality sensor", "Gas detector sensor", "Smoke detector sensor", "Luminance sensor", "Thermo-hygrometric sensor", "User presence sensor"). A set of classes to further classify the appliances according to the type of residents with disability they can support is also developed: As an example for all the classes of appliance above identified, a dishwasher can be further specified as a "Dishwasher suitable for Visually-impaired Resident", "Dishwasher suitable for Cognitive-impaired Resident", "Dishwasher suitable for Hearing-impaired Resident", "Dishwasher suitable for Motor-impaired Resident".

This module did not reuse any of the several existing ontologies developed for the classification and description of appliances or sensors (such as "SAREF—Semantic Appliance Reference ontology" [66] or "SSNO—Semantic Sensor Network Ontology" [67]); most of them contain a grade of detail that exceed the scope of the DSS, therefore a development from scratch has been chosen.

4.3.2. Empirical Methodology for Populating the Appliances and Sensors Module

To populate the "Appliances and Sensors" module with instances, a group of experts (composed by an architect, a designer and a biomedical engineer) was appointed to select a list of appliances and to classify them as being suitable for particular categories of residents with impairments. The appliances were selected by searching the main online vendors on the web for appliances designed for people with disabilities. For an appliance to be evaluated by the group of experts, its webpage had to be provided with the following information:

Full specifications for the appliance (dimensions, accessories, buttons and controls description, power requirements and energy performances, programs installed):

- A description of the appliance's program(s)—especially those programs intended for people with disabilities;
- A photo gallery to allow the group to evaluate the relevant design features of the appliances.

The result of this search led to the inclusion of both ADA compliant (appliances compliant to the Americans with Disabilities Act [68]) and non-ADA compliant appliances in the list, which is composed of a total of 25 appliances (five ovens, five refrigerators, five cooktops, four dishwashers, three washers, three microwave ovens; see Appendix A for the complete list).

The group identified the selected appliances according to at least one of these features:

- The appliance has (at least) a program that is able to help a person with a specific disability in performing activities in the kitchen (cooking, cleaning, etc.);
- The appliance's design features (colors, design, shape, etc.) makes it easy to use for people with disabilities.

The 25 appliances found were then classified according to the benefit(s) they can supply: The group worked to empirically assess whether an appliance was able to help the resident to cope with one or more of their impairments, selecting specific ICF domains where appliance's features could enhance the performing of activities or mitigate a disability. For instance, cooktops characterized by large button controls, digital and wide backlit display, high contrast design (such as a dark-colored surface with bright-colored controls) have been classified as somehow helpful for people with specific visual impairments (b21002, b21000 for the acuity of near/distant vision). Lift ovens, whose door opens following a vertical movement, can be particularly suited for wheelchair users (thus helping users with impairments in the structures specified in "s120 Spinal cord and related structures", "s110 Structure of brain" and in the functions specified in the codes from "b760 Control of voluntary movement functions" to "b780 Sensations related to muscles and movement functions"); nonetheless, this type of oven can help people who cannot bend ("d4105 Bending") or suffers from muscular problems (b7300, b7356).

The impossibility to physically evaluate each specimen of the selected appliances led to the application of the empirical methodology described above. By relying merely on manufacturer provided information, the DSS's knowledge base can be incremented by applying the same methodology to appliances not previously enlisted. The group of experts substantially acted as prospects (persons motivated to purchase an item) usually do when they want to purchase an appliance: They search information on the products (on the internet or in stores) they are interested in, but only rarely they can test it (contrary to automotive industry, home appliance industry does not allow to test the products before purchasing them).

Appliances' assessment has been conducted assuming that all appliances have to be installed in a house following the appropriate specifications and expedients, which means for example that in order for a lift oven to be of some advantage for a wheelchair user, the appliance must be installed taking into account the user's height on their wheelchair (the height can indeed vary according to the type of wheelchair adopted and its settings).

The results of this work make use of a specific object property ("helpsCopingWith"), to state where an appliance can provide support for specific impairments, as illustrated in the following Figure 5.

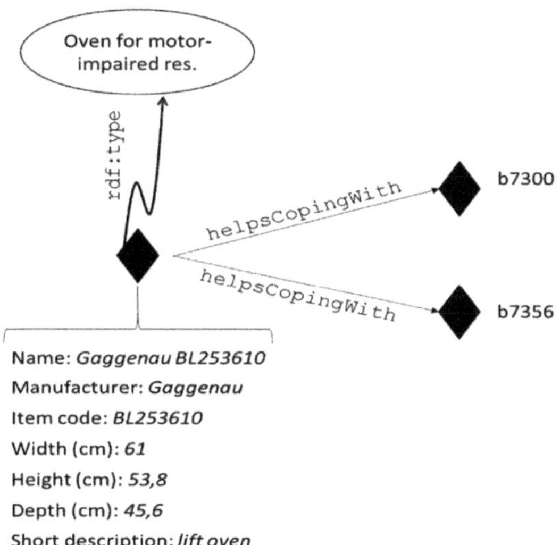

Figure 5. An example of an oven, classified as helpful for dwellers with motor impairments. Individuals are represented with diamonds, concepts are represented with circles, and roles are represented with arrows. The type of an individual is stated with a curved arrow, while datatype properties are collected under the square bracket.

Evidently an appliance can be classified as suitable to help different categories of dwellers with disabilities, thus belonging to two or more of the subclasses discussed above.

Sensors can also be classified following a similar approach. For instance, smoke and gas detectors can be helpful for people whose sense of smell is compromised ("b255 Smell functions"), while luminance sensors can be used to assess the environmental conditions for individuals with vision-related impairments. Sensors do not take advantage of the "helpsCopingWith" object property since they provide measurements and observations that can be used to monitor the safety and the quality of the environment regardless of the user.

4.3.3. Programs Description

The lists of appliances' programs are detailed with the subclasses "Dishwasher Program", "Washer Program", "Microwave oven Program" and "Oven Program", the only categories of appliances that foresee specific programs for their functioning. Each of the programs is described with datatype properties that specify the program name, providing a textual description of the program. Programs are associated to an appliance through the object property "isProgramOf", which is the inverse of "hasProgram".

4.3.4. Reconfiguration Projects Module

The last module of the application ontology provides the means to formalize the reconfiguration projects executed by the designers. This simple module consists in a class ("Project") collecting all the projects performed by a designer. For each individual belonging to this class, it is possible to specify the following information: The resident for which the project has been designed (via the "isDesignedFor" object property); the appliances selected by the designer and their features, choosing them from the results generated by the reasoning process of the DSS ("includesAppliances"); the designer executing the project ("designedBy"); an identification number for the project (with the datatype property "hasID").

4.4. Reasoning with the Application Ontology of the DSS

The application ontology can support reasoning processes and querying. Reasoning in ontologies allows to derive facts which are not explicitly expressed in the knowledge base. The DSS exploits the reasoner Pellet [69] to classify residents' modelled health conditions into the classification, described in Section 4.2.2, and to retrieve a list of appliances suitable for a resident. With a set of SWRL rules it is possible to define the conditions for matching appliances with dwellers' health conditions, basing on the ICF domains specified both for persons and appliances.

Classification of dwellers' health condition is performed with a simple SWRL:

```
Dweller (?p), hasHealthCondition (?p, ?hc),
HealthCondition (?hc), isDescribedBy (?hc, ?des), Descriptor (?des), describes (?des,
?icf), SeeingAndRelatedFunctions(?icf) ->
HealthConditionWithVisualImpairment (?hc)
```

To further classify the health condition according to the value of the generic qualifier, a set of rules is specified; the following SWRL rule specifies the conditions for which a health condition is inferred to suffer for a moderate vision-related impairment:

```
Dweller (?p), hasHealthCondition (?p, ?hc), HealthCondition (?hc),
isDescribedBy (?hc, ?des), Descriptor (?hc), describes (?des,
?icf), SeeingAndRelatedFunctions(?icf), qualif-value (?des, 2) ->
ModerateVisualImpairment (?hc)
```

Classes, described in Section 4.2.2, are further detailed with the use of OWL restrictions, as the following excerpt in XML/RDF syntax [70] illustrates:

```
<owl:Class rdf:id="DwellerWithVisionImpairment">
<owl:equivalentClass>
<owl:Restriction>
<owl:onProperty rdf:resource="#hasHealthCondition" />
        <owl:someValuesFrom
        rdf:resource="#HealthConditionWithVisualImpairment" />
</owl:Restriction>
</owl:equivalentClass>
</owl:Class>
```

Once the residents are classified according to their health condition, it is possible to retrieve a list of appliances that have been classified as able to help dwellers to cope with some of their impairments. This matching can be performed with a set of SWRL rules, like the following one, which is associated with appliances to a specific health condition with visual impairments:

```
DwellerWithVisionImpairment (?p), hasHealthCondition (?p, ?hc),
HealthConditionWithVisualImpairment (?hc), isDescribedBy (?hc,
?des), Descriptor (?des), describes (?des, ?icf), SeeingAndRelatedFunctions(?icf1),
OvenSuitableForVisualImpairedResident (?app), helpsCopingWith
(?app, ?icf), SameAs (?icf, ?icf) -> suitableApplianceFor (?app, ?p)
```

This rule allows each appliance recognized as helping residents in coping with a specific impairment of their health condition to be linked to the dwellers via the object property "suitableApplianceFor".

The application ontology, uploaded on a semantic repository, can be queried using the SPARQL Protocol and RDF Query Language (SPARQL) [23]. In this way, it is possible to retrieve the results inferred by the reasoner with a simple SPARQL query like the following:

```
PREFIX r: <http://www.stiima.cnr.it/RecAAL/>
SELECT ?appliance~WHERE
{?appliance r:isSuitableFor r:Silvia }.
```

Querying with SPARQL also allows to retrieve the list of all appliances belonging to specific classes, retrieve the list of residents with specific impairments, the list of programs and details specified for each appliance.

5. The RecAAL Application

To ease the exploitation of the results of the reasoning deriving from the DSS, the RecAAL application is developed. RecAAL is a PC-based application developed using Unity 3D [71]. Once the designer has acquired the blueprints of the resident's current kitchen, the resident is able to design a virtual 3D model of the domestic environment in the application. Then, the designer opens the application, selects the resident, and reconfigures the kitchen, as illustrated in Figure 6. The selection of the resident triggers SPARQL querying of the ontology and allows the retrieval of the appliances suitable for the resident.

Within the virtual 3D environment, the designer can add the appliances into the kitchen's model, choosing them among the ones provided by the semantic reasoning process. Suitable appliances' list is updated in real-time querying the application ontology with SPARQL, as illustrated in Section 4.4, and depicted in Figure 7.

The use of a 3D model allows the designer to apply changes to the 3D environment, while the residents can see the modifications in the appearance of the kitchen. For each appliance that can be selected, the designer can open an interface illustrating the options provided by the DSS; designer and resident can choose together which of the available options can help most the dweller in their activities in the kitchen.

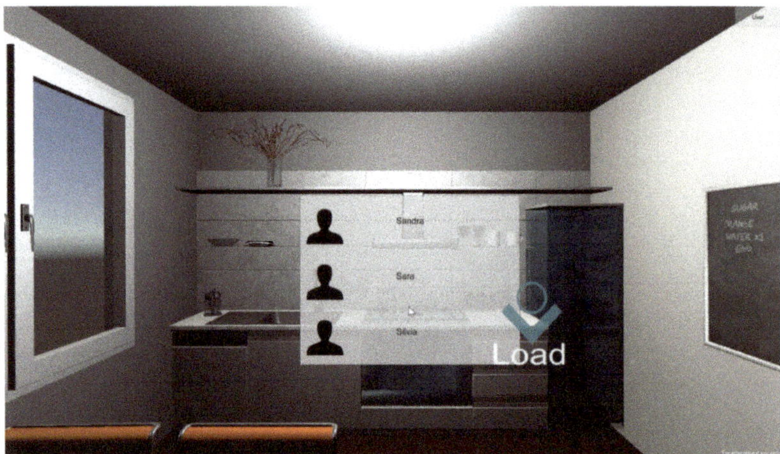

Figure 6. A snapshot of the RecALL: The designer selects the resident for which the reconfiguration project is executed. Once the resident is selected, SPARQL queries interrogate the knowledge base to retrieve the appliances suitable for the chosen resident, according to their health condition.

Figure 7. A snapshot of RecAAL: The designer chooses the appliance from those suggested by the Decision Support System (DSS), as suitable for the resident.

The designer can also select sensors to be installed in the kitchen. The list of sensors selected appears on the blackboard (as illustrated in Figure 8). At the end of the reconfiguration activity, the reconfigured project can be saved, and can be saved in the semantic knowledge base with a SPARQL query inserting a new project or modifying an existing one.

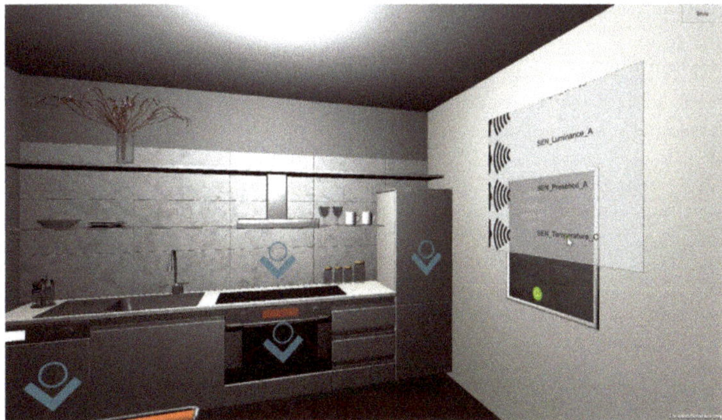

Figure 8. A snapshot of RecAAL: The list of sensors selected during the reconfiguration process is shown on the blackboard in the 3D environment.

5.1. Preliminary Evaluation of RecAAL

The interface interaction experience of RecAAL for domestic environment reconfiguration has been tested in a preliminary study aimed at providing an expert evaluation of the interface functioning. The sample involved seven subjects (five males, and two females, with a mean age 30; the sample is composed of PhD candidates and students from Engineering and Informatics disciplines). The main goal and the general functioning of the application were illustrated to the involved subjects prior to the execution of the test.

Subjects were then asked to test RecAAL knowing resident's impairment conditions. All of participants' comments and feedback were noted.

In order to evaluate perception of prospective usefulness, the following outcomes were evaluated at the end of each participant's experience through the administration of questionnaires:

- Technology Acceptance Model 2 (TAM2) questionnaire [72]—the original version of TAM aimed at assessing how a user come to accept and use a certain technology, through the evaluation of its perceived usefulness and its perceived ease of use [73]. With the respect to this first version, TAM2 has been extended to evaluate technology acceptance also in terms of social influence (subjective norm, voluntariness, and image) and cognitive instrumental (job relevance, output quality, result demonstrability, and perceived ease of use) processes. All the questionnaire's items are assessed using a 7-point Likert scale, ranging from 1 ("strongly disagree") to 7 ("strongly agree").
- System Usability Scale (SUS) [74]—it consists of a ten-item questionnaire with five response options for respondents (from 1, "strongly disagree" to 5, "strongly agree"). SUS allows evaluating a wide variety of products and services in terms of user-friendliness, consistency, ease in learning their functioning, cumbersomeness.
- Section C of Mobile App Rating Scale (MARS) [75]—the rating scale assesses app quality on four dimensions, i.e., engagement, functionality, aesthetics, information. In this case, the evaluation was limited to the graphical aspects (Section C). All items are rated on a 5-point scale from 1 "Inadequate" to 5 "Excellent".

5.2. Results

5.2.1. Technology Acceptance Model 2 Questionnaire for evaluating the interaction

Overall mean of TAM2 questionnaire is 5.25 (SD = 0.61), corresponding to "somewhat agree" on the 7-points Likert scale. Highest scores are reported on items 8 ("Interacting with the system does not require a lot of my mental effort"), 9 ("I find the system to be easy to use"), and 10 ("I find it easy to get the system to do what I want it to do"), belonging to the "Perceived Ease of Use" scale. Lower scores are reported for items 11 ("In my job, usage of the system is important"), and 14 ("I have no problem with the quality of the system's output".) They correspond to the "Job Relevance" and "Output Opportunity" scales (Table 2).

Table 2. The results of the administered Technology Acceptance Model 2 (TAM2) questionnaire.

Item	Item Description	Mean	Standard Deviation
	Intention to use		
1	Assuming I have access to the system, I intend to use it.	5.5	0.97
2	Given that I have access to the system, I predict that I would use it.	5	0.81
	Perceived usefulness		
3	Using the system improves my performance in my job.	5.33	1.10
4	Using the system in my job increases my productivity.	5	1
5	Using the system enhances my effectiveness in my job.	5.17	1.06
6	I find the system to be useful in my job.	5.16	1.21
	Perceived ease of use		
7	My interaction with the system is clear and understandable.	5.5	0.96
8	Interacting with the system does not require a lot of my mental effort.	6	0.81
9	I find the system to be easy to use.	5.83	1.07
10	I find it easy to get the system to do what I want it to do.	5.83	1.06
	Job relevance		
11	In my job, usage of the system is important.	4.33	0.74
12	In my job, usage of the system is relevant.	5	1
	Output opportunity		
13	The quality of the output I get from the system is high.	5.16	0.37
14	I have no problem with the quality of the system's output.	4.66	1.10

5.2.2. System Suability Scale

According to literature data [76], scores of 68 are considered as "usability average". RecAAL's overall score is 72.5 (SD = 9.61), a borderline result that indicate an average outcome with improvements needed (as shown in Figure 9). In particular, lower scores are related to perception of various function integration and to the interaction with the 3D environment.

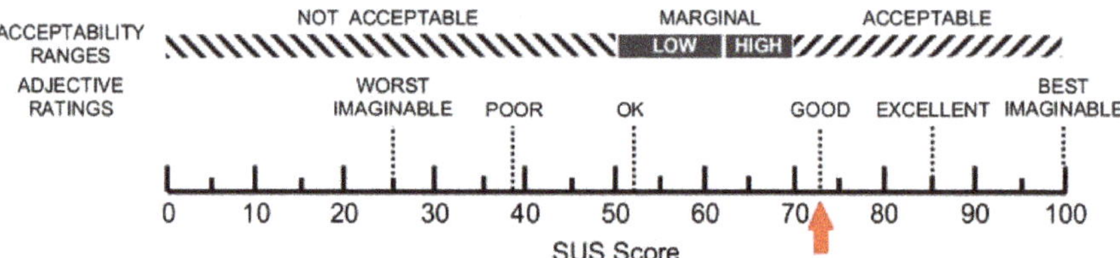

Figure 9. A representation of System Usability Scale (SUS): The red arrow indicates RecAAL's score.

5.2.3. Mobile Application Rating Scale

Mobile Application Rating Scale (MARS)_section C mean score is 3.38 (SD = 0.25), corresponding to "acceptable value" (Table 3). Critical aspects highlighted by participants' comments include mainly graphic elements.

Table 3. The results of the administer Mobile App Rating Scale (MARS)_section C test.

Item	Mean	Standard Deviation
Layout: Is the arrangement and size of buttons/icons/menus/content on the screen appropriate or zoomable if needed?	3.16	0.75
Graphics: How high is the quality/resolution of graphics used for buttons/icons/menus/content?	3.33	0.51
Visual appeal: How good does the app look?	3.6	0.81

5.2.4. Participants' Comments

During the execution of the tests, participants manifested some comments and concerns regarding the application. These outputs are briefly reported hereinafter:

- Low readability of appliances names because of the small font (five subjects);
- User needs or clinical condition are not made explicit in the application when the designer starts the reconfiguration project (four subjects);
- Lack of residents customized icon (three subjects);
- Dweller choice is not well shown (three subjects);
- Concerns related to a low understanding of the logical link between residents and appliances choices—without a preliminary explanation (three subjects);
- Redundant icons on the appliance choice menu (two subjects);
- Need for emphasizing appliances when the cursor hovers over one of the selectable options (three subjects).

5.3. Discussion

Applied technology research uses extensively models of Technology Acceptance in order to predict the intended use. In particular, TAM was used in many works in order to examine acceptance of different technologies [77]. Regarding the DSSs evaluation, TAM model has been used to understand acceptance inclination of manager's in business organization [78]; evaluation of a DSS is also conducted in Reference [79], where a sample of airline companies' employees assessed the benefits deriving from the use of a DSS. Other examples of DSS evaluation with TAM can be traced in research fields related to the planning of environmental development [80] and to the clinical setting [81,82]. The authors of this work are not aware of any study that measures TAM's variables in a DSS designed for AAL. Moreover, since DSSs' interface plays a pivotal role in technology acceptance, and it constitutes the only means through which the operator exploits the system, a comparison with similar systems is not possible.

Generally, we can observe that DSS technologies are well accepted by users working in professional fields, especially if they are designed to help in specific phases of the work. In accordance, our tool received positive evaluations at the overall score and, in particular at the scales that are most considered (i.e., "Perceived Usefulness" and "Perceived ease of use"). The SUS score was 72.5 (SD = 9.61), corresponding to a borderline level between "Marginal" and "Acceptable" according to the Acceptability ranges, and between the "Ok" and "Good" Adjective ratings. For this reason, enhancements are necessary. Finally, overall mean score at the section C of MARS was 3.38 (SD = 0.25), corresponding to the median value of the Likert scale, which corresponds to "satisfaction with few problems"; "moderate quality graphics aspects" and "average visual appeal". It is evident that some graphics aspects are to be reviewed and modified.

Subjects' comments noted during test session are relevant to deepen emerged issues and to understand which improvements are to be carried out. Small font used to indicate of appliances' name and resident's characteristics should be enlarged with attention to the color contrast; dwellers' icons customization should be allowed. Subjects emphasized the need to make explicit clinical conditions of the dwellers, during the initial configuration phase. Logical links between dwellers and appliances choices must be explicitly stated. Other improvable graphics aspects are: Emphasizing appliances when the cursor hovers over them, and eliminating redundant icons from the menu.

6. Limitations of RecAAL's DSS and Future Perspectives

The authors acknowledge that this work has some limitations and that further improvements are needed before the actual use of the described DSS and application.

6.1. Extending and Mapping the DSS Ontology

The possibility to rely on a referenced ontology of ICF eased the reuse of the whole standard classification for RecAAL's DSS. However, in order for an ontology to be reused, it is important to define how it aligns with other models describing the same domains; this process is defined as ontology alignment (also known as ontology mapping or ontology matching). Mapping one ontology with another means that for each concept in the first ontology we try to find a corresponding concept that has the same or similar semantics in the second ontology [83]. Nevertheless, the creation of high-quality ontology mapping in an automatic way is still a challenge—and a cornerstone for the whole Semantic Web [84].

The ontology developed for the DSS (whose concepts and properties are here introduced by the namespace recAAL) can be mapped to other relevant ontologies, in order to foster its better interoperability and reusability. An ontology reused in many projects and developed within the framework of appliances' energy-efficiency is SAREF. This model, developed with experts working in the appliance industry [66], was developed to foster interoperability among different devices. The concepts recAAL:Appliance and recAAL:Sensor can be semantically matched respectively with saref:Appliance and saref:Sensor, since they describe the same concept, as well as the respective subclasses representing specific categories of appliances or sensors (such as saref:WashingMachine, saref:SmokeSensor and saref:TemperatureSensor). Moreover, datatype properties used in the DSS's ontology for appliances' description (Section 4.3.1) can be aligned with the equivalent datatype properties modelled in SAREF (saref:hasDescription, saref:hasManufacturer, saref:hasName; etc.). MonErgy ontology [85] is another example of semantic model developed to provide a description of appliances and their energy ratings. This ontology classifies the monergy:ApplianceType in a set of subclasses, each of which corresponding to appliances' types (monergy:MicrowaveOven, monergy:Oven, monergy:DishWasher, etc.). These classes can be semantically aligned with those modelled to classify DSS's appliances (Section 4.3.1). Similarly, DomoML-env [86] (an ontology aimed at describing domestic devices to enhance their interoperability within a smart home) foresees a domoml-env:BuildingEquipment class that is detailed in domoml-env:HouseholdAppliance, which is further deepened into the subclasses domoml-env:WhiteGoods and domoml-env:BrownGoods; each appliance type is here represented as a concept, and can be semantically aligned with the classes modelled in the DSS's otology. Moreover, some of DomoML-env's properties modelled to describe appliances can be matched with the ones used in the DSS's ontology. Device description is the aim of the FIPA Device Ontology Specification [87], a model aimed at fostering interoperability when communicating about devices and their capabilities. The class fipa:Device corresponds to recALL:Appliance ∪ recAAL:Sensor and therefore FIPA's properties can be used to describe DSS's devices. DSS's Sensors (recAAL:Sensor) can be semantically matched with their equivalent concept in the Sensor-Observation-Sampling-Actuator ontology (SOSA), which is a core ontology reused in the W3C-endorsed SSN [67]. This ontology can also provide the means for the formal representation of actuators (sosa:Actuator) and for the description of the measurements performed by sensors, as well as the actuation provided by the actuators.

DSS's ontology residents' registry records (Section 4.2.1) can be aligned with the core properties of the Friend Of a Friend (FOAF) specification [88], a vocabulary widely-used for the description of networks of people.

Since the DSS's aim is to suggest appliances for the reconfiguration of different domestic environments (not limited to the kitchen) an extension of the ontology should encompass also describing the appliances' location; reconfiguration projects that tackles two or more rooms could benefit from a formal description of the environments. To this purpose, DogOnt [89] can provide the means to describe how a domestic environment is composed (including architectural elements and furniture) and the location of the various devices in the home.

6.2. Including More Personae

The two personae described in Section 3.2 were selected, taking into account the impact of the respective disabilities in the population. Silvia, the first person affected by frailty, represents one of the 962 million people aged over 60 years old in the world [90]. Frailty develops as a consequence of age-related decline, and nowadays afflicts half of the population aged 85 or more [91]; while evidences suggest that the incidence of this condition can affect also people aged 65–74 years old [92]. Giovanni, suffering from a visual impairment, is a person who represents a common situation in older groups of people. In fact, according to World Health Organization's report "Universal Eye Health: A Global Action Plan 2014–2019" [93], 285 million people are affected by vision-related issues (39 million people are blind, with a complete impairment); visual impairments are more frequent among elderlies and the 65% of people affected by a moderate and severe impairment are older than 50 years of age.

Following the same methodology, described in Sections 3.2 and 3.3, it is possible to sketch other personae, starting with the identification of ICF domains involved in the description of their impairments. Moreover, other personae with different health conditions, not enlisted in Section 3.2 can be modelled and described too, e.g., taking advantage of ICF core sets [94].

6.3. Using Machine Learning to Increase Ontology Population

A limit related to the current version of the DSS relies on its limited number of instances, in particular appliances, used for the proof of concepts. As described in Section 4, a group of experts worked to identify a certain number of appliances to be modelled into the application ontology. The group empirically selected a number of appliances and then classified it according to the benefits these can provide to particular categories of residents with impairments; the ontological population of appliances' list can include both ADA and non-ADA compliant appliances, since the evaluation of the suitability of a device is performed by considering both its design features and programs. Such an empirical approach requires a lot of work to be carried out in order to:

- Identify the appliances on vendors' and/or brands websites;
- Agree on appliances' specifics to be evaluated and on the methodology to evaluate them;
- Manually classify them according to their specifics.

RecAAL's DSS could therefore benefit from the application of Machine Learning (ML) techniques to populate the appliances' ABox: Trying to automatically classify the appliances according to a set of appliances already classified by experts can, from the one hand, increase the number of individuals, while on the other hand can speed up application ontology's population process.

Another application of ML techniques can concern the possibility to classify the appliances, not only as suitable for some specific impairments, but also to the severity of the impairments. In RecAAL, the selection of an appliance from the suggested list is performed by the designer together with the resident; by exploiting ML to further classify appliances according also to the magnitude of the impairments they can help coping with, the designer can potentially have a more limited—but more fitting—selection to choose from. This approach requires anyway clinical personnel to supervise the results generated from the automatic classification performed by ML techniques, since the complete automation of this classification process involves a sensitive domain—people with impairments everyday life and habits.

Additionally, the list of appliances could be flanked with a list of kitchen aids (such as cutting boards and tools for slicing foods designed for one-handed people, automatic and/or electric can openers, ergonomic peelers, etc.). These tools should undergo the same evaluation from a group of experts to be classified conveniently and may require the full extent of ICF "Body Structures" qualifiers to specify the type of disability the tools can mitigate; for this case, the DSS's application ontology already provides the means to support this kind of body structures-related descriptions.

Finally, dwellers' feedback regarding their experiences with the appliances selected and installed in their houses can constitute a validation means for experts' group work, helping in better defining the classification methodology, illustrated in Section 4.3.2. Residents' feedbacks can potentially be organized in a semantic knowledge base to be integrated to the original RecALL's ontology.

6.4. Validation with Professionals

Regarding RecAAL's validation, the protocol described in Section 6, needs to be administered to those professionals who could take some advantages from the application's work: Interior designers, architects, smart home designers, caregivers, and vocational therapists could potentially be interested in knowing which appliances can be of some help for particular categories of dwellers. Moreover, to validate the approach of the empirical methodology, tests with both designers and residents with impairments need to be conducted. The preliminary tests described above highlighted that RecAAL can benefit from some enhancement in the graphical interface; appliances' features need to be shown to application's users, as well as an aggregate data regarding resident's health condition.

7. Conclusions

In this work, the development of a Decision Support System (DSS) for the reconfiguration of a domestic environment is presented; while most of AAL solutions rely on complex systems and architectures, the DSS suggests a set of appliances to support residents affected by mild or moderate disabilities, thus enabling a simpler reconfiguration of living environments. The development process starts with the identification of specific residents, elderlies affected by impairments related to ageing and users affected by sensory or motor systems pathologies. To define the health condition of the residents, the International Classification of Functioning, Disability and Health (ICF) was selected as a standard tool able to ease communication among clinical and non-clinical stakeholders.

The DSS relies on a semantic application ontology, whose development is performed following the NeOn Methodology; the application ontology reuses ICF's ontology and develops other parts from scratch. The result of this process is an application ontology that takes into account the residents' health status and providing the means to describe the appliances to be placed within the reconfiguration process. Reasoning with the DSS allows to match residents with a set of appliances able to help them to cope with their impairments.

The DSS constitutes the base of the RecAAL application, which replicates the resident domestic environments in a 3D model; in this model a designer can select and place the appliances according to the results generated by reasoning process, then he can save the reconfiguration project.

Further works foresee the possibility to enhance some aspects of the DSS and the RecAAL application, by applying ML techniques for the automatic classification of appliances and kitchen aids.

Author Contributions: D.S. designed the study, developed the ontology and RecAAL, wrote the first draft of the manuscript. M.S. contributed to the development of RecAAL and revised the manuscript.

Funding: This work has been founded by "Convenzione Operativa No. 19365/RCC" in the framework of the project "Future Home for Future Communities".

Acknowledgments: Authors would like to acknowledge the contribution of the group of experts, who cooperated to the classification of the 25 test appliances used to develop the Decision Support System.

Conflicts of Interest: The authors declare no conflict of interest.

Appendix A

#	Type	Name	Manufacturer	W	H	D	ICF domains	Feature/program
1	oven	GE café CT9070SHSS	GE Appliances	75,56	72,4	70,5	b710.(≤2); b7300(≤1); b7356(≤1); b760(≤1); d4450(≤1); s750(≤3)	French door.
2	oven	N 90	NEFF	59,5	59,6	54,8	b710.(≤2); b7300(≤1); b7356(≤1); b760(≤1); d4450(≤1); s750(≤3)	Slide and hide door.
3	microwave	Cook magic 87108	Cook Magic	53,4	30,5	43,2	b140.1; b1560.1; b1561.1; b2100(≤2); b21022(≤2);	Talking microwave (instructions); easy to feel buttons.
4	microwave	Talking microwave oven	Magic chef	54,6	30,5	38,1	b140.1; b1560.1; b1561.1; b2100(≤2); b21022(≤2);	Talking microwave (instructions).
5	microwave	Stainless Design	RCA	53,97	29,51	40,26	b140.1; b1561.1; b2100(≤1); b21022(≤1);	Tactile marks on buttons to help discriminating appliance's functions; wide button panel.
6	cooktop	GE café CHP9536SJSS	GE Appliances	91	ns	50,8	b140.1; b1561.1; b2100(≤1); b21022(≤1);	Backlit display; central position of the button panel; cool to touch induction stoves.
7	cooktop	GE café PHP9036SJSS	GE Appliances	91	ns	50,8	b140.1; b1561.1; b2100(≤1); b21022(≤1);	Digital backlit display; high contrast button panel (white on black); cool to touch induction stoves.
8	dishwasher	DD24SI9_N Integrated style	Fisher & Paykel	59,85	41,4	58	b140.1; b1561.1; b2100(≤1); b21022(≤1); d4105.1	Few operating buttons; knock on the panel to stop the device from washing.
9	cooktop	37" Electric Smoothtop Cooktop	Electrolux	91,4	ns	52,1	b140.1; b1561.1; b2100(≤1); b21022(≤1);	Lateral high-contrast (light azure on black) button panel; backlit digital display; cool to touch induction stoves.
10	washer	Duet	Whirlpool	80	97	69	b140.1; b1561.1; b2100(≤2); b21022(≤2);	Tactile buttons; each choiche is combined with tones; backlit display.
11	cooktop	Thermador CIT36XKBB	Thermador	94	ns	54	b140.1; b1561.1; b2100(≤2); b21022(≤2);	Backlit and full color button panel; sensors for automatic detection of cookware; larger cooking surface.
12	refrigerator	Amana AFI2539ERW	Amana	91,12	178,12	89,54	b140.1; b1561.1; b2100(≤2); b21022(≤2);	French door; exterior ice and water dispenser; backlit button panel with intuitive icons.
13	cooktop	Franke FH 604-1E 4I T	Franke	76	ns	51	b2100(≤2); b21022(≤2);	High contrast (black on white) control panel and cooking surface.
14	oven	Gaggenau 200 Series BL253610	Gaggenau	61	53,8 (86)	45,6	b710.(≤3); b7300(≤2); b7356(≤3); b760(≤1); d4450(≤3); d4105(≤3); d430(≤2); s750(≤3)	Automatic elevating base (lift oven).
15	oven	Siemens Wall-mounted lift oven	Siemens	59,9	53,8 (158)	45,5	b710.(≤3); b7300(≤2); b7356(≤3); b760(≤1); d4450(≤3); d4105(≤3); d430(≤2); s750(≤3)	Automatic elevating base (lift oven).
16	oven	30" Single Wall Oven with Even-Heat True Convection	Kitchen aid	76,2	71,1	68,6	b2100(≤2); b21022(≤2);	Easy to feel buttons; high contrast button panel (white on black).
17	refrigerator	BP 2850 Premium BioFresh	Liebherr	66,5	125	60	b710.(≤1); b7300(≤2); b7356(≤1); d4450(≤3); s750(≤3)	Compact sizes.
18	refrigerator	Avanti RA31B0W Freestanding	Avanti	47	85	49,5	b710.(≤1); b7300(≤2); b7356(≤1); d4450(≤3); s750(≤3)	Compact sizes.
19	dishwasher	Miele G4780SCVI Dimension series	Miele	45	80,64	57,1	b2100(≤2); b21022(≤2);	Easy to feel buttons; backlit digital display; high contrast buttons (black on steel).
20	washer	GE GFW480SSKWW	GE Appliances	71	100	87,3	b140.1; b1561.1; b2100(≤2); b21022(≤2); b710.(≤3); b7300(≤2); b7356(≤3); b760(≤1); d4450(≤3); d4105(≤3); d430(≤2); s750(≤3)	Knob for program selection; warning lights to highlight programs' selections; high-contrast (white on black) control panel; front load (porthole door glass).
21	dishwasher	Bosch SPE68U55UC 800 Series	Bosch	44,7	81,4	57,3	b140.1; b1561.1; b2100(≤2); b21022(≤2); b710.(≤3); b7300(≤2); b7356(≤3); b760(≤1); d4450(≤3); d4105(≤3); d430(≤2); s750(≤3)	Easy to feel buttons; backlit digital display; high contrast buttons (black on steel).
22	washer	Bosch WAT28400UC	Bosch	59,7	84,4	61,6	b140.1; b1561.1; b2100(≤1); b21022(≤1); b710.(≤3); b7300(≤2); b7356(≤3); b760(≤1); d4450(≤3); d4105(≤3); s750(≤3)	Knob for program selection; digital backlit display; front load (porthole door glass).
23	dishwasher	Fisher Paykel DD24SAX9N	Fisher & Paykel	59,8	40,96	57,3	b140.1; b1561.1; b2100(≤1); b21022(≤1); b710.(≤3); b7300(≤2); b7356(≤3); b760(≤1); d4450(≤3); d4105(≤3); d430(≤2);s750(≤3)	Exterior control panel with limited number of buttons and digital display; drawer opening and loading.
24	refrigerator	LG LFX25974ST	LG	90,8	177,16	87	b2100(≤2); b21022(≤2); b710.(≤2); b7300(≤1); b7356(≤1); b760(≤1); d4450(≤1); s750(≤3)	French door opening; internal LED lighting.
25	refrigerator	K 3130 Comfort	Liebherr	63	144,7	60	b710.(≤1); b7300(≤2); b7356(≤1); d4450(≤3); s750(≤3)	Door opening mechanism; compact sizes.

Figure A1. A recapitulatory schema of the work conducted by the expert group on a set of 25 appliances.

References

1. Giannakouris, K. Ageing characterises the demographic perspectives of the European societies. *Stat. Focus* **2008**, *72*, 2008.
2. Christensen, K.; Doblhammer, G.; Rau, R.; Vaupel, J.W. Ageing populations: The challenges ahead. *Lancet* **2009**, *374*, 1196–1208. [CrossRef]
3. Chan, M.; Campo, E.; Estève, D.; Fourniols, J.Y. Smart homes—Current features and future perspectives. *Maturitas* **2009**, *64*, 90–97. [CrossRef] [PubMed]
4. Demiris, G.; Rantz, M.J.; Aud, M.A.; Marek, K.D.; Tyrer, H.W.; Skubic, M.; Hussam, A.A. Older adults' attitudes towards and perceptions of "smart home"technologies: A pilot study. *Med. Inf. Internet Med.* **2004**, *29*, 87–94. [CrossRef] [PubMed]
5. Demiris, G.; Hensel, B.K.; Skubic, M.; Rantz, M. Senior residents' perceived need of and preferences for "smart home" sensor technologies. *Int. J. Technol. Assess. Health Care* **2008**, *24*, 120–124. [CrossRef] [PubMed]
6. Courtney, K.L. Privacy and Senior Willingness to Adopt Smart Home Information Technology in Residential Care Facilities. Available online: http://hdl.handle.net/1828/6616 (accessed on 7 August 2018).
7. Katz, S. Assessing self-maintenance: Activities of daily living, mobility, and instrumental activities of daily living. *J. Am. Geriatr. Soc.* **1983**, *31*, 721–727. [CrossRef] [PubMed]
8. Åkesson, K.P.; Bullock, A.; Rodden, T.; Koleva, B.; Greenhalgh, C. A Toolkit for User Re-Configuration of Ubiquitous Domestic Environments. Available online: http://citeseerx.ist.psu.edu/viewdoc/download?doi=10.1.1.120.7276&rep=rep1&type=pdf (accessed on 7 August 2018).
9. Humble, J.; Crabtree, A.; Hemmings, T.; Åkesson, K.P.; Koleva, B.; Rodden, T.; Hansson, P. Playing with the BitsUser-configuration of Ubiquitous Domestic Environments. In Proceedings of the International Conference on Ubiquitous Computing, Seattle, WA, USA, 12–15 October 2003; pp. 256–263.
10. Criel, J.; Geerts, M.; Claeys, L.; Kawsar, F. Empowering elderly end-users for ambient programming: The tangible way. In Proceedings of the International Conference on Grid and Pervasive Computing, Oulu, Finland, 11–13 May 2011; pp. 94–104.
11. Giner, P.; Cetina, C.; Fons, J.; Pelechano, V. Building self-adaptive services for ambient assisted living. In Proceedings of the International Work-Conference on Artificial Neural Networks, Salamanca, Spain, 10–12 June 2009; pp. 740–747.
12. Ruiz-López, T.; Rodríguez-Domínguez, C.; Noguera, M.; Garrido, J.L. Towards a reusable design of a positioning system for AAL environments. In Proceedings of the International Competition on Evaluating AAL Systems through Competitive Benchmarking, Lecce, Italy, 26 September 2011; pp. 65–79.
13. Design for All. Project Website. Available online: www.d4all.eu (accessed on 7 August 2018).
14. Future Home for Future Communities. Project Website. Available online: www.fhffc.it (accessed on 7 August 2018).
15. Blomqvist, E. The use of Semantic Web technologies for decision support—A survey. *Semant. Web* **2014**, *5*, 177–201.
16. Cheung, K.H.; Prud'hommeaux, E.; Wang, Y.; Stephens, S. Semantic Web for Health Care and Life Sciences: A review of the state of the art. *Eur. PMC* **2009**. [CrossRef] [PubMed]
17. Liaw, S.T.; Taggart, J.; Yu, H.; de Lusignan, S.; Kuziemsky, C.; Hayen, A. Integrating electronic health record information to support integrated care: Practical application of ontologies to improve the accuracy of diabetes disease registers. *J. Biomed. Inf.* **2014**, *52*, 364–372. [CrossRef] [PubMed]
18. Xu, B.; Xu, L.D.; Cai, H.; Xie, C.; Hu, J.; Bu, F. Ubiquitous data accessing method in IoT-based information system for emergency medical services. *IEEE Trans. Ind. Inf.* **2014**, *10*, 1578–1586.
19. Khan, W.A.; Khattak, A.M.; Hussain, M.; Amin, M.B.; Afzal, M.; Nugent, C.; Lee, S. An adaptive semantic based mediation system for data interoperability among health information systems. *J. Med. Syst.* **2014**, *38*, 28. [CrossRef] [PubMed]
20. Shaban-Nejad, A.; Lavigne, M.; Okhmatovskaia, A.; Buckeridge, D.L. PopHR: A knowledge-based platform to support integration, analysis, and visualization of population health data. *Ann. N. Y. Acad. Sci.* **2017**, *1387*, 44–53. [CrossRef] [PubMed]
21. Ullah, F.; Habib, M.A.; Farhan, M.; Khalid, S.; Durrani, M.Y.; Jabbar, S. Semantic interoperability for big-data in heterogeneous IoT infrastructure for healthcare. *Sustain. Cities Soc.* **2017**, *34*, 90–96. [CrossRef]

22. Pan, J.Z. Resource description framework. In *Handbook on Ontologies*; Springer: Berlin, Germany, 2009; pp. 71–90.
23. Pérez, J.; Arenas, M.; Gutierrez, C. Semantics and Complexity of SPARQL. In Proceedings of the International Semantic Web Conference, Athens, GA, USA, 5–9 November 2006; pp. 30–43.
24. del Carmen Legaz-García, M.; Martínez-Costa, C.; Menárguez-Tortosa, M.; Fernández-Breis, J.T. A semantic web based framework for the interoperability and exploitation of clinical models and EHR data. *Knowl.-Based Syst.* **2016**, *105*, 175–189. [CrossRef]
25. Gomez, J.; Oviedo, B.; Zhuma, E. Patient monitoring system based on internet of things. *Procedia Comput. Sci.* **2016**, *83*, 90–97. [CrossRef]
26. Datta, S.K.; Bonnet, C.; Gyrard, A.; Da Costa, R.P.F.; Boudaoud, K. Applying Internet of Things for personalized healthcare in smart homes. In Proceedings of the 2015 24th Wireless and Optical Communication Conference (WOCC), Taipei, Taiwan, 23–24 October 2015; pp. 164–169.
27. Bikakis, A.; Patkos, T.; Antoniou, G.; Plexousakis, D. A survey of semantics-based approaches for context reasoning in ambient intelligence. In Proceedings of the European Conference on Ambient Intelligence, Darmstadt, Germany, 7–10 November 2007; pp. 14–23.
28. Osman, T.; Lotfi, A.; Langensiepen, C.; Chernbumroong, S.; Saeed, M. Semantic-based decision support for remote care of dementia patients. In Proceedings of the 2014 IEEE Symposium on Intelligent Agents (IA), Orlando, FL, USA, 9–12 December 2014; pp. 89–96.
29. Horrocks, I.; Patel-Schneider, P.F.; Boley, H.; Tabet, S.; Grosof, B.; Dean, M. SWRL: A Semantic Web Rule Language Combining OWL and RuleML. Available online: http://www.daml.org/swrl/proposal/rules-all.html (accessed on 6 August 2018).
30. Zentek, T.; Marinc, A.; Rashid, A. Methods and tools for ontology-based configuration processes of AAL environments. In *Ambient Assisted Living*; Springer: Berlin, Germany, 2014; pp. 213–224.
31. Zhang, Y.F.; Gou, L.; Tian, Y.; Li, T.C.; Zhang, M.; Li, J.S. Design and development of a sharable clinical decision support system based on a semantic web service framework. *J. Med. Syst.* **2016**, *40*, 118. [CrossRef] [PubMed]
32. Fotopoulou, E.; Zafeiropoulos, A.; Terroso-Sáenz, F.; Simsek, U.; González-Vidal, A.; Tsiolis, G.; Gouvas, P.; Liapis, P.; Fensel, A.; Skarmeta, A. Providing personalized energy management and awareness services for energy efficiency in smart buildings. *Sensors* **2017**, *17*, 2054. [CrossRef] [PubMed]
33. Fensel, A.; Tomic, D.K.; Koller, A. Contributing to appliances' energy efficiency with Internet of Things, smart data and user engagement. *Future Gener. Comput. Syst.* **2017**, *76*, 329–338. [CrossRef]
34. Madrazo, L.; Massetti, M.; Sicilia, A.; Wadel, G.; Ianni, M. SEíS: A semantic-based system for integrating building energy data. *Informes de la Construcción* **2015**, *67*, 11. [CrossRef]
35. Bonino, D.; Corno, F.; De Russis, L. Poweront: An ontology-based approach for power consumption estimation in smart homes. In *Internet of Things. User-Centric IoT*; Springer: Berlin, Germany, 2015; pp. 3–8.
36. Huang, C.C.; Liu, A.; Zhou, P.C. Using ontology reasoning in building a simple and effective dialog system for a smart home system. In Proceedings of the 2015 IEEE International Conference on Systems, Man, and Cybernetics, Kowloon, China, 9–12 October 2015; pp. 1508–1513.
37. Ni, Q.; de la Ivan, P.; García Hernando, A.B. A foundational ontology-based model for human activity representation in smart homes. *J. Ambient Intell. Smart Environ.* **2016**, *8*, 47–61. [CrossRef]
38. Hardie, G.J. ACC0SSible EnVirOnments TOWard Universal Design. In *Design Intervention (Routledge Revivals): Toward a More Humane Architecture*; Van Nostrand Reinhold: Washington, DC, USA, 2015.
39. Organization, W.H. International classification of functioning, disability and health: ICF. In *World Health Organization*; World Health Organization: Geneva, Switzerland, 2001.
40. Arlati, S.; Spoladore, D.; Mottura, S.; Zangiacomi, A.; Ferrigno, G.; Sacchetti, R.; Sacco, M. Architecture of a virtual reality and semantics-based framework for the return to work of wheelchair users. In Proceedings of the International Conference on Augmented Reality, Virtual Reality and Computer Graphics, Ugento, Italy, 12–15 June 2017; pp. 74–85.
41. Spoladore, D. Ontology-based decision support systems for health data management to support collaboration in ambient assisted living and work reintegration. In Proceedings of the Working Conference on Virtual Enterprises, Vicenza, Italy, 18–20 September 2017; pp. 341–352.
42. Okochi, J.; Utsunomiya, S.; Takahashi, T. Health measurement using the ICF: Test-retest reliability study of ICF codes and qualifiers in geriatric care. *Health Qual. Life Outcomes* **2005**, *3*, 46. [CrossRef] [PubMed]

43. Freedman, V.A. Adopting the ICF language for studying late-life disability: A field of dreams? *J. Gerontol. Ser. A Biomed. Sci. Med. Sci.* **2009**, *64*, 1172–1174. [CrossRef] [PubMed]

44. Buono, S.; Zagaria, T. ICF-Classificazione Internazionale del funzionamento, della Disabilità e della Salute. *Ciclo Evolutivo e Disabilità/Life Span Disabil.* **2003**, *6*, N1.

45. Scherer, M.J.; Craddock, G.; Mackeogh, T. The relationship of personal factors and subjective well-being to the use of assistive technology devices. *Disabil. Rehabil.* **2011**, *33*, 811–817. [CrossRef] [PubMed]

46. Andronache, A.S.; Simoncello, A.; Della Mea, V.; Daffara, C.; Francescutti, C. Semantic aspects of the International Classification of Functioning, Disability and Health: Towards sharing knowledge and unifying information. *Am. J. Phys. Med. Rehabil.* **2012**, *91*, S124–S128. [CrossRef] [PubMed]

47. Della Mea, V.; Simoncello, A. An ontology-based exploration of the concepts and relationships in the activities and participation component of the international classification of functioning, disability and health. *J. Biomed. Semant.* **2012**, *3*, 1. [CrossRef] [PubMed]

48. Kumar, A.; Smith, B. The ontology of processes and functions: A study of the international classification of functioning, disability and health. In Proceedings of the AIME 2005 Workshop on Biomedical Ontology Engineering, Aberdeen, UK, 23–27 July 2005.

49. BioPortal. International Classification of Functioning, Disability and Health Ontology. Available online: https://www.bioportal.bioontology.org/ontologies/ICF (accessed on 5 August 2018).

50. Cooper, A. *The Inmates Are Running the Asylum: [Why High-Tech Products Drive Us Crazy and How to Restore the Sanity]*; Sams Indianapolis: Indianapolis, IN, USA, 2004.

51. Pruitt, J.; Grudin, J. Personas: Practice and theory. In Proceedings of the 2003 Conference on Designing for User Experiences, San Francisco, CA, USA, 6–7 June 2003; pp. 1–15.

52. Fried, L.P.; Tangen, C.M.; Walston, J.; Newman, A.B.; Hirsch, C.; Gottdiener, J.; Seeman, T.; Tracy, R.; Kop, W.J.; Burke, G. Frailty in older adults: Evidence for a phenotype. *J. Gerontol. Ser. A Biol. Sci. Med. Sci.* **2001**, *56*, 146–157. [CrossRef]

53. Gauthier, S.; Reisberg, B.; Zaudig, M.; Petersen, R.C.; Ritchie, K.; Broich, K.; Belleville, S.; Brodaty, H.; Bennett, D.; Chertkow, H. Mild cognitive impairment. *Lancet* **2006**, *367*, 1262–1270. [CrossRef]

54. Blasco, R.; Marco, Á.; Casas, R.; Cirujano, D.; Picking, R. A smart kitchen for ambient assisted living. *Sensors* **2014**, *14*, 1629–1653. [CrossRef] [PubMed]

55. Angermann, A.; Bauer, R.; Nossek, G.; Zimmermann, N. *Injuries in the European Union: Statistics Summary 2003–2005*; Eurosafe, KFV: Vienna, Austria, 2007.

56. Gruber, T.R. A translation approach to portable ontology specifications. *Knowl. Acquis.* **1993**, *5*, 199–220. [CrossRef]

57. Menzel, C. Reference Ontologies-Application Ontologies: Either/Or or Both/And? Available online: http://ceur-ws.org/Vol-94/ki03rao_menzel.pdf (accessed on 6 August 2018).

58. Fernández-López, M.; Gómez-Pérez, A. Overview and analysis of methodologies for building ontologies. *Knowl. Eng. Rev.* **2002**, *17*, 129–156. [CrossRef]

59. Suárez-Figueroa, M.C.; Gómez-Pérez, A.; Fernández-López, M. The NeOn methodology for ontology engineering. In *Ontology Engineering in a Networked World*; Springer: Berlin, Germany, 2012; pp. 9–34.

60. Fernández-López, M.; Gómez-Pérez, A.; Juristo, N. Methontology: From ontological art towards ontological engineering. In Proceedings of the AAAI-97 Spring Symposium Series, Stanford, CA, USA, 24–26 March 1997.

61. Sure, Y.; Staab, S.; Studer, R. Ontology engineering methodology. In *Handbook on Ontologies*; Springer: Berlin, Germany, 2009; pp. 135–152.

62. Suárez-Figueroa, M.C.; Gómez-Pérez, A.; Villazón-Terrazas, B. How to write and use the ontology requirements specification document. In Proceedings of the OTM Confederated International Conference On the Move to Meaningful Internet Systems, Vilamoura, Portugal, 1–6 November2009; pp. 966–982.

63. McGuinness, D.L.; Van Harmelen, F. OWL Web Ontology Language Overview. Available online: http://www.citeulike.org/group/2170/article/100176 (accessed on 6 August 2018).

64. Grüninger, M.; Fox, M.S. Methodology for the Design and Evaluation of Ontologies. Available online: http://citeseerx.ist.psu.edu/viewdoc/summary?doi=10.1.1.44.8723 (accessed on 7 August 2018).

65. Gangemi, A. Ontology design patterns for semantic web content. In Proceedings of the International semantic web conference, Galway, Ireland, 6–10 November 2005; pp. 262–276.

66. Daniele, L.; den Hartog, F.; Roes, J. Created in close interaction with the industry: The smart appliances reference (SAREF) ontology. In Proceedings of the International Workshop Formal Ontologies Meet Industries, Berlin, Germany, 5 August 2015; pp. 100–112.

67. Compton, M.; Barnaghi, P.; Bermudez, L.; García-Castro, R.; Corcho, O.; Cox, S.; Graybeal, J.; Hauswirth, M.; Henson, C.; Herzog, A. The SSN ontology of the W3C semantic sensor network incubator group. *Web Semant. Sci. Serv. Agents World Wide Web* **2012**, *17*, 25–32. [CrossRef]

68. Act, D. Americans with Disabilities Act. Available online: https://www.ada.gov/ (accessed on 7 August 2018).

69. Sirin, E.; Parsia, B.; Grau, B.C.; Kalyanpur, A.; Katz, Y. Pellet: A practical owl-dl reasoner. *Web Semant. Sci. Serv. Agents World Wide Web* **2007**, *5*, 51–53. [CrossRef]

70. Beckett, D.; McBride, B. RDF/XML Syntax Specification (Revised). Available online: http://citeseerx.ist.psu.edu/viewdoc/download?doi=10.1.1.454.3972&rep=rep1&type=pdf (accessed on 7 August 2018).

71. Kim, S.L.; Suk, H.J.; Kang, J.H.; Jung, J.M.; Laine, T.H.; Westlin, J. Using Unity 3D to facilitate mobile augmented reality game development. In Proceedings of the 2014 IEEE World Forum on Internet of Things (WF-IoT), Seoul, Korea, 6–8 March 2014; pp. 21–26.

72. Venkatesh, V.; Davis, F.D. A theoretical extension of the technology acceptance model: Four longitudinal field studies. *Manag. Sci.* **2000**, *46*, 186–204. [CrossRef]

73. Davis, F.D. Perceived usefulness, perceived ease of use, and user acceptance of information technology. *MIS Q.* **1989**, 319–340. [CrossRef]

74. Brooke, J. SUS-A quick and dirty usability scale. *Usabil. Eval. Ind.* **1996**, *189*, 4–7.

75. Stoyanov, S.R.; Hides, L.; Kavanagh, D.J.; Zelenko, O.; Tjondronegoro, D.; Mani, M. Mobile app rating scale: A new tool for assessing the quality of health mobile apps. *JMIR mHealth uHealth* **2015**, *3*, e27. [CrossRef] [PubMed]

76. Bangor, A.; Kortum, P.; Miller, J. Determining what individual SUS scores mean: Adding an adjective rating scale. *J. Usabil. Stud.* **2009**, *4*, 114–123.

77. Casas, C.A. Factors That Determine Attitudes toward the Use Technology to Plan for Retirement: An Empirical Analysis. Available online: https://academyfinancial.org/resources/Documents/Proceedings/2010/6B-Casas.pdf (accessed on 7 August 2018).

78. Dulcic, Z.; Pavlic, D.; Silic, I. Evaluating the intended use of Decision Support System (DSS) by applying Technology Acceptance Model (TAM) in business organizations in Croatia. *Procedia-Soc. Behav. Sci.* **2012**, *58*, 1565–1575. [CrossRef]

79. Alshibly, H.H. Investigating decision support system (DSS) success: A partial least squares structural equation modeling approach. *J. Bus. Stud. Q.* **2015**, *6*, 56.

80. Adagha, O.; Levy, R.M.; Carpendale, S.; Gates, C.; Lindquist, M. Evaluation of a visual analytics decision support tool for wind farm placement planning in Alberta: Findings from a focus group study. *Technol. Forecast. Soc. Chang.* **2017**, *117*, 70–83. [CrossRef]

81. Grout, R.W.; Cheng, E.R.; Carroll, A.E.; Bauer, N.S.; Downs, S.M. A six-year repeated evaluation of computerized clinical decision support system user acceptability. *Int. J. Med. Inf.* **2018**, *112*, 74–81. [CrossRef] [PubMed]

82. Omar, A.; Ellenius, J.; Lindemalm, S. Evaluation of Electronic Prescribing Decision Support System at a Tertiary Care Pediatric Hospital: The User Acceptance Perspective. In *ITCH*; IOS Press: Amsterdam, The Netherlands, 2017; pp. 256–261.

83. Navas-Delgado, I.; Aldana-Montes, J.F. Data Integration: Introducing Semantics. In *Handbook of Research on Innovations in Database Technologies and Applications: Current and Future Trends*; IGI Global: Hershey, PA, USA, 2009; pp. 460–470.

84. Noy, N.F. Ontology mapping. In *Handbook on Ontologies*; Springer: Berlin, Germany, 2009; pp. 573–590.

85. Elmenreich, W.; Khatib, T.; Monacchi, A. Smart Microgrids: Optimizing Local Resources toward Increased Efficiency and a More Sustainable Growth. In *Research and Development Evolving Trends and Practices-towards Human, Institutional and Economic Sectors Growth*; InTechOpen: Lodon, UK, 2017.

86. Sommaruga, L.; Perri, A.; Furfari, F. DomoML-env: An ontology for Human Home Interaction. In Proceedings of the SWAP 2005—Semantic Web Applications and Perspectives, Trento, Italy, 14–16 December 2005; p. 166.

87. FIPA Ontology Service Specification 2000. Available online: http://www.fipa.org/specs/fipa00086/XC00086C.html. (accessed on 1 August 2018).

88. Brickley, D.; Miller, L. FOAF Vocabulary Specification 0.91 2010. Available online: http://xmlns.com/foaf/spec/ (accessed on 1 August 2018).

89. Bonino, D.; Corno, F. Dogont-ontology modeling for intelligent domotic environments. In Proceedings of the International Semantic Web Conference, Karlsruhe, Germany, 26–30 October 2008; pp. 790–803.

90. World Population Prospects: The 2017 Revision, Key Findings and Advance Tables. Available online: https://www.esa.un.org/unpd/wpp/publications/files/wpp2017_keyfindings.pdf (accessed on 7 August 2018).

91. Clegg, A.; Young, J.; Iliffe, S.; Rikkert, M.O.; Rockwood, K. Frailty in elderly people. *Lancet* **2013**, *381*, 752–762. [CrossRef]

92. Xue, Q.-L. The frailty syndrome: Definition and natural history. *Clin. Geriatr. Med.* **2011**, *27*, 1–15. [CrossRef] [PubMed]

93. Organization, W.H. *Universal Eye Health: A Global Action Plan 2014–2019*; World Health Organization: Geneva, Switzerland, 2013.

94. Bickenbach, J.; Cieza, A.; Rauch, A.; Stucki, G. *ICF Core Sets: Manual for Clinical Practice for the ICF Research Branch, in Cooperation with the WHO Collaborating Centre for the Family of International Classifications in Germany (DIMDI)*; Hogrefe Publishing: Boston, MA, USA, 2012.

 *electronics*

Article

An Unpowered Sensor Node for Real-Time Water Quality Assessment (Humic Acid Detection)

Rashid Mirzavand [1,*], Mohammad Mahdi Honari [1], Bahareh Laribi [2], Behnam Khorshidi [3], Mohtada Sadrzadeh [3] and Pedram Mousavi [1]

[1] Intelligent Wireless Technology Lab (IWTL), University of Alberta, Edmonton T6G 1H9, Canada; honarika@ualberta.ca (M.M.H.); pmousavi@ualberta.ca (P.M.)

[2] Li Ka Shing Centre for Health Research Innovation, University of Alberta, Edmonton T6G 2E1, Canada; laribi@ualberta.ca

[3] Advanced Water Research Lab (AWRL), University of Alberta, Edmonton T6G 1H9, Canada; behnam@ualberta.ca (B.K.); sadrzade@ualberta.ca (M.S.)

* Correspondence: mirzavan@ualberta.ca; Tel.: +1-587-557-6800

Received: 7 September 2018; Accepted: 2 October 2018; Published: 3 October 2018

Abstract: A zero-power microwave sensor is reported for the real-time assessment of water quality. The proposed structure is able to transmit sensed data directly to a base-station without additional data processing at the wireless sensor node (WSN) which results in less power consumption. The base-station propagates a single tone signal at the frequency of $f_0/2$. At the sensing node, an antenna absorbs that signal and a passive frequency doubler makes its frequency twice, i.e., f_0, which will be used as the carrier signal. Two pairs of open-ended coaxial probes are used as liquid sensors; one inside a known reference sample and the other one inside the water under test. A combination of both sensors' data will be sent to the base-station. A special six-port structure is used for modulation of sensed data over the carrier. At the base-station, a receiver will demodulate the received signal for extracting the sensed data. As an example, the system has been evaluated at $f_0 = 2.45$ GHz for the detection of Humic-Acid levels as a common contaminant of river waters.

Keywords: Internet of things (IoT); real-time assessment; reflection-based; six-port structure; unpowered; wireless sensor node (WSN)

---

1. Introduction

Water crisis, according to the Global Risks Report by World Economic Forum in 2017, is consistently among the top-ranked global risks since 2012 [1]. Improved technologies make water harvesting possible from rainwater, seawater desalination, and industrial/municipal waste-waters, even at homes [2,3]. These utilities are required to periodically monitor water quality. To prevent unhealthy water usage, the automated in-line sensors are required to detect various pollutions [4,5]. However, most of these systems are not real-time and/or Internet of Things (IoT) compatible, as they need special laboratory equipment. Using wireless sensor nodes and Internet of distributed water systems are a step toward smarter cities [6–9]. A wireless sensor node (WSN) in a wireless network senses a physical/chemical variation in a desired environment [10–12], analyze them, and transmit the extracted data to a receiver which can be a mobile phone or a base-station [13]. In this regard, the WSN usually has a small processing unit, one or more sensors, a telecommunication subsystem, and a source of energy in the form of battery or energy harvesting module. A few un-powered sensor systems were proposed which comprises receiving, frequency conversion, sensing, and transmitting elements [14–16].

There are a couple of architecture reported for sensor nodes in the literature which usually include radio frequency identification (RFID). The interferometry systems send a signal and measure the reflection from sensor nodes by a direct conversion receiver [17–20]. The chip-based sensing nodes have a separate sensor, a digitizer, and a direct conversion modulator [21,22]. Using chips make multi-node networks possible but a higher received signal strength is required for powering-up the sensor and micro-controller chips. The chipless structures in [23–26] work based on the shift in the operating frequency. These frameworks are sensitive to the undesirable condition varieties that change the frequency response of system and need an accurate frequency discovery at the receiver. This detriment is a major point of confinement on the actualizing functional remote systems based on these type of sensors. The six-port structures (SPS), as a vector modulator, only consists of some passive elements [27–30] and is an ideal choice for a near-to-zero (N-zero) or zero-power systems. The direct conversion sensors, as of late proposed in [31,32], need a signal generator and a power source with the occasional support or trade necessities at the sensor node. Therefore, these kind of nodes cannot be utilized in applications with restricted access or troubles for upkeep.

This paper proposes real-time water quality assessment using a Base-Station (BS) and sensor nodes in a water harvesting system. The adaptive and switched-beam antenna at the BS makes an exclusive connection with each node possible. The sensor node senses the effects of filter's output and reference sample on the reflection coefficients of open-ended coaxial probes, simultaneously. This information can be used to determine the quality of filtered water. For systems with exchangeable filters, the reference sample can be taken when the filter is new and works perfectly. After that, the quality of filtering and thus the replacement time of the filter can be determined.

The proposed direct conversion sensor is based on the SPS that simplify the sensing system by eliminating digitizer and integrating the sensor into the modulator. Using the vector modulator eliminates the frequency up-converting chain and leads to a low-cost and straightforward realization of modulation scheme for transmitting data. The introduced unpowered WSN comprises a dual-band receiving/transmitting antenna, a frequency diplexer, a frequency doubler, a SPS, and two pairs of open-ended coaxial probes for sensing in which one pair senses the desired variations in the water under test (WUT) while the other one is in contact with the pure water, as a reference. These probes provide broadband and non-destructive sensing of liquids. The variations in sensing parts modulate the input signal and the reference data can be used in the calibration procedure of six-port receiver at the BS.

For evaluation, the system has been implemented at the frequency of 2.45 GHz. As a common contaminant sample, various concentrations of humic acid in water were used as the WUTs to resemble dissolved organic matter in the river. The measurement results show that the proposed sensor node can detect the level of pollution with a good accuracy.

2. Materials and Methods

The proposed wireless quality sensing system consists of a base station and one or more zero-power sensor nodes, as shown in Figure 1a. The BS transmits the pure and receives the modulated signals at the frequencies of $f/2$ and f, respectively. The node receives the pure signal at $f/2$, modulates it with sensed data, and transmits it back at f. In the next sections, both parts are presented in detail.

2.1. The Sensing Node

The sensing mechanism is shown in Figure 1b, which is based on a comparison between the water filter's output as the water under test and a fixed pure water as the reference sample. The open-ended coaxial line is selected as the sensitive circuit that can provide a good accuracy for liquid detection. The material around the open end of the line affects its fringing fields, as shown in Figure 1c. Considering the open-ended coaxial probe as a truncated transmission line, the electromagnetic waves propagate along it and reflected back at the end of line because of an impedance mismatch between the probe and the sample. This mismatch, and thereafter the reflection coefficient, is related to the ratio of dielectric constants for sample and probe, or equivalently ratio of their capacitances.

For a WUT with permittivity of ε_{WUT}, the reflection coefficient (Γ_{WUT}) of the open-ended line can be represented by [33],

$$\Gamma_{WUT} = \frac{1 - j\omega Z_0 \left(\varepsilon_{WUT} C_0 + C_f\right)}{1 + j\omega Z_0 \left(\varepsilon_{WUT} C_0 + C_f\right)},$$ (1)

where ω is angular frequency, Z_0 is characteristic impedance of coaxial line, i.e., 50 Ω, C_0 and C_f are capacitances of air outside and fringing field inside the coaxial line, respectively. For a reference sample with permittivity of ε_{Ref} close to ε_{WUT}, the first approximation of (1) can be obtained as,

$$\Gamma_{WUT} = \Gamma_{Ref} - 2j\omega Z_0 \left(\varepsilon_{WUT} - \varepsilon_{Ref}\right) C_0.$$ (2)

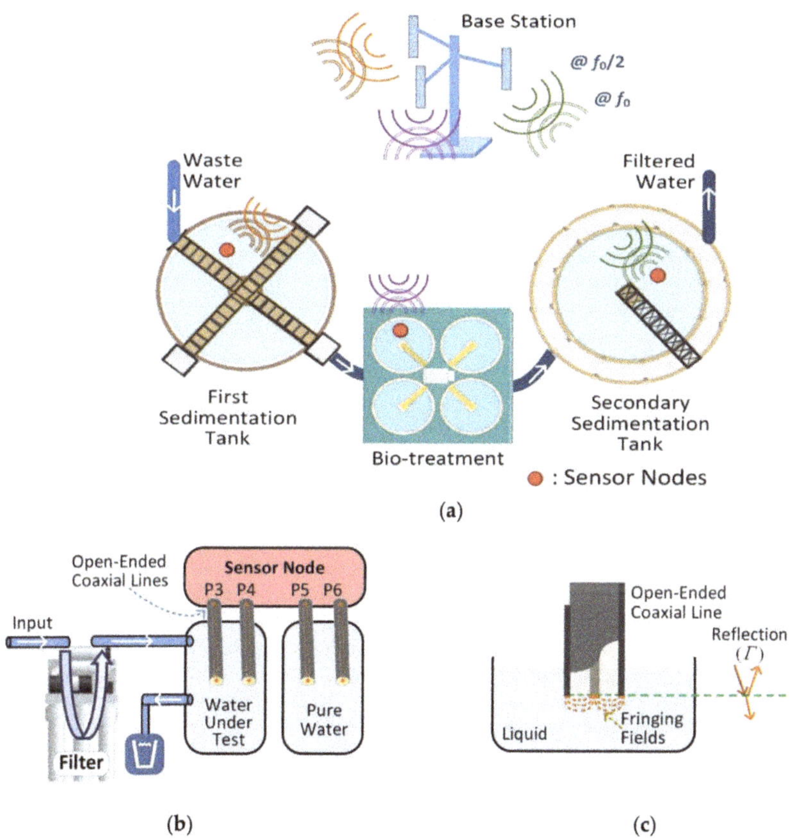

Figure 1. Schematic presentation of real-time water quality assessment: (**a**) A water sensor network; (**b**) A sensor node; (**c**) Open-ended coaxial line sensing of water.

The proposed sensor node uses the same sensitive circuits for the WUT and reference samples. The node consists of a six-port sensor, a dual-band antenna, a diplexer, and a frequency doubler, as shown in Figure 2a. The antenna absorbs the transmitted signal of BS at $f/2$ and the diplexer passes it to the frequency doubler. The output signal of the doubler is used as the input signal of the SPS, at f. The output port of SPS is connected to the f branch of diplexer and transmits the output modulated-signal back to the BS through the antenna. The other four ports of SPS are connected to two pairs of open-ended coaxial line for sensing, as described previously. One pair senses the WUT while the other one with a known sample is used as a reference for calibration procedure at the receiver.

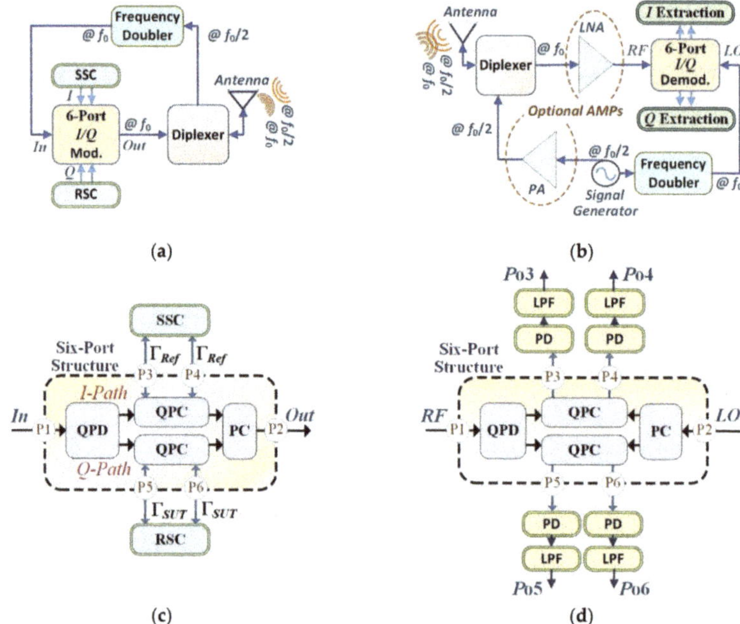

Figure 2. Functional block diagrams of system's sub-circuits: (**a**) The sensor node; (**b**) The base station; (**c**) The six-port sensor; (**d**) The six-port receiver.

The modified SPS as a sensor node uses a 90° hybrid coupler, two pairs of variable reflectors and one power combiner, as shown in Figure 2c. In the first stage, the input signal at port #1 (P_1) is quadrature divided between two branches, named by *I*- and *Q*-path. At each path, a pair of sensitive structures reflects the signal at reflection ports, i.e., P_3, P_4, P_5, and P_6, while the phase and amplitude of reflected signals change according to the WUT. The power combiner adds two reflected signals at the output port P_2. Considering the SPS as a linear circuit with ideal power combiner (equal power division with 0 degrees phase shift) and quadrature couplers (equal power division with 90 degrees phase shift), its scattering parameters are related as follows,

$$S_{31} = jS_{41} = -S_{32} = jS_{42} = jS_{51} = -S_{61} = -S_{52} = jS_{62},$$
$$\text{and } S_{mn} = S_{nm}, \tag{3}$$

where S_{mn} is the reflected power waves from port m due to the incident power waves at port n, for n and m from 1 to 6. Then, the reflection coefficient at the input (R_{11}) and transmission from input to output (T_{21}) of SPS can be represented as,

$$R_{11} = S_{31}\Gamma_3 S_{13} + S_{41}\Gamma_4 S_{14} + S_{51}\Gamma_5 S_{15} + S_{61}\Gamma_6 S_{16}$$
$$= S_{31}^2(\Gamma_3 - \Gamma_4) + S_{51}^2(\Gamma_5 - \Gamma_6), \tag{4}$$

$$T_{21} = S_{31}\Gamma_3 S_{23} + S_{41}\Gamma_4 S_{24} + S_{51}\Gamma_5 S_{25} + S_{61}\Gamma_6 S_{26}$$
$$= S_{31}^2(\Gamma_3 + \Gamma_4) - jS_{51}^2(\Gamma_5 + \Gamma_6). \tag{5}$$

Based on (3) and (4), the input reflection coefficient will be equal to zero ($R_{11} = 0$) if $\Gamma_{Ref} \triangleq \Gamma_3 = \Gamma_4$ and $\Gamma_{WUT} \triangleq \Gamma_5 = \Gamma_6$. Then, the normalized transmission coefficient from the input to the output port (T_N) is simplified to:

$$T_N \triangleq \frac{1}{2S_{31}^2} T_{21} = \Gamma_{Ref} + j\Gamma_{WUT}, \tag{6}$$

which is normalized to the known value of S_{31}. Hence, for a single tone input signal, the output signal is composed of two reflected components, i.e., Γ_{Ref} and $j\Gamma_{WUT}$, which are in a semi-orthogonal vector space and easy to separate at the receiver.

2.2. The Base Station

At the BS, as shown in Figure 2b, a signal generator provides the main signal at the frequency of $f/2$. An unequal power divider separates a low-power part of this signal for subsequent demodulation. A frequency doubler, which consists of a nonlinear element and its matching circuits, upconverts the frequency to f and feeds it to the input port of the SPS as a direct conversion receiver. Using the same signal source for modulation and demodulation makes the synchronization much easier as there is no frequency difference between the received and local oscillator (LO) signals at the receiver. The high-power part is passed to the $f/2$ branch of a diplexer which is connected to a dual-band transmitting at $f/2$ and receiving at f antenna. Therefore, the BS can propagate a single tone signal at the frequency of $f/2$. The other branch of diplexer separates the received signal at f and feeds it to the input port of SPS for detection. As there is no critical limitation on the power consumption of BS, the transmitted and received signals can be amplified by a power amplifier (PA) and a low noise amplifier (LNA), respectively, to increase the wireless coverage or improve the signal to noise ratio. In the SPS as a direct conversion receiver, various $90°$ phase shifted versions of received (RF) and local oscillator (LO) signals at the same frequency are combined, as shown in Figure 2d. Then, signals at the output port #3 through #6 are applied to four power detectors and low-pass filters to find the output powers P_{03}-P_{06}. The normalized coefficient between the (RF) and (LO) signals is defined by T_B, with real and imaginary parts of I_B and Q_B. In a lossless SPS, T_B can be calculated from the linear compositions of the output signals, $P_{03,...,06}$, as [28],

$$T_B \triangleq I_B + jQ_B = I_B = \frac{P_{04} - P_{03}}{2} + j\frac{P_{06} - P_{05}}{2}. \tag{7}$$

As in an ideal communication channel $T_B = T_N = (\Gamma_{Ref} + j\Gamma_{WUT})$, the value of Γ_{WUT} can be calculated from the measured T_B and known Γ_{Ref}. Based on this demodulated data, the pollution index of water and the quality of WUT can be estimated.

3. Experimental Verification

The proposed system is evaluated at the power and data transmit frequencies of 1.225 GHz and 2.45 GHz, respectively, as shown in Figure 3a. The circuits are fabricated with printed circuit technology on Rogers' RO4003 material with relative permittivity of 3.55, thickness of 0.508 mm, and loss tangent of 0.0027. The antennas is fabricated on Rogers' RT/duroid 5880 material with relative permittivity of 2.2, thickness of 0.508 mm, and loss tangent of 0.0009.

An R&S ZVA67 (Rohde & Schwarz: Munich, BY, Germany) vector network analyzers is used for reflection coefficient measurements. An ADF4350 (Analog Devices: Norwood, MA, USA) frequency synthesizer generates both frequencies at the base station. An AD7605 (Analog Devices: Norwood, MA, USA) data acquisition system converts received signals from analog to digital domain for demodulation in a personal computer. The output power of transmitter was +5 dBm and distance between the sensor node and base-station was selected as 1.5 m. The sensor is zero power but there is no critical limitation on the power consumption of base-station. Therefore, the transmitted and received signals can be amplified by a power amplifier (PA) and a low noise amplifier (LNA), respectively, to increase the wireless coverage or improve the signal to noise ratio.

The detailed schematics of all sub-circuits are presented in Figure 3 with the dimensions provided in Tables 1 and 2. A HSMS-2850 (Broadcom Inc.: San Jose, CA, USA) conventional diode and an open stub are used to generate and filter the second harmonic of the input signal in the output branch. A dual-band low-profile antennas [34] is designed to transmit and receive the frequencies of 1.225 GHz and 2.45 GHz. Figure 4 shows the implemented overall system, sensing node, receiver, diplexer, the combined structure of diplexer and frequency doubler, and dual-band antenna.

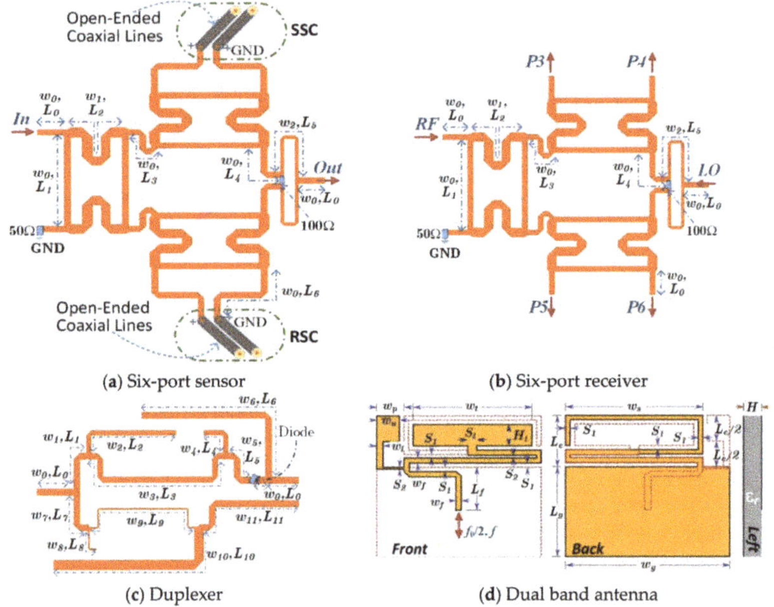

Figure 3. Detailed schematic of designed circuits: (**a**) The six-port sensor; (**b**) The six-port receiver; (**c**) The duplexer at sensor node including frequency doubler; (**d**) The dual band antenna.

Table 1. Six-Port Sensor and Demodulator Dimensions.

Parameter	(mm)	Parameter	(mm)
w_0	1.13	L_0	5.00
w_1	1.91	L_1	18.8
w_2	0.62	L_2	8.50
w_3	0.30	L_3	22.4
s	0.70	L_4	10.2

The measured parameters of various parts are presented in Figure 5. The SPS provides the acceptable transitions about −6 dB while its isolation and reflection coefficients are better than −10 dB, at the operating frequency of 2.45 GHz. The required phase shifts of 0° and 90° in a conventional SPS are also achieved, as shown in Figure 5a. The antenna response in Figure 5b shows that despite the small size, it can be used in both frequencies with the acceptable gains (more than 1.7 dBi). The diplexer has less than −0.5 dB loss in the pass bands and better than 15 dB isolation in the rejection bands for both branches of 1.225 GHz and 2.45 GHz, as seen in Figure 5c. The performance of frequency doubler in Figure 5d shows about 10 dB conversion loss from main to the second harmonic signals.

Table 2. Diplexer, Frequency Doubler, and Dual-Band Compact Antenna Dimensions.

Parameter	(mm)	Parameter	(mm)	Parameter	(mm)	Parameter	(mm)
w_0	1.13	L_0	5.00	w_1	1.13	L_1	7.00
w_2	0.85	L_2	18.8	w_3	1.02	L_3	30.3
w_4	0.85	L_4	7.20	w_5	1.13	L_5	4.80
w_6	1.13	L_6	32.6	w_7	1.13	L_7	7.00
w_8	0.3	L_8	4.40	w_9	0.25	L_9	4.3
w_{10}	1.70	L_{10}	31.2	w_{11}	1.13	L_{11}	20.3
W_t	36.5	W_p	10.1	S_t	2.525	W_u	8.67
H_t	9.1	W_l	1.11	H	0.508	W_g	62
S_2	0.47	L_g	111.67	S_1	1.22	W_f	2.225
W_s	53.3	L_f	29.67	ε_r	2.2	L_e	18.65

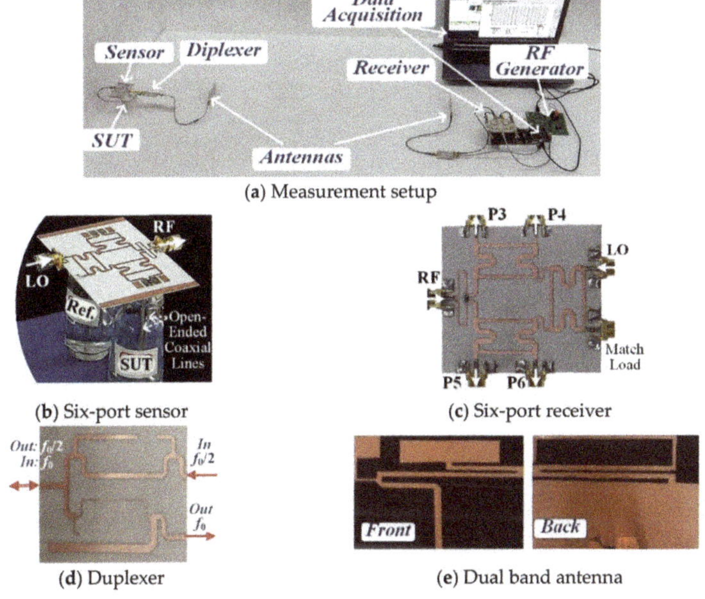

(**a**) Measurement setup

(**b**) Six-port sensor

(**c**) Six-port receiver

(**d**) Duplexer

(**e**) Dual band antenna

Figure 4. Fabricated water quality sensing system.

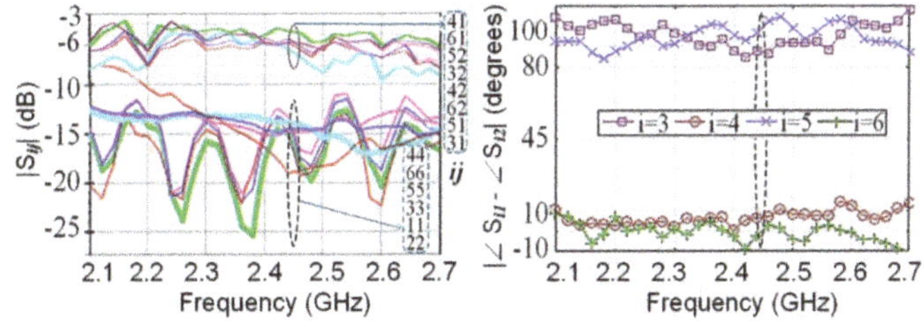

(**a**) Scattering parameters of Six-Port Structure (i = 3–6)

Figure 5. *Cont.*

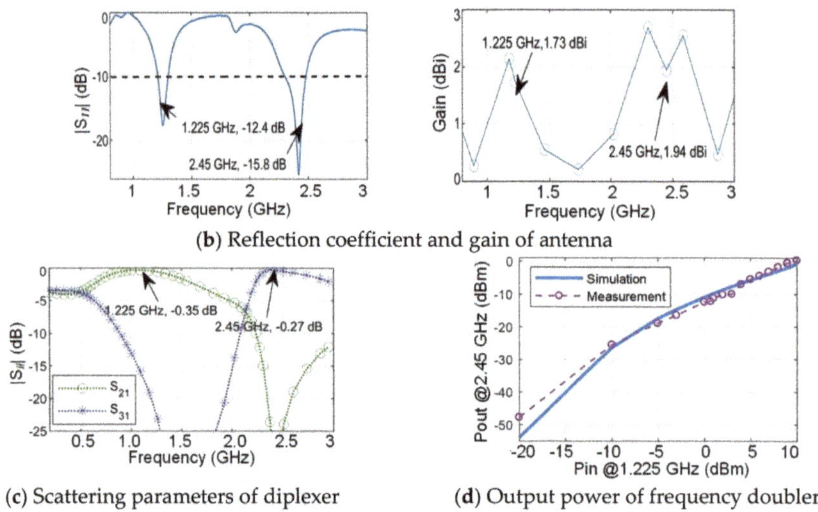

(b) Reflection coefficient and gain of antenna

(c) Scattering parameters of diplexer   **(d)** Output power of frequency doubler

Figure 5. Measurement results of sub-circuits.

To evaluate the sensor in the first step, the sensitive circuit has been tested to find its response to various samples which will be used as the reference to calculate concentrations of contaminant (CoC) in the water at the BS. The system is tested with three water samples with 5, 11, and 28 ppm of humic acid and for each sample the measurements were repeated 10 times. A commercial humic acid (Sigma-Aldrich, CAS no: 1415-93-6) was used in sample preparation. The amplitude and phase of Γ_{WUT} versus CoC are approximately linear, as can be seen in Figure 6a,b. These curves can be used at the BS to extract the CoC from the calculated Γ_R.

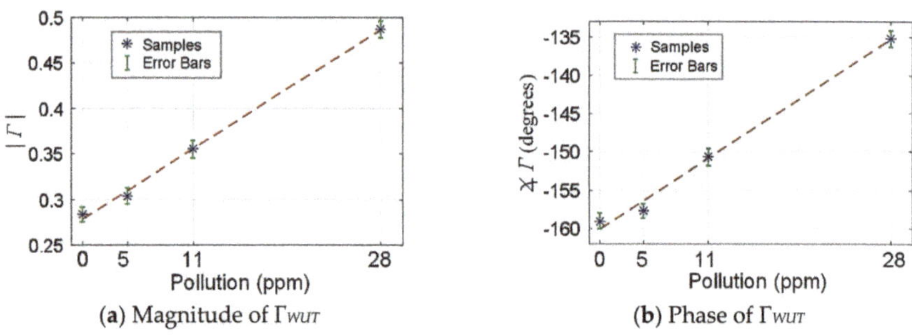

(a) Magnitude of Γ_{WUT} **(b)** Phase of Γ_{WUT}

Figure 6. Measurement results of Γ_{WUT} versus concentrations of pollution (ppm).

The calculated constellation at the BS for all samples and 10 times measurements are presented in Figure 7. All data are normalized to a reference case which is obtained by using the pure water as WUT. Using a nonlinear interpolation, we can fit a curve to the measurement points. The errors of demodulated points, $(I, Q)_{Dem}$, with the points on the fitted curve, $(I, Q)_{Fit}$, can be defined as,

$$Error \triangleq \frac{\sqrt{(I_{Dem} - I_{Fit})^2 + (Q_{Dem} - Q_{Fit})^2}}{\sqrt{I_{Fit}^2 + Q_{Fit}^2}} \times 100\%, \tag{8}$$

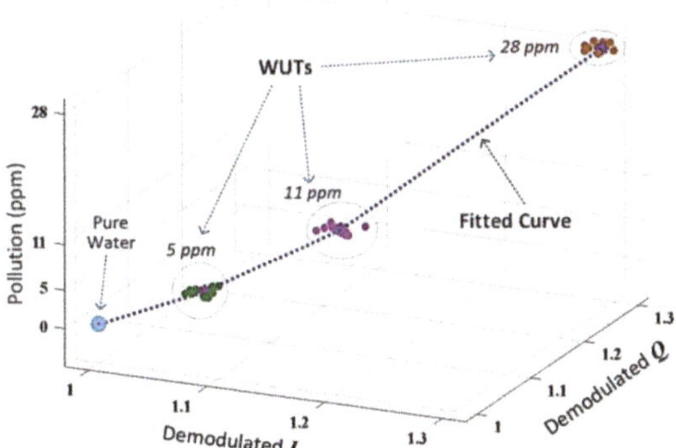

Figure 7. Demodulated data at the receiver (I: real part, Q: imaginary part).

In the above measurements, errors are less than 4% for a laboratory test environment using a +5 dBm transmitter at 1.225 GHz and about 1.5 m wireless range. Undoubtedly, this error depends on the propagation channel conditions, such as propagation power, distance between transmitter and receiver, and environmental noises.

In a real scenario, first, two similar volume of pure water are used as the test and the reference samples. This test gives us a reference node which will be mapped to (1,1,0). Then, the test ports will be put inside the WUT samples while the reference ports remain in the pure water. By using (7), demodulated I and Q will be extracted from the received signal and normalized to the reference values. The demodulated constellation point $(I, Q)_{Dem}$ will be mapped to Figure 7 and the concentration of contaminant can be determined. In a water treatment system, a pre-defined level of pollution is considered for water quality assessment and the proportional limit point, $(I, Q)_{Lim}$, can be determined for that level of pollution from the fitted curve. Then, the base station can simply compare $(I, Q)_{Dem}$ with $(I, Q)_{Lim}$ and find if the water quality is acceptable or not. Therefore, the system provides a simple real-time assessment without local power sources at the sensor node. This is true that some water quality assessment systems can provide higher wireless ranges and various pollution detection but they need very long processing times and periodic battery maintenances at the sensor nodes.

4. Conclusions

This paper proposed a zero-power direct conversion sensor. The six-port structure was used at the node as a sensing data modulator and at the base station as the IQ data demodulator. The input signal of this sensor was generated by a passive frequency doubler from a pure wave received from the BS at $f/2$. A dual band antenna was used as the receiver of power-up signal at $f/2$ and transmitter of modulated signal at f. As an example for validation, a system is fabricated at f = 2.45 GHz and its results for various polluted water samples have been presented. The ability of sensing and directly transmitting its data at the RF frequencies, without local power source and signal processing at the node, expand applications of the proposed system as sensor nodes in real-time water quality assessment with low complexity, power consumption, and cost. In this paper, the system was designed and evaluated by using the conventional microwave structures and inexpensive printed circuit board (PCB) technology. In the next step, the sensor nodes have been optimized and miniaturized for mass production and WSN applications by using compact building blocks and integrated circuit (IC) technologies. Moreover, the application can be extended to human body sensors for wireless measurement of biological tissues [35].

Author Contributions: R.M. conceived design and experiments. M.M.H. assisted in experiments. B.L. and P.M. participated in developing approach and methodology. B.K. and M.S. prepared the samples and assisted with discussion and interpretation of results. All authors reviewed the manuscript.

Funding: This research was funded by NSERC-AITF industrial research chair program.

Conflicts of Interest: The authors declare no conflicts of interest.

Abbreviations

QPD	Quadrature Power Divider
QPC	Quadrature Power Coupler
PC	Power Combiner
PD	Power Detector
LPF	Low Pass Filter
RSC	Reference Sensitive Circuits
SSC	Sample Sensitive Circuits

References

1. World Economic Forum. *The Global Risks Report 2017*; World Economic Forum: Geneva, Switzerland, 2017.
2. Allwood, G.; Wild, G.; Hinckley, S. Fiber bragg grating sensors for mainstream industrial processes. *Electronics* **2017**, *6*, 92. [CrossRef]
3. Khorshidi, B.; Thundat, T.; Fleck, B.A.; Sadrzadeh, M. A novel approach toward fabrication of high performance thin film composite polyamide membranes. *Sci. Rep.* **2016**, *6*, 22069. [CrossRef] [PubMed]
4. Park, S.J.; Hong, J.T.; Choi, S.J.; Kim, H.S.; Park, W.K.; Han, S.T.; Park, J.Y.; Lee, S.; Kim, D.S.; Ahn, Y.H. Detection of microorganisms using terahertz metamaterials. *Sci. Rep.* **2014**, *4*, 4988. [CrossRef] [PubMed]
5. Højris, B.; Christensen, S.C.B.; Albrechtsen, H.-J.; Smith, C.; Dahlqvist, M. A novel, optical, on-line bacteria sensor for monitoring drinking water quality. *Sci. Rep.* **2016**, *6*, 23935. [CrossRef] [PubMed]
6. Culler, D.E.; Mulder, H. Smart sensors to network the world. *Sci. Am.* **2004**, *290*, 84–91. [CrossRef] [PubMed]
7. Tucker, R.; Ruffini, M.; Valcarenghi, L.; Campelo, D.R.; Simeonidou, D.; Du, L.; Marinescu, M.-C.; Middleton, C.; Yin, S.; Forde, T. Connected OFCity: Technology innovations for a smart city project. *IEEE/OSA J. Opt. Commun. Networking* **2017**, *9*, A245–A255. [CrossRef]
8. Bouk, S.H.; Ahmed, S.H.; Kim, D.; Song, H. Named-data-networking-based ITS for smart cities. *IEEE Commun. Mag.* **2017**, *55*, 105–111. [CrossRef]
9. Li, M.; Lin, H.-J. Design and implementation of smart home control systems based on wireless sensor networks and power line communications. *IEEE Trans. Ind. Electron.* **2015**, *62*, 4430–4442. [CrossRef]
10. Im, H.; Lee, S.; Naqi, M.; Lee, C.; Kim, S. Flexible PI-Based Plant Drought Stress Sensor for Real-Time Monitoring System in Smart Farm. *Electronics* **2018**, *7*, 114. [CrossRef]
11. Mirzavand, R.; Honari, M.M.; Mousavi, P. High-Resolution Balanced Microwave Material Sensor with Extended Dielectric Range. *IEEE Trans. Ind. Electron.* **2017**, *64*, 1552–1560. [CrossRef]
12. Mirzavand, R.; Honari, M.M.; Mousavi, P. High-Resolution Dielectric Sensor Based on Injection-Locked Oscillators. *IEEE Sens. J.* **2017**, *18*, 141–148. [CrossRef]
13. Donelli, M.; Manekiya, M. Development of Environmental Long Range RFID Sensors Based on the Modulated Scattering Technique. *Electronics* **2018**, *7*, 106. [CrossRef]
14. Visser, H.J.; Vullers, R.J.M. RF energy harvesting and transport for wireless sensor network applications: Principles and requirements. *Proc. IEEE* **2013**, *101*, 1410–1423. [CrossRef]
15. Huang, H.; Chen, P.-Y.; Hung, C.-H.; Gharpurey, R.; Akinwande, D. A zero power harmonic transponder sensor for ubiquitous wireless μL liquid-volume monitoring. *Sci. Rep.* **2016**, *6*, 18795. [CrossRef] [PubMed]
16. Zhang, J.; Tian, G.Y.; Marindra, A.M.J.; Sunny, A.I.; Zhao, A.B. A review of passive RFID tag antenna-based sensors and systems for structural health monitoring applications. *Sensors* **2017**, *17*, 265. [CrossRef] [PubMed]
17. Linz, S.; Oesterle, F.; Talai, A.; Lindner, S.; Mann, S.; Barbon, F.; Weigel, R.; Koelpin, A. 100 GHz reflectometer for sensitivity analysis of MEMS sensors comprising an intermediate frequency six-port receiver. In Proceedings of the 2015 IEEE Topical Conference on Wireless Sensors and Sensor Networks (WiSNet), San Diego, CA, USA, 25–28 January 2015.
18. Vinci, G.; Koelpin, A. Progress of six-port technology for industrial radar applications. In Proceedings of the 2016 IEEE Topical Conference on Wireless Sensors and Sensor Networks (WiSNet), Austin, TX, USA, 24–27 January 2016.

19. Mann, S.; Linz, S.; Erhardt, S.; Lindner, S.; Lurz, F.; Maune, H.; Weigel, R.; Koelpin, A. Differential measuring dual six-port concept and antenna design for an inline foil thickness sensor. In Proceedings of the 2016 German Microwave Conference (GeMiC), Bochum, Germany, 14–16 March 2016.
20. Kuo, H.-C.; Lin, C.-C.; Yu, C.-H.; Lo, P.-H.; Lyu, J.-Y.; Chou, C.-C.; Chuang, H.-R. A fully integrated 60-GHz CMOS direct-conversion Doppler radar RF sensor with clutter canceller for single-antenna noncontact human vital-signs detection. *IEEE Trans. Microwave Theory Tech.* **2016**, *64*, 1018–1028. [CrossRef]
21. Von der Mark, S.; Huber, M.; Boeck, G. 24 GHz direct conversion transceiver for sensor networks. In Proceedings of the 2007 IEEE Wireless Communications and Networking Conference, Kowloon, China, 11–15 March 2007.
22. Cook, B.S.; Vyas, R.; Kim, S.; Thai, T.; Le, T.; Traille, A.; Aubert, H.; Tentzeris, M.M. RFID-based sensors for zero-power autonomous wireless sensor networks. *IEEE Sens. J.* **2014**, *14*, 2419–2431. [CrossRef]
23. Adhikary, M.; Biswas, A.; Akhtar, M.J. Active Integrated Antenna Based Permittivity Sensing Tag. *IEEE Sens. Let.* **2017**, *1*, 1–4. [CrossRef]
24. Lobato-Morales, H.; Corona-Chavez, A.; Olvera-Cervantes, J.L.; Chávez-Pérez, R.A.; Medina-Monroy, J.L. Wireless sensing of complex dielectric permittivity of liquids based on the RFID. *IEEE Trans. Microwave Theory Tech.* **2014**, *62*, 2160–2167. [CrossRef]
25. Bouaziz, S.; Chebila, F.; Traille, A.; Pons, P.; Aubert, H.; Tentzeris, M. Novel micro-fluidic structures for wireless passive temperature telemetry medical systems using radar interrogation techniques in Ka-band. *IEEE Antennas Wirel. Propag. Lett.* **2012**, *11*, 1706–1709. [CrossRef]
26. Cole, A.J.; Young, P.R. Chipless Liquid Sensing Using a Slotted Cylindrical Resonator. *IEEE Sens. J.* **2017**, *18*, 149–156. [CrossRef]
27. Li, J.; Bosisio, R.G.; Wu, K. Computer and measurement simulation of a new digital receiver operating directly at millimeter-wave frequencies. *IEEE Trans. Microwave Theory Tech.* **1995**, *43*, 2766–2772. [CrossRef]
28. Mirzavand, R.; Mohammadi, A.; Abdipour, A. Low-cost implementation of broadband microwave receivers in Ka-band using multiport structures. *IET Microwaves Antennas Propag.* **2009**, *3*, 483–491. [CrossRef]
29. Mirzavand, R.; Mohammadi, A.; Ghannouchi, F.M. Five-port microwave receiver architectures and applications. *IEEE Commun. Mag.* **2010**, *48*, 30–36. [CrossRef]
30. Beikmirza, M.R.; Mohammadi, A.; Mirzavand, R. Power amplifier linearisation using digital predistortion and multi-port techniques. *IET Sci. Meas. Technol.* **2016**, *10*, 467–476. [CrossRef]
31. Mirzavand, R.; Honari, M.M.; Mousavi, P. N-ZERO direct conversion wireless sensor based on six-port structures. In Proceedings of the 2017 IEEE MTT-S International Microwave Symposium (IMS), Honolulu, HI, USA, 4–9 June 2017.
32. Mirzavand, R.; Honari, M.M.; Mousavi, P. Direct-conversion sensor for wireless sensing networks. *IEEE Trans. Ind. Electron.* **2017**, *64*, 9675–9682. [CrossRef]
33. Berube, D.; Ghannouchi, F.M.; Savard, P. A comparative study of four open-ended coaxial probe models for permittivity measurements of lossy dielectric/biological materials at microwave frequencies. *IEEE Trans. Microwave Theory Tech.* **1996**, *44*, 1928–1934. [CrossRef]
34. Li, R.; Pan, B.; Laskar, J.; Tentzeris, M.M. A Novel Low-Profile Broadband Dual-Frequency Planar Antenna for Wireless Handsets. *IEEE Trans. Antennas Propag.* **2008**, *56*, 1155–1162. [CrossRef]
35. La Gioia, A.; Porter, E.; Merunka, I.; Shahzad, A.; Salahuddin, S.; Jones, M.; O'Halloran, M. Open-Ended Coaxial Probe Technique for Dielectric Measurement of Biological Tissues: Challenges and Common Practices. *Diagnostics* **2018**, *8*, 40. [CrossRef] [PubMed]

Article

Evolution of Wireless Sensor Network for Air Quality Measurements

Patricia Arroyo, Jesús Lozano * and José Ignacio Suárez

Industrial Engineering School, University of Extremadura, 06071 Badajoz, Spain; parroyoz@unex.es (P.A.); jmarcelo@unex.es (J.I.S.)
* Correspondence: jesuslozano@unex.es; Tel.: +34-924-289-300

Received: 30 October 2018; Accepted: 19 November 2018; Published: 22 November 2018

Abstract: This study addresses the development of a wireless gas sensor network with low cost, small size, and low consumption nodes for environmental applications and air quality detection. Throughout the article, the evolution of the design and development of the system is presented, describing four designed prototypes. The final proposed prototype node has the capacity to connect up to four metal oxide (MOX) gas sensors, and has high autonomy thanks to the use of solar panels, as well as having an indirect sampling system and a small size. ZigBee protocol is used to transmit data wirelessly to a self-developed data cloud. The discrimination capacity of the device was checked with the volatile organic compounds benzene, toluene, ethylbenzene, and xylene (BTEX). An improvement of the system was achieved to obtain optimal success rates in the classification stage with the final prototype. Data processing was carried out using techniques of pattern recognition and artificial intelligence, such as radial basis networks and principal component analysis (PCA).

Keywords: chemical sensors; wireless sensor network; cloud computing; air quality

---

1. Introduction

In most cities, air quality improved (significantly) over the past decades. Visible air pollution (smoke, dust, and smog) disappeared from many cities due to local, national, and European initiatives. However, the current air quality still affects the health of the population. According to the World Health Organization (WHO), 1.7 million children die as a result of contaminated environments (indoor and outdoor) [1]. On the other hand, the Health Effect Institute concludes from its studies that long-term exposure to air pollution in 2016 was responsible for the deaths of 6.1 million people due to strokes, heart attacks, lung diseases, and lung cancer [2]. Air quality is, therefore, a problem common to almost all major cities.

Volatile organic compounds (VOCs) are among the main pollutants in the atmosphere. These are organic compounds that evaporate or sublimate at room temperature and pressure, and are derived from products such as fuels and solvents from anthropogenic and natural sources. These compounds are directly associated with chronic effects on health, as well as the formation of ozone and mists. The health effects of VOCs depend on the type of component, although benzene (C_6H_6) is the most relevant compound, since it is considered a potent human carcinogen by the International Agency for Research on Cancer (IARC). Specifically, it causes acute myeloid leukemia, and there is some evidence that it may cause lymphocytic leukemia [3]. In addition, like toluene ($C_6H_5CH_3$), it is a precursor pollutant of ozone and secondary organic aerosols.

Because of the great global damage caused by the presence of pollutants in the atmosphere, many organizations and countries around the world established monitoring systems that provide the data needed to improve air quality. While, for the vast majority of these observations, the established analytical reference methods continue to be used, miniaturization led to a growth in the prominence of a generation of low-cost devices. Such devices are also smaller, lighter, and have a lower power consumption. Thanks to their appearance, an increase in the spatial density of the measurements was achieved, even though they are less precise devices than the reference systems. Although they are not a direct substitute for reference instruments, they are a complementary source of information on air quality to validate atmospheric models and predictions at high temporal and spatial resolution [4]. This potential increase in the spatial density of the measurements is mainly achieved using sensor networks.

The wireless sensor network (WSN) is a growing technology that is applied in many different monitoring situations [5]. WSNs are composed of small devices called nodes that collect information from the environment with sensors, process it, and communicate wirelessly with other nodes in the network. The main fields in which the WSNs are used include (according to Reference [6]) military and crime prevention, health, environment, industry and agriculture, and urbanization and infrastructure. However, this technology offers significant benefits especially in applications where large spaces must be covered, such as in the measurement of air quality. As a result, there are numerous related works in this field, many of which were recently collected by some authors [7,8]. Nevertheless, WSNs have a limited lifespan due to energy consumption. Therefore, much of the current and future research focuses on the use of different techniques in order to maximize lifetime [9]. Among them are the architectures of tiered systems, medium access control (MAC) protocols of low energy consumption, "duty-cycle" strategies, and the redundant placement of nodes to ensure coverage. As of yet, these techniques only manage to optimize and adapt energy consumption to maximize battery life of the sensor node. However, it is also worth highlighting energy-harvesting techniques, which use renewable energy sources to address the problem, and can be an important step forward in achieving the continuous operation of the WSNs over time [10].

Within the different technologies and standards of WSN, ZigBee stands out for applications of low cost, low consumption, and low data rate [11]. ZigBee is a model that defines a set of communication protocols that overlaps the IEEE.802.15.4 [12,13] specification. In addition, devices that use this communication protocol allow working in power-saving mode, thereby further reducing the consumption of the system. Consequently, this communication protocol was used in numerous applications related to air quality [14–16].

Also noteworthy is the need for quick access from anywhere to the information of the WSN nodes. To this end, Internet of things (IoT) and cloud computing can be used [17]. Cloud computing refers to internet servers responsible for responding to requests at any time. On the other hand, the Internet of things technology is the interconnection of a network of objects through the internet. These two technologies are complementary: IoT can benefit from the unlimited storage and communication offered by cloud technology, while cloud computing can extend its reach to the "real world" with IoT. The integration of these technologies with the WSN was already carried out in some works due to its great utility [18–20].

In regards to low-cost gas sensors, there are different technologies available, mainly including resistive sensors, electrochemical sensors, nondispersive infrared (NDIR) detectors, absorption sensors, and photoionization detectors (PIDs) [21]. Resistive metal oxide (MOX) gas sensors are one of the most used due to their low cost, low consumption, lightweight nature, and small size. In addition, MOX sensors react with a large number of gases and have a very quick response time. Because of this versatility, they are very useful in various fields, especially in the environmental monitoring and detection of pollutants [22,23].

The results presented in this work study the discrimination capacity of the system for benzene, toluene, ethylbenzene, and xylene (BTEX) compounds. Other methods and technologies were previously used for this purpose. The most common method for the detection of these VOCs is gas chromatography/mass spectrometry [24–27]. These systems are of high precision and selectivity. However, they are expensive and due to the large size and weight of the equipment; as such, their field detection capacity is limited. In addition, although these methods are very useful for low-level detection, they require a lot of time due to sample transport, analyte desorption, preconcentration, and data transmission. Numerous authors also used devices based on colorimetric methods [28]. However, although they are portable, they do not allow the creation of a spatial matrix of numerous nodes that allows studying the presence of BTEX at different points.

Notably, it is usually necessary to apply data processing techniques in the use of devices with MOX gas sensors. The main used pattern recognition techniques in the field of gas detection were summarized in numerous articles in recent years [29,30].

Therefore, in this work a low-cost system was developed for the measurement of air quality. Throughout the article, the architecture and the evolution in the development of the electronic and communication system are described.

In this work, the following contributions are presented:

- Design and development of a wireless gas sensor network for low-cost air quality measurements, with low size and low consumption.
- Description of the different prototypes corresponding to the evolution of the designed system across several years and projects: electronics and communication.
- Use of artificial neural networks for processing the collected data.
- The discrimination capability of the module was tested with BTEX volatile compounds. These tests also allowed studying the evolution of system operation.

2. Materials and Methods

This paper describes the development of a wireless sensor network (WSN) for gas sensors to detect air quality. During the evolution of the project, four different prototypes of the device were developed: prototype version 1 (PV1) [31], prototype version 2 (PV2), prototype version 3 (PV3) [32], and prototype version 4 (PV4). In general, the scheme of the different designs is similar (shown in Figure 1). The corresponding energy source in each case powers the entire device through different voltage converters. Firstly, an optional pumping system carries the gas samples to the sensors cell. These sensors change their electrical resistance in the presence of the different gaseous compounds, which is translated into a voltage change. The signal is conditioned and filtered so that it can be received by the chosen radio frequency (RF) module. This module is responsible for wirelessly sending all the information received to a central station, where the data processing can be performed to obtain the final results in terms of concentration prediction or classification of gas. On the other hand, the RF module is also responsible, in some cases, for controlling the pump system and the sensor heaters (necessary for proper operation of gas sensors).

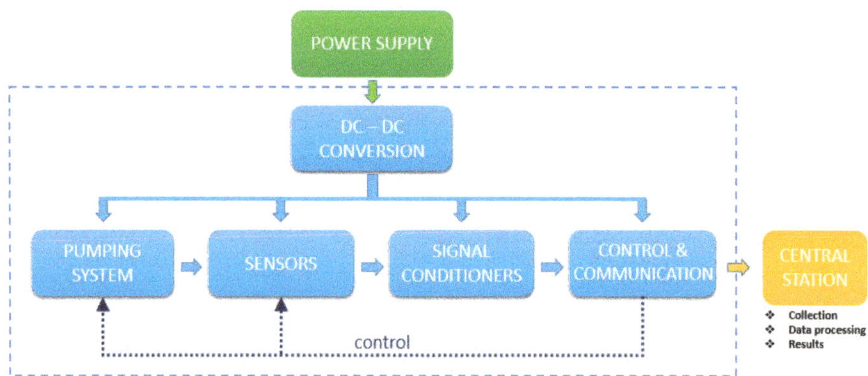

Figure 1. Block diagram of each node of the WSN.

Throughout the evolution of the system, four different prototypes were designed and developed, depending on the context of the application and also improving on the previous ones. The first version was a homemade prototype created to study the operation of ZigBee communication and gas sensors. The second system incorporated improvements in system autonomy and a greater versatility for using different types of sensors. The third one included changes in communication and data acquisition (incorporating the use of a data cloud), and improved the adaptation of the sensors signals and their stability. Finally, the last system is the most optimized, incorporating solar power and greater autonomy, greater adaptation and control of the sensors, and improvements in the acquisition and processing of data.

2.1. Evolution of Power Supply

2.1.1. Battery Chargers

The first prototype (PV1) was powered by a 9-V nickel metal hydride battery with a capacity of 155 mAh that allowed portability. However, an autonomy of more than 1.5 h was not achieved (3.5 h while maintaining the RF module in low-consumption mode in measurements with low sampling frequency, ≤ 1 sample per hour). For this reason, in PV2 and PV3, a lithium-ion battery of 3.7 V and 1350 mAh was incorporated. In addition, in PV2, a charger circuit was also included to facilitate charging through an external jack connector. The core of this circuit was the MCP73113/4 chip (Microchip, Chandler, AZ, USA), an integrated lithium-ion battery charge management controller with overvoltage protection. In particular, it provides specific charging algorithms for the batteries and, thus, achieves an optimal and safe capacity in the shortest possible charging time. The load current is programmed from the value of an external resistor connected to a 10-pin chip. In this case, a limiting value of 1000 mA was chosen (Figure 2).

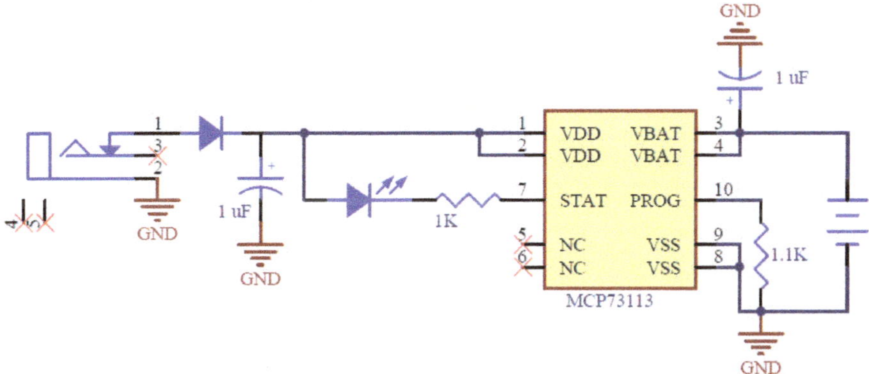

Figure 2. Electrical diagram of battery charging system corresponding to prototype version 2 (PV2).

This circuit was eliminated in the third prototype because the location where it was going to be used had no external source, thus allowing the optimization of the size of the PCB (Printed Circuit Board).

The last and current prototype (PV4) includes a 3.7-V and 2050-mAh battery that, together with a solar panel, greatly improves the autonomy of the system. For this purpose, the LT3652 charger integrated circuit (Linear Technology, Milpitas, CA, USA), optimized for solar panel applications, is used (Figure 3). This circuit keeps the solar panel at the maximum output power and the charging current is modified according to the battery state at each moment. In addition, it has temperature protection and a timer.

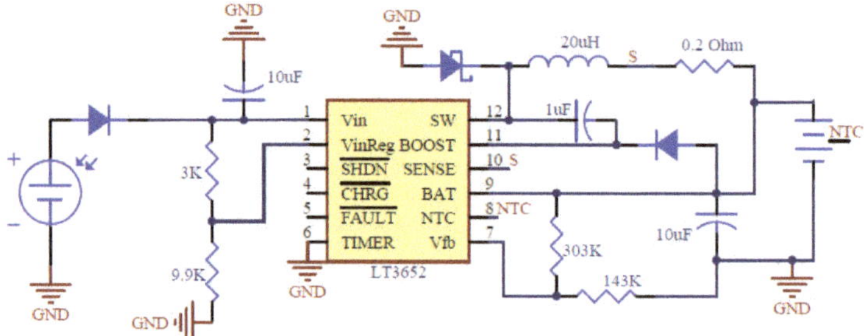

Figure 3. Electrical diagram of battery charging system from solar panels corresponding to PV4.

2.1.2. Voltage Converters

With respect to the voltage transformation, different converters were used in the different versions of the device. In PV1, linear regulators with up to 250 mA of 3.3 V (for the XBee module) and 5 V (for the sensors) were used. PV2 had an adjustable and disconnectable step-up converter for the sensors, since the battery voltage was changed from 9 V to 3.7 V. This was replaced by two direct current (DC)–DC converters with fixed output voltage (5 V) in PV3 and PV4. This change was due to the high instability in the voltage that distorted the functioning of the sensors. Both converters have different functions: one is used to power the pumping system (pump and electrovalve), while the other allows powering the sensor devices (heating resistor and sensor) more accurately and efficiently.

Figure 4 shows the electrical scheme in the case of PV4. It shows that the step-up DC–DC converter NCP1402 (ON Semiconductor, Phoenix, AZ, USA), capable of providing 200 mA, was used to power the pumping system (5V_P); the high efficiency step-up DC–DC converter LTC3525-5 (Linear Technology, Milpitas, CA, USA), capable of supplying 400 mA at the output, was used to power the sensors (5V_S); and the step-down DC–DC converter LM3671MF-3.3 (Texas Instruments, Dallas, TX, USA) was used to power the XBee communication module (3.3 V).

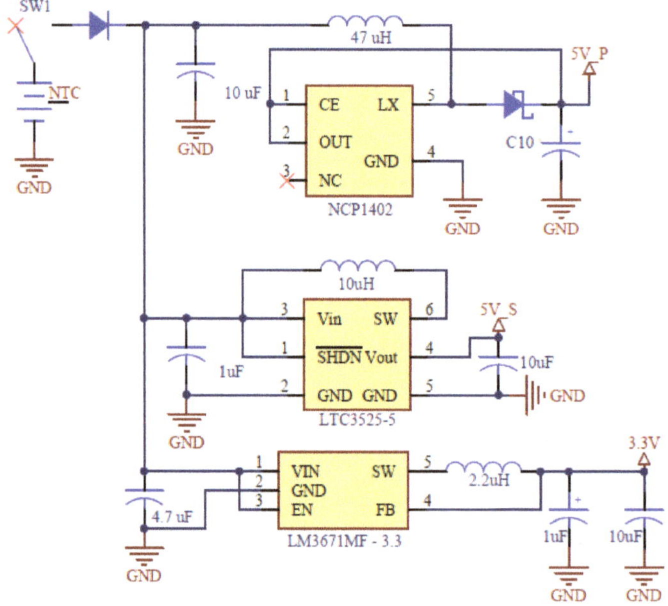

Figure 4. Electrical diagram of voltage conversion corresponding to PV4.

2.2. Sensors and Evolution of Signal Conditioning

2.2.1. Gas Sensors

All sensors used in this work are commercial resistive gas sensors. Specifically, they are semiconductor metal oxide (MOX) sensors whose electrical conductivities are modulated as a result of a reaction between the semiconductor and the gases in the atmosphere. These types of sensors need to be heated in a localized and uniform way or using a pulsed mode between 200 and 450 °C to keep them at an optimum temperature for gas detection [33,34]. It is necessary to carefully control the temperature because the sensitivity of the sensor is strongly dependent on it. Therefore, such sensors include an integrated heating element. The pulsed-temperature operating mode [35] consists of using short heating or cooling pulses from a reference temperature (ambient, high, or intermediate temperature). This mode of operation promotes transient chemical reactions.

The equivalent circuit for these sensors is composed of heating resistance (R_H) and a sensor resistance (R_S) components. Figure 5 shows the general circuit recommended by the manufacturers, where a heating voltage (V_H) is applied to R_H and a supply voltage (V_{CC}) to R_S. In addition, a load resistance (R_L) is used to obtain an output voltage (V_S), which depends on the following equation:

$$V_S = (V_{CC} \times R_L)/(R_S + R_L). \tag{1}$$

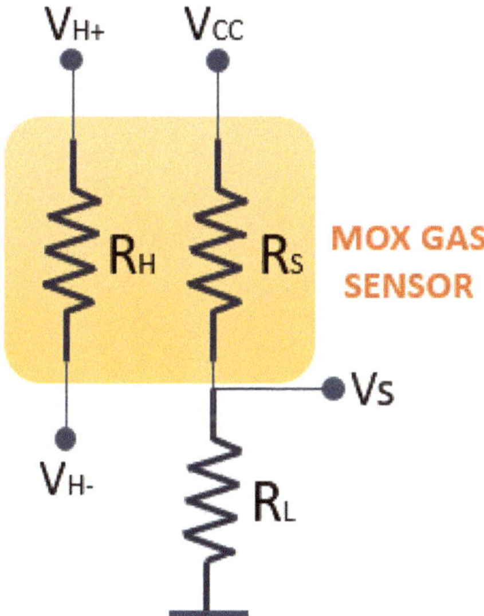

Figure 5. Equivalent circuit for MOX sensors.

2.2.2. Signal Conditioning Circuits

Regarding the conditioning circuit of the sensor signal, PV1 was only composed of the load resistor together with a capacitor to reduce electromagnetic noise and provide low impedance to the analog input of the XBee communication module. In the second and third prototypes, a voltage follower was added to avoid the loading effect. Furthermore, in the second prototype, a variable resistor was used as load resistance (seeking more versatility of the system). However, because it destabilized the system, a fixed resistor was again used in the third version. Finally, the final prototype added the ability to amplify the signal for applications with low-signal sensors.

On the other hand, the power circuits of the heating resistance of the sensors also evolved. In the first device, a voltage of 5 V was directly applied to the heating resistor. Then, a variable resistor was added, since not all the sensors needed the same power for proper operation. In the third version, this variable resistor was replaced by a fixed one (as in the case of the conditioning circuit for the sensor signal), and the heating element activation and deactivation functionality was incorporated using a digital output of the XBee module and a bipolar transistor. Thus, it managed to reduce consumption when sensors were not necessarily working. Finally, PV4 added a heater power control through a PWM (Pulse-Width Modulation) output and a MOSFET transistor, thereby achieving the possibility of modifying the operating temperatures of the gas sensors and of using the pulsed-temperature operating mode.

Figure 6 shows the final electrical diagram of the sensor signal conditioning and of the heating power control in PV4. RH corresponds to the heating resistance, R3 is the resistor placed in series to limit the maximum current in RH, Rg is the gate resistor, VS is the output voltage of the gas sensor, R2 and R1 are the resistors corresponding to the amplification circuit of the signal, RS is the resistance of the sensor, RL the load resistor corresponding to the sensor, and VA is the output voltage of the amplifier stage, and the input to the analog/digital converter of the XBee module.

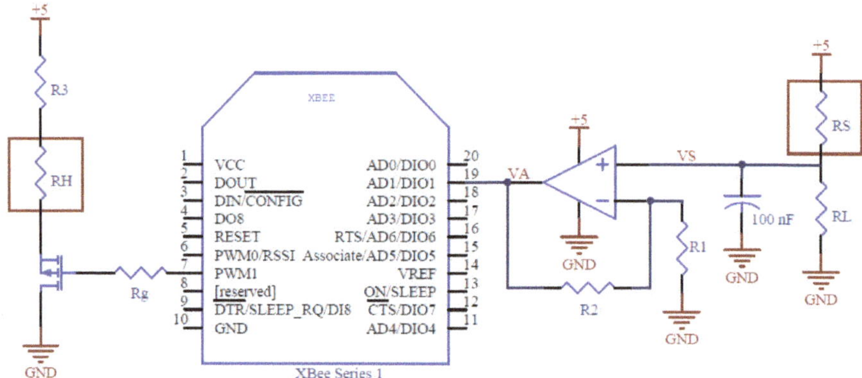

Figure 6. Electrical diagram of the sensor signal conditioning circuits and of the control of the heating power in PV4.

According to this, the input voltage in the XBee module is defined by the following equation (corresponding to the non-inverting amplifier):

$$VA = (1 + R2/R1) \times VS. \tag{2}$$

2.3. Sampling System

The sampling system takes a representative sample of the air to be analyzed, which is carried to the sensor cell. From the second prototype onward, the sampling system included a pump and an electrovalve in the sensor nodes in order to be connected to the system and to control the headspace from liquid samples for doing several measurements in the laboratory. In this way, it was possible to switch between a reference gas and a target gas and lead it to the sensor cell. For this purpose, a PWM output was used for adjusting pump speed, and a digital output was used for controlling the electrovalve state. In the first case, a MOSFET transistor and a gate resistor were used, while, in the second case, a bipolar transistor and the corresponding base resistor were used (Figure 7).

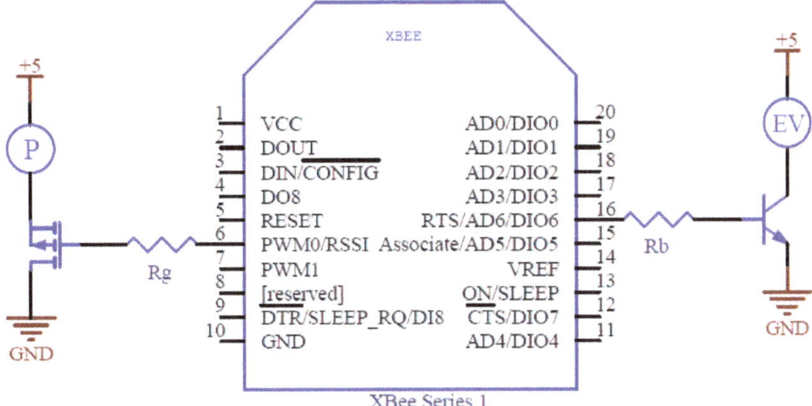

Figure 7. Electrical diagram of the activation circuits of the pump and the electrovalve (PV2, PV3, and PV4).

2.4. RF Module (XBee) and Evolution of Wireless Communication

The wireless communication devices used were the XBee radio frequency modules [36], which work in the 2.4-GHz band and with the IEEE 802.15.4 communication protocol. These are developed by Digi International (Minnetonka, MN, USA), and allow the creation of ZigBee networks (oriented to systems of low data transfer and consumption). They also incorporate a microcontroller (M9S08GT60, Freescale, Austin, TX, USA) to control all other peripherals. The module has seven ports configurable as digital inputs/outputs or analog inputs, along with two more digital inputs and outputs, and two PWM outputs.

In the first and second prototypes developed in this work (PV1 and PV2), the communication network was formed by the sensor nodes and a coordinator node responsible for receiving information from all others. To implement this coordinator node, a commercial interface card was used to communicate the XBee module with a computer via universal serial bus (USB). For receiving data and for configuration and monitoring of the entire network, an application was developed in LabVIEW. Then, data were stored on the computer for further processing.

In PV3, as before, the network consisted of some sensor nodes responsible for receiving the information and sending it, following the ZigBee protocol. However, in this case, the network coordinator node was the gateway "ConnectPort X4" (Digi, Minnetonka, MN, USA). It was connected to the internet via ethernet, and was responsible for submitting the information collected by the sensor nodes to the commercial cloud "Device Cloud" from Digi, where it is stored in XML format.

For programming, the "ConnectPort X" gateways offer a built-in Python® engine, providing a powerful open-source software tool to develop custom applications that run on the gateway. In this study, several Python® applications were developed for controlling the network. Among them, two stand out, which allow the information received by the nodes to be separated and pre-processed and then sent and stored in the data cloud. The difference between these two applications is that one was designed for laboratory measurements and, therefore, controls the pump and the electrovalve for switching between a reference gas and the target gas. The other application was designed for field applications, with an uncontrolled gas inlet to the sensor cell.

Finally, in the latest version, a self-developed data cloud was created in order to receive data from the sensor network and to provide storage services, classification, and requests.

2.5. Summary of Evolution of Prototypes

Table 1 shows the different main characteristics of each of the developed versions of the wireless sensor network for air quality measurements. It specifies the different sizes, the maximum and minimum consumption, and the autonomy, whether the gas sensors were integrated within the node or were connectable from an external PCB, as well as the tools used to receive, store, and process the collected data by the sensor nodes, whether they included a connection and control capacity for the pumping system, and the main features of improvement with respect to the previous version. The evolution was geared toward greater autonomy, smaller size, and greater flexibility and versatility.

Table 1. Main characteristics of each of the prototype versions (PVs) designed.

	PV1	PV2	PV3	PV4
SIZE	91 × 59 mm	68 × 47 mm	69 × 36 mm	60 × 40 mm
CONSUMPTION	45 to 100 mA	205 to 355 mA	196 to 355 mA	104 to 270 mA
AUTONOMY	1.5 to 3.4 h	3.6 to 6.4 h	3.6 to 6.7 h	7.59 h to months
POWER	9 V NiMH battery	3.7 V Li-ion battery with charger	3.7 V Li-ion battery	3.7 V Li-ion battery with solar panel
SENSORS	Integrated	Interchangeable	Integrated	Interchangeable
RECEPTION AND PROCESSING	▪ Coordinator node ▪ LabVIEW application ▪ Manual processing	▪ Coordinator node ▪ LabVIEW application ▪ Manual processing	▪ Gateway ▪ Commercial data cloud ▪ Automatic preprocessing and manual processing	▪ Gateway ▪ Self-developed cloud ▪ Automatic processing
PUMPING SYSTEM	No	Yes	Yes	Yes
FEATURES OF IMPROVEMENT		▪ Greater adaptability	▪ Better signal conditioning ▪ Disconnectable heating	▪ Signal amplification capacity ▪ Heating power control

Pictures of the evolution of the wireless gas sensor nodes described in this paper are presented in Figure 8.

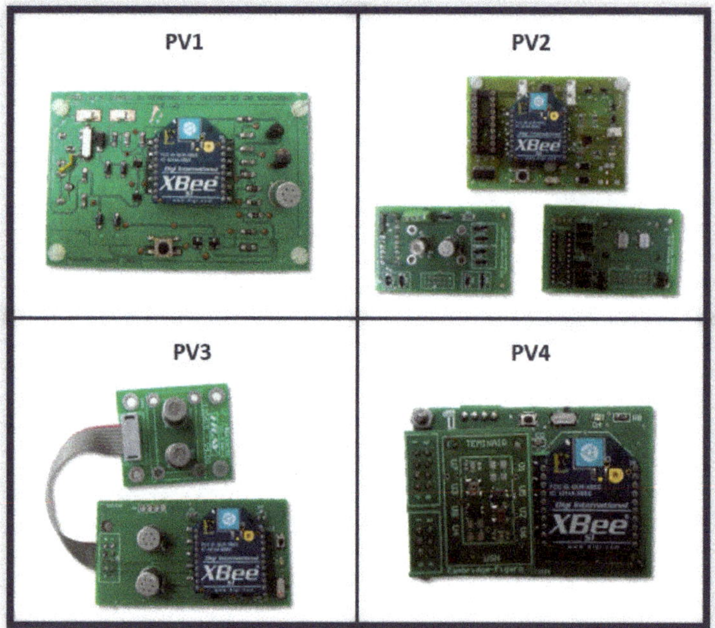

Figure 8. Real images of the prototypes developed.

2.6. Data Processing

For proper device operation, it is necessary to use data processing techniques and artificial intelligence algorithms. In this process, four stages are typically performed (Figure 9): preprocessing, reduction of the number of variables, prediction, and decision-making.

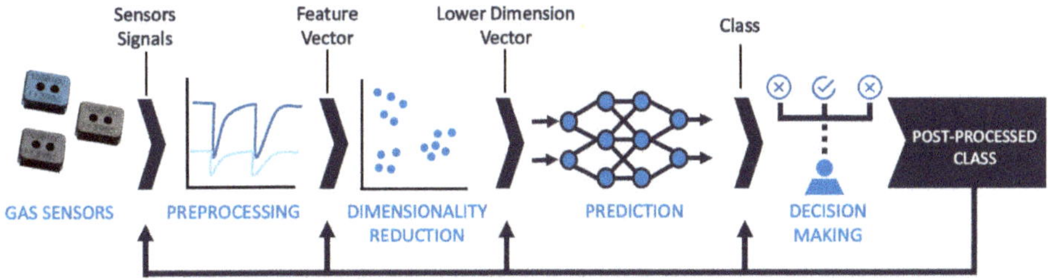

Figure 9. Data processing block diagram.

Firstly, pre-processing techniques are applied to the collected data. In this case, this stage is performed in real time on the gateway. One of the existing feature extraction algorithms in the literature according to Gutierrez-Osuna [30] was used, namely the relative resistance algorithm (RR). Following this algorithm, the characteristic value of each measurement is defined by the following equation:

$$RR = R_V/R_N, \tag{3}$$

where R_V is the resistance value in exposure to the reference compound (air) and R_N is the resistance value in exposure to the target compound, both in steady-state situations.

To reduce the size of the extracted data, the principal component analysis (PCA) [37] technique was used. This technique reduces the dataset, losing the least amount of information possible. It employs linear combinations of the original variables resulting in linearly independent variables. This phase and the following phase are performed in the cloud system.

Next, the prediction phase is carried out. At this stage, regression techniques can be applied to quantify concentrations, while classification techniques can be applied to discriminate contaminating compounds, or clustering techniques can be applied to group similar responses. In the results shown in this article, classification tasks were applied. To this end, probabilistic neural networks (PNN) were used, also called radial basis networks due to the use of a neuron activation radial basis function (RBF) [38]. These networks are made up of four layers. The input layer corresponds to the PCA components used. The next one is the pattern layer, with a number of neurons equal to the training vectors, grouped by classes, where the distance between the input layer vector and each element of the training set was evaluated. The third layer, i.e., the summation layer, contains a neuron for each class and adds the outputs of the pattern neurons belonging to the same class. Lastly, the output layer is a "limiter" that seeks the maximum value of the sum layer. Then, the highest value is selected and set to 1 as a result, while the other outputs are set to 0.

Finally, to determine the validity of the system, predictions of known values were made to compare the estimate values with the real results. Leave-one-out cross-validation (LOOCV) was used to determine the performance of the trained model in this case. This validation technique proposes to perform as many iterations as samples present in the dataset.

3. Results and Discussion

3.1. Measurement Set-Up

The same measurements were made for each of the versions of the designed wireless networks, except in the case of the PV1, which was developed in order to make first contact with the technology used, and only had one gas sensor (TGS2600, Figaro, Japan).

The array of sensors used in each prototype for the following measurements are as follows:

- 2 × TGS2600 (Figaro, Japan) and 2 × TGS2620 (Figaro, Japan) in PV2 and PV3.
- 2 × TGS8100 (Figaro, Japan), 1 × CCS801, and 1 × CCS803 (ams, UK) in PV4.

These tests attempted to analyze the ability of devices to discriminate the BTEX (benzene, toluene, ethylbenzene, and xylene) volatile organic compounds dissolved in water. For this purpose, the static head space technique was used in 22-mL vials. Samples of 10 mL were prepared at a 5% concentration of each compound. Then, the headspace was drawn into the sensor cell using a pump. The vials were kept at 20 °C. Each measurement cycle lasted 10 min: 140 s for the passage of the target compound to the sensor cell, and 460 s for the flow of the reference gas (in this case, clean air). In the measurements made with the final prototype, these times were updated to 60 s (target) and 540 s (reference) to ensure the signal stabilization in the reference gas phase. Figure 10 shows a diagram of the measurement process.

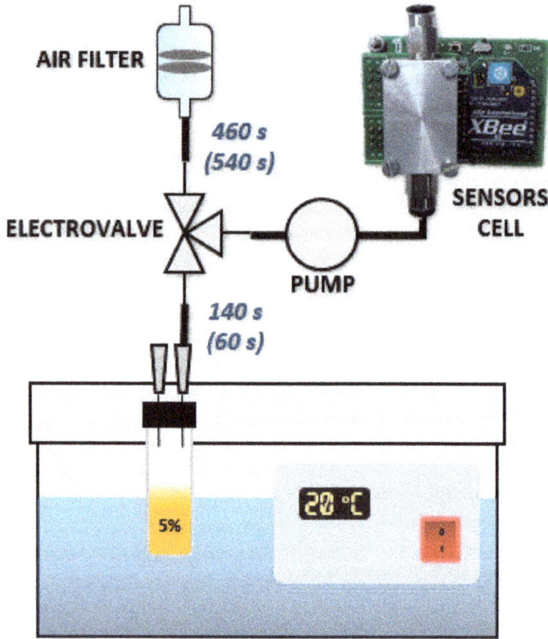

Figure 10. Measurements set-up scheme.

More than 15 measurements were taken for each one of the BTEX compounds and distilled water (in order to have a reference of absence of simulated contaminants in the environment).

3.2. Results

The signals obtained from one of the sensors of each of the four sets of measurements are shown in Figure 11. The selected signals correspond to eight measurement cycles of xylene in each case. One of the sensors (model TGS2600) was selected for PV2 and PV3. Because PV4 did not use this sensor model, the signal of sensor model TGS8100, from the same manufacturer, was selected. The evolution shows the improvement achieved in each version due to changes in the power and conditioning circuits, pump power, and timing optimization. Thus, between the first two sets of measurements, noise reduction was achieved thanks to the changes introduced in the conditioning and power circuits of the sensors, and changes in the heater temperature. Then, between the second and third package (made with the same version of the device, PV3), further noise reduction and a greater stabilization of the signal were achieved by decreasing the flow rate of the sample (by controlling the power of the pump). Finally, between the last two sets of measurements, in addition to the changes introduced in the adaptation and control circuitry, a faster response was achieved due to the use of a sensor of smaller size and consumption.

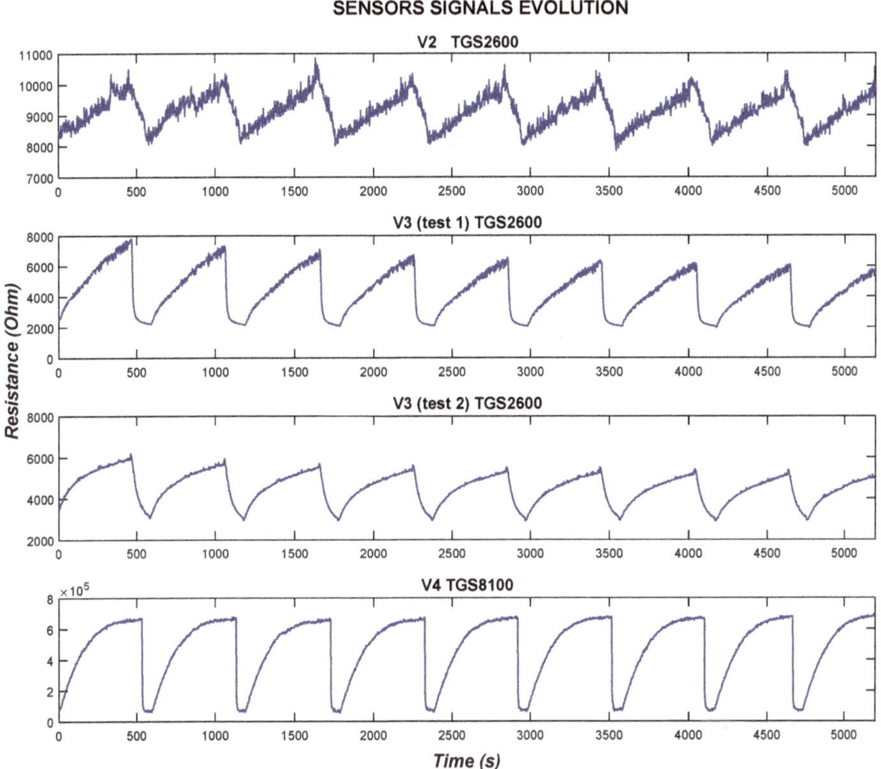

Figure 11. Evolution of sensor signals (resistance versus time), corresponding to the eight xylene measurements.

Once all the data from the measurements were collected, data processing was performed. In the case of PV2, the preprocessing phase was done manually through the Matlab software. However, in the third and fourth versions, this process was performed automatically (while measurements were made) by the program developed in Python that ran on the gateway. As explained above, this preprocessing phase used the relative resistance algorithm. It extracted the value of the ratio between the resistance value of the baseline and the resistance value during exposure to the target compound. In this way, it was possible to extract the main information, while considerably reducing the size of the data.

In all cases, the first two measures were discarded, since the systems were not yet stabilized and the conditions were not the same. Therefore, 13 measurements of each compound were used for data processing.

Then, an analysis of the main component (PCA) was carried out for a graphical representation of the measurements. Figure 12A shows the first two principal components of the measurements made with PV2. A high overlap can be observed between some compounds such as toluene, benzene, and xylene. In addition, short-term drift and dispersion effects appear, resulting from high noise in the measurements and non-stable temperature of the gas sensor heaters. The PCA of the same measurements made with PV3 is presented in Figure 12B. It shows that the clusters are further apart than in the previous case, although there is still overlap between those of toluene and xylene. Furthermore, a high drift effect is still present, possibly due to depletion of the sample. A similar test was repeated using lower pump power in the extraction phase of the sample (test 2). Moreover, the preprocessing program was improved, achieving greater accuracy of obtaining the characteristic value of each measurement. In Figure 12C, it can be observed that the PCA plot improved significantly, managing to reduce the drift effect and the overlaps between zones (only a small overlap between the areas of benzene and toluene, although they are generally very close to each other). Finally, Figure 12D shows the first two principal components of the values of the measurements made with the latest version of the device (PV4), where it can be observed that different areas concerning each compound are clearly separated and non-dispersed.

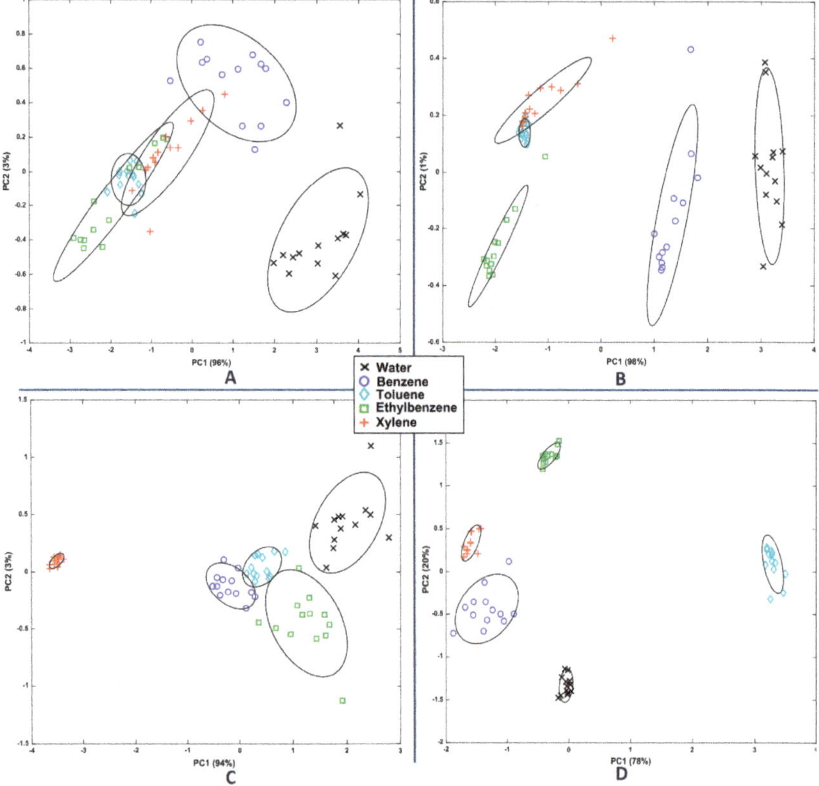

Figure 12. Principal component analysis (PCA) plot for benzene, toluene, ethylbenzene, and xylene (BTEX) compounds of the different datasets: (**A**) PV2; (**B**) PV3 (test 1); (**C**) PV3 (test 2); (**D**) PV4.

Next, PNN was used in order to discriminate the compounds. Then, the LOOCV validation technique was used to study the classification capacity in each case. The results of each of the four studied cases are presented in Table 2, which contains the confusion matrix obtained, allowing us to observe the system performance. The matrix columns represent the predicted class, and the rows represent the real class. As a result, the main diagonal contains correct predictions, while values outside it correspond to erroneous ones. Red data represent the matrix corresponding to the results of PV2. Blue data correspond to the first test performed with PV3 (without preprocessing and pump power correction), while green data correspond to the second test (with correction) of PV3. Finally, the black columns refer to the data resulting from PV4. The resulting success rates were 80%, 93.84%, 96.82%, and 100% for the four datasets, respectively.

Table 2. Confusion matrix obtained in leave-one-out cross-validation (LOOCV) validation. Red: PV2; blue: PV3 (test1); green: PV3 (test2); black: PV4.

Real/Predicted	Water	Benzene	Toluene	Ethylbenzene	Xylene
Water	13 13 13 13				
Benzene		12 13 13 13			1
Toluene			13 12 13 13		1
Ethylbenzene		1	3 1	7 12 11 13	3 1
Xylene		2	4 2		7 11 13 13

4. Conclusions

In this paper, a wireless gas sensor network focusing on the study of air quality was presented. For this purpose, the electronic evolution of the designed sensor nodes was described, until a node of low cost, low consumption, and small size was obtained. Up to four gas microsensors can be connected to the nodes. In addition, they incorporate a control and RF module with ZigBee protocol that allows communication with a central node. This, in turn, is responsible for collecting and storing the data, controlling some aspects of the sensor nodes, and, in the most advanced prototype, preprocessing the data and uploading it to a data cloud.

The system was designed to be used in pollutant detection applications and air quality control in large areas. In order to verify the proper operation and discrimination capacity of the system, discrimination tests of BTEX volatile organic compounds were carried out. These tests also allowed studying the evolution of system operation. As a result, the signals were observed to improve significantly, and the discrimination success rates increased from 80% (PV1) to 100% (PV4).

Author Contributions: P.A. designed the hardware and performed the measurements; J.I.S. and J.L. designed the control architecture and the experiments. All authors wrote the article.

Funding: The authors want to thank the Spanish Ministry of Economy and Competitiveness and Junta de Extremadura for supporting the TEC2013-48147-C6-5-R and IB16048 projects.

Acknowledgments: The authors want to thank José Luis Herrero for help with the cloud system, and Pablo Carmona, Juan Álvaro Fernandez, and Carlos Sánchez for help with the data processing methods.

Conflicts of Interest: The authors declare no conflict of interest.

References

1. WHO. *The Cost of a Polluted Environment: 1.7 Million Child Deaths a Year, Says WHO*; World Health Organization: Geneva, Switzerland, 2017.
2. McCarthy, N. *Air Pollution Contributed to More Than 6 Million Deaths in 2016*; Forbes: New York, NY, USA, 2018.
3. WHO. *Esposure to Benzene: A Major Public Health Concern*; World Health Organization: Geneva, Switzerland, 2010.

4. Lung, C.; Jones, R.; Zellweger, C.; Karppinen, A.; Penza, M.; Dye, T.; Hüglin, C.; Ning, Z.; Leigh, R.; Hagan, D.; et al. *Low-Cost Sensors for the Measurement of Atmospheric Composition: Overview of Topic and Future Applications (WMO)*; Lewis, A.C., Von Schneidemesser, E., Peltier, R., Eds.; World Meteorological Organization: Geneva, Switzerland, 2018; ISBN 9789263112156.

5. Yick, J.; Mukherjee, B.; Ghosal, D. Wireless sensor network survey. *Comput. Netw.* **2008**, *52*, 2292–2330. [CrossRef]

6. Rawat, P.; Singh, K.D.; Chaouchi, H.; Bonnin, J.M. Wireless sensor networks: A survey on recent developments and potential synergies. *J. Supercomput.* **2014**, *68*, 1–48. [CrossRef]

7. Yi, W.Y.; Lo, K.M.; Mak, T.; Leung, K.S.; Leung, Y.; Meng, M.L. A Survey of Wireless Sensor Network Based Air Pollution Monitoring Systems. *Sensors* **2015**, *15*, 31392–31427. [CrossRef] [PubMed]

8. Othman, M.F.; Shazali, K. Wireless Sensor Network Applications: A Study in Environment Monitoring System. *Procedia Eng.* **2012**, *41*, 1204–1210. [CrossRef]

9. Baranov, A.; Spirjakin, D.; Akbari, S.; Somov, A. Optimization of power consumption for gas sensor nodes: A survey. *Sens. Actuators A Phys.* **2015**, *233*, 279–289. [CrossRef]

10. Shaikh, F.K.; Zeadally, S. Energy harvesting in wireless sensor networks: A comprehensive review. *Renew. Sustain. Energy Rev.* **2016**, *55*, 1041–1054. [CrossRef]

11. Farahani, S. Chapter 3—ZigBee and IEEE 802.15.4 Protocol Layers. In *ZigBee Wireless Networks and Transceivers*; Elsevier: Amsterdam, The Netherlands, 2008; pp. 33–135.

12. De Guglielmo, D.; Brienza, S.; Anastasi, G. IEEE 802.15.4e: A survey. *Comput. Commun.* **2016**, *88*, 1–24. [CrossRef]

13. Baronti, P.; Pillai, P.; Chook, V.W.C.; Chessa, S.; Gotta, A.; Hu, Y.F. Wireless sensor networks: A survey on the state of the art and the 802.15.4 and ZigBee standards. *Comput. Commun.* **2007**, *30*, 1655–1695. [CrossRef]

14. Huang, Y.; Hu, L.; Yang, D.; Liu, H. Air-Sense: Indoor environment monitoring evaluation system based on ZigBee network. *IOP Conf. Ser. Earth Environ. Sci.* **2017**, *81*, 12208. [CrossRef]

15. Kasar, A.R.; Khemnar, D.S.; Tembhurnikar, N.P. WSN Based Air Pollution Monitoring System. *Int. J. Sci. Eng. Appl.* **2013**, *2*, 2319–7560. [CrossRef]

16. Yang, C.-T.; Chen, S.-T.; Den, W.; Wang, Y.-T.; Kristiani, E. Implementation of an Intelligent Indoor Environmental Monitoring and management system in cloud. *Future Gener. Comput. Syst.* **2018**. [CrossRef]

17. Botta, A.; de Donato, W.; Persico, V.; Pescapé, A. Integration of Cloud computing and Internet of Things: A survey. *Future Gener. Comput. Syst.* **2016**, *56*, 684–700. [CrossRef]

18. Herrero, J.L.; Lozano, J.; Santos, J.P.; Suárez, J.I. On-line classification of pollutants in water using wireless portable electronic noses. *Chemosphere* **2016**, *152*, 107–116. [CrossRef] [PubMed]

19. Li, W.; Kara, S. Methodology for Monitoring Manufacturing Environment by Using Wireless Sensor Networks (WSN) and the Internet of Things (IoT). *Procedia CIRP* **2017**, *61*, 323–328. [CrossRef]

20. Kumar, P.M.; Lokesh, S.; Varatharajan, R.; Gokulnath, C.; Parthasarathy, P. Cloud and IoT based disease prediction and diagnosis system for healthcare using Fuzzy neural classifier. *Future Gener. Comput. Syst.* **2018**. [CrossRef]

21. Aleixandre, M.; Gerboles, M. Review of small commercial sensors for indicative monitoring of ambient gas. *Chem. Eng. Trans.* **2012**, *30*, 169–174. [CrossRef]

22. Fine, G.F.; Cavanagh, L.M.; Afonja, A.; Binions, R. Metal oxide semi-conductor gas sensors in environmental monitoring. *Sensors* **2010**, *10*, 5469–5502. [CrossRef] [PubMed]

23. Peterson, P.J.D.; Aujla, A.; Grant, K.H.; Brundle, A.G.; Thompson, M.R.; Vande Hey, J.; Leigh, R.J. Practical use of metal oxide semiconductor gas sensors for measuring nitrogen dioxide and ozone in urban environments. *Sensors* **2017**, *17*, 1653. [CrossRef] [PubMed]

24. Kubinec, R.; Adamuščin, J.; Jurdáková, H.; Foltin, M.; Ostrovský, I.; Kraus, A.; Soják, L. Gas chromatographic determination of benzene, toluene, ethylbenzene and xylenes using flame ionization detector in water samples with direct aqueous injection up to 250 µL. *J. Chromatogr. A* **2005**, *1084*, 90–94. [CrossRef] [PubMed]

25. Hazrati, S.; Rostami, R.; Fazlzadeh, M. BTEX in indoor air of waterpipe cafés: Levels and factors influencing their concentrations. *Sci. Total Environ.* **2015**, *524–525*, 347–353. [CrossRef] [PubMed]

26. Niri, V.H.; Mathers, J.B.; Musteata, M.F.; Lem, S.; Pawliszyn, J. Monitoring BTEX and aldehydes in car exhaust from a gasoline engine during the use of different chemical cleaners by solid phase microextraction-gas chromatography. *Water Air Soil Pollut.* **2009**, *204*, 205–213. [CrossRef]

27. Zali, S.; Jalali, F.; Es-haghi, A.; Shamsipur, M. New nanostructure of polydimethylsiloxane coating as a solid-phase microextraction fiber: Application to analysis of BTEX in aquatic environmental samples. *J. Chromatogr. B* **2016**, *1033–1034*, 287–295. [CrossRef] [PubMed]

28. Allouch, A.; Le Calvé, S.; Serra, C.A. Portable, miniature, fast and high sensitive real-time analyzers: BTEX detection. *Sens. Actuators B Chem.* **2013**, *182*, 446–452. [CrossRef]

29. Marco, S.; Gutiérrez-Gálvez, A. Signal and Data Processing for Machine Olfaction and Chemical Sensing: A Review. *IEEE Sens. J.* **2012**, *12*, 3189–3214. [CrossRef]

30. Gutierrez-Osuna, R. Pattern analysis for machine olfaction: A review. *IEEE Sens. J.* **2002**, *2*, 189–202. [CrossRef]

31. Lozano, J.; Suárez, J.I.; Arroyo, P.; Ordiales, J.M.; Álvarez, F. Wireless sensor network for indoor air quality monitoring. *Chem. Eng. Trans.* **2012**, *30*, 319–324. [CrossRef]

32. Arroyo, P.; Lozano, J.; Suárez, J.I.; Herrero, J.L.; Carmona, P. Wireless sensor network for indoor air quality monitoring and Control. *Chem. Eng. Trans.* **2016**, *54*, 217–222. [CrossRef]

33. Kohl, D. Fundamentals and Recent Developments of Homogeneous Semiconducting Sensors. In *Sensors and Sensory Systems for an Electronic Nose*; Gardner, J.W., Bartlett, P.N., Eds.; Springer: Dordrecht, The Netherlands, 1992; pp. 53–76.

34. Moseley, P.T.; Stoneham, A.M.; Williams, D.E. Oxide semiconductors: Patterns of gas response behaviour according to materials type. In *Techniques and Mechanisms in Gas Sensing*; Moseley, P.T., Norris, J., Williams, D.E., Eds.; Adam Hilger: Bristol, UK, 1991; pp. 108–138.

35. Presmanes, L.; Thimont, Y.; El Younsi, I.; Chapelle, A.; Blanc, F.; Talhi, C.; Bonningue, C.; Barnabé, A.; Menini, P.; Tailhades, P. Integration of P-Cuo thin sputtered layers onto microsensor platforms for gas sensing. *Sensors* **2017**, *17*, 1409. [CrossRef] [PubMed]

36. Eady, F. Maxstream/XBee. In *Hands-On ZigBee*; Newnes, Ed.; Elsevier: Amsterdam, The Netherlands, 2007; pp. 131–152.

37. Esbensen, K.H.; Geladi, P. Principal Component Analysis: Concept, Geometrical Interpretation, Mathematical Background, Algorithms, History, Practice. *Compr. Chemom.* **2009**, 211–226. [CrossRef]

38. Specht, D.F. Probabilistic neural networks. *Neural Netw.* **1990**, *3*, 109–118. [CrossRef]

 *electronics*

Article

RoomFort: An Ontology-Based Comfort Management Application for Hotels

Daniele Spoladore [1,*], Sara Arlati [1,†], Sara Carciotti [2], Massimiliano Nolich [2] and Marco Sacco [1]

[1] Institute of Intelligent Industrial Technologies and Systems for Advanced Manufacturing, National Research Council, Via Previati 1/E, 23900 Lecco, Italy; sara.arlati@stiima.cnr.it (S.A.); marco.sacco@stiima.cnr.it (M.S.)

[2] Department of Engineering and Architecture, University of Trieste, Via Alfonso Valerio 6/3, 34127 Trieste, Italy; scarciotti@units.it (S.C.); mnolich@units.it (M.N.)

* Correspondence: daniele.spoladore@stiima.cnr.it; Tel.: +39-0341-2350202

† Current address: Department of Electronics, Information and Bioengineering, Politecnico di Milano, Via Giuseppe Ponzio 34, 20133 Milano, Italy.

Received: 23 October 2018; Accepted: 19 November 2018; Published: 22 November 2018

Abstract: Business traveling is attracting growing attention due to the expansion of international markets. This fact calls for an increasing attention of the tourism sector toward the needs of business travellers, who often require services that are different from the ones desired by leisure tourists. The application of smart solutions coming from Context Awareness and Ambient Intelligence aimed at promoting guests' comfort and well-being, also in cases in which they have special needs, represents a promising solution to tackle business travellers' requirements and thus, to increase hotels attractiveness and incomes. In this context, this work introduces RoomFort, a smart comfort management system aimed at enhancing comfort of hotel room guests and leveraging on semantic representations of comfort, environment, and sensors. RoomFort provides a set of domain ontologies to formalize comfort-related metrics and to exploit the automatic reasoning capabilities provided by Semantic Web technologies, while gathering data through a network of sensors to ensure guests are provided with tailored comfort profiles during their stays in the hotel. Particular focus has been placed on visual comfort, since indoor lighting features constitute one of the main factors influencing the two main activities that most business travellers accomplish in their hotel room: working and relaxing.

Keywords: ontology-based application; ontology development; context awareness; hotel room comfort; indoor comfort

---

1. Introduction

Business travelling has been assuming a growing trend in the last years due to the globalization and expansion of international markets. World Travel & Tourism Council stated that there is a relation between business travel and economic growth, highlighting a direct correlation between international travel tourism and global trade growth [1]. The increase in demand will lead to higher tariffs, with a consequent increase of 3.7% for hotels incomes [2]. This trend, though with different rates, is the same worldwide: the Global Business Travel Association [3] has declared that the business travel sector has been undergoing a strong increase in the last years.

In such context, several sources have started highlighting that business travellers need to rely on comfortable hotel rooms, in which comfort metrics (temperature, illuminance and humidity rate) can be adjusted according to the guests' needs [4,5]. Moreover, frequent business travellers would like to customize comfort metrics according to the activities they are performing [6].

The requested features call for a novel idea of comfort, which can be approached to the holistic comfort, a concept that takes into account the traveller and both tangible and intangible environmental factors to deliver an optimal and tailored experience during guests' stay. This is particularly relevant for business travellers, who, in addition to normal activities performed in the hotel room by leisure tourists, may need to work in their room. They need to be alert, concentrated and not distracted by unpleasant or uncomfortable environments; thus, it is imperative for hotel owners to provide them with the highest and most tailored comfort possible. For this purpose, Ambient Intelligence (AmI) and Context Awareness (CA) are two fields of study that can provide some interesting features to the hotellerie industry, by making rooms and services "smarter". AmI and CA, in fact, can enhance the comfort quality of the guests' stay in the hotel by providing them tailored comfort sets and services.

This work presents RoomFort, a system that aims at providing guests with comfort metrics that are tailored to their needs (intended as both physical and physiological necessities, as well as desires) and adjusted according to the activities they are performing in their hotel room. RoomFort exploits formal (i.e., ontological) representations of "domains of knowledge" related to the guests and to the room's comfort metrics, and a network of sensors to measure, analyze and customize comfort metrics. Ontologies can provide a logic-based, formal and sharable interpretation of knowledge and can foster information integration, support automatic reasoning processes and allow to infer new information; therefore, they represent a promising tool for fostering the decision making in contexts—as hotellerie—where several domains of knowledge are involved [7]. The system can be exploited to customize temperature, humidity rate, air temperature (with Heating, Ventilation and Air Conditioning (HVAC) system) and air quality (by triggering the opening and closing of room's windows); nevertheless, the achievement of the optimal visual comfort has been chosen as the main objective of this work. This is due to both the strong influence that light conditions have on human alertness and performances [8] and to the ease with which light installations could be made in the hotel rooms, with respect to the renewal of the heating or of the air-conditioning systems. Finally, RoomFort grants data privacy for both customers and hotel manager, as personal data and hotel data are stored in separate private cloud space and only the parameters need to optimize the guest comfort inside a given hotel room are merged together, inside a private cloud enclave, to perform a reasoning in order to obtain the best actuation for the activity performed by that guest in that given room of that hotel.

The remainder of this work is organized as follows: Section 2 underlines some of the remarkable papers in the field of semantic and intelligent based technologies for comfort management in indoor environments; this Section highlights the lack of standard reference ontologies in a pivotal field of knowledge (i.e., representation of indoor comfort metrics). Section 3 introduces the concept of holistic comfort and links it to the hotel industry, highlighting some of the issues and desiderata belonging to business travellers, target of this work. Section 4 presents the current status of hotels' categorization in Europe, United States of America, Canada and other countries; this section also introduces the sample hotel room adopted for this work. Section 5 describes RoomFort system's architecture and delves into the description of the domain ontologies developed, with a specific focus on the methodology adopted for modelling, the RoomFort application and the information exchange among the architectural actors. Section 6 introduces the preliminary tests conducted to define the best luminous metrics for reading and relaxing in a hotel room; the results deriving from this tests are then discussed and modelled in the ontologies. Section 7 briefly points the attention on some particular use-cases, showing how RoomFort could be of potential benefit for a variety of travellers and how it can meet the concept of comfort understood as a service to be provided to guests. Finally, Section 8 summarizes the main outcome of this work and sketches the future directions it will undertake.

2. Related Work

Research on comfort has acquired a growing importance in the last decade with the spreading of CA systems, Ambient Assisted Living (AAL) and AmI. However, very few works relied on ontologies to provide a sound, sharable and reasonable knowledge base describing comfort-related concepts and measurements. The above-mentioned domains of knowledge share some similarities: they rely on sensors to capture environmental information and they exploit technologies to ease dweller's life, with a particular focus on frail segments of the population. Ontology also plays a pivotal role in tourism, where the exploitation of knowledge bases has lead to a variety of smart solutions.

2.1. Comfort in CA, AAL and AmI Systems

Most of the studies focusing on indoor comfort customization are for CA systems, AmI and AAL solutions and Smart Homes. Nevertheless, only a few of these works tackled the issue of modelling comfort metrics and measurements within ontologies, thus, limiting the semantic description to a restricted number of comfort-related concepts and neglecting the representation of measurements. Although leveraging on semantic web technologies, these works are more focused on the interoperability capabilities provided by ontologies rather than the possibility to provide a sound representation of comfort metrics. Tila et al. [9] described an indoor environmental comfort system taking advantage of a context ontology, in which concepts for the description of sensors and actuators were modelled with Resource Description Framework (RDF) [10]. The authors leveraged the ontology's capabilities to provide semantic interoperability among different data and to back-up the deployment of an IoT system for indoor environment control. Thus, this study is more focused toward the description of the interoperability among sensors and actuators, neglecting a formal description of comfort metrics involved in the system, and reasoning capabilities are dedicated to this goal as well. An ontological approach is the base of Flexergy [11], an ontology aimed at representing the domain of sustainable comfort; the semantic modelling of sensors, actuators, devices, environments and comfort is used as a tool to ease the interoperability of various data coming from different sources. The work links the possibility to provide tailored comfort metrics (air quality and thermal comfort) with energy-saving needs; anyhow, Flexergy's exploitation of ontologies is limited to the design of the energetic infrastructure of the indoor environment and does not involve the modelling of comfort-related concepts. Recently, Mahroo et al. [12] investigated the use of semantic-based technologies to enable a CA system and the possibility to deliver tailored services within a Smart Home, highlighting some of the challenges connected to the exploitation of ontologies and reasoning. In this work ontologies play a pivotal role in managing several aspects of the Smart Home, but no direct reference to indoor comfort management is described.

2.2. Modelling Comfort with Domain Ontologies

The growing interest for AAL, AmI and CA technologies and the possibility offered by ontologies to provide a formal and sharable description of domains of knowledge raised researchers' interest in the exploitation of semantic models for a variety of purposes. DogOnt [13], a widely known ontology dedicated to home automation, refers to the possibility to implement "comfort and energy savings", but the model lacks specific concepts for the description of indoor comfort metrics. Although there is a lack of comfort reference ontologies, several studies developed their own domain ontologies to represent some comfort-related concepts. In [14], ontology is used as a decision support system to improve the quality of three comfort metrics (temperature, humidity and CO_2 concentration) in indoor environments; leveraging on data acquired by sensors, reasoning processes can suggest to the human user the actions that could improve the quality of one or more comfort metrics in the environment. The ontology of this system is developed with Ontology Web Language (OWL) [15] and exploits Semantic Web Rule Language (SWRL) [16] rules to describe more complex actions—such as the influence of opening a window on indoor temperature. Adeleke et al. [17] proposed an "Indoor Environmental Quality" (IEQ) ontology for indoor air quality monitoring and control, formalizing some of the knowledge of the standard ISO 7730:2005; the aim of this semantic model is to analyze potential health risks related to comfort metrics and determine control actions. The IEQ ontology provides representations of several comfort-related concepts, such as human activities, observations and buildings. Stavropoulos et al. [18] developed BOnSAI (Smart Building Ontology for Ambient Intelligence), an ontology for smart building and AmI, mainly focusing on services, hardware energy management, and encompassing some concepts regarding the context. Developed in OWL-S [19],

BOnSAI takes into account the possibility to describe "environmental parameters", such as CO_2 level, Illuminance, Pressure, Humidity to express the functionality of smart devices and services. These parameters are used to express the functionalities of the devices deployed within the environment and, secondary, to increase user's comfort. Similarly, in [20] the authors developed the ThinkHome ontology to represent the whole smart home ecosystem, thus, encompassing some comfort-related concepts. ThinkHome encompasses the possibility to deduce the default comfort parameters according to dweller's age and gender leveraging reasoning mechanisms. The ontology, developed with OWL, provides the means to describe temperature, humidity and air quality. More detailed indoor comfort metrics are modelled in the Smart Home Simulator [21], an AAL Virtual Reality-based application leveraging semantic representations of concepts to provide inhabitants with customized services and comfort metrics (CO_2 concentration, humidity rate, illuminance and temperature) according to their health conditions.

2.3. Ontology and Tourism

Two recent surveys on recommender systems [22] and mobile technologies [23] applied in tourism highlighted how knowledge representation with ontologies is widely adopted to enable intelligent systems in providing customized suggestions tourists. This approach encompasses both the reuse of existing ontologies and the development of new ones from scratch. In particular, Petrina et al. [24] describe the provision of smart and personalized services to tourists interested in historical Points of Interest (POIs). Leveraging on an ontological representation of POIs, this recommender system can show tourists the nearest POIs taking into account tourist's preferences; moreover, it can also provide a list of other POIs historically related to the suggested POI. Smirnov et al. [25] rely on ontology to provide ad-hoc transportation scheduling able to take into account available schedules, foreseen availability and occupancy of the transportation means. As a result, a cyber-physical infomobility recommender system is developed, in which ontologies provide the common vocabulary for the description of transportation services, POIs and attractions. In [26], Moreno et al. describe a web-based system providing personalized recommendations of touristic activities in a Spanish region, Tarragona. Using specific ontologies, this system takes into account demographic data, travel preferences, tourists' ratings and opinions, to provide tailored suggestions.

These works are examples of how ontology can be adopted as a promising technology for the provision of personalized touristic information, also in the context of mobile technologies.

RoomFort exploits ontologies to provide a formal, sharable and simple conceptualizations of the most relevant indoor comfort metrics and their measurements, focusing its attention on the possibility to provide holistic and tailored comfort metrics to business travellers staying in a hotel. It is also worth noticing that no applications of such technologies in the field of hotel industry have been traced in literature.

3. The Concept of Holistic Comfort and Hotel Industry

Holistic comfort is a theory developed in the field of nursing care that asserts the measurability of comfort [27]. This theory encompasses the environment as one of the key features to reach an adequate level of comfort; although holistic comfort has been developed within a health-related context, its principles can be applied to the all the fields involving the humans and their interactions within an indoor environment, thus, to the hotellerie sector too.

3.1. Business Traveller

Tourism is a dynamic industry experiencing an increasing phase throughout the world. This industry encompasses both people travelling for leisure (leisure tourists) and people travelling for business (business travellers). In 2017, business travelling counted for the 23% of total tourism expenses, according to [2]. As further analyzed in the following subsections, business travellers' needs cover a pivotal role in the selection of the hotel where they decide to stay. In particular, the characteristics of the room and its services are important factors which strongly influence the choice of the hotel [28]. Recent research showed how business travellers are more inclined to take into account comfort-related services while choosing hotel rooms [29], thus, indicating that the attention towards Indoor Environmental Quality (IEQ) represents an economic value for them. Also, it is worth noticing that, contrary to leisure tourists, business travellers never consider their travel as a vacation, but always as a business and work-related issue. Therefore, they do not experience the travel as pleasant, but rather as a burden to bear to obtain better professional positions. Many business travellers report to work many hours—even beyond normal working hours—to finish their duties sooner, so that they can come back home earlier. This is due both to job-related concerns (e.g., more demanding workload on return) and to the willingness of seeing again family members and friends. These pressing—and often auto-imposed—demands turn into stress, burnout syndromes and unhealthy behaviours [30]. This is the main reason why comfort has become a relevant concern for business travellers: the hotel room alone cannot contribute in changing such behaviours, but may limit business travellers' unease by providing, from the one hand, a comfortable working environment promoting workers' concentration and alertness, and, on the other hand, a relaxing space to restore and recover after long working shifts [31].

3.2. Comfort in the Hotel Industry

Ariffin et al. argued that "tourist satisfaction is a psychological concept that involves the feeling of well-being and pleasure that results from obtaining what one hopes for and expects from an appealing product and/or service" [32]. Moreover, in the same work, the authors showed that the business travellers are more concerned with comfort and amenities of the hotel room than others quality factors. Thus, the enhancement of the experience passes through the consideration of air quality, temperature, acoustic (i.e., intangible environmental factors [33]), and furnishings, materials, smells, humidity, ventilation, brightness and hygiene (i.e., tangible factors) to design and provide comfortable and pleasant environments. The growing interest toward all these features has been highlighted by a recent study, which underlined how guests are willing to pay an extra charge on the room rate for enjoying more comfortable indoor conditions [29].

Thus, if the aim of hotels is to provide a more comfortable environment for customers, it is essential to satisfy their needs by proposing a holistic experience in the whole hotel building, and especially in the customers' room. However, to satisfy the holistic concept of comfort, taking care of all the above mentioned factors may still be not enough: it is necessary to consider also single person's needs and his/her personal feelings within the room environment.

For instance, the complaints of customers after an accommodation period in a hotel are commonly related to uncomfortable air temperatures and to the difficulty or impossibility of setting the preferred comfort metrics [34]. A survey of the literature showed that a more flexible thermal comfort standard brings environmental and economic improvement [34], while music influenced customers' relaxation [35]. Lighting and colour combinations influence the way guests perceive various spaces, and may also induce some modifications in their behaviour [32] and increase their productivity [36]. Other environmental conditions can produce effects on indoor environments' inhabitants, especially on their health. Asthma, allergies and respiratory diseases, for instance, can be tackled by intervening directly on air quality and temperature comfort metrics [36]. Finally, it has also been proven that having the chance of regulating a comfort-related parameter (i.e., illuminance) is something that people appreciate [37]; illuminance and light features could thus, be exploited to meet business travellers' expectations and promote their revisiting to the same hotel for their next trips.

3.3. Luminous Comfort: Meeting the Needs of Business Travellers

Lighting contributes in creating a mood and atmosphere inside a room, and thus, it may be adjusted to design an environment whose characteristics corresponds to the user's demand and expectation [38]. e.g., the lights of lamps projected on a table in a working area should be designed for reading and working with a laptop, thus, limiting reverberation and promoting paper-based text clearness. Indeed, lighting can influence working performances, especially those performances directly depending on vision. Several characteristics of lighting (such as illuminance, glare, spectrum of the light) can help a worker to stay alert and to focus his/her attention or motivation. In 1989, the National Electrical Manufacturers Association of the USA had already pointed out the link between lighting and rapidity of production of drawings in an indoor environment where bright reflections were reduced [4].

Baron et al. [39] investigated the role of illuminance and spectral distribution (i.e., the colour) of light on the performance of different tasks. Variations in illuminance and lamp typologies were found to exert a significant effect on several cognitive and work-related tasks, such as word categorization, preferring cooperation for resolving interpersonal conflicts (instead of avoidance), willingness to help others, sense of ability in performing a clerical task [40].

More recently, it was also demonstrated how lighting and students' learning performance are connected, better lighting leads to an increase in students' learning motivation [41]. Because of these reasons, a hotel room that allows being customized by the guests according to their needs or desires could play an important role in promoting the hotel's revenue. Indeed, it is attractive for the more demanding travellers and, consequently, can be considered as an added value for the hotel owner, who can improve the quality of the services he/she provides and increase the rate of returning visitors. This represents a strong need for hotel owners, who aim more and more at creating memorable experiences in their guests: travellers are usually prone to look for different accommodations in order to enrich their experience [5,42], and thus, they must be provided with strong motivations to return to an already-visited place. In fact, the increasing awareness of importance of comfort has led people to be more demanding and search for more and more the quality in their living environments, and thus, in the hotels' rooms as well. Light intensity and colour are two factors with impact on people's activity in the space that can help in achieving these objectives. Since illumination is known to cause behavioural responses in humans, such knowledge can be exploited in order to help hotel guest in staying either alert or concentrated, or relaxed [43]. According to the results of the study conducted in [44], the cool colours are perceived as pleasant, comfortable, and activating, while warm colours are perceived as more relaxing. Because of this, and considering the small economical effort required to change the room's lighting, hotel managers should consider applying these known concept on light colours in their facilities, so to influence guests' emotions and feelings [45].

With regard to business travellers' needs, highlighted in the subsection above, the possibility to provide a customized luminous comfort setting appears promising in easing their staying by helping them in better performing their jobs, or relaxing when needed.

To do this, it is necessary to go beyond what is defined in the "lighting standards" in working environments, which are regulated by the European norm EN 12464-1 that sets the minimum requirements for indoor illuminance of working places. This standard sets the minimum illuminance requirements of an actual working area (also defined as "task area") rather than of the entire room. For each of the working activities identified by the EN 12464-1, the norm specifies the ranges for a set of parameters concurring in the definition of the luminous environment (luminance distribution, illuminance, glare, colour rendering and colour appearance of light, daylight, glare, flicker). The norm also recommends the minimum amount of illuminance for each task area according to a set of factors:

- Psycho-physiological aspects such as visual comfort and well being;
- Requirements for visual tasks;
- Visual ergonomics;
- Safety;
- Economy.

In particular, EN 12464-1 stresses how the required maintained illuminance (E_m) should be increased in case of particular conditions, e.g., when there is the necessity of higher productivity, when the visual capacity of a worker is below normal, when the task requires a great amount of attention and/or time, etc. On the contrary, the maintained illuminance can be decreased in other particular conditions, e.g., the task is undertaken for an unusually short time or details on which worker's attention must focus are large or highly contrasted. In any case, the normative states that in continuously occupied area, the E_m cannot be less than 200 lux. The European standard considers only white light, though literature pointed out that the overall impression that a person gets of a space is contributed by three atmospheric elements: colour, light and style; the colour seems to be the most influential [46].

4. Hospitality Services in the Tourism Sector

Since providing a comfortable experience to its guest is usually a hotel's main goal, comfort in hotels is defined by the interactions that guests have with the environment (i.e., the hotel room and communal areas), which plays an important role in making the experience more memorable to the guests. The guest's interactions with the environment, when positive, have been proven to increase their satisfaction, and studies pointed out that the physical environment constitutes a fundamental component of hospitality itself [32]. Despite this known importance, when travellers search for their ideal hotel, they have to face a very large set of choices: environmental characteristics are usually not well described and making an informed decision is not easy, especially considering the lack of a unified international classification system for the hotel rooms and their comforts. In fact, different countries adopt various classification systems for hotels and diverse evaluation criteria for services and facilities [47].

For instance, in Europe, a star-based classification is commonly used, but the rooms belonging to the same category could have different characteristics from one country to another.

- France adopts a seven categories classification, ranging from "no star", to five stars and including also the "Palace" class for five-star hotels;
- Spain does not rely on a national classification system for hotels; each Regional Government ratifies its own classification systems—although the differences among the various regional classifications are minimal. Generally, hotels are classified according to a system of stars ranging from the one to five;
- in Germany, under the patronage of HOTREC (Hotels, Restaurants and Cafés in Europa) [48], a one to five stars system is used to classify hotel rooms and their services;
- in the United Kingdom a star rating system is adopted to describe all accommodations (hotels, B&Bs, inns, etc.).

Australia, South Africa and India also adopt a star rating system; in the United State of America and Canada the accommodations are classified according to a one to five rating system developed in 1977 by the American Automobile Association. The system is divided in five categories and uses "diamonds" instead of stars (one diamond being the lowest category and five diamonds being the highest category).

Italy has a hotel rating system that ranges from one to five stars (the higher the number of stars is, the higher is the quality level of the accommodation) and that aims at guaranteeing more competitiveness to the national tourism in the global market [49]. The Italian rating system is mandatory and managed by public authorities.

Such rating system defines the minimum national standards for services and facilities and classifies hotels according to a code represented by a number of stars. As the number of stars increases, the services provided by the hotel and its rooms proportionally increase. For example, a one-star room needs a minimum 14 m^2 of for a double bed (8 m^2 for single bed) and a five-star room requires 16 m^2 for a double bed (9 m^2 for single bed). For the purpose of this work, a typical Italian three-star room has been taken as sample. The characteristics of this type of room, are:

- services: 16/24 h of reception, daily cleaning of rooms, at least 1 foreign language and TV service in each room;
- minimum dimensions: 8 m^2 one single bedroom, 14 m^2 double bedroom, 3 m^2 bathroom;

- furniture: bed, table, chair, desk, wardrobe, mirror, luggage stool and bath furniture.

As the reader can see, the above-mentioned classification systems do not take into account IEQ metrics, but focuses on rooms' dimensions and on the services the hotel can provide to its guests. Therefore, improving IEQ would not act on improving the hotel rating, but rather toward promoting travellers' revisit and supporting an (appropriate) increase of the hotel room cost with respect to other rooms belonging to the same rating category.

5. A Modular Ontology-Based Architecture for Managing the Comfort in Hotel Room Environments

RoomFort system architecture encompasses both hardware and software technologies and its aim is to manage room environmental comfort in a personalized way. RoomFort measures indoor comfort metrics, and saves the acquired data using Semantic Web Standards (RDF and OWL). These data are stored in a private cloud repository, where they can be reasoned over to foster the optimal personalized actuation of indoor comfort. RoomFort has a two-sided authentication process: from one side the hotel shall register on the system, providing a description of all the equipment and of the environmental comfort facilities for both sensing and actuation; on the other side, the client, i.e., the hotel guest, shall describe his/her characteristics that can affect the perceived comfort during the staying at the hotel. The matching among these data is performed in the private cloud enclave of the guest, so that no personal data is directly transferred to the hotel; only the actuations to tailor guest's comfort—which are the results of the reasoning process computed on the private cloud of the guest—are visible to the guest. The association between the user and his/her room is allowed by the hotel personnel, which enables to transfer room ontology to the private user cloud. Guest data are stored in a protected enclave on a smart device, so that privacy and security related to sensitive personal data are safeguarded, as proposed in an application in the health-care sector [50]. Also, it is worth noticing that the information about the equipment of the hotel are preserved, since, in the reasoning process, only the parameters to be controlled are involved. The specific characteristics of each device, instead, remain in the hotel private cloud space. As all the personal and sensitive data are collected on a private secure enclave, and that the data are not transferred to any other party during the reasoning process, the RoomFort system architecture fulfills the General Data Protection Regulation (GDPR) principles of personal data privacy in the European Union.

The RoomFort system architecture is composed by the following elements:

- a set of sensors to detect illuminance, CO_2 concentration, temperature and humidity rate inside the room;
- a framework for semantic annotation of data gathered by the sensors, according to [51];
- a repository for indoor measurements (data gathered by sensors and semantically annotated);
- a reasoner able to provide customization of comfort metrics according to a set of conditions, described in ontologies;
- a set of ontologies, formalizing both the conditions and the rules to tailor indoor comfort metrics (described in detail in Sections 5.2–5.4);
- actuators, in this case a set of nine Philips Hue Lamps (six mounted on the ceiling and three on the table); the complete set of actuators encompasses also a PCE thermo-hygrometer and a Cozir Amb CO_2 concentration sensor;
- an application running on Android devices and allowing the guest to declare the activities he/she wants to perform and in which area of the room;
- a secure cloud service for hosting the hotel and the guest data, and for running the reasoning processing and producing the optimal comfort actuations for that guest performing a given activity inside such hotel room.

Therefore, to operate in the RoomFort framework, both hotel and guest characteristics are described in a set of ontologies. More in details, each hotel room needs to be described in an ontology encompassing concepts and measurements related to spaces, furniture and installed devices in order to provide interoperability among devices and a safe and sound control of comfort metrics. The guest should have his/her own data related to his/her health condition in an ontology-compliant format too; in fact, these data are retrieved by RoomFort in order to customize the room's indoor comfort metrics according to the guests' desires and activities.

Figure 1 shows a business traveller booking a room in a hotel which uses the RoomFort framework, bringing together his/her own personal and health-related ontologies. Leveraging on the possibility to access to all the knowledge formalized in the ontologies, RoomFort can operate as an application that configures the comfort metrics in the room according to the guest's needs and preferences [52]. The key feature of this proposed architecture is the focus on the guest, as an individual with specific needs or desires. In this context, RoomFort aims at providing him/her with tailored comfort metrics, with the final goal of increasing his/her satisfaction. As shown in Figure 2, RoomFort relies on a cloud-based architecture. The application operates on a private cloud enclave that stores the information of the booked room, the environmental sensing data and the ontologies related to the guest. In this way, the reasons behind an actuation are only available on the private enclave and stay hidden to hotel personnel, thus, safeguarding guests' privacy.

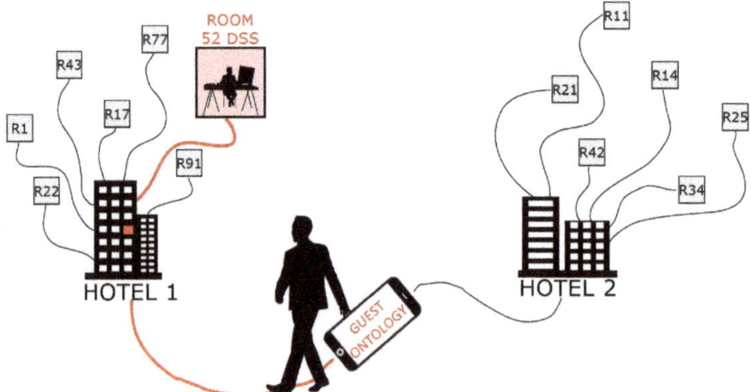

Figure 1. A schema describing the functioning of RoomFort: a business traveller can choose any hotel adopting the system and import his/her preferences.

Figure 2. A schema describing RoomFort's architecture.

5.1. RoomFort's Ontologies: Modelling Methodology

Ontologies-explicit, shared and Description Logic-based conceptualizations of the knowledge and the relationships of the concepts composing a domain [53]—in RoomFort are used to model comfort-related concepts with W3C-endorsed languages Resource Description Framework (RDF) [10], Ontology Web Language (OWL) [15] and Semantic Web Rule Language (SWRL) [16]. Another interesting feature related to the use of ontologies is the possibility to derive new facts—which are not explicitly expressed in the ontology—through reasoning, thus, discovering new chunks of knowledge and adding value to several knowledge-based businesses and fields. RoomFort's ontologies were developed following the methodology described by Suárez-Figueroa et al. [54], the NeOn Methodology. Among the variety of semantic modelling methodologies, NeOn was chosen since it considerably simplifies the identification of the knowledge to be represented through the compiling of the Ontology Requirements Specification Document (ORSD) [55]; the ORSD allows to acquire useful indications regarding the granularity of the semantic models, their extents, the scope of the models, the identification of the end-users of the ontologies, the functional and non-functional requirements the ontologies must satisfy. Together with the NeOn Methodology, ORSD can simplify the development of the ontologies by specifying their extents. Following the scenarios depicted in the NeOn Methodology, the development of RoomFort's models foresees the reuse of already existing ontological resources and the development from scratch of new models.

As mentioned above, the domains of interest of this study regard:

- the guests and their health conditions Section 5.2; the International Classification of Functioning, Disability and Health (ICF) was found as a suitable ontology for the description of health-related conditions [56];
- the hotel room and the devices (sensors and actuators) in it Section 5.3, a domain divided into:

    - the hotel room, for the description of which the Accommodation Ontology Language Reference (ACCO) [57] and DogOnt [13] were the reused ontologies;
    - the devices deployed in the room, whose formal description is performed referring to the Smart Appliance REFerence Ontology (SAREF) [58];

- the comfort metrics to be monitored in order to provide a comfortable environment to the guest Section 5.4, for which RoomFort relies on ontologies developed from scratch and led by the embryonic work presented in [21,59]. A particular attention is posed on the luminous comfort, as stated in the previous Sections, as one of the most sensitive domains for business travellers.

These modules composing RoomFort ontology are developed using OWL-DL [60], a subset of OWL combining enough expressive power with full reasonability. The open-source ontology editor Protégé (version 5.3) was used for the development of the semantic models.

The following subsections delve into the description of the semantic modules developed for RoomFort architecture.

5.2. Guest Ontology

5.2.1. A Holistic Framework for Guest's Health Status Description

The description of the guests' health condition relies on a World Health Organization-endorsed standard: the International Classification of Functioning, Disability and Health (ICF) [61]. This classification conceptualizes the functioning of a person as an interaction between his/her health condition and the environment where the person lives. ICF is organized in two main parts: the first, "Functioning and Disability", provides a description of the components Body functions, Body structures and Activities and participation; and the second, "Contextual Factors", provides the means to describe the impact of the components Environmental factors and Personal factors. Each component can be further specified into Chapters, sections of the classification identifying a health-related domain. Through a progressive specification of chapters, ICF allows to assess the domains of the functioning and the disability of an individual. Each ICF component is characterized by a letter (b for Body functions, s for Body structures, e for Environmental factors, d for Activities and participation) and can be deepened by adding digits, as shown in Figure 3.

The magnitude of an impairment is determined by adding a qualifier to the corresponding ICF code (0 indicates the absence of impairments in a specific code, 1 stands for a mild impairment, 2 denotes a moderate impairment, 3 indicates a severe impairment, while 4 states a complete impairment). Therefore, the qualified code b21020.2 indicates a moderate impairment in the "Colour vision".

b "Body functions"	Component	
b2 "Sensory functions and pain"	Chapter	
b210 "Seeing functions"	**b230** "Hearing functions"	Second level item
b2102 "Quality of vision"	**b2300** "Sound detection"	Third level item
b21020 "Colour vision"	- - -	Fourth level item

Figure 3. An example of ICF illustrating the structure of the classification.

ICF is often exploited as a practical tool to ease the communication between health professionals and other stakeholders [59,62]; moreover, the classification is suited also to describe each context where health and environment interact: work reintegration [63], domestic age-care [64], AAL [65]. ICF has also been represented into an ontological model in RDF/OWL [56], which can be used as reference in the modelling of more complex ontologies. However, it has to be underlined that this model inherits some shortcomings belonging to the whole classification, such as problems regarding incongruent classification of some concepts, a lack of clarity between activities and their qualities, incorrect parent-child relationships [66] and overemphasis on subsumption [67].

5.2.2. Describing the Guest's Personal and Health Data

This module gathers the guest's registry records, data provided by the guest when he/she reserves his/her room. These data are modelled as objects of datatype properties and provide the means to represent the first name, last name, date of birth, tax identification number of the guest—who is represented as an individual. Using an object property, each guest is connected to his/her health condition, represented as an individual. The modelling of each health condition reuses the ICF ontology, as illustrated in Figure 4.

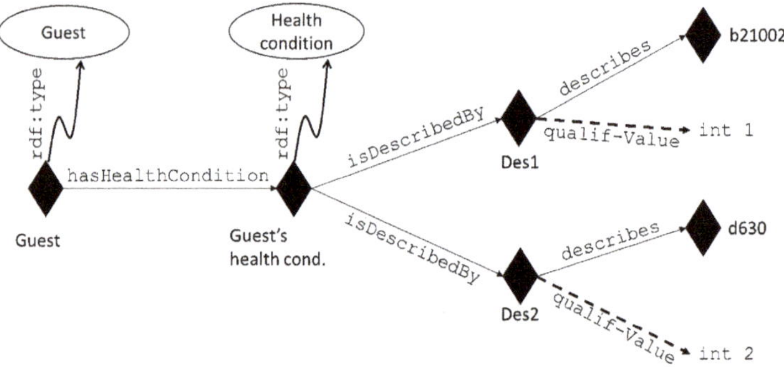

Figure 4. An example of the modelling of a guest's health condition; individuals are represented with diamonds, concepts are represented with circles, and roles are represented with arrows (dashed arrows indicate datatype properties, full-line arrows represent object properties). The type of an individual is stated with a curved arrow.

For each ICF code involved in the description of an impairment, a "descriptor" individual is used; descriptors are used to provide a univocal link for each ICF code and its qualifier, avoiding the use of a reification [68].

In this way, it is possible to represent the full extent of ICF qualifiers and to model complex health conditions, enabling the semantic representation of n-ary relationships without adding complexity to the whole application ontology.

5.2.3. Addressing the Needs of Travellers With Impairments

As described above, RoomFort relies on ICF to provide a description of travellers' health status. Having this piece of information, it is possible to further customize the luminous metrics according to traveller's specific disability. For instance, a traveller characterized by photophobia (hypersensitivity to light due to e.g., albinism or corneal abrasion) may be characterized by an impairment in the ICF code b21020-Light sensitivity—and may benefit from suffused lighting, also when working; a person characterized by macular degeneration can be described as having impairments in the following codes (according to Silva et al. [69]):

- b21001 Monocular acuity of distant vision;
- b21002 Binocular acuity of near vision;
- b2101 Visual field functions;
- b21020 Light sensitivity;
- b21021 Colour vision;
- b21022 Contrast sensitivity;
- b21023 Visual picture quality.

People suffering from maculopathy have issues in performing activities low illuminance and at night-time and reported to have difficulties in reading [70]. In this case, it is thus, recommendable to provide them with an intense and focused light, which can help them in distinguishing written text. RoomFort can provide these type of users with more appropriate environmental conditions by automatically adjusting the maintained illuminance, light colour and wall colour while they are performing working activities in the room. Of course, RoomFort cannot address all the physiological problems related to these conditions, neither it provides a permanent solution; instead, the system can make the working activity more comfortable to those who are particularly fragile in some vision-related dimension. Similarly, RoomFort can provide personalized comfort metrics related to persons who have some form of impairment in the perception of temperature (described by ICF codes b2700 Sensitivity to temperature; b550 Thermoregulatory functions; b5501 Maintenance of body temperature), respiratory issues (described with ICF range of codes related to the functions of the respiratory system b440-b449). In these cases, a guest travelling to a hotel equipped with RoomFort can upload (or ask his/her physician to upload) his/her physiological status (formalized in an RDF/OWL ontology) and a set of SWRL rules to adapt comfort metrics of the customized comfort set by increasing or decreasing the illuminance and changing light colour. The SWRL acquires the following form:

```
Guest_with_mild_b21002_imp(?g), selectsActivity(?g, ?a),
Activity (work), CustomizedLuminousComfortSetting (?clcs)->
provideComfortSetting (?clcs)
```

The Customized Luminous Comfort Setting (CLCS) is modelled as a "regular" comfort setting, but for instance in the case of a business traveller characterized by hypersensitivity to light, its comfort setting is adjusted as shown in the following Figure 5.

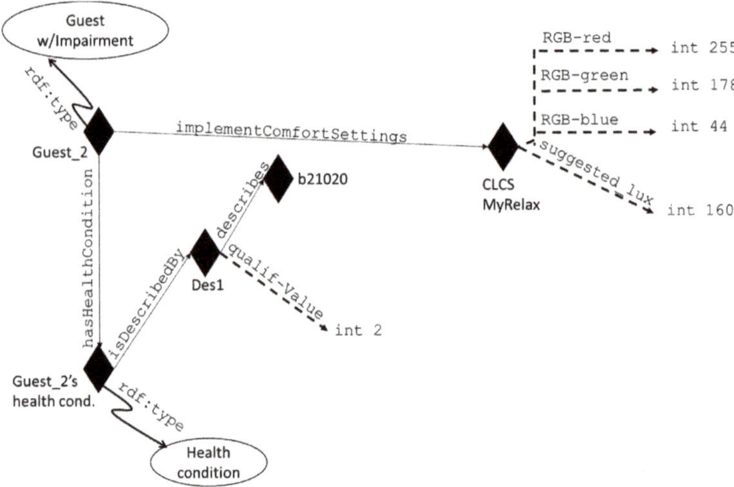

Figure 5. An example of the modelling of a Customized Luminous Comfort Setting (CLCS) for a traveller characterized by visual impairment. Individuals are represented with diamonds, concepts are represented with circles, and roles are represented with arrows (dashed arrows indicate datatype properties, full-line arrows represent object properties). The type of an individual is stated with a curved arrow.

5.3. The Room Ontology

5.3.1. Hotel Room and Its Features Description

The description of the hotel room relies on the Accommodation Ontology Language Reference (ACCO) [57], a vocabulary for modelling hotels, vacation homes, camping sites and other accommodations; originally thought for the description of these accommodations for e-commerce, ACCO can be adopted to provide sharable information regarding, for instance, a hotel room. It allows to specify the star-rating of a hotel and the star-rating adopted standard, the hotel features, the price of a specific room per night. ACCO also allows to specify the hotel room's features, such as: maximum number of occupants, the possibility to allow pets in the premises, the duration of the stay, etc. ACCO does not allow the description of the physical room, therefore to complete the modelling of a room DogOnt [13] was selected. This model is widely used to provide descriptions of smart environments, specifying the location in the built environment of devices (both sensors and actuators) with `dogont:isIn` object property, applicable for appliances, sensors and actuators. DogOnt also allows to model devices independently from the specific technologies, referring to their typology, functionality (the tasks a device can accomplish, `dogont:Functionality`) and state (the condition of the device, such as "on", "off" or "stand-by", `dogont:hasState`); these features and the classes and properties describing it can be mapped to other relevant device ontologies, as illustrated in the following subsection

5.3.2. Devices Deployed in the Room Module

Devices' description leverages the Smart Appliance REFerence Ontology (SAREF) [58] to describe some of the features of a device and to complete DogOnt's provided device location in the space; starting from the concept of Device, this reference ontology provides the means to describe device's properties, location in the space, type; moreover, SAREF models the function of a device, such as a sensor and the metrics it measures. For example, a smoke sensor (belonging to the class `saref:Sensor`), performs a `saref:SensingFunction`. SAREF is suited to describe indoor environment devices and is created with RDF/OWL, as well as already exploited in several studies on interoperability among devices [71]. SAREF has been adopted to describe the devices deployed in the room used for RoomFort tests (see further Section 5); in particular, for each device its type (sensor, actuator, appliance, light, etc.) and specific ID are specified.

5.4. Comfort Metrics, Measurements and Luminous Comfort Settings Module

As stated above, there are no canonical and widely used comfort ontologies. Therefore, RoomFort's application ontologies relied on a different approach. The comfort metrics involved in a hotel room and analyzed in this work are "Temperature", "Humidity rate", "Illuminance": these metrics, modelled as classes, are further detailed with the respective "Comfortable" and "Uncomfortable" subclasses (respectively: "ComfortableIlluminance", "UncomfortableIlluminance"; "ComfortableTemperature", "UncomfortableTemperature"; "ComfortableHumidityRate", "UncomfortableHumidityRate"). Measurements acquired by a sensor are semantically annotated providing for each: a unique ID, the value of the performed measurement, a DateTime stamp of the measurement, the unit of measurement involved, the comfort metrics it is referred to. An example of measurements modelling is provided in Figure 6.

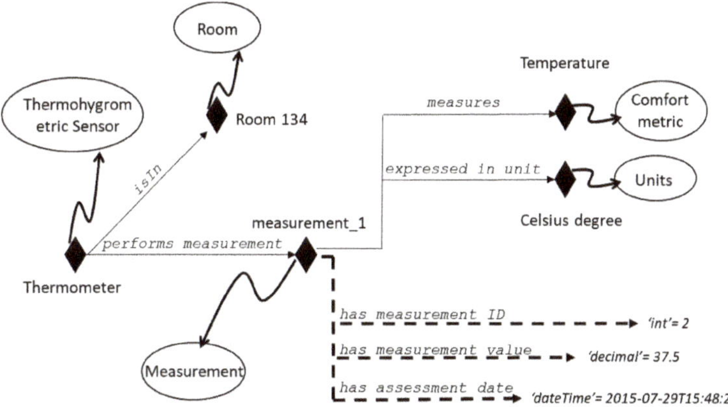

Figure 6. An example of the modelling of a measurement performed in the hotel room; individuals are represented with diamonds, concepts are represented with circles, and roles are represented with arrows (dashed arrows indicate datatype properties, full-line arrows represent object properties). The type of an individual is stated with a curved arrow.

Each measurement acquired by a sensor is then classified thanks to a set of SWRL rule. For instance, the following rule:

```
Guest(?g), selectsActivity(?g, ?a), Activity (work),
IlluminanceSensor(?ls), acquiresMeasurement (?ls, ?m),
Measurement(?m), hasMeasurementValue (?m, ?value),
greaterThanOrEqual(?value, 200), lessThanOrEqual(?value, 300)
-> ComfortableIlluminance(?m)
```

allows to classify an illuminance measurement when the guest specifies he/she wants to read in the room as comfortable or uncomfortable; in the latter case, uncomfortable measurements enable actuation and are used to suggest corrective actions. Moreover, as seen above, a similar modelling can be adopted for the description of both Luminous Comfort Settings (LCS) and CLCS. In this case, an individual representing the LCS is linked with its characteristics (through datatype properties indicating the RGB code of the color of the light and the E_m expressed in lux), as illustrated in Figure 7.

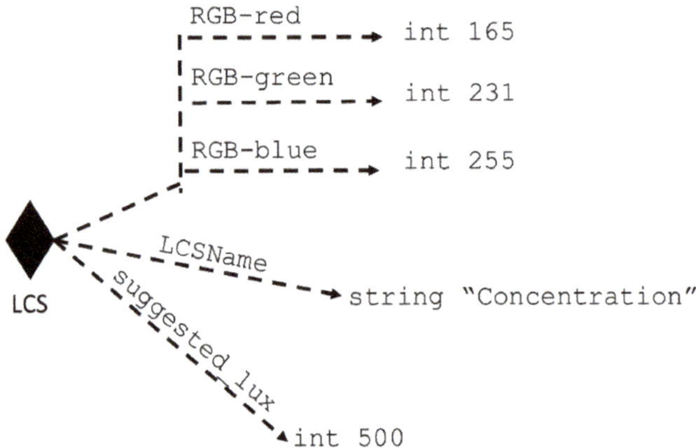

Figure 7. An example of the modelling of Luminous Comfort Setting (LCS); individuals are represented with diamonds, concepts are represented with circles, and roles are represented with arrows (dashed arrows indicate datatype properties). Please note that this specific LCS here represented is one of the results coming from the evaluation of visual comfort in a hotel room (described in Section 6).

5.5. The Semantic Repository and Reasoning Engine

The ontologies described above are hosted on a semantic repository, also defined as triple-store or RDF store [72], since it allows to query and retrieve data in semantic-compliant format. RoomFort's ontologies are hosted on Stardog, a widely known knowledge graph platform that supports querying activities and reasoning with RDF, OWL and SWRL.

Reasoning in Stardog is performed at query time, which means that the triples resulting from the reasoning process are not materialized (and automatically added into the ontologies) but, instead, for each query requiring the result deriving from the application of one or more SWRL, the reasoner solves only those rules necessary to solve the query. Consequently, the reasoning profile selected for RoomFort deployment on Stardog (version 5.3.4) [73] allows the treatment of rules in the SWRL form like those presented in the previous subsections.

5.6. The RoomFort Application: Querying and Retrieving Data From the Ontology

RoomFort application is developed with Unity 3D [74] to run on Android devices (smartphone and tablets). The applications' interface has been designed to be user-friendly and the more intuitive as possible. It allows the guest to select the activities and the area of the room (the bed or the desk, for example) in which he/she wants to perform such activity. Moreover, the application can be used to create novel CLCS according to guest's responses and save them in the semantic repository. Figure 8 shows a user while experiencing the RoomFort application.

The application can exchange information with the semantic repository (and the ontologies hosted in it) via a semantic middleware, a software developed with Java that allows to query the semantic knowledge base using predefined SPARQL (SPARQL Protocol and RDF Query Language) [75] queries. This program is run each time the guest decides to perform an activity inside the room and taps the related button on the smartphone application interface to state her/his intention. The moment the passenger taps the button on the application to perform an activity, the middleware program runs to generate a proper SPARQL query with necessary input data to be able to retrieve information regarding guest's health condition. These input data are passed from application to the middleware through a JSON (JavaScript Object Notation) file indicating the passenger's name, the activity she/he would like to perform, health-related data, the location where the activity is going to happen; the JSON file is fed into the middleware as an input to generate the precise SPARQL queries to insert that specific situation inside the ontology, retrieve the inferred data according to the new data inserted, and finally delete the inserted data to have the ontology ready for the next execution. After generating the correct SPARQL query, the middleware program runs the Stardog server, on which a query similar to the following is performed:

```
PREFIX rf: <http://www.stiima.cnr.it/RoomFort>
PREFIX dog: <http://www.elite.polito.it/ontologies/dogont.owl>
SELECT ?lcs
WHERE
{ ?guest rf:selectsActivity rf:Relaxing ;
rf:setsActivityLocation dog:Bed .
?lcs rf:isSuitableForActivity rf:Relaxing .
}
```

a query that allows retrieving the luminous conditions suitable for relaxing on the bed. Similarly, though the use of the SPARQL command INSERT a guest can add one or more LCS to the ontology—in this case, to his/her preferences. The middleware operates by translating SPARQL queries' results into JSON files and feeding them to the actuators, the lamps near the bed, in this specific case.

Figure 8. A screenshot of the RoomFort application for Android devices. The user (identified by his/her own ID number) selects an activity.

6. Evaluation of the Visual Comfort

The development of the above-mentioned ontology constitutes a key feature to enable the adaptation of the comfort conditions according to the guest's current activity and to his/her preference. Such adaptation occurs automatically when the guest has set his/her own preferences or has introduced his/her health status description in the system; however, the first time the guest (without impairments) starts an activity in the hotel room, the system is unaware of his/her preference and thus, requires some initial conditions, which have to be decided and described in RoomFort in advance. A possible solution may be the application of European standard EN 12464-1 as initial conditions. Nevertheless, this has two possible drawbacks: (1) standards often correspond to the minimum requirements, and not to a "comfortable" condition [76]; (2) standards are applied according to the activity that guests are expected to perform in a certain place: e.g., at the desk, people are expected to read or to write, not to relax while listening to music. Therefore, light conditions at the desk will correspond to the standard value for reading, i.e., 200–500 lux, which is indeed too bright for a relaxing activity. To try to reduce the level of discomfort caused by the strict application of normative-based values, setting "activity-related" initial conditions (namely, the LCS)—regardless of the place in which such an activity occurs, appears as a reasonable solution. To verify this hypothesis, we designed a repeated-measure study whose aim is evaluating whether specific light conditions can improve the user's perceived comfort, while staying sit at the hotel room desk and accomplishing two different activities resembling the two main activities of a business travellers: reading while being concentrated and relaxing.

6.1. Methods

6.1.1. Participants

Twenty-eight adults aged 44.25 ± 17.09 have been enrolled in the study. All were in a good general health status. Exclusion criteria were: moderate to severe vision or motor impairment; severe pain; cognitive decline; inability to read Italian language; inability to provide informed written consent. All the other demographic and clinical characteristics of the study participants are reported in Table 1.

Table 1. Sample's characteristics; M = male; F = female.

Participants	28	
Gender (M/F)	12/16	
Age	44.25 ± 17.09	
Education (Years)	15.63 ± 3.13	
Mild vision impairment 71% :	*Astigmatism* :	43%
	Myopia :	46%
	Presbyopia :	21%
	Hyperopia :	11%

The subjects participating in the study provided informed written consent.

6.1.2. Equipment

The test took place in an indoor environment simulating a three-star hotel room. As depicted in Figure 9, the guest enters the room through the entrance area that acts as an anteroom between the bathroom and sleeping area. From this area, the guest can then access to the outdoor terrace. The room dimensions—including the bathroom— were 3×6 m^2; room height was 2.20 m. The room's three functional areas were furnished as follows:

- Entrance: wardrobe
- Sleeping area: bed 1 and 2, bedside Tables 1 and 2, chair 1, desk, minibar, TV
- Terrace: chair 2, table

The space and furniture organization inside the room matches the characteristics of the environment described in the ontology. The room and the terrace were equipped with networked devices able to monitor the environment and to deliver appropriate comfort metrics according to each guest's preferences and to the activity he/she is performing. For luminous comfort provision, six Philips Hue spotlights were mounted on the ceiling and three table lamps mounting Philips Hue bulbs were placed close to the table (see Figure 9). The light beams of these three lamps were directed toward the white wall behind the table, so that light colors and temperature could be experienced at their best by an individual sit at the table; this also allows to change the colour of the wall, according to the selected LCS. A window allowing the daylight illumination of the room was present on the shortest wall, however, not to influence the test results, it was covered with a dark curtain for the whole tests' duration (with the exception of the questionnaires' answering time). To accomplish the reading task, the users were provided with white-paper pages; the texts were taken from the Italian edition of the books "*La coscienza di Zeno*" (Zeno's Conscience, Italo Svevo, 1923) and "*Utopia*" (Utopia, Thomas Moore, 1516). The choice of extracts not too easy to comprehend was intentional, to encourage the user in concentrating during the activity accomplishment. Both texts were written with a serif typeface (Georgia), pt. 12.

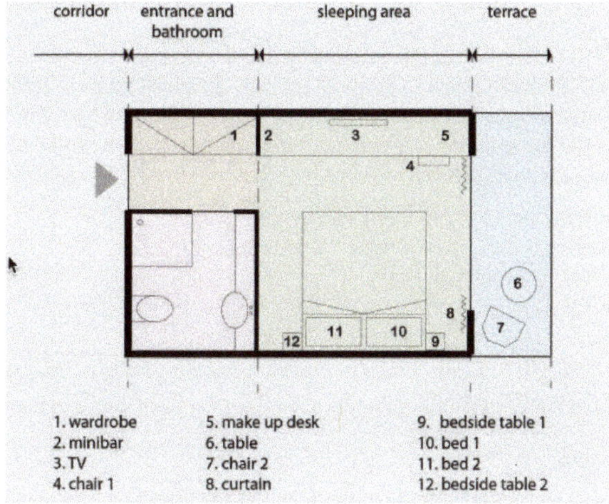

Figure 9. Functional areas in a room.

6.1.3. Protocol

Each subject performed the test in the above-mentioned environment, been administered with all light conditions for the duration of both the activities. Each session started with one minute of dark adaptation [77]. Each light condition lasted 2 min per activity, thus, resulting in: 2 min of reading with condition (1), administration of the questionnaire (see Measures paragraph), 2 min of relaxing with condition (1), administration of the questionnaire. At the end of such a series, one minute of dark adaptation was performed and the light condition was changed. The whole test lasted about 25–30 min per subjects. The four light conditions are presented in Table 2 and in Figure 10. Standards represent the average illumination required for reading, i.e., the general condition that one can expect to find in correspondence with a hotel room's table. The other three conditions, namely "Relax", "Concentration" and "Red" were similar to the Philips Hue predefined light sets.

The choice of using predefined lighting sets is justified from the lack of scientific literature regarding this topic; since to our knowledge no other studies investigating lighting comfort while reading and relaxing in a hotel room have been conducted, we relied on the know-how and the knowledge of a world-known manufacturer, such as Philips.

Table 2. Characteristics of the four light conditions used for the validation. RGB (Red, Green and Blue) is the color model adopted.

	Relax	Concentration	Red	Normative
Illuminance (lux)	200	500	300	400
RGB	(255, 178, 44)	(165, 231, 255)	(255, 15, 15)	(255, 255, 255)
Correlated Color Temperature (K)	2600	7500	1000	5600

Figure 10. The four light conditions: "Normative", "Relax", "Concentration" and "Red".

6.1.4. Measures

To evaluate the rates of perceived comfort, an ad-hoc questionnaire—adapted from [37,78]—has been developed. The questionnaire foresees three items aimed at investigating the satisfaction of the users with respect to the light conditions during the accomplishment of a specific activity, and two items about the user's personal feelings.

(Q1) I am satisfied with the amount of light for reading;
(Q2) I am satisfied with the amount of light for relaxing;
(Q3) I like the vertical surface brightness;
 Q4) I feel concentrated;
(Q5) I feel relaxed.

In all cases, the user had to indicate his/her level of agreement on a 7-point Likert scale ranging from 1 (strongly disagree) to 7 (strongly agree).

6.1.5. Statistical Analyses

Data resulting from the questionnaire were analyzed using one-way repeated measures ANOVA; post-hoc tests were performed using Turkey range test and 95% confidence. Matrix of inter-correlations were used to assess whether a correlation exists between age and light preferences and between visual impairments (i.e., wearing glasses) and light preferences. All tests were performed using MiniTab 18.

6.2. Results

Results of the questionnaires for the two considered activities are reported in Table 3.

Table 3. Results of the questionnaires. Grouping information using the Turkey method and 95% confidence level (means that do not share a letter are significantly different). Conc. = Concentration.

Reading				*Relaxing*			
Relax	**Conc.**	**Red**	**Normative**	**Relax**	**Conc.**	**Red**	**Normative**
5.11 $\pm$1.26 ^{A}	4.39 $\pm$1.26 ^{A}	3.39 $\pm$1.69 ^{B}	4.50 $\pm$1.32 ^{A}	5.39 $\pm$1.17 ^{A}	4.21$\pm$1.77 ^{B}	4.14 $\pm$1.63 ^{B}	4.36 $\pm$1.81 ^{A,B}
4.64 $\pm$1.6 ^{B}	6.11 $\pm$1.23 ^{A}	2.86 $\pm$1.65 ^{C}	5.89 $\pm$1.10 ^{A}	4.61 $\pm$1.59 ^{B}	5.82 $\pm$1.49 ^{A}	3.04 $\pm$1.86 ^{C}	5.50 $\pm$1.35 ^{A,B}
4.64 $\pm$1.62 ^{A}	5.21 $\pm$1.45 ^{A}	3.54 $\pm$1.77 ^{B}	4.89 $\pm$1.47 ^{A}	4.54 $\pm$1.88 ^{A,B}	5.11 $\pm$1.66 ^{A,B}	3.75 $\pm$1.82 ^{B}	4.43 $\pm$1.57 ^{A,B}
4.93 $\pm$1.68 ^{A}	4.43 $\pm$1.57 ^{A,B}	3.36 $\pm$1.75 ^{B}	4.61 $\pm$1.50 ^{A}	5.21 $\pm$1.57 ^{A}	4.32 $\pm$1.66 ^{A,B}	4.00 $\pm$1.75 ^{B}	4.14 $\pm$1.76 ^{A,B}
4.74 $\pm$1.72 ^{A}	5.36 $\pm$1.57 ^{A}	3.00 $\pm$1.72 ^{B}	5.04 $\pm$1.57 ^{A}	4.46 $\pm$1.53 ^{A}	4.89 $\pm$1.73 ^{A}	3.11 $\pm$1.77 ^{B}	4.43 $\pm$1.73 ^{A}

No correlations were found between demographic characteristics and light preferences.

6.3. Discussion of Test Results

The results showed that, in general, users preferred the "relax" condition (i.e., a low color temperature and a quite low illuminance) for the reading activity and the "concentration" condition (medium color temperature and medium illuminance) for the relax. "Red" was judged as not suitable for any activities, while the normative-based conditions were evaluated always as quite good (between 4 and 5 points of the Likert-scale). Beside the "red" condition, which was expected [78] to be worse than the others, the obtained results are in contrast with both Philips definitions and previous studies. Iszo [79], for instance, found that people reported to feel more relaxed when the illuminance was lower and more active when the light was more intense. Viola et al. [80] reported and increased alertness with blue-enriched white light (17,000 K); Wang et al. [78] demonstrated that relatively lower CCTs are regarded as more comfortable and preferred for relaxing, while higher CCTs are considered more comfortable and preferred for working. A possible explanation for the results of the present study may be found in the different setup and, in particular, in the quantity of light diffused in the environment or in the glare present on the papers. This lack of generalizability has been already highlighted [78] and luminance (i.e., the luminous power perceived by the human eye) has been suggested as the variable to estimate when evaluating visual comfort, instead of illuminance (i.e., the measurement of the amount of light falling onto (illuminating) and spreading over a given surface area) [37]. This aspect calls for more studies aimed at defining new light-related metrics and motivates the implementation of the above-mentioned light conditions in RoomFort ("**relax**" for reading and "**concentration**" for relaxing), though in contrast with what reported by other studies. One last important point to mention is the inefficacy of the normative-based lights to elicit visual comfort for both the two tested activities.

6.4. Luminous Comfort Settings Deriving from the Tests

The two LCSs, "**relax**" for the reading activity and "**concentration**" for the relaxing activity, depicted in Table 2—obtained by the above-mentioned tests are modelled into the RoomFort ontology, according to the design pattern presented in Section 5.4. The results of the modelling are provided in Figure 11, which summarizes the two LCSs and their suggested use inside the hotel room.

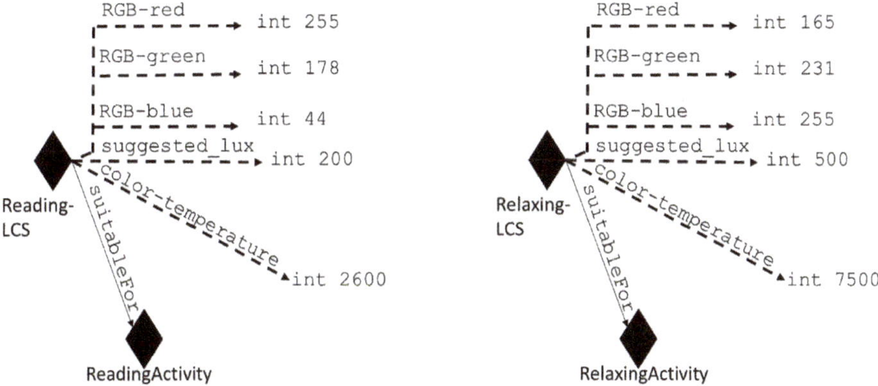

Figure 11. The modelling of the two Luminous Comfort Setting (LCS) deriving from the tests conducted on luminous comfort evaluation. Individuals are represented with diamonds, concepts are represented with circles, and roles are represented with arrows (dashed arrows indicate datatype properties).

7. Considerations on the Applicability of RoomFort and Its Validation

This Section highlights some aspects related to RoomFort's applicability in hotels, the proposed validation for the prototypical application developed and contextualizes the work in the field of a novel paradigm for IEQ.

7.1. Comfort as a Service

As RoomFort aims at providing guest-based comfort for some indoor metrics, a novel paradigm for indoor comfort management has starting to spread: Comfort as a Service (CaaS). In a recent research paper, Juan Gómez-Romero et al. [81] suggest that dwellers should hand over the control of their comfort-management systems to a energy-savings companies. The purpose of this action aims at generating an automatic optimal control strategy for the indoor domestic equipment, able to provide the inhabitants with adequate comfort levels while ensuring energy-savings. Moreover, CaaS approach releases building occupants from operating with the comfort equipment, which usually generates energy wasting, uncomfortable indoor comfort and an increase in costs. The idea suggested in [81] turns the traditional model of paying per consumed energy in favor of a model of paying per provided comfort, thus, making comfort a service.

In relation to RoomFort, CaaS relies on a different technological AmI framework, including also IoT, predictive computing and Big Data to deliver comfort management and energy-saving. Nevertheless, with particular reference to the hotel industry, the idea of CaaS, in which the guests can purchase tailored and energy-saving comfort settings, seems to be supported by studies in the tourism field, as underlined by [32,33]; besides, Buso et al. [29] recently pointed out how guest are willing to pay an extra charge on the room rate for enjoying more comfortable indoor conditions.

Therefore, RoomFort can potentially be seen as a component of a CaaS system, thus, providing more comfortable rooms, sustaining energy-saving and meeting guests' needs, and also generating a win-win situation for both guests and hotel owners.

7.2. Applicability of RoomFort to Hotellerie

RoomFort relies on semantic representations of comfort, health and device-related concepts leveraging ontologies to formalize the relationships among these domains of knowledge. Although Semantic Web technologies are widely used in several fields and applications, their adoption in everyday life is still a work in progress. Nevertheless, RoomFort's deployment relies on an architecture that exploits several well-established concepts and technologies AmI, AAL and CA applications. One of the limits of RoomFort's current configuration consists in the possibility to provide to the hotel guest's ICF-health data. Although this problem does not jeopardize the adoption of the whole application, it is mainly caused by the following issues.

ICF is an international standard fully understandable by clinical personnel, but, even if its terms are quite transparent in their meanings—people who are unaware of the classification functioning may find it difficult to use. A solution to this issue is represented by the possibility for the guest to have an ICF-based representation of his/her health condition performed by his/her physician. In this way, the guest's health condition will always be portable and can be delivered as (ontological) data.

With regard to the portability of the guest's health data, it worths noticing that the same approach can be adopted also for personalized LCS: in this sense, a guest arriving in a hotel can set up his/her own personalized LCS. This means that the customization of visual comfort inside an indoor environment can potentially be done even without recurring to reasoning processes; in this particular case the guest, when booking a hotel room, submits his LCS together with his/her health-related data.

Being a semantic-based application, RoomFort's wide adoption in hotel industry requires single accommodations to agree on a common representation of the knowledge related to the guests, their health condition, the comfort metrics measured, the measurements performed in the room and the devices to be deployed in the environment (i.e., sensors and actuators). In this way, each hotel may rely on a safe and shared model to formalize guests' data and comfort. Therefore, for a pervasive adoption of RoomFort hotel industry must agree on a shared and sound ontological description of the domains of interest, even considering the lack of ontological standards, as described in Sections 2 and 5. Using a shared vocabulary (as the one described in Section 5), each hotel can therefore describe itself, its rooms and the services it provides. Nonetheless, RoomFort's horizontal scalability allows the system to be exploited also for the customization of comfort metrics in relation to other activities performed in the room (eating, working with a laptop, watching the television, etc.).

RoomFort can be further developed into a Decision Support System (DSS); in fact, being aware of the guests' health condition and his/her needs, RoomFort can potentially provide the guest with a set of most suitable LCS, CO_2 concentration, indoor temperature and humidity rate to maximize his/her comfort; in the particular case of guests afflicted by vision-related, respiratory-related or sensitivity to temperature-related health problems the expedients provided by the DSS can potentially help the guests in coping with their impairments while performing specific activities.

Finally, RoomFort—even if originally thought for business travellers due to their particular necessities—can be adjust to work also for leisure tourists, especially in the context of CaaS, in which leisure tourists can decide whether to purchase or not an additional, automatic and optimal comfort settings.

7.3. Proposed Validation Framework of RoomFort Application

Once the RoomFort mobile application will be completed including the possibility of varying all the comfort metrics potentially changeable within the RoomFort framework, it will be validated in a study enrolling healthy adults. Participants will be asked to work for half a day (4 h) in the environment reprising the hotel room (described in Section 6.1.2) with their own laptop (and paper-based documents) and to relax whenever they like, either on the bed or while staying at the desk. Before undergoing the study, all the participants will be briefly instructed on the RoomFort application functionalities and on the variables which they can modify throughout the day. No further instructions will be given. After the end of the test, participants will be administered a questionnaire aimed at evaluating (1) whether they liked the possibility to change the environmental conditions, (2) whether they liked the predefined sets for each activity and (3) whether they would have preferred not having an application to adjust the different comfort metrics, through 7-point Likert questions. In addition, System Usability Scale (SUS) [82] and Technology Acceptance (TAM) [83] questionnaires will be administered too, to evaluate respectively the user-friendliness of the application and its perceived ease-of-use and usefulness.

8. Conclusions and Future Works

To satisfy guest's needs, the research proposes RoomFort, a semantic-based application aimed at providing a holistic comfort experience in the business travellers' rooms; RoomFort leverages a novel ontology-based architecture able to personalize indoor comfort metrics inside the room according to guests' needs, desires and activities. In this work, the authors focused on the possibility to provide customized luminous comfort settings suited for two pivotal activities for business travellers: working and relaxing. The results of a study conducted on 28 participants allowed to model into ontologies the best luminous comfort settings, which can be included in RoomFort's semantic knowledge base with the aim of providing business travellers with the best indoor conditions to ensure alertness and well-being.

RoomFort's ontologies can also provide the means to manage indoor CO_2 concentration, temperature and humidity rate, thus, actuating responses from the HVAC system of the hotel room. Furthermore, leveraging on an international representation of humans' health conditions, the system provides the possibility to customize the indoor comfort of the hotel room basing on guest's needs and characteristics. This feature can play an important role as an attraction tool for the more demanding customers but, consequently, can be also a valuable asset for hotel owner—in fact, by reducing the uncomfortable feeling and increasing the comfort perception, the attractiveness of the hotel could exponentially increases. RoomFort's system architecture assures that no guest personal data is stored in the hotel environment, so that privacy is preserved.

Future studies foresee the evaluation of RoomFort application for smartphones, following the validation framework proposed in this work. A set of tests, aimed at validating RoomFort's capabilities to actuate modifications in temperature and humidity rate—by triggering the activation of the HVAC system of the room—will also be deployed; then a test with participants will be aimed at evaluating the quality of the provided actuation. Together with the management of visual comfort, this feature can constitute a step towards the adoption of tailored holistic comfort in indoor environments. Moreover, RoomFort will be tested also with leisure tourists, to understand their possible acceptance of this technology in the context of providing optimal and energy-saving comfort management as an additional service.

Author Contributions: D.S. developed the ontologies presented in this work, set the semantic repository, contributed to the development of RoomFort architecture and supervised the writing of the first draft of this paper. S.C. provided the description of the room and contributed to the enrollment of the 28 participants and to the administration of the study together with M.N.; S.A. developed the study protocol, analyzed the outcomes, wrote the study methods and results, and revised the whole manuscript; M.N. developed the application with the help of S.A. and D.S., contributed to the development of RoomFort architecture and to the administration of the study; M.S. contributed to the development of RoomFort and revised the manuscript together with S.A.

Funding: This research received no external funding.

Acknowledgments: This work has been founded by "Convenzione Operativa No. 19365/RCC" in the framework of the project "Future Home for Future Communities". Authors would like to acknowledge the 28 participants who took part to the study.

Conflicts of Interest: The authors declare no conflict of interest.

Abbreviations

The following abbreviations are used in this manuscript:

AmI	Ambient Intelligence
CA	Context Awareness
HVAC	Heating, Ventilation and Air Conditioning
RDF	Resource Description Framework
OWL	Ontology Web Language
SWRL	Semantic Web Rule Language
IEQ	Indoor Environmental Quality
ICF	International Classification of Functioning, Disability and Health
CLCS	Customized Luminous Comfort Setting
LCS	Luminous Comfort Setting
DSS	Decision Support System

References

1. World Travel & Tourism Council. Available online: https://www.wttc.org (accessed on 18 October 2018).
2. WTTC. *Travel & Tourism Global Economic Impact & Issues 2018*; WTTC: London, UK, 2018; p. 11.
3. Global Business Travel Association. Available online: https://www.gbta.org/membership-and-communities/chapters-and-regions/europe (accessed on 18 October 2018).
4. Boyce, P.R.; Berman, S.M.; Collins, B.L.; Lewis, A.L.; Rea, M.S. *Lighting and Human Performance: A Review*; National Electrical Manufacturers Association (NEMA) and Lighting Research Institute: Washington, DC, USA, 1989.
5. Lovelock, C.; Wirtz, J.; Tat Keh, H.; Lu, X. *Services Marketing in Asia: Managing People , Technology and Strategy*, 2nd ed.; Prentice Hall, Pearson: Singapore, 2005; Volume 13.
6. Veitch, J.A.; Hine, D.W.; Gifford, R. End users: Knowledge, beliefs, and preferences for lighting. *J. Inter. Des.* **1993**, *19*, 15–26. [CrossRef]

7.   Blomqvist, E. The use of Semantic Web technologies for decision support—A survey. *Semant. Web* **2014**, *5*, 177–201.

8.   Vimalanathan, K.; Ramesh Babu, T. The effect of indoor office environment on the work performance, health and well-being of office workers. *J. Environ. Health Sci. Eng.* **2014**, *12*, 113. [CrossRef] [PubMed]

9.   Tila, F.; Kim, H. Semantic IoT System for Indoor Environment Control—A Sparql and SQL based hybrid model. *Adv. Sci. Technol. Lett.* **2015**, *120*, 678–683.

10.   Pan, J.Z. Resource Description Framework. In *Handbook on Ontologies*; Springer: Berlin/Heidelberg, Germany, 2009; pp. 71–90.

11.   Zeiler, W.; Van Houten, M.; Savanović, P.; Zeiler, W.; Van Houten, R.; Boxem, G.; Savanovic, P.; Van Der Velden, J.; Wortel, W.; Haan, J.F.; et al. *Flexergy: An Ontology to Couple Decentrilised Sustainable Comfort Systems with Centralised Energy Infrastructures*; Technical Report; Technische Universiteit Eindhoven: Eindhoven, The Netherlands, 2009.

12.   Mahroo, A.; Spoladore, D.; Caldarola, E.G.; Modoni, G.; Sacco, M. Enabling the Smart Home Through a Semantic-Based Context-Aware System. In Proceedings of the PerLS'18—Second International Workshop on Pervasive Smart Living Spaces IEEE International Conference on Pervasive Computing and Communication, Athens, Greece, 19–23 March 2018.

13.   Bonino, D.; Corno, F. DogOnt—Ontology modeling for intelligent domotic environments. In *International Semantic Web Conference*; Springer: Berlin/Heidelberg, Germany, 2008; pp. 790–803.

14.   Frešer, M.; Cvetković, B.; Gradišek, A.; Luštrek, M. Anticipatory system for T–H–C dynamics in room with real and virtual sensors. In Proceedings of the 2016 ACM International Joint Conference on Pervasive and Ubiquitous Computing Adjunct—UbiComp '16, Heidelberg, Germany, 12–16 September 2016; pp. 1267–1274.

15.   McGuinness, D.L.; Van Harmelen, F. OWL Web Ontology Language Overview. W3C Recomm. 2004. Available online: http://www.w3.org/TR/owl-features/ (accessed on 18 October 2018).

16.   Horrocks, I.; Patel-schneider, P.F.; Boley, H.; Tabet, S.; Grosof, B.; Dean, M. SWRL: A Semantic Web Rule Language Combining OWL and RuleML. *W3C Memb. Submiss.* **2004**, *21*, 1–20.

17.   Adeleke, J.A.; Moodley, D. An Ontology for Proactive Indoor Environmental Quality Monitoring and Control. In Proceedings of the 2015 Annual Research Conference on South African Institute of Computer Scientists and Information Technologists—SAICSIT '15, Stellenbosch, South Africa, 28–30 September 2015; pp. 1–10.

18.   Stavropoulos, T.G.; Vrakas, D.; Vlachava, D.; Bassiliades, N. BOnSAI. In Proceedings of the 2nd International Conference on Web Intelligence, Mining and Semantics—WIMS '12, Craiova, Romania, 6–8 June 2012; p. 1.

19.   Martin, D.; Burstein, M.; Hobbs, J.; Lassila, O.; McDermott, D.; McIlraith, S.; Narayanan, S.; Paolucci, M.; Parsia, B.; Payne, T.; et al. OWL-S: Semantic markup for web services. *W3C Memb. Submiss.* **2004**. Available online: https://www.w3.org/Submission/OWL-S/ (accessed on 18 October 2018).

20.   Reinisch, C.; Kofler, M.J.; Kastner, W. ThinkHome: A smart home as digital ecosystem. In Proceedings of the 4th IEEE International Conference on Digital Ecosystems and Technologies, Dubai, UAE, 13–16 April 2010; pp. 256–261.

21.   Spoladore, D.; Arlati, S.; Sacco, M. Semantic and Virtual Reality-Enhanced Configuration of Domestic Environments: The Smart Home Simulator. *Mob. Inf. Syst.* **2017**, *2017*, 3185481. [CrossRef]

22.   Borràs, J.; Moreno, A.; Valls, A. Intelligent tourism recommender systems: A survey. *Expert Syst. Appl.* **2014**, *41*, 7370–7389. [CrossRef]

23.   Kim, D.; Kim, S. The role of mobile technology in tourism: Patents, articles, news, and mobile tour app reviews. *Sustainability* **2017**, *9*, 2082. [CrossRef]

24.   Petrina, O.; Petrina, O.B. Smart Spaces Based Construction and Personalization of Recommendation Services for Historical e-Tourism of Recommendation Services for Historical e-Tourism. *Int. J. Adv. Intell. Syst.* **2016**, *9*, 85–95.

25.   Smirnov, A.; Shilov, N.; Kashevnik, A.; Ponomarev, A. Cyber-physical infomobility for tourism application. *Int. J. Inf. Technol. Manag.* **2017**, *16*, 31. [CrossRef]

26.   Moreno, A.; Valls, A.; Isern, D.; Marin, L.; Borràs, J. SigTur/E-Destination: Ontology-based personalized recommendation of Tourism and Leisure Activities. *Eng. Appl. Artif. Intell.* **2013**, *26*, 633–651. [CrossRef]

27.   Kolcaba, K.Y. Holistic comfort: Operationalizing the construct as a nurse-sensitive outcome. *Adv. Nurs. Sci.* **1992**, *15*, 1–10. [CrossRef]

28. Chu, R.K.; Choi, T. An importance-performance analysis of hotel selection factors in the Hong Kong hotel industry: A comparison of business and leisure travellers. *Tour. Manag.* **2000**, *21*, 363–377. [CrossRef]

29. Buso, T.; Dell'Anna, F.; Becchio, C.; Bottero, M.C.; Corgnati, S.P. Of comfort and cost: Examining indoor comfort conditions and guests' valuations in Italian hotel rooms. *Energy Res. Soc. Sci.* **2017**, *32*, 94–111. [CrossRef]

30. Striker, J.; Luippold, R.S.; Nagy, L.; Liese, B.; Bigelow, C.; Mundt, K.A. Risk factors for psychological stress among international business travellers. *Occup. Environ. Med.* **1999**, *56*, 245–252. [CrossRef] [PubMed]

31. Gilbert, D.C.; Morris, L. The relative importance of hotels and airlines to the business traveller. *J. Contemp. Hosp. Manag.* **1995**, *7*, 19–23. [CrossRef]

32. Ariffin, A.A.M.; Aziz, N.A. The Effect of Physical Environment's Innovativeness on the Relationship between Hosting Quality and Satisfaction in Hotel Services. *Int. J. Trade Econ. Financ.* **2012**, *3*, 337–342. [CrossRef]

33. Ryu, K.; Jang, S.C.S. The Effect of Environmental Perceptions on Behavioral Intentions Through Emotions: The Case of Upscale Restaurants. *J. Hosp. Tour. Res.* **2007**, *31*, 56–72. [CrossRef]

34. Bohdanowicz, P.; Martinec, I.; Martinac, I. Thermal comfort and energy-savings in the hotel industry. In Proceedings of the Conference on Biometeorology and Aerobiology Joint with the 16th International Congress on Biometeorology, Kansas City, MI, USA, 28 October–1 November 2002; Volume 1, pp. 396–400.

35. Magnini, V.P.; Parker, E.E. The psychological effects of music: Implications for hotel firms. *J. Vacat. Mark.* **2009**, *15*, 53–62. [CrossRef]

36. Fisk, W.J. Health and Productivity Gains from Better Indoor Environments and their Relationship with Building Energy Efficiency. *Annu. Rev. Energy Environ.* **2000**, *25*, 537–566. [CrossRef]

37. Van Den Wymelenberg, K.; Inanici, M. A critical investigation of common lighting design metrics for predicting human visual comfort in offices with daylight. *LEUKOS J. Illum. Eng. Soc. N. Am.* **2014**, *10*, 145–164. [CrossRef]

38. Abbas, N.; Kumar, D.; McLachlan, N. The psychological and physiological effects of light and colour on space users. In Proceedings of the IEEE Engineering in Medicine and Biology 27th Annual Conference, Shanghai, China, 17–18 January 2006; Volume 2, pp. 1228–1231.

39. Baron, R.A.; Rea, M.S.; Daniels, S.G. Effects of indoor lighting (illuminance and spectral distribution) on the performance of cognitive tasks and interpersonal behaviors: The potential mediating role of positive affect. *Motiv. Emot.* **1992**, *1*, 1–33. [CrossRef]

40. Samani, S.A.; Samani, S.A. The impact of indoor lighting on students' learning performance in learning environments: A knowledge internalization perspective. *Int. J. Bus. Soc. Sci.* **2012**, *3*, 127–136.

41. Shamsul, B.; Sia, C.; Ng, Y.; Karmegan, K. Effects of Light's Colour Temperatures on Visual Comfort Level, Task Performances, and Alertness among Students. *Am. J. Public Health Res.* **2013**, *1*, 159–165. [CrossRef]

42. Ariffin, A.A.M.; Maghzi, A. A preliminary study on customer expectations of hotel hospitality: Influences of personal and hotel factors. *Int. J. Hosp. Manag.* **2012**, *31*, 191–198. [CrossRef]

43. Küller, R.; Ballal, S.; Laike, T.; Mikellides, B.; Tonello, G. The impact of light and colour on psychological mood: A cross-cultural study of indoor work environments. *Ergonomics* **2006**, *49*, 1496–1507. [CrossRef] [PubMed]

44. Odabaşioğlu, S.; Olguntürk, N. Effects of Coloured Lighting on the Perception of Interior Spaces. *Percept. Mot. Skills* **2015**, *120*, 183–201. [CrossRef] [PubMed]

45. Siamionava, K.; Slevitch, L.; Tomas, S.R. Effects of spatial colors on guests' perceptions of a hotel room. *Int. J. Hosp. Manag.* **2018**, *70*, 85–94. [CrossRef]

46. Countryman, C.C.; Jang, S. The effects of atmospheric elements on customer impression: The case of hotel lobbies. *Int. J. Contemp. Hosp. Manag.* **2006**, *18*, 534–545. [CrossRef]

47. Minazzi, R. Hotel Classification Systems: A Comparison of International Case Studies. *Economica* **2012**, *4*, 64–86.

48. HOTREC Hotels, Restaurants & Cafés in Europa. Available online: https://www.hotrec.eu (accessed on 18 October 2018).

49. Gazzetta Ufficiale. Decree 21 October 2001, in the Gazzetta Ufficiale n. 34, 11 February 2009. Available online: http://www.gazzettaufficiale.it/eli/gu/2009/02/11/34/sg/pdf (accessed on 18 October 2018).

50. Cuzzocrea, A.; Grasso, G.M.; Nolich, M. Effective and efficient distributed management of big clinical data: A framework. *Int. J. Data Min. Model. Manag.* **2018**, in press.

51. Wei, W.; Barnaghi, P. Semantic annotation and reasoning for sensor data. In *European Conference on Smart Sensing and Context*; Springer: Berlin/Heidelberg, Germany, 2009; pp. 66–76.

52. Buqi, R.; Carciotti, S.; Cipriano, M.; Ferrari, P.; Nolich, M. Cruise cabin as a home: Smart approaches to improve cabin comfort. In Proceedings of the NAV 2018: 19th International Conference on Ship and Maritime Research, Trieste, Italy, 20–22 June 2018; pp. 647–654.

53. Gruber, T.R. A Translation Approach to Portable Ontology Specifications. *Knowl. Acquis.* **1993**, *5*, 199–220. [CrossRef]

54. Pérez, A.; Baonza, M.D.F.; Villazón, B. *Neon Methodology for Building Ontology Networks: Ontology Specification*; Technical Report February; Departamento de Inteligencia Artificial, Facultad de Informática, Universidad Politécnica de Madrid: Madrid, Spain, 2008.

55. Fernández-López, M.; Gómez-Pérez, A.; Juristo, N. METHONTOLOGY: From Ontological Art Towards Ontological Engineering. In Proceedings of the AAAI-97 Spring Symposium on Ontological Engineering, Stanford, CA, USA, 24–26 March 1997; pp. 33–40.

56. International Classification of Functioning, Disability and Health. Available online: https://www.bioportal.bioontology.org/ontologies/ICF (accessed on 18 October 2018).

57. Hepp, M. *Accommodation Ontology Language Reference*; Technical Report; Hepp Research GmbH: Innsbruck, Austria, 2013.

58. Daniele, L.; den Hartog, F.; Roes, J. Created in Close Interaction with the Industry: The Smart Appliances REFerence (SAREF) Ontology. In *Lecture Notes in Business Information Processing*; Springer: Cham, Switzerland, 2015; Volume 225, pp. 100–112.

59. Spoladore, D.; Arlati, S.; Nolich, M.; Carciotti, S.; Rinaldi, A. Ontologies' definition for modeling the cabin comfort on cruise ships. In Proceedings of the NAV 2018: 19th International Conference on Ship and Maritime Research, Trieste, Italy, 20–22 June 2018; pp. 877–884.

60. Motik, B.; Sattler, U.; Studer, R. Query answering for OWL-DL with rules. *Web Semant. Sci. Serv. Agents World Wide Web* **2005**, *3*, 41–60. [CrossRef]

61. World Health Organization. *International Classification of Functioning, Disability and Health: ICF*; World Health Organization: Geneva, Switzerland, 2001.

62. Spoladore, D. Ontology-based decision support systems for health data management to support collaboration in ambient assisted living and work reintegration. In Proceedings of the 18th IFIP WG 5.5 Working Conference on Virtual Enterprises, Vicenza, Italy, 18–20 September 2017; Volume 506, pp. 341–352.

63. Arlati, S.; Spoladore, D.; Mottura, S.; Zangiacomi, A.; Ferrigno, G.; Sacchetti, R.; Sacco, M. Architecture of a virtual reality and semantics-based framework for the return to work of wheelchair users. In *International Conference on Augmented Reality, Virtual Reality and Computer Graphics*; Springer: Cham, Switzerland, 2017; Volume 10325, pp. 74–85.

64. Okochi, J.; Utsunomiya, S.; Takahashi, T. Health measurement using the ICF: Test-retest reliability study of ICF codes and qualifiers in geriatric care. *Health Qual. Life Outcomes* **2005**, *3*, 46. [CrossRef] [PubMed]

65. Spoladore, D.; Sacco, M. Semantic and Dweller-Based Decision Support System for the Reconfiguration of Domestic Environments: RecAAL. *Electronics* **2018**, *7*, 179. [CrossRef]

66. Della Mea, V.; Simoncello, A. An ontology-based exploration of the concepts and relationships in the activities and participation component of the international classification of functioning, disability and health. *J. Biomed. Semant.* **2012**, *3*, 1. [CrossRef] [PubMed]

67. Andronache, A.S.; Simoncello, A.; Della Mea, V.; Daffara, C.; Francescutti, C. Semantic aspects of the International Classification of Functioning, Disability and Health: Towards sharing knowledge and unifying information. *Am. J. Phys. Med. Rehabil.* **2012**, *91*, S124–S128. [CrossRef] [PubMed]

68. Noy, N.; Rector, A.; Hayes, P.; Welty, C. Defining N-Ary Relations on the Semantic Web. W3C Work. Group Note. 2006. Available online: https://www.w3.org/TR/swbp-n-aryRelations/ (accessed on 18 October 2018).

69. Da Silva, M.R.; de Souza Nobre, M.I.R.; de Carvalho, K.M.; de Cássia Ietto Montilha, R. Visual impairment, rehabilitation and International Classification of Functioning, Disability and Health. *Rev. Bras. Oftalmol.* **2014**, *73*, 291–301. [CrossRef]

70. Owsley, C.; McGwin, G.; Scilley, K.; Kallies, K. Development of a questionnaire to assess vision problems under low luminance in age-related maculopathy. *Investig. Ophthalmol. Vis. Sci.* **2006**, *47*, 528–535. [CrossRef] [PubMed]

71. Daniele, L.; den Hartog, F.; Roes, J. How to keep a reference ontology relevant to the industry: A case study from the smart home. In *International Experiences and Directions Workshop on OWL*; Springer: Cham, Switzerland, 2016; Volume 9557, pp. 117–123.

72. Rohloff, K.; Dean, M.; Emmons, I.; Ryder, D.; Sumner, J. An Evaluation of Triple-Store Technologies for Large Data Stores. In *OTM Confederated International Conferences "On the Move to Meaningful Internet Systems"*; Springer: Berlin/Heidelberg, Germany, 2007; pp. 1105–1114.

73. Stardog 5—Knowledge Graph Platform. Available online: https://www.stardog.com/docs/ (accessed on 18 October 2018).

74. Unity. Available online: https://unity3d.com/ (accessed on 18 October 2018).

75. Sirin, E.; Parsia, B. SPARQL-DL: SPARQL query for OWL-DL. In Proceedings of the OWLED 2007 Workshop on OWL: Experiences and Directions, Innsbruck, Austria, 6–7 June 2007.

76. Oral, G.K.; Yener, A.K.; Bayazit, N.T. Building envelope design with the objective to ensure thermal, visual and acoustic comfort conditions. *Build. Environ.* **2004**, *39*, 281–287. [CrossRef]

77. Ohta, N.; Robertson, A. *Colorimetry: Fundamentals and Applications*; John Wiley & Sons: Hoboken, NJ, USA, 2006.

78. Wang, Q.; Xu, H.; Zhang, F.; Wang, Z. Influence of color temperature on comfort and preference for LED indoor lighting. *Optik* **2017**, *129*, 21–29. [CrossRef]

79. Izsó, L.; Láng, E.; Laufer, L.; Suplicz, S.; Horváth, Á. Psychophysiological, performance and subjective correlates of different lighting conditions. *Light. Res. Technol.* **2009**, *41*, 349–360 [CrossRef]

80. Viola, A.U.; James, L.M.; Schlangen, L.J.M.; Dijk, D.J. Blue-enriched white light in the workplace improves self-reported alertness, performance and sleep quality. *Scand. J. Work Environ. Health* **2008**, *34*, 297–306. [CrossRef] [PubMed]

81. Gómez-Romero, J.; Molina-Solana, M.; Ros, M.; Ruiz, M.D.; Martin-Bautista, M.J. Comfort as a service: A new paradigm for residential environmental quality control. *Sustainability* **2018**, *10*, 3053. [CrossRef]

82. Brooke, J. SUS-A quick and dirty usability scale. *Usabil. Eval. Ind.* **1996**, *189*, 4–7.

83. Venkatesh, V.; Davis, F.D. A Theoretical Extension of the Technology Acceptance Model: Four Longitudinal Field Studies. *Manag. Sci.* **2000**, *46*, 186–204. [CrossRef]

 *electronics*

Article

Using Entropy of Social Media Location Data for the Detection of Crowd Dynamics Anomalies

Carlos Garcia-Rubio [1], Rebeca P. Díaz Redondo [2], Celeste Campo [1,*] and Ana Fernández Vilas [2]

[1] Department of Telematic Engineering, University Carlos III of Madrid, Avda. Universidad 30, Leganés, E-28911 Madrid, Spain; cgr@it.uc3m.es
[2] Information & Computing Lab., AtlantTIC Research Center, School of Telecommunications Engineering, University of Vigo, E-36310 Vigo, Spain; rebeca@det.uvigo.es (R.P.D.R.); avilas@det.uvigo.es (A.F.V.)
* Correspondence: celeste@it.uc3m.es

Received: 31 October 2018; Accepted: 27 November 2018; Published: 3 December 2018

Abstract: Evidence of something unusual happening in urban areas can be collected from different data sources, such as police officers, cameras, or specialized physical infrastructures. In this paper, we propose using geotagged posts on location-based social networks (LBSNs) to detect crowd dynamics anomalies automatically as evidence of a potential unusual event. To this end, we use the Instagram API media/search endpoint to collect the location of the pictures posted by Instagram users in a given area periodically. The collected locations are summarized by their centroid. The novelty of our work relies on using the entropy of the sequence of centroid locations in order to detect abnormal patterns in the city. The proposal is tested on a data set collected from Instagram during seven months in New York City and validated with another data set from Manchester. The results have also been compared with an alternative approach, a training phase plus a ranking of outliers. The main conclusion is that the entropy algorithm succeeds inn finding abnormal events without the need for a training phase, being able to dynamically adapt to changes in crowd behavior.

Keywords: city behavior; anomaly detection; location-based social networks; data mining algorithms

---

1. Introduction

Any city management department is interested in detecting unusual events in the urban area as early as possible. Being aware of any unexpected situation going on in the city allows city management departments to take action, for instance by controlling traffic or public transportation or informing the city inhabitants. Many of the detection techniques are based on noticing the unexpected behavior of groups of people (e.g., abnormally high or low number of citizens) using cameras or other advanced devices in smart cities. The main drawback of this approach is the need to deploy a specialized physical infrastructure in the area under study.

To overcome this limitation, location-based social networks (LBSNs) seem to be an interesting approach: no specific infrastructure is needed to collect the data, but the citizens themselves are the ones who buy, maintain, and carry the needed mobile devices; and they freely disclose their location throughout the day by proactively posting pictures or tweets, thus making the process seamless to them. This paradigm allows collecting a high volume of data, coming from many different users, distributed throughout all the city, thus becoming a good proxy for representing the behavior of the city. However, collecting the continuous stream of LBSN data, summarizing and analyzing it, and actually detecting the anomalies are tasks that may lead to an important computational cost, thus making it difficult to be applied in real time.

With this trade-off in mind, we propose a novel approach to detect potential anomalies as they happen with an efficient methodology. The idea is to sample at intervals the location data of Instagram posts to represent the behavior of citizens. The collected locations at each interval will be summarized by their centroid. The novelty of our work relies on the use of entropy to analyze the sequence of centroid locations (one per interval) in order to detect anomalies. Since entropy measures the uncertainty of the next event in a sequence, when something unusual happens and the citizens' locations greatly vary, we expect changes in the value of entropy.

This approach is shown to be quick enough to spot changes in the city behaviors as they happen, since entropy calculation is an easy iterative process. Although entropy has been traditionally used for outlier detection in many areas, to our knowledge, there are no previous approaches applying this strategy to detect crowd dynamics anomalies in urban areas. In this paper, we propose how to go from location information of a crowd to a sequence of symbols to which Shannon's entropy definition can be applied.

The rest of the paper is as follows: Section 2 overviews other alternatives to detect anomalies in crowd behavior, whereas our approach is detailed in Section 3; after that, we present the data set and how the parameters of the algorithm are selected in Section 4. In Section 5, we validate the entropy-based methodology for crowd anomalies detection in the city. In Section 6, we discuss the limitations of our approach. Finally, we discuss the conclusions in Section 7.

2. Related Work

Early detection of unusual events in urban areas is a challenge that has been tackled from different sides. Besides the video-processing techniques [1,2], the use of public posts shared in social media has recently constituted a novel focus of attention [3]. Some approaches focus on the shared content, for example the analysis of text messages to detect events, like in [4] or [5], where Twitter and Instagram were the data sources. Other proposals go further and try to detect natural disasters, such as earthquakes [6] or forest fires [7].

However, users' locations are becoming more important, especially since LBSNs are so popular. In [8], tweets were collected and assigned to previously-defined regions in intervals of six hours, which makes the possibility of the early detection of events difficult. Twitter was also used in [9], where a high activity triggers the system. Later, those tweets were analyzed to know if the event was already expected or not. In this case, the detection does not work for low activity behaviors, even if they are rare indeed. The proposal in [10] tried to detect and monitor local social events by applying clustering (k-means), although this technique requires specifying the number of cluster in advance, which is not flexible enough for detection purposes.

Previous work also faced crowd detection based on geolocated posts by using density-based clustering [11,12] without imposing an a priori decision about the number of clusters or their shape. In spite of having obtained sound and accurate results, its computation cost suggests applying this approach only when other evidence of unexpected behavior has been detected.

All works above face the problem of identifying events that do not match an expected pattern, which is established by applying both supervised or unsupervised machine learning approaches. Once a regular pattern is defined, any anomaly detection technique may be applied. However, a pattern-based approach implies a two-step process, whose success depends on the availability of training data and, more importantly, on the ability to maintain an up-to-date pattern throughout time. On the contrary, entropy-based outlier detection, the novel approach in this paper, exploits the entropy behavior to minimize both drawbacks: (i) anomalous data increase the entropy values, so no previous patterns are needed, and (ii) the entropy levels are continuously adapted as long as new geolocated data are extracted from social media.

3. Problem Definition and Methodology

The goal of the methodology proposed in this paper is to detect potential anomalies quickly in the city by inspecting the behavior of the crowds populating it. These anomalies serve as proxies of unexpected or unusual events happening in the city now. Therefore, they could serve as warnings for the city service managers to react in time when needed.

The problem scenario is as follows. We consider the locations of the people distributed throughout a specific city and summarize them by their centroid. The centroid location changes throughout the day and also depends on the day itself. However, how the location changes throughout a particular day is similar if we compare the same day of the week (e.g., Tuesdays) across different weeks, except when an abnormal or unexpected event is taking place. Thus, we need to determine and track the location of the centroid at intervals, to detect deviations from the normal weekly track, for each day of the week.

Breaking the problem into its parts, the general methodology proposed is as follows:

1. First, we need to obtain the data representing the distribution of the people all over the considered city.
2. The next step is to identify the location of the people's concentration. Then, the crowd tracking generates a sequence of locations that represent the crowd behavior, for each day, separately.
3. Then, we need to measure how "normal" or "unexpected" the behavior represented by the locations sequence is.
4. In order to deal with such an amount of data, we need to summarize the data through some indicator that is fast to retrieve, as well as expressive enough so as to reflect anomalies.
5. Finally, we need to detect possible abnormal behaviors from the previous measurements.

Our proposal is implemented as follows. In order to determine people locations, we used data collected from Instagram: we obtained the location of the pictures posted by this LBSN's users throughout the city, and we grouped them into time periods, T.

Three time intervals, T, were tested: 15, 30, and 60 min. For shorter time intervals (less than 15 min), the number of posts would not be statistically significant in order to detect behavioral variations reliably (with the Instagram API, we obtained up to 200 posts on average every 15 min). On the other hand, longer time intervals would introduce too much delay when detecting an event. Thus, each day of the week was divided into 15–60 min chunks, and the data about the posts in each chunk provided by Instagram were aggregated to compute the distribution of the geotagged Instagram posts in the city.

We assumed that the variations in the geographical distribution of geotagged posts in Instagram could be used to track variations in the location of the whole population in the city. In other words, we assumed that any event that produced an abnormally high or low number of citizens in an area would reflect in the geotagged post distribution on Instagram. See Section 6 for a discussion on content bias in crowd-sourced geographic information.

Once we had the locations of posts in the last T period, the centroid of the locations was calculated to summarize the data at each interval, using the Haversine distance, since the points are on the Earth's surface.

After that, we need to transform the centroid coordinates (one per interval) into the symbolic domain, which allows computing the entropy of the sequence later on. In order to do so, the city was split into $S \times S$ non-overlapping cells of the same size. Then, each cell was labeled with a symbol. The position of the centroid at each temporal interval was identified by the symbol of the cell that enclosed that position. Thus, the city behavior was expressed as a sequence of symbols. We tested different grid resolutions, from 3×3–9×9.

Next, we quantified the behavior of the centroid movement as the deviation from the expected uncertainty of that centroid movement. People movements have some degree of randomness, as shown in [13], and so does the behavior of the resulting crowd. However, big deviations from the expected value of uncertainty can potentially unveil unexpected events. This way, we allowed the centroid movement to have the expected level of randomness, but we aimed to capture the times in which that randomness was too different from the expected value. One way to measure the expected uncertainty of a sequence of symbols pertaining to an alphabet $\mathscr{L}$ is through the information theory concept of Shannon entropy. We will now introduce the concept of entropy and its practical interpretation. A wider review on this topic can be found in [14,15].

Let X be a discrete random variable taking values on an alphabet $\mathscr{L}$, $|\mathscr{L}|$ being the cardinality of the alphabet, with Probability Mass Function (PMF) $\Pr(X = l) = p(l), \forall l \in \mathscr{L}$. Then, the Shannon entropy of X can be written as:

$$H = -\sum_{l \in \mathscr{L}} p(l) \log_2 p(l) \tag{1}$$

where the base two logarithm denotes that the resulting entropy value is measured in bits and where $p(l)$ is the probability of symbol l. Paying attention to the practical meaning of entropy, H measures the expected "surprise" or uncertainty enclosed by the random variable X.

Since the probability mass function $p(l)$ is not available, and our data were not an infinite sequence of symbols, we approximate it by a maximum likelihood estimator based on the observable data:

$$p(l, i) = \frac{N_{l,i}}{i}, 0 \leq i \leq n \tag{2}$$

where $N_{l,i}$ is the number of appearance of location l in the sequence from the beginning up to time interval i and n is the total number of time intervals.

Applying this to the entropy formula, for each time interval, i, we have:

$$H(i) = -\sum_{l \in \mathscr{L}} p(l, i) \log_2 p(l, i) \tag{3}$$

As we will explain later, at each interval, we will calculate the entropy from the beginning of the sequence up to that interval, H, and also the entropy considering just the last *win* symbols of the sequence, H_{win}, with *win* ranging from 2 weeks–2 months. For H_{win} we will use Equation (3), but with $p(l, i)$ being:

$$p(l, i) = \frac{N_{wl,i}}{win}, win \leq i \leq n \tag{4}$$

where $N_{wl,i}$ is the number of appearances of location l in the last *win* symbols of the sequence (from $i - win + 1$–i).

Finally, we inspect the values of the entropy calculated at each time interval i, $H(i)$, or $H_{win}(i)$, depending on whether we consider the entropy from the beginning of the last win symbols, and label as potential anomalies those samples with higher entropy differences with respect to the previous value.

In the next section, this methodology is applied to a specific scenario, analyzing the parameter selection (time interval duration, grid size, entropy calculation details) and discussing the results obtained.

4. Experiment and Parameter Selection

4.1. Data Set

After analyzing the pros and cons of different LBSNs, we finally decided to use Instagram as our data source, since at the time of beginning our investigation (January 2016): (i) it did not limit the location linked to posts, directly being the GPS location, so its posts were not biased by the venues' locations (as happens with Foursquare); (ii) it was possible to collect posts shared within a specific geographic area; Instagram has already more monthly active users than Twitter, thus becoming important to be able to bound the posts we are interested in; and (iii) its API goes also further than Twitter since it imposes less call restrictions (500 calls/hour for Sandbox mode, 5000 calls/hour for Live mode (The Sandbox mode is a test mode with more restricted call limits. After submitting your application for review to Instagram, the application can be switched to Live mode, with higher request limits).

We used the Instagram API media/search endpoint (https://www.instagram.com/developer/endpoints/media/) to extract the posts published in real time in a given area, setting the latitude and longitude of the center and using a maximum radius of up to 5 km. Each call to the media/search endpoint returns the most recent posts, up to 20 results. The data were extracted using a script in R, which performs iterative calls to the API, obtaining the data in JSON format and converting them to an R data frame, which can be saved in R native format.

In this section, we apply the previous methodology to the specific scenario of New York City during a time span of 7 months. We extracted geotagged data using the Instagram API media/search endpoint, setting the center of the area in Times Square (40.756667 N, 73.986389 W) and using the maximum radius allowed (5 km), from 23 August 2015–28 February 2016, which covered: (a) special days, when the city is traditionally more crowded like Christmas time; (b) unusual days, such as the weekend when Storm Jonas hit the United States, as we will see later; and (c) days that are considered normal, when no special events or phenomena are expected to happen. During this period, 4,335,880 posts were collected, an average of 22,677.48 post per day. They were grouped into time intervals of 15 min (greater time intervals were obtained by aggregating the post of one or more consecutive chunks).

4.2. Parameter Selection

As explained in Section 3, there are two parameters related to the centroid tracking step: the frequency at which the centroid location is sampled, T (i.e., the time interval length during which location data are aggregated); and the square size, S, when splitting the city into a labeled grid. Besides, when calculating entropy, we realized that considering the location sequence from the beginning to each interval, i, led to very small variations in the results after a few weeks. This is because as more samples are available to calculate $p(l,i)$, more samples are needed to notice a change, whereas unexpected events last, at most, one day, i.e., 96 samples with $T = 15$. For this reason, we tested a windowed version of the entropy calculation with the window size, *win*, ranging from 2 weeks–2 months. Finally, to avoid changes when comparing work days with weekends, we divided the data set by day of the week and applied the analysis comparing the same day. Figure 1 shows some combinations of parameters for one of the days of the week (Thursdays). Other combinations were tested, which are not shown here for brevity.

Figure 1 shows clear differences among all the versions, the main one being the window used for entropy calculation, which allows for changes to be noticed. We can see that with large T and small S, we observe too many variations in entropy to allow detecting real anomalies, while large S flatten the variations too much, not allowing them to be detected. On the other hand, without the window, the entropy flattens when the sequence is sufficiently long, which prevents detecting changes. In conclusion, T of 15 or 30 min, S between 5×5 and 7×7, and *win* between 4 and 6 weeks seem good.

To decide which combination of parameters T, S. and *win* works best, we applied the following procedure. First, we identified known special days and annotated the specific dates (Table 1). Next, using the data represented in Figure 1, we ordered the days regarding the entropy difference with respect to the previous value in descending order (i.e., we ordered the entropy values from the first more likely to reflect an unexpected behavior in the city to the least likely one, and annotated its date), aggregating all days of the week. Then, we checked for each of the ordered days if it corresponded to any of the ones in Table 1. Figure 2 represents the percentage of special days in that table detected when considering the ordered list from top to bottom. For instance, if there are 10 special days out of 100 total days and in the first 10 ordered days, there are 2 special ones, then that means that we can spot 20% of the special days (y-axis) when considering 10% (x-axis) of the total number of days. The ideal case would be to spot 100% of special days by analyzing the minimum total days (i.e., all special days are the ones with the highest entropy difference with respect to the previous day).

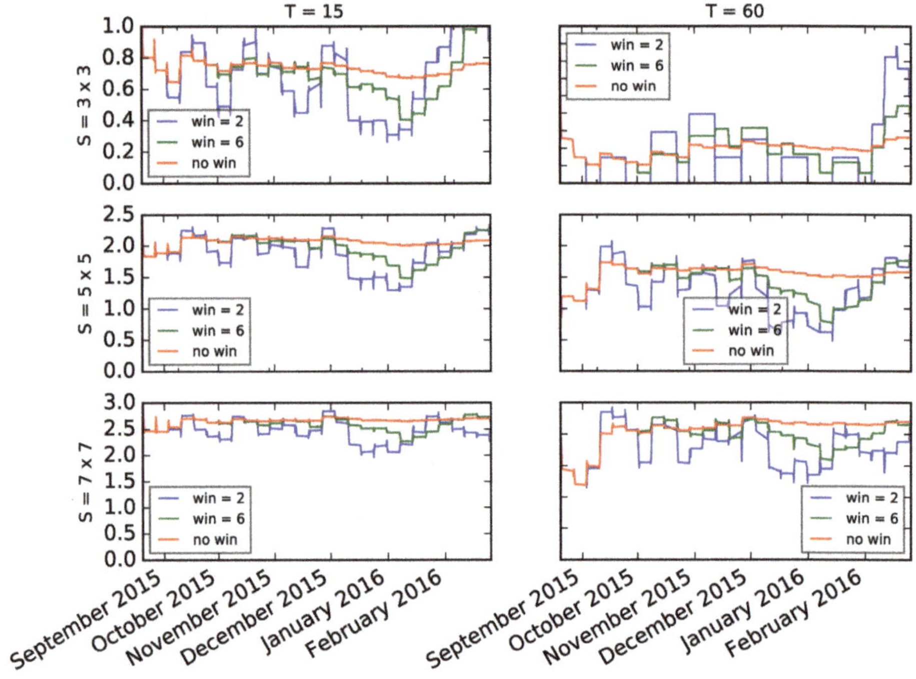

Figure 1. Entropy evolution of Thursdays for different values of time interval (*T* min), grid resolution (*S*), and sequence window (*win* weeks).

Table 1. Special events considered.

Date	Event
12 October 2015	Columbus Day
12 October 2015	Halloween
11 November 2015	Veterans Day
26 November 2015	Thanksgiving Day
24 December 2015	Christmas' Eve
25 December 2015	Christmas
31 December 2015	New Year's Eve
1 January 2016	New Year

In Figure 2, we plot the results of this analysis for different parameter combinations of *T*, *S*, and *W*. With *W* = 4 weeks, we can spot up to 55% of special days in the first 20% of the total ordered days. Therefore, in order to identify the highest number possible by considering the least number of total days, a window of 4 weeks is preferable, combined with $T = 15$ min and any grid size (both $S = 5 \times 5$ and $S = 7 \times 7$ overlap). Besides these results, something even more interesting came up during the analysis. Taking a look at the steepest changes in entropy (the top values in the ordered list), we further analyzed the contents of the posts and discovered that three of the days at the top of the list corresponded to an unknown event for us: the Comic Con conference, held in New York during 8–11 October (The identification of the cause of the event was made in this work by manually inspecting the posts of that day. In another independent work, we showed how a story detection process can be used (using natural language processing) to find out what is happening in an area [16]). That discovery ignited the expectations regarding the method proposed as one to capture unexpected behaviors quickly in the city for further analysis using more computationally-expensive techniques to understand exactly what is going on.

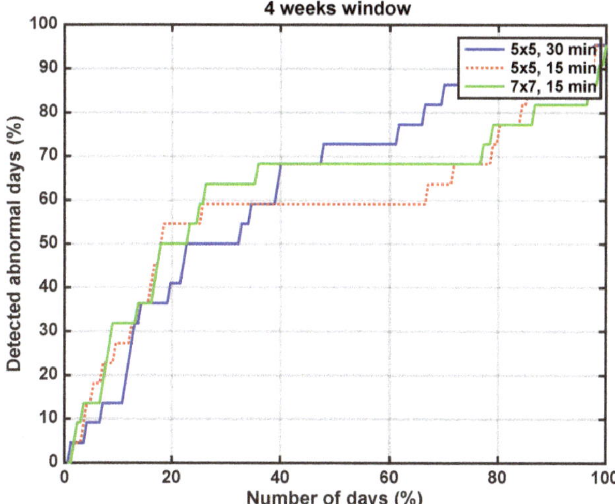

Figure 2. Abnormal day detection percentages for *win* = 4 weeks.

5. Validation

In this section, we validate the entropy-based methodology for crowd anomalies detection. First, we compare the abnormal days detected in the data set described in Section 4.1 using our technique with the ones detected using a different approach. Second, we test the effectiveness of our technique with a different data set.

5.1. Comparison with Results Obtained Using an Alternative Approach

In Section 4.2, we compared the abnormal days detected using the entropy evolution against a list of special days (mainly holidays) previously identified in Table 1. In this section, we will compare the consistency of our results with the ones obtained using a different approach. We will first explain the alternative approach considered and then compare the results.

5.1.1. Alternative Approach

In [12], we defined the criteria to identify moderate and extreme outliers by comparing (i) the clusters obtained applying the clustering algorithm to the real-time data (real-time clustering) and (ii) the clusters in the reference clustering (the behavioral pattern of the city). Both clustering results (reference clustering and real-time clustering) are characterized by a set of clusters, which are specified by two features per cluster: the number of data points and their location.

Note that this approach uses, from the 22 weeks of the data set, 20 weeks as the training set and the other two as a test set. With the training set, we obtain the average location and size of the crowds in the area for each day of the week at each half-hour interval (reference clustering). With the test set, we check the validity of the model (real-time clustering).

Four values or thresholds that define four types of outliers characterize the reference clustering: LMO (Lower Moderate Outlier; LEO (Lower Extreme Outlier); UMO (Upper Moderate Outlier); and UEO (Upper Extreme Outlier). In order to obtain these four thresholds, we adopted the traditional approach [17,18] as our starting point. As explained in [19], an outlier is an observation that lies an abnormal distance from other values. We can display the observations in a box plot with the median and the lower and upper quartiles (defined as the 25th and 75th percentiles). We define the lower quartile as Q_1, the upper quartile as Q_3, and the difference $(Q_3 - Q_1)$ as the interquartile range (IQR). Then, according to [17], we define the following values (often called fences):

$$UpperOutlier(UO) = Q_3 + \delta \times IQR$$

$$LowerOutlier(LO) = Q_1 - \delta \times IQR$$

where $\delta = 1.5$ is used for moderate outliers (UMO and LMO) and $\delta = 3$ for extreme outliers (UEO and LEO). These values of δ are the standards in exploratory data analysis ([17,19]). However, and in order to avoid negative numbers, we have redefined the lower limits as follows:

$$LMO = min(Q_1 - 1.5 \times IQR, minPoints)$$

$$LEO = min(Q_1 - 3 \times IQR, 0)$$

This definition reflects that a cluster in the real-time clustering should be considered with an unusually low number of points when it is lower than the $minPoints$ used to obtain the reference clustering, and extremely low when the cluster is empty.

Therefore, identifying an outlier is as simple as comparing the number of data points in a cluster belonging to the real-time clustering with the number of points in the correspondent cluster in the reference cluster. Consequently, if the value is greater than the UEO, we know that the activity should be considered highly abnormal; if the value is greater than the UMO, but lower than the UEO, we know that the activity should be considered as unexpected; if the value is lower than the LEO, we know that the activity should be considered highly abnormal; and finally, if the value is lower than the LMO, but greater than the LEO, the activity should be considered as unexpected.

The essential issue here is to know which is the cluster in the reference cluster that should be used for the previous comparison, i.e., which is the cluster in the reference cluster that fits the cluster under study. In order to determine this important aspect, we have defined the distance between two clusters C_x and P_y as follows:

$$dist_{xy} = \frac{1}{n_{C_x}} \sum_{i=0}^{n_{C_x}} dist_{x_{iy}}$$

were n_{C_x} is the number of points in the cluster C_x and $dist_{x_{iy}}$ is the distance between a point c_{x_i}, which belongs to cluster C_x, and the cluster P_y. Our definition of this distance, between a point and a cluster, is the following one:

$$dist_{x_{iy}} = min(dist(c_{xi}, p_{y_j})), \forall p_{y_j} \in P_y$$

i.e., it is the distance between the point c_{x_i} and the closest point that belongs to P_y.

Finally, a cluster C_x is considered to fit the reference cluster P_y if it holds that:

$$P_y = \arg\min(dist_{xy})/dist_{xy} \leq \epsilon \tag{5}$$

The definitions above allow us to compare both clustering by comparing individually each cluster in the real-time clustering with all the clusters in the reference clustering as follows:

1. When a cluster in the real-time clustering fits (according to Equation (5)) a cluster in the reference clustering, the number of points in the former is compared to the four thresholds in order to find out if there is any kind of anomaly.

2. If more than one cluster in the real-time clustering fits the same cluster in the reference clustering, they will be considered as a unique cluster, i.e., they are merged. Then, the number of points in

the merged clusters is compared with the four thresholds in order to find out if there is any kind of anomaly.

3. All the clusters in the real-time clustering that do not fit any cluster in the reference clustering are considered as Position Outliers (PO), since it entails that we have detected activity in the real-time clustering in areas where it was not expected according to the reference clustering.

4. If no cluster in the reference clustering fits a cluster in the real-time clustering, we consider that the cluster exists with zero points, and it is considered as a Position Outlier (PO), since there is not activity in a specific area where it is expected according to the reference clustering.

As a result of the comparison between the real-time clustering and the reference clustering, we will have a set of clusters that constitutes the difference clustering. The analysis of this difference clustering allowed us to infer if the activity in the area under study was the expected one or if it shows some outliers [12].

5.1.2. Ranking of Outliers with the Alternative Approach

The analysis of the difference clustering in [12] is not enough to obtain an ordered ranking of the detected outliers. This ranking, although it is not essential to detect anomalies, is useful to compare different detection methods, the main objective of the work introduced in this paper.

With this aim, we have established the following set of rules that jointly constitutes a metric that allows us to assign a value or mark, the DoA (Degree of Anomaly), to each cluster in the difference clustering:

1. if the cluster has a Number of Points (NoP) greater than the LMO and lower than the UMO, the DoA is zero, i.e., the cluster represents an expected or normal behavior.

2. If the cluster has an NoP greater than the UMO, the DoA is the result of subtracting the UMO from the NoP. This applies for those clusters.

3. If the cluster has an NoP lower than the LMO, the DoA is the result of subtracting the NoP form the LMO.

4. If the cluster is a Position Outlier (PO), the DoA is the result of adding its NoP to the maximum DoA calculated for the other clusters in the difference clustering.

The result of adding the obtained values for all the clusters in the difference clustering is the Degree of Anomaly (DoA) of the difference clustering.

5.1.3. Results and Discussion

In Figures 3 and 4, we show the days in the data set ordered according to entropy-based anomaly detection and to the (DoA) of the difference clustering, respectively.

First, we have to establish a threshold (both in entropy and in DoA) between the days that we consider normal and anomalous. To set this threshold, we considered the point where the slope of the graphs was -1. In Figures 3 and 4, we show in dotted lines the trend line, which is exponential in the case of the entropy and follows a power trend line in the case of DoA. We also show the point where the slope of the trend line equals -1. Considering this threshold, the number of abnormal days detected is 16 with the entropy approach and 11 with the DoA approach. Visually examining the graphs, we see that the threshold chosen in the case of DoA corresponds to where there is a rapid rise in the DoA value, while in the case of entropy, we observe a change in trend around Day 27. However, we stick to the thresholds obtained above.

With these thresholds, the list of abnormal days detected with both approaches is shown in Table 2, together with the position in the rank of each algorithm. We can see that three days appear as anomalous in both algorithms: 10 October 2015, 24 Dedember 2015, and 24 January 2016. One of them corresponds to Christmas Eve, while the two others correspond to events not predicted in Table 1: the New York Comic Con 2015 https://en.wikipedia.org/wiki/New_York_Comic_Con and the winter storm Jonas https://en.wikipedia.org/wiki/January_2016_United_States_blizzard. Other potentially abnormal days identified in Table 2 are not pointed out as such by any of the algorithms, e.g., Columbus Day or Veterans Day.

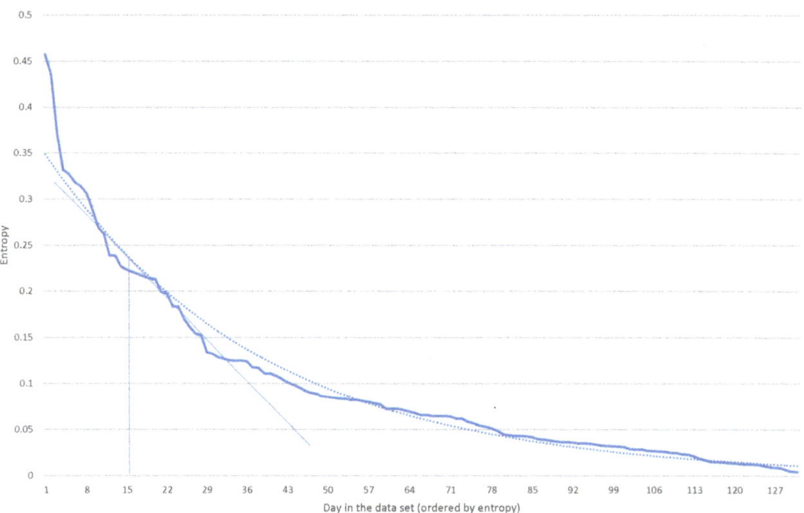

Figure 3. Days in the data set ordered according to entropy.

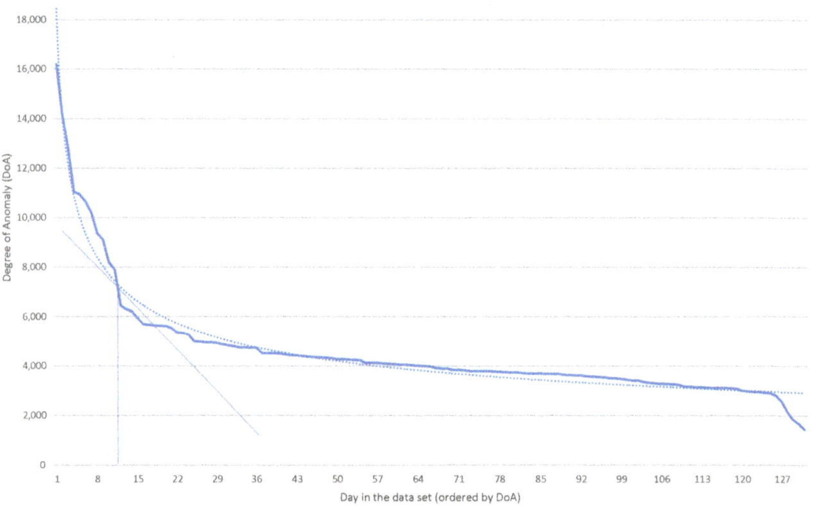

Figure 4. Days in the data set ordered according to the degree of anomaly of the difference clustering.

Table 2. Abnormal days detected using entropy and DoA.

Date	Entropy Rank	DoA Rank	Event
16 September 2015	9		-
8 October 2015		3	Comic Con
9 October 2015		1	Comic Con
10 October 2015	15	2	Comic Con
11 October 2015		9	Comic Con
14 October 2015	4		-
24 October 2015		10	-
1 November 2015	10		Day after Halloween
2 November 2015	13		-
25 November 2015	5		Thanksgiving long weekend
28 November 2015	7		Thanksgiving long weekend
29 November 2015	11		Thanksgiving long weekend
22 December 2015	3		Days before Christmas
23 December 2015	1		Days before Christmas
24 December 2015	6	8	Christmas' Eve
25 December 2015		5	Christmas
31 December 2015		11	New Year's Eve
1 January 2016		7	New Year
14 January 2016		4	-
15 January 2016	14		-
19 January 2016	16		-
21 January 2016	8		Storm Jonas
23 January 2016	12		Storm Jonas
24 January 2016	2	6	Storm Jonas

Examining the list of abnormal days in Table 2, we observe the following:

- The algorithms needed some history to compare past behaviors with present behaviors and to be able to decide if one day was abnormal or not. We have established this initial transient in four weeks. 16 September was the fist day after this transient period, and it was still considered abnormal by the entropy algorithm, not so by the DoA algorithm.
- The entropy algorithm better detected consecutive abnormal days, for example long weekends around a holiday, e.g., Thanksgiving, or events lasting several days, e.g., the winter storm Jonas. Note that a travel ban was instituted for New York City for 23–24 January during the storm Jonas and that this was one of the top abnormal days for both algorithms.
- On the other hand, the entropy algorithm tended to point out as anomalous wrongly the days following really anomalous days. As it used a four-week window for calculating the entropy, if in the last four weeks, there were several abnormal days, e.g., the Christmas holidays, then the days of the week after Christmas appeared to be different from the previous ones and appeared high in the entropy rank. However, this feature is important for adapting to city changes, e.g., street closures for long-term works.

With these results, we can validate that the entropy approach worked well at detecting abnormal events in the city when compared with an algorithm that was trained with the whole data set but two weeks. The first advantage of the entropy-based outlier detection is that no previous patterns for training are needed, since it is continuously learning from the location of the posts obtained from Instagram. After an initial transient period of four weeks, anomalous data increase the entropy values and abnormal events start to be detected. The second advantage is that the entropy levels are continuously adapted as long as new geolocated data are extracted from social media. New patterns are learned. and older patterns are forgotten, adapting to the evolution of the city.

Regarding the computational cost of the entropy algorithm, it is very simple and can be implemented in real time with low resource consumption. Since we used the windowed version of the entropy, H_{win}, the computation cost of the entropy depended on the number of symbols in the sequence, *win*, and the cardinality of the alphabet $|\mathcal{L}|$ (i.e., the number of possible different symbols in our distribution). In our case, the cardinality of the alphabet was the number of cells in the grid in which we divided the city. Assuming a grid of $S \times S$ cells, $|\mathcal{L}| = S^2$. Both quantities are constant and small, and Equation (3) can be computed in a fixed, short time.

All the results presented so far were obtained using the New York data set. We will check next if the algorithm works well with the same parameters used before in a very different data set.

5.2. Validation with a Different Data Set

To validate the selected parameters, we applied them to another data set obtained in a city with different characteristics. We collected geolocated Instagram posts in Manchester for four months.

Figure 5 shows the entropy evolution of Tuesdays using the same parameters chosen for the New York data set in Section 4.2: $win = 4$, $T = 15$, $S = 5 \times 5$. We can observe a remarkable increase in entropy on 23 May, following the terrorist attack on the evening of 22 May 2017 https://en.wikipedia.org/wiki/Manchester_Arena_bombing. This was by far the day with the highest entropy increase in all the data set, with an increment of 0.22.

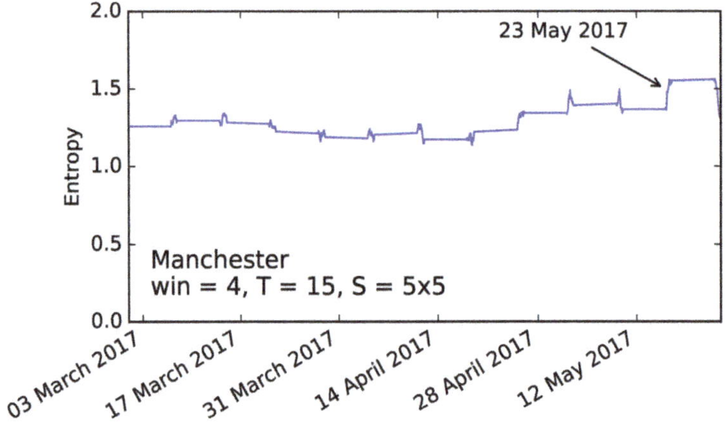

Figure 5. Entropy evolution in the Manchester data set with the selected parameters.

6. Limitations

One of the limitations of using Instagram or any other social network to detect anomalous events is that it is very sensitive to changes in API policies. At the time we carried out the New York data capture campaign (end of 2015 and beginning of 2016), the Instagram API media/search endpoint allowed recovering data from any moment in the past, between two timestamps (you can see the API at the time of our data capture campaign at the Internet Archive: http://web.archive.org/web/20150531210319/https://instagram.com/developer/endpoints/media/), so our data set could be re-extracted later by anyone (for example, if she/he would like to reproduce our study). This is not possible anymore. Besides, since June 2016, for privacy reasons, the media/search endpoint in Sandbox mode was limited to return just the media you uploaded from that location. To have access to the public content published by others, you need to submit your application to Instagram for approval for the Live mode. This was not required when we made the New York capture campaign.

Another limitation of our approach is about how the Instagram API media/search endpoint provides geolocated posts. The location of the post was obtained from the latitude and longitude where the photo was taken (provided by the device). However, Instagram does not provide public information about the percentage of Instagram posts that contain geolocation. According to the survey study in [20], 30% of the respondents said they geotag all posts, and 30% said they never geotag posts; however, 60% claimed to geotag some of their posts, and about 10% claimed to geotag half or more of their posts. Although an accurate percentage cannot be provided without the official data from Instagram, taking into consideration the information in [21], it could be claimed that geotagged posts increase engagement up to 79%. Additionally, we can argue that Instagram is one of the most geolocated social networks, since the percentage of geolocated posts in Twitter was just 1% in 2014 [22], the same year as the study in [21].

A possible question is whether there may be events of interest that may not be detected using Instagram because they were not attractive to their users. In this work, we are interested in detecting unusual events such as emergencies. In [23], the authors presented the results of a study on citizens' perception of social media in emergencies conducted in Germany. The study highlighted that around 24% of people have used social media during an emergency to share information. When asked about what types of information they share, 37% of the times they share the location and some photo or video. According to this study, we expect emergency events to be identifiable on Instagram, as we have found in the two study cases (New York and Manchester) presented in this paper.

Finally, some recent papers ([24,25]) studied content bias in crowd-sourced geographic information in OpenStreetMap, depending on the country and the culture. Another work presented a similar study during disasters ([26]). It is difficult to know if there are deviations of this nature in the data we obtained from Instagram. We do not know the information that could be relevant to study these biases, such as age, nationality, cultural level, etc., of post authors. However, we believe that our use of social networks (specifically Instagram) differs from that of OpenStreetMap in these works in two important aspects. First, the posts we obtained were generated in a very limited are (radius of 5 km), so we did not expect great differences in demographic and social characteristics of the post authors. Second, in OpenStreetMap, the geographic information is explicitly crowd-sourced by the users (they make an explicit action to send the information), while in our work, we collected the geographic information from Instagram without the users being aware that they were participating in this process. We believe that this unnoticed collection process protects against the biases that occur when the user explicitly sends the information. Anyway, these aspects remain open and need further investigation.

7. Conclusions

This paper proposes a new entropy-based methodology for early detection of anomalies in urban areas that exploits the location data of the posts published on LBSNs. The proposal uses a centroid as the single geographic point summarizing the pulse of the city, the location of which is tracked to detect changes in its entropy evolution. Although more than one point could be used to represent the citizens' movement all around the area under study, working only with one centroid allows obtaining quick and sound results.

From the time sequence of centroids that summarize the pulse of the city, just the last W weeks were considered, and the centroids were discretized into an $S \times S$ grid. We studied different values of the parameters, and we found the best results with $W = 4$ and $S = 5$. We then used the entropy of the discretized sequence of centroid locations in the last W weeks to detect anomalies.

The main advantage of our algorithm is that there is no training phase, so the algorithm starts detecting abnormal days from the beginning, with good results after the first W weeks. Another advantage of our approach is that it can adapt to changes in the dynamics of the city, since at the same time it learns new patterns from current posts, it forgets old (more than W weeks old) patterns. The algorithm is simple and fast, so it can be executed in real time with low resource consumption.

The validation was done with seven months of geolocated data from Instagram posts published in NYC. Apart from correctly identifying up to 55% of expected abnormal days (Christmas, holidays, etc.), the solution was able to discover events we were not aware of, where an unusual pattern was clearly detected by our proposed methodology, and further analysis of the content of the posts uncovered the reason. The parameters selected were also validated with other data set, from Manchester, where the effects of a terrorist attack in the entropy of the crowd dynamics can be observed.

We are currently working on two lines: on the one hand, extending the algorithm to work with more than one centroid (two, three) representing the movement of the whole population in the city; on the other hand, the analysis presented in this paper shows the changes (of entropy or DoA) at a day level. This analysis can be presented at shorter intervals (every 15 or 30 min) to show sudden changes in the city as they occur.

In this work, we have considered aggregation of Instagram posts at fixed time intervals (15, 30, and 60 min). As future work, other forms of aggregation of posts can be investigated. Posts could be aggregated in variable length time intervals, aggregating a constant number of posts (e.g., 200 post) per time interval, so that the time intervals would be shorter or larger depending on the activity (the number of posts) on Instagram. Surely, this could help detect the events that cause a large number of posts faster.

Author Contributions: All the authors participated in the conceptualization of this paper. C.G.-R. and C.C. contributed to the design, implementation, and validation of the entropy-based abnormal events detection algorithm. R.P.D.R. and A.F.V. contributed to the data sets and the DoA approach to abnormal events detections.

Funding: This research was partially funded by the Ministry of Economy and Competitiveness through TEC2017-84197-C4-1-R, TEC2017-84197-C4-2-R, TEC2014-54335-C4-2-R, and TEC2014-54335-C4-3-R, and the European Regional Development Fund (ERDF) and the Galician Regional Government under agreement for funding the Atlantic Research Center for Information and Communication Technologies (AtlantTIC).

Acknowledgments: C.G.-R. and C.C. would like to acknowledge Alicia Rodriguez-Carrion for her help in the initial stages of this work.

Conflicts of Interest: The authors declare no conflict of interest. The founding sponsors had no role in the design of the study; in the collection, analyses, or interpretation of data; in the writing of the manuscript, and in the decision to publish the results.

References

1. Ghidoni, S.; Cielniak, G.; Menegatti, E. Texture-based crowd detection and localization. In *Intelligent Autonomous Systems 12*; Springer: Berlin/Heidelberg, Germany, 2013; pp. 725–736.

2. Zhang, Y.; Qin, L.; Ji, R.; Yao, H.; Huang, Q. Social attribute-aware force model: Exploiting richness of interaction for abnormal crowd detection. *IEEE Trans. Circuits Syst. Video Technol.* **2015**, *25*, 1231–1245. [CrossRef]

3. Atefeh, F.; Khreich, W. A survey of techniques for event detection in twitter. *Comput. Intell.* **2015**, *31*, 132–164. [CrossRef]

4. Watanabe, K.; Ochi, M.; Okabe, M.; Onai, R. Jasmine: A real-time local-event detection system based on geolocation information propagated to microblogs. In Proceedings of the 20th ACM international conference on Information and Knowledge Management, Glasgow, UK, 24–28 October 2011; pp. 2541–2544.

5. Ranneries, S.B.; Kalør, M.E.; Nielsen, S.A.; Dalgaard, L.N.; Christensen, L.D.; Kanhabua, N. Wisdom of the local crowd: Detecting local events using social media data. In Proceedings of the 8th ACM Conference on Web Science, Hannover, Germany, 22–25 May 2016; pp. 352–354.

6. Sakaki, T.; Okazaki, M.; Matsuo, Y. Earthquake shakes Twitter users: Real-time event detection by social sensors. In Proceedings of the 19th International Conference on World Wide Web, Raleigh, NC, USA, 26–30 April 2010; pp. 851–860.

7. De Longueville, B.; Smith, R.S.; Luraschi, G. "OMG, from here, I can see the flames!": A use case of mining location based social networks to acquire spatio-temporal data on forest fires. In Proceedings of the 2009 International Workshop on Location Based Social Networks, Seattle, WA, USA, 3 November 2009; pp. 73–80.

8. Wakamiya, S.; Lee, R.; Sumiya, K. Crowd-based urban characterization: Extracting crowd behavioral patterns in urban areas from twitter. In Proceedings of the 3rd ACM SIGSPATIAL International Workshop On Location-Based Social Networks, Chicago, IL, USA, 1 November 2011; pp. 77–84.

9. Walther, M.; Kaisser, M. Geo-spatial event detection in the twitter stream. In Proceedings of the ECIR'13 Proceedings of the 35th European Conference on Advances in Information Retrieval, Moscow, Russia, 24–27 March 2013.

10. Lee, R.; Sumiya, K. Measuring geographical regularities of crowd behaviors for Twitter-based geo-social event detection. In Proceedings of the 2nd ACM SIGSPATIAL International Workshop On Location Based Social Networks, San Jose, CA, USA, 2–5 November 2010; pp. 1–10.

11. ben Khalifa, M.; Redondo, R.P.D.; Vilas, A.F.; Rodríguez, S.S. Identifying urban crowds using geo-located Social media data: A Twitter experiment in New York City. *J. Intell. Inf. Syst.* **2017**, *48*, 287–308. [CrossRef]

12. Domínguez, D.R.; Redondo, R.P.D.; Vilas, A.F.; Khalifa, M.B. Sensing the city with Instagram: Clustering geolocated data for outlier detection. *Expert Syst. Appl.* **2017**, *78*, 319–333. [CrossRef]

13. Gonzalez, M.C.; Hidalgo, C.A.; Barabasi, A.L. Understanding individual human mobility patterns. *Nature* **2008**, *453*, 779–782, doi:10.1038/nature06958. [CrossRef] [PubMed]

14. Gao, Y.; Kontoyiannis, I.; Bienenstock, E. Estimating the entropy of binary time series: Methodology, some theory and a simulation study. *Entropy* **2008**, *10*, 71–99. [CrossRef]

15. Cover, T.M.; Thomas, J.A. *Elements of Information Theory*, 2nd ed.; Wiley: New York, NY, USA, 2006.

16. Cerezo-Costas, H.; Fernández-Vilas, A.; Martín-Vicente, M.; Díaz-Redondo, R.P. Discovering geo-dependent stories by combining density-based clustering and thread-based aggregation techniques. *Expert Syst. Appl.* **2018**, *95*, 32–42. [CrossRef]

17. Tukey, J.W. *Exploratory Data Analysis*; Addison-Wesley Reading: Boston, MA, USA, 1977.

18. Acuna, E.; Rodriguez, C. *A Meta Analysis Study of Outlier Detection Methods in Classification*; Technical paper; Department of Mathematics, University of Puerto Rico at Mayaguez: Mayaguez, Puerto Rico, 2004.

19. Natrella, M. NIST/SEMATECH e-Handbook of Statistical Methods; NIST/SEMATECH. 2013. Available online: https://www.itl.nist.gov/div898/handbook/ (accessed on 29 November 2018).

20. Menfors, M.; Fernstedt, F. Geotagging in Social Media: Exploring the Privacy Paradox. Bachelor's Thesis, University of Borås, Borås, Sweden, 2015.

21. Heine, C. 14 Instagram Data Findings That Every Marketer Needs to Know. 2014. Available online: https://www.adweek.com/digital/14-instagram-data-findings-every-marketer-needs-know-160969/ (accessed on 29 November 2018).

22. Graham, M.; Hale, S.A.; Gaffney, D. Where in the World are You? Geolocation and Language Identification in Twitter. *Prof. Geogr.* **2014**, *66*, 568–578. [CrossRef]

23. Reuter, C.; Kaufhold, M.A.; Spielhofer, T.; Hahne, A.S. Social Media in Emergencies: A Representative Study on Citizens' Perception in Germany. *Proc. ACM Hum.-Comput. Interact.* **2017**, *1*, 90:1–90:19, doi:10.1145/3134725. [CrossRef]

24. Quattrone, G.; Capra, L.; De Meo, P. There's No Such Thing As the Perfect Map: Quantifying Bias in Spatial Crowd-sourcing Datasets. In Proceedings of the 18th ACM Conference on Computer Supported Cooperative Work & Social Computing (CSCW '15), Vancouver, BC, Canada, 14–18 March 2015; pp. 1021–1032. [CrossRef]

25. Dittus, M.; Quattrone, G.; Capra, L. Mass Participation During Emergency Response: Event-centric Crowdsourcing in Humanitarian Mapping. In Proceedings of the 2017 ACM Conference on Computer Supported Cooperative Work and Social Computing (CSCW '17), Portland, OR, USA, 25 February–1 March 2017; pp. 1290–1303. [CrossRef]

26. Anderson, J.; Soden, R.; Keegan, B.; Palen, L.; Anderson, K.M. The Crowd is the Territory: Assessing Quality in Peer-Produced Spatial Data During Disasters. *Int. J. Hum.-Comput. Interact.* **2018**, *34*, 295–310. [CrossRef]

Article

Proactive Content Delivery with Service-Tier Awareness and User Demand Prediction

Jing Hu [1], Yaling Lai [1], Ao Peng [1,*], Xuemin Hong [2] and Jianghong Shi [2]

[1] School of Information Science and Engineering, Xiamen University, Xiamen 361005, Fujian, China; 23320161153403@stu.xmu.edu.cn (J.H.); 23320151154036@stu.xmu.edu.cn (Y.L.)

[2] Key Laboratory of Underwater Acoustic Communication and Marine Information Technology, Ministry of Education of China, Xiamen University, Xiamen 361005, Fujian, China; xuemin.hong@xmu.edu.cn (X.H.); shijh@xmu.edu.cn (J.S.)

* Correspondence: pa@xmu.edu.cn; Tel.: +86-592-258-0150

Received: 14 November 2018; Accepted: 24 December 2018; Published: 2 January 2019

Abstract: Cost-effective delivery of massive data content is a pressing challenge facing modern mobile communication networks. In the literature, two primary approaches to tackle this challenge are service-tier differentiation and personalized proactive content caching. However, these two approaches have not been integrated and studied in a unified framework. This paper proposes an integrated proactive content delivery scheme that jointly exploits the availability of multiple service tiers and multi-user behavior prediction. Three optimal algorithms and one heuristic algorithm are introduced to solve the cost-minimization problems of multi-user proactive content delivery under different modelling assumptions. The performance of the proposed scheme is systematically investigated to reveal the impacts of proactive window size, service-tier price ratio, and traffic cost model on the system performance.

Keywords: proactive content delivery; differentiated services; redundant capacity; secondary traffic

---

1. Introduction

The rapid proliferation of smart phones and mobile Internet has driven an explosive growth of mobile data traffic demand. According to Cisco's report [1], global mobile data traffic will reach 49 exabytes per month by 2021. Among various types of mobile applications, content delivery (e.g., web browsing, video streaming) consumes the majority of the mobile data traffic. A Cisco report [1] estimated that video content will account for 78% of the world's total mobile traffic in 2021. However, the high price of mobile data plan (e.g., cost per Mbyte) is still one of the main factors prohibiting the ubiquitous adoption of mobile video applications. Therefore, significant research interests have been attracted in designing a mobile content delivery network that is cost-friendly to massive content delivery services.

Contradicting the high price of mobile data plan, the overall utilization of the mobile communication network's capacity is relatively low. This is because the mobile traffic demand varies significantly across space and time [2–5], while the network is typically built to accommodate the peak traffic demand. Consequently, a large amount of "redundant capacity" (i.e., the difference between the actual traffic load and the network capacity) is not used during off-peak hours [6], resulting in a low overall utilization of the network. It is widely anticipated that improving the network utilization can help to reduce the cost per bit for mobile operators and ultimately the price per bit for mobile users.

A wide range of different approaches have been studied to improve the network capacity utilization. These approaches can be broadly categorized into two types: network-centric approach and price-centric approach. The former focuses on improving the technical efficiency of the network, which can ultimately reduce the operational expenses (OPEX) and/or capital expenses (CAPEX) of mobile operators. Within this category, "green radio" [7–9] aims to dynamically adjust the number of powered-on base stations (BSs) to match the actual traffic demand, so that the OPEX (mainly the cost of electricity consumption) can be reduced. Another approach called "proactive mobile edge caching" [10–18] aims to push popular (i.e., frequently requested) content in advance and cache them in the mobile edge network or even in end-user devices, so that on-demand traffic is off-loaded to the edge network or to off-peak hours. In practice, Netflix's content delivery network (CDN), named Open Connect, can deploy servers at Internet exchange points (IXPs) and inside Internet service providers (ISPs) without operating either a backbone network or data centers, and pre-load contents on its servers during off-peak times to reduce the amount of transit traffic [19]. Furthermore, the hybrid CDN–P2P solutions, integrating P2P into the current CDN architectures, were proposed to maximize throughput and reduce expenses [20]. This load-balancing approach helps to ease the pressure of network capacity expansion, so that the CAPEX can be reduced.

The second category is the price-centric approach. The rationale is to introduce diverse communication service tiers [21,22] with differentiated prices to end users. The service tiers and prices are allowed to be changed flexibly, such that the network utilization can be improved via market dynamics. Within this category, time-based data pricing schemes [23–30] (i.e., different traffic pricing during different hours in a day) are designed to attract users through special discounts in off-peak hours. This coarse-grain approach can help to smooth the temporal variation of traffic load, but is unable to balance the spatial traffic variation. Moreover, traffic from cheaper data plans may affect the quality-of-service (QoS) of traffic from normal data plans, resulting in a degraded quality-of-experience (QoE) for normal users in off-peak hours.

An alternative price-centric approach is service-based data pricing schemes [31–38], which allow the mobile operator (i.e., mobile ISP) to offer differentiated communication service tiers associated with different prices. Paper [31] derived the optimal service qualities and associated prices for an ISP with the consideration of capacity constraints and user characteristics. Paper [32] addressed the problem of ISP service tier design based on specific requirements of the applications such as web browsing and video streaming. Financial portfolio theory was applied to develop an optimization model in [33]. Various technical, economical, and social aspects of Internet service differentiation were discussed in [34–38]. Generally speaking, compared with time-based data pricing schemes, service-based data pricing schemes offer more flexibility and greater commercial incentive. Therefore, the 5th generation (5G) mobile communication network has incorporated new technologies, such as network slicing, to enable mobile ISPs to offer differentiated service tiers.

The above-mentioned studies on mobile content delivery have mostly taken a perspective from the mobile ISPs, who are essentially data pipes and have limited knowledge about user behavior and preference. In a parallel research field of content recommendation [39–42], it has been established that the content providers (CPs), such as YouTube and Netflix, can play an active role in content delivery. The reason is that CPs hold the data of users' content preferences and historical access behavior. For general human behavior [39,40], especially for wireless data users [41,42], there is substantial evidence showing that their content consumption behaviors are fairly predictable at a fine-grain timescale (from minutes to hours). Such personalized, fine-grain information enables CPs to predict users' content demand, so that traditional proactive caching schemes can be personalized and become more effective. As a result, CP-centric personalized content delivery, as an alternative to the traditional ISP-centric content delivery, has attracted increasing research interests lately.

Previous studies on mobile content delivery have either taken an ISP-centric perspective or a CP-centric perspective. To our best knowledge, studies that unify both perspectives are still rare. In this paper, we propose a content delivery scheme that integrates both perspectives. Our scheme can simultaneously exploit the availability of differentiated services tiers and the predictability of user behavior. The main contributions of our paper are as follows. First, we propose a proactive content delivery scheme with service-tier awareness and user behavior prediction for the purpose of cost reduction. Second, considering a baseline scheme of proactive content delivery with one time-slot, we derive the optimal content delivery policy that can minimize the long-term cost. Third, considering a generalized scheme of multi-time-slot proactive content delivery, we propose a near-optimal heuristic algorithm for cost reduction. The performances of the proposed schemes are systematically evaluated to reveal key insights into the impacts of various system parameters on the cost.

The remainder of this paper is organized as follows. Section 2 describes the system model. Sections 3 and 4 formulate and analyze the problems of proactive content delivery in single-time-slot and multi-time-slot cases, respectively. Numerical results are presented in Section 5. Finally, conclusions are drawn in Section 6.

2. System Model

2.1. Model of Communication Service Tiers

We consider a system consisting of a CP, an ISP, and N users. The content data is delivered from the CP to users via the ISP, as shown in Figure 1. For simplicity, we assume that the ISP offers two service tiers: a primary traffic (PT) service and a secondary traffic (ST) service. For concreteness, we further assume that the ST only utilizes the redundant capacity of the network [6]. This assumption has two implications. First, ST has a strictly lower priority than PT, therefore the unit cost of ST (e.g., dollar per kilo bytes) is also cheaper than PT. The ratio of ST cost over PT cost is denoted as β, where $0 \leq \beta \leq 1$. Second, the capacity of ST is upper bounded by the redundant capacity of the network. The total system capacity is dependent on the infrastructure deployment and network planning of the ISP. Once a network is rolled out, the system capacity is relatively stable. Redundant capacity is given by the difference between the system capacity and the primary traffic volume. Because the primary traffic volume fluctuates over time, the redundant capacity also changes dynamically. In practice, redundant capacity can be estimated by subtracting the pre-defined system capacity by the primary traffic load, which can be measured in real-time. We note that our paper focuses on the problem of proactive content delivery, which has a time-scale of seconds or minutes. Within such a time scale, the volume of redundant capacity can be treated as fixed. Therefore, our model captures the daily traffic fluctuation by a single parameter Cr_t, which indicates the currently available redundant capacity, i.e., the upper limit for ST at time t.

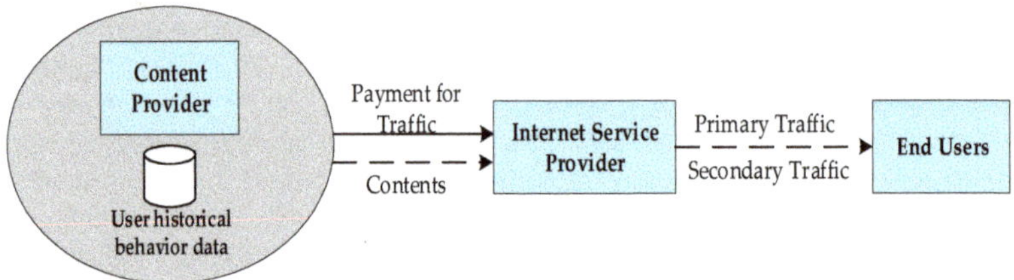

Figure 1. Illustration of the system model.

Within each service tier, the total traffic cost $C(L)$ is a function of the traffic load L. The cost is interpreted as the cost to the ISP for secondary service provision (i.e., transmit more data using redundant capacity). It is assumed that such a cost of the ISP is proportional to the cost of CP to access communication services provided by the ISP. Two cost models are considered in our paper. One is the simple case of volume-based or linear cost, which means the cost per unit traffic remains unchanged regardless of the traffic load L. In this case, we have $C_l(L) = k_l L$, where the cost is linearly proportional to the traffic load. Another case is quadratic cost, where $C_q(L) = k_q L^2$. This is a commonly used model in the literature [18] to reflect the fact that the cost to the ISP to support higher data rates scales non-linearly with the data rate. Such a nonlinear scaling is rooted in Shannon's capacity formula: once the physical bandwidth is fixed, the data rate can be improved by increasing the transmit power, but with diminishing returns. In the literature, the cost–traffic volume function is commonly approximated by a quadratic function for analytical convenience [18].

2.2. Model of User Behavior

We assume that time is slotted into unit intervals and indexed by t. It is assumed that the CP is able to make probabilistic predictions on the users' content request behavior based on historical trace. The prediction tells that user n ($n \in \{1, 2, \ldots, N\}$) will consume a total of $\zeta_{n,t}$ amount of data at time slot t with probability $p_{n,t}$, where $0 \leq \zeta_{n,t} < \infty$ and $0 \leq p_{n,t} \leq 1$. A random binary variable is used to indicate whether the nth user's request actually occurs at time t, i.e.,

$$I_{n,t} = \begin{cases} 1, & p_{n,t}, \\ 0, & 1 - p_{n,t} \end{cases} \tag{1}$$

It is assumed that multiple users' arrival and content consumption behaviors are independent from each other. Furthermore, user demands are assumed to be cyclic-stationary. This assumption is supported by various measurements showing that the user demand fluctuates in a periodic pattern [40,43] (e.g., on a daily basis). As a result, we can group multiple time slots into a cyclic period. The number of time slots in a period is denoted as T. It follows that

$$\zeta_{n,t} = \zeta_{n,t+T}, \; p_{n,t} = p_{n,t+T}, \; \forall n, t \tag{2}$$

2.3. Protocols of Proactive Content Delivery

We propose a protocol that is simultaneously aware of the service tiers and user behavior predictions. This requires certain degrees of collaboration and information sharing between the ISPs and CPs. At time slot t, the protocol uses the PT service tier to satisfy users' instantaneously content demand in the current slot. This is called reactive content delivery (RCD). Meanwhile, if redundant capacity is available, the protocol will proactively push a portion of the forecasted content demand in the upcoming several time slots using the ST service tier. This is called proactive content delivery (PCD). As the process iterates, the content demand at time t will be partly delivered by RCD via the PT service tier and partly by PCD via the ST service tier. Unlike traditional proactive caching schemes, the main difference here is that RCD and PCD are associated with the PT service tier and ST service tier, respectively.

Suppose that PCD is conducted over a length of W time-slots, where $1 \leq W \leq T$ and $\tau \in \{1, 2, \ldots, W\}$. When $W = 0$, the content delivery mechanism is purely reactive, which serves as our baseline case. The case of $W = 1$ is called single-slot PCD (SPCD), while the more general case of $1 < W \leq T$ is called multi-slot PCD (MPCD). We use $x_{n,t}(\tau)$ to denote the portion of data expected for user n at time $t + \tau$ but is proactively pushed to the user at time-slot t. Here τ denotes how many time slots are ahead for proactive caching. The main parameters in this paper are summarized in Table 1.

Table 1. Main parameters used in our model.

Variable	Definition
N	Number of users
T	Number of time-slots in a cyclic period
W	Window size for proactive content caching
$\zeta_{n,t}$	User n's demand at time-slot t (unit: MB)
$p_{n,t}$	User n's arrival probability at time-slot t
$I_{n,t}$	Random variable of user n's demand at time-slot t
Cr_t	System's redundant capacity at time-slot t (unit: MB)
$x_{n,t+1}$	Portion of proactively delivered data to be consumed at time-slot $t+1$ (unit: MB)
$x_{n,t}(\tau)$	Portion of proactively delivered data to be consumed at time-slot $t+\tau$ (unit: MB)
β	Ratio of the cost of the ST service tier over the PT tier

3. Proactive Content Delivery with Single Time-Slot

3.1. Problem Formulation

This section considers the case of proactive content delivery with single time-slot, where forecasted user demands can be sent one time-slot ahead using the ST service tier. At a given time- slot t, the cost is composed of two parts. One is the cost generated by RCD through the PT service tier, and the other part is the cost generated by PCD through the ST service tier. The time-average expected cost can be written as:

$$\eta_s(\mathbf{x}) = \frac{1}{T} \sum_{t=1}^{T} E\left[C\left(\sum_{n=1}^{N} (\zeta_{n,t} - x_{n,t}) I_{n,t} \right) + \beta \cdot C\left(\sum_{n=1}^{N} x_{n,t+1} \right) \right] \tag{3}$$

where we define a $N \times T$ matrix $\mathbf{x}$, the elements of which are $x_{n,t}$, $\forall n, t$. In Equation (3), $x_{n,t+1}$ represents the portion of proactively pushed data for the next time slot $t + 1$, and the expectation is taken over the random variable $I_{n,t}$. The received data for each user should not exceed the user's demand at time t, i.e.,

$$0 \leq x_{n,t} \leq \zeta_{n,t} \tag{4}$$

and the total amount of proactively pushed data cannot exceed the upper limit of the redundancy capacity at the current time-slot t, i.e.,

$$\sum_{n=1}^{N} x_{n,t+1} \leq Cr_t \tag{5}$$

The main objective is to minimize the total cost over the feasible space of $\mathbf{x}$. The optimization problem can be formulated as

$$s.t. \begin{cases} \min_{\mathbf{x}} \eta_s(\mathbf{x}) \\ 0 \leq x_{n,t} \leq \zeta_{n,t} & \forall n, t \\ x_{n,t} = x_{n,t+T} & \forall n, t \\ \sum_{n=1}^{N} x_{n,t} \leq Cr_t & \forall n, t \\ I_{n,t} \in \{0, 1\} & \forall n, t \end{cases} \tag{6}$$

For comparison purposes, also consider the baseline case of pure RCD. The time-average expected cost in this case is given by

$$\eta = \frac{1}{T} \sum_{t=1}^{T} E\left[C\left(\sum_{n=1}^{N} \zeta_{n,t} I_{n,t} \right) \right] \tag{7}$$

where $\sum_{n=1}^{N} \zeta_{n,t} I_{n,t}$ is the actual traffic load requested at time t. In this case, the system is purely reactive to the users' request and there is no decision variable to be optimized.

3.2. Linear Cost Model

Assuming the linear cost model, we can substitute $C_l(L)$ into Equation (3) to yield

$$
\begin{aligned}
\eta_s^l(\mathbf{x}) \;&=\; \tfrac{1}{T}\sum_{t=1}^{T} E\left[k_l\left(\sum_{n=1}^{N} (\xi_{n,t}-x_{n,t})\mathrm{I}_{n,t}\right) + \beta\cdot k_l\left(\sum_{n=1}^{N} x_{n,t+1}\right)\right] \\
&\overset{(a)}{=}\; \tfrac{1}{T}\sum_{t=1}^{T}\sum_{n=1}^{N} k_l\!\left((\beta-p_{n,t})x_{n,t}+\xi_{n,t}p_{n,t}\right)
\end{aligned}
\tag{8}
$$

We note that the property of cyclic-stationary user demand (i.e., $x_{n,t}=x_{n,t+T}$) is used in Equation (8) to give $\sum_{t=1}^{T} x_{n,t+1}=\sum_{t=1}^{T} x_{n,t}$. From Equation (8), we can see that the optimization problem in Equation (6) becomes a linear programming problem, such that the problem can be easy solved by classic methods such as the dual interior point method.

A closer look at Equation (8) reveals a key insight that both the cost and the PCD decision variable x are determined by the relative difference between the cost ratio β and users' arrival probabilities $p_{n,t}$. When $p_{n,t} > \beta$, PCD for the nth user is beneficial for cost reduction; when $p_{n,t} < \beta$, PCD for the nth user becomes harmful because there is a higher likelihood that the pushed data will not be actually consumed by the user, so that the resource used for PCD is wasted. When $p_{n,t} = \beta$, PCD for the nth user makes no difference.

3.3. Quadratic Cost Model

When the cost is a quadratic function of the traffic load, the costs increase rapidly as the load increases. In this case, PCD becomes more useful because it helps to smooth the traffic load and reduce fluctuations over time. Substituting $C_q(L)$ into (3) yields:

$$
\begin{aligned}
\eta_s^q(\mathbf{x}) \;&=\; \tfrac{1}{T}\sum_{t=1}^{T} E\left[k_q\left(\sum_{n=1}^{N} (\xi_{n,t}-x_{n,t})\mathrm{I}_{n,t}\right)^2 + \beta\cdot k_q\left(\sum_{n=1}^{N} x_{n,t+1}\right)^2\right] \\
&=\; \tfrac{1}{T}\sum_{t=1}^{T} k_q\left(\sum_{n=1}^{N} (\xi_{n,t}-x_{n,t})^2 p_{n,t} + \sum_{n=1}^{N}\sum_{m\neq n} (\xi_{n,t}-x_{n,t})p_{n,t}(\xi_{m,t}-x_{m,t})p_{m,t}\right. \\
&\qquad\left. +\beta\sum_{n=1}^{N} x_{n,t+1}^2 + \beta\sum_{n=1}^{N}\sum_{m\neq n} x_{n,t+1}x_{m,t+1}\right) \\
&=\; \tfrac{1}{T}\sum_{t=1}^{T} k_q\left(\sum_{n=1}^{N} (p_{n,t}+\beta)x_{n,t}^2 + \sum_{n=1}^{N}\sum_{m\neq n} (p_{n,t}p_{m,t}+\beta)x_{n,t}x_{m,t} - 2\sum_{n=1}^{N} \xi_{n,t}p_{n,t}x_{n,t}\right. \\
&\qquad\left. -2\sum_{n=1}^{N}\sum_{m\neq n} \xi_{m,t}p_{m,t}p_{n,t}x_{n,t} + \sum_{n=1}^{N} \xi_{n,t}^2 p_{n,t} + \sum_{n=1}^{N}\sum_{m\neq n} \xi_{n,t}\xi_{m,t}p_{n,t}p_{m,t}\right)
\end{aligned}
\tag{9}
$$

We can see that in this case, we no longer have a simple intuitive solution for x. However, it can be proved that the problem in Equation (9) is a convex optimization problem (see Appendix A). Hence, the optimal solution can be readily solved using standard convex optimization techniques.

4. Proactive Content Delivery with Multiple Time-Slots

4.1. Problem Formulation

As a generalization from the single-time slot case, portions of user's predicted demand can be pushed to users by multiple time-slots ahead through the ST service tier. The time-average expected cost in this case is given by:

$$\eta_m(\mathbf{x}) = \frac{1}{T}\sum_{t=1}^{T} E\left[C\left(\sum_{n=1}^{N} \left(\zeta_{n,t} - \sum_{\tau=1}^{W} x_{n,t-\tau}(\tau) \right) I_{n,t} \right) + \beta \cdot C\left(\sum_{n=1}^{N}\sum_{\tau=1}^{W} x_{n,t}(\tau) \right) \right] \tag{10}$$

where the decision variable $\mathbf{x}$ is a $N \times T \times W$ matrix, whose elements are given by $x_{n,t}(\tau)$, $\forall n, t, \tau$. Here, what differs from the single-time-slot case is that user n's cached data at time t is the accumulated data pushed from the previous W time-slots. PCD for each user is constrained by the individual user demand, i.e.,

$$x_{n,t-\tau}(\tau) \geq 0,$$
$$\sum_{\tau=1}^{W} x_{n,t-\tau}(\tau) \leq \zeta_{n,t} \tag{11}$$

in addition, the total amount of PCD data of all users at any time-slot t cannot exceed the current redundant capacity, i.e.,

$$\sum_{n=1}^{N}\sum_{\tau=1}^{W} x_{n,t}(\tau) \leq Cr_t \tag{12}$$

the optimization problem can then be formulated as:

$$\min_{\mathbf{x}} \eta_m(\mathbf{x})$$
$$s.t. \begin{cases} x_{n,t}(\tau) \geq 0 & \forall n, t, \tau \\ x_{n,t}(\tau) = x_{n,t+T}(\tau) & \forall n, t, \tau \\ \sum_{\tau=1}^{W} x_{n,t-\tau}(\tau) \leq \zeta_{n,t} & \forall n, t, \tau \\ \sum_{n=1}^{N}\sum_{\tau=1}^{W} x_{n,t}(\tau) \leq Cr_t & \forall n, t, \tau \\ I_{n,t} \in \{0,1\} & \forall n, t \end{cases} \tag{13}$$

4.2. Linear Cost Model

Substituting the linear cost function $C_l(L)$ into Equation (10) we get

$$\begin{aligned} \eta_m^l(\mathbf{x}) &= \frac{1}{T}\sum_{t=1}^{T} E\left[C_l\left(\sum_{n=1}^{N} \left(\zeta_{n,t} - \sum_{\tau=1}^{W} x_{n,t-\tau}(\tau) \right) I_{n,t} \right) + \beta \cdot C_l\left(\sum_{n=1}^{N}\sum_{\tau=1}^{W} x_{n,t}(\tau) \right) \right] \\ &= \frac{1}{T}\sum_{t=1}^{T} k_l\left(\sum_{n=1}^{N} \left(\zeta_{n,t} - \sum_{\tau=1}^{W} x_{n,t-\tau}(\tau) \right) p_{n,t} \right) + \beta \cdot k_l\left(\sum_{n=1}^{N}\sum_{\tau=1}^{W} x_{n,t}(\tau) \right) \\ &\overset{(b)}{=} \frac{1}{T}\sum_{t=1}^{T} k_l \sum_{n=1}^{N} \left(\sum_{\tau=1}^{W} x_{n,t}(\tau)(\beta - p_{n,t}) + \zeta_{n,t} p_{n,t} \right) \end{aligned} \tag{14}$$

In (14), the equality (b) follows by $\sum_{t=1}^{T}\sum_{\tau=1}^{W} x_{n,t-\tau}(\tau) = \sum_{t=1}^{T}\sum_{\tau=1}^{W} x_{n,t}(\tau)$. We can see that the optimization problem reduces to a linear programing problem. Similar to the case of single time-slot, the effectiveness of PCD still depends on the relative difference between the traffic cost ratio β and user n's arrival probability $p_{n,t}$. However, the proactive data user n received from different time-slot, i.e., $x_{n,t-\tau}(\tau)$, depends on the redundant capacity of the previous W time-slots. This requires proper monitoring of real-time redundant capacity over multiple time slots.

4.3. Quadratic Cost Model

Substituting the quadratic cost function $C_q(L)$ into Equation (10), we have

$$
\begin{aligned}
\eta_m^q(\mathbf{x}) \;=\; & \frac{1}{T}\sum_{t=1}^{T} E\left[k_q\left(\sum_{n=1}^{N}\left(\xi_{n,t} - \sum_{\tau=1}^{W} x_{n,t-\tau}(\tau) \right) I_{n,t} \right)^2 + \beta k_q \left(\sum_{n=1}^{N}\sum_{\tau}^{W} x_{n,t}(\tau) \right)^2 \right] \\[4pt]
=\; & \frac{1}{T}\sum_{t=1}^{T}\Bigg\{ E\Bigg[k_q \sum_{n=1}^{N}\left(\xi_{n,t} - \sum_{\tau=1}^{W} x_{n,t-\tau}(\tau) \right)^2 I_{n,t}^2 \\[4pt]
& + k_q \sum_{n=1}^{N}\sum_{n\neq m}\left(\xi_{n,t} - \sum_{\tau=1}^{W} x_{n,t-\tau}(\tau) \right)\left(\xi_{m,t} - \sum_{\tau=1}^{W} x_{m,t-\tau}(\tau) \right) I_{n,t} I_{m,t} \Bigg] + \beta k_q \left(\sum_{n=1}^{N}\sum_{\tau}^{W} x_{n,t}(\tau) \right)^2 \Bigg\} \\[4pt]
=\; & \frac{1}{T}\sum_{t=1}^{T}\Bigg\{ k_q \sum_{n=1}^{N}\left(\xi_{n,t} - \sum_{\tau=1}^{W} x_{n,t-\tau}(\tau) \right)^2 p_{n,t} \\[4pt]
& + k_q \sum_{n=1}^{N}\sum_{n\neq m}\left(\xi_{n,t} - \sum_{\tau=1}^{W} x_{n,t-\tau}(\tau) \right)\left(\xi_{m,t} - \sum_{\tau=1}^{W} x_{m,t-\tau}(\tau) \right) p_{n,t} p_{m,t} + \beta k_q \left(\sum_{n=1}^{N}\sum_{\tau}^{W} x_{n,t}(\tau) \right)^2 \Bigg\}
\end{aligned}
\tag{15}
$$

This yields a complicated non-linear optimization problem and there is no straightforward proof for its convexity. However, because the utility function can be easily evaluated in closed-form, general purpose heuristic search algorithms such as the pattern search [44] can be used to solve the problem effectively.

5. Simulation Results

This section presents numerical results to our previous analysis. For illustration purposes, we set $T = 10$ and $N = 3$. User n's demand at time t is drawn from a uniform distribution on $[0, 500]$; the arrival probability of user n at time t follows a uniform distribution on $[0, 1]$. The scaling constants in the linear and quadratic cost models are given by $k_l = 2$ and $k_q = 0.005$, respectively. The case of pure RCD, where there is no proactive caching, is also presented as a performance benchmark.

5.1. Case of Single Time-Slot

Using the linear cost model, Figure 2 shows how the time-average expected cost and the redundant capacity utilization changes as a function of the ST/PT cost ratio β. The results are obtained by solving the linear optimization problem defined in Section 3.2 and averaging over 100 realizations. It is observed that a smaller value of β leads to a lower cost and a higher utilization of the redundant capacity. This is expectable because a smaller value of β would better encourage the use of PCD using the ST service tier. When $\beta = 1$, which means the two service tiers have the same cost, there is no performance gain to use PCD at all. Moreover, we can see that larger amount of redundant capacity helps to reduce the cost because more user demand can be accommodated via the ST service tier.

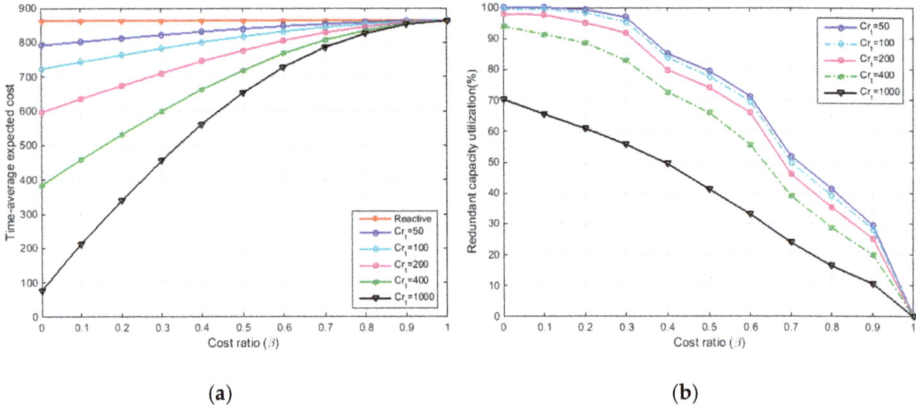

Figure 2. (**a**) The time-average expected cost as a function of the ST/PT cost ratio β; (**b**) the redundant capacity utilization as a function of the ST/PT cost ratio β (linear cost model, varying redundant capacity Cr_t).

Using the quadratic cost model, Figure 3 shows how the time-average expected cost and the redundant capacity utilization changes as a function of the ST/PT cost ratio β. The results are obtained by solving the convex optimization problem defined in Section 3.3. The general trend observed in Figure 3 is similar to that in Figure 2, i.e., a smaller value of β leads to a lower cost and a higher utilization of the redundant capacity. However, a key difference to Figure 2 occurs when β approaches 1, where PCD is shown to be useful for cost reduction even when the cost of ST and PT are the same. For example, at $Cr_t = 400$ and $\beta = 1$, the time-average cost can be reduced by nearly 32% (as opposed to 0% in Figure 2) and the redundant traffic utilization is about 43% (as opposed to 0% in Figure 2). This is because the PCD can help to smooth the user demand in time, while a more balanced user demand yields a lower cost under the quadratic cost model.

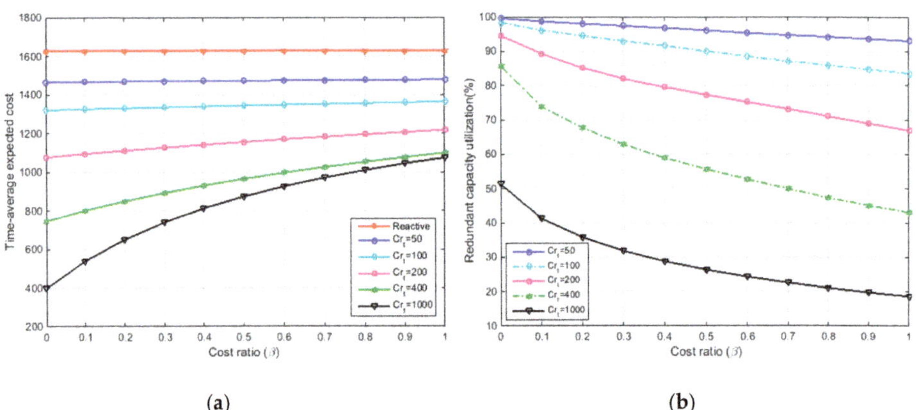

Figure 3. (**a**) The time-average expected cost as a function of the ST/PT cost ratio β; (**b**) the redundant capacity utilization as a function of the ST/PT cost ratio β (quadratic cost model, varying redundant capacity Cr_t).

5.2. Case of Multiple Time-Slot

Figure 4 shows three figures related to the performance of multi-time-slot PCD under the linear cost model. The results are obtained by solving the linear optimization problem defined in Section 4.2.

The general conclusions drawn from Figure 4 are the same as that in Figure 2, i.e., PCD is not useful when there is no cost difference between ST and PT service tiers. Apart from this, Figure 4a–c further reveal the impact of proactive window size on the performance. It is observed that increasing the window size does help to further reduce the cost, but the improvement is limited and becomes insignificant when W is greater than five. In Figure 4c, we can see that when the value of β increases, the effectiveness of cost reduction by increasing W decreases. This suggests that when the costs of the two service tiers are comparable, increasing the proactive window size W will become less effective for cost saving.

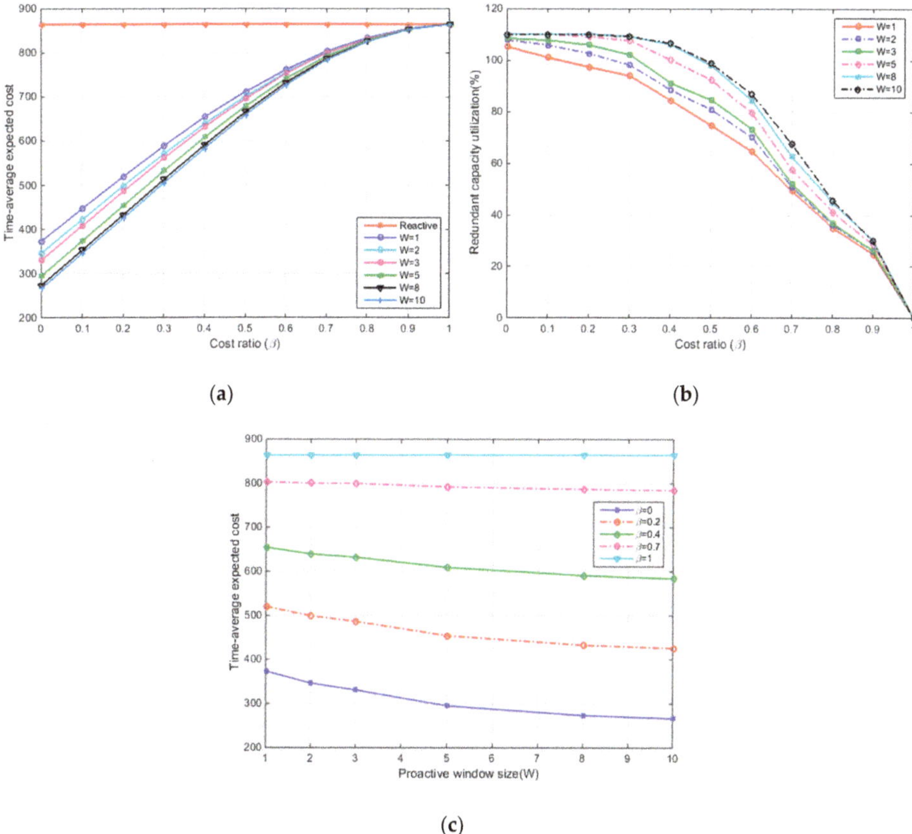

Figure 4. (**a**) The time-average expected cost as a function of the ST/PT cost ratio β; (**b**) the redundant capacity utilization as a function of the ST/PT cost ratio β; (**c**) the time-average expected cost as a function of the proactive window size W (linear cost model, $Cr_t = 400$, varying window size W).

Finally, Figure 5 shows three figures related to the performance of multi-time-slot PCD under the quadratic cost model. The results are obtained by solving the non-linear optimization problem defined in Section 4.3 using pattern search. Compared with Figure 4, Figure 5 shows that using PCD is always useful for cost reduction regardless of the values of β. Even when $\beta = 1$, the cost can still be reduced by 53% thanks to the load smoothing effect. Moreover, increasing the window size also helps for load smoothing, and is hence considered beneficial for all values of β. Table 2 further demonstrates the smoothing effect of multi-time-slot PCD on network traffic load. Given $Cr_t = 400$ and $\beta = 0.5$, the variances of the actual traffic across different time slots is shown as a function of the window size. We can see that increasing W helps to reduce the variance of the traffic load, but has diminishing returns especially when W becomes greater than five.

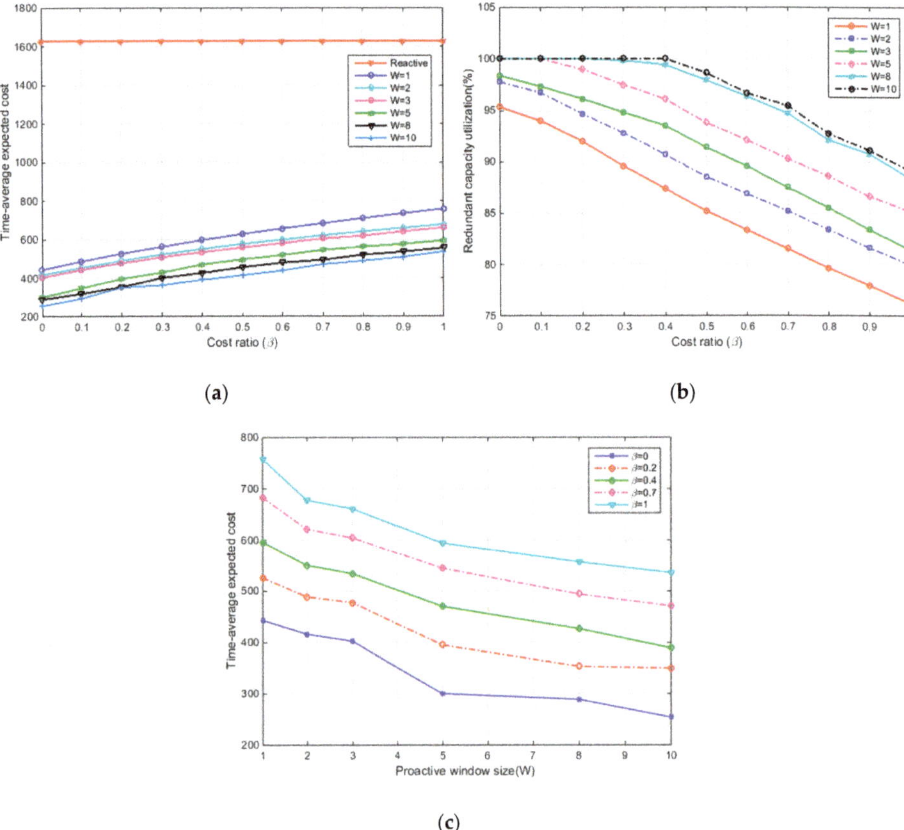

(a)

(b)

(c)

Figure 5. (a) The time-average expected cost as a function of the ST/PT cost ratio β; (b) the redundant capacity utilization as a function of the ST/PT cost ratio β; (c) the time-average expected cost as a function of the proactive window size W (quadratic cost model, $Cr_t = 400$, varying window size W).

Table 2. The variance of traffic demand.

W	1	2	3	5	8	10
Variance $(\times 10^4)$	8.3188	5.7479	5.0893	4.2842	3.4933	3.3491

The above simulation results show that both single time-slot and multiple time-slot PCD can bring good performance gain for CP. The performance gain increases with lower cost rate β and larger window size W. However, the performance gain is fundamentally constrained by the volume of redundant capacity. In practice, this means close cooperation must be established between CP and ISP so that the volume of redundant capacity in the current network can be measured and shared in real time. For the ISP, our model helps to improve the overall utilization of network infrastructure and generate additional revenue. For CP, our model helps to attract users and promote content consumption by reducing the cost of content delivery per bit. In summary, our model can offer a win-win situation for ISP and CP.

6. Conclusions

This paper proposes a personalized PCD scheme that aims to minimize the total cost of content delivery by means of multiple service-tier transmission and multi-user behavior prediction. The problem of personalized PCD has been systematically investigated in single-time-slot and multi-time-slot cases, under both linear and quadratic cost models. Three optimal algorithms and one heuristic algorithm have been presented to solve the respective optimization problems. Simulation results have demonstrated the effectiveness of the proposed PCD scheme and revealed the impacts of proactive window size, service-tier cost ratio, and traffic cost model on the cost of content delivery. We conclude that personalized PCD over multiple service tiers can effectively reduce the cost when the cost is sensitive to the total traffic load and/or the type of service tiers.

Author Contributions: Conceptualization, J.H. and Y.L.; Formal analysis, J.H.; Investigation, Y.L.; Methodology, A.P.; Project administration, A.P. and X.H.; Resources, J.S.; Supervision, J.S.; Validation, Y.L.; Writing—Original draft, J.H.; Writing—Review & editing, A.P. and X.H.

Funding: This research was funded by the National Natural Science Foundation of China (NSFC) (Grant No.: 61571378) and the National Key Research and Development Program of China (Grant No.: 2018YFB0505202).

Conflicts of Interest: The authors declare no conflict of interest.

Appendix A

Substituting Equation (9) into Equation (6), the problem of single-slot cost optimization becomes:

$$
\min_{\mathbf{x}} \frac{1}{T} \sum_{t=1}^{T} \left\{ \sum_{n=1}^{N} k_q(\beta + p_{n,t}) x_{n,t}^2 + \sum_{n=1}^{N} \sum_{m \neq n} k_q(p_{n,t} p_{m,t} + \beta) x_{n,t} x_{m,t} \right.
$$
$$
\left. - \sum_{n=1}^{N} 2k_q \left(\zeta_{n,t} p_{n,t} + \sum_{m \neq n} \zeta_{m,t} p_{n,t} p_{m,t} \right) x_{n,t} \right\} + cons
$$
$$
s.t. \begin{cases} 0 \leq x_{n,t} \leq \zeta_{n,t} & \forall n,t \\ x_{n,t} = x_{n,t+T} & \forall n,t \\ \sum_{n=1}^{N} x_{n,t} \leq Cr_t & \forall n,t \\ I_{n,t} \in \{0,1\} & \forall n,t \end{cases} \tag{A1}
$$

where, $cons = \frac{k_q}{T} \sum_{t=1}^{T} \sum_{n=1}^{N} \left(\zeta_{n,t}^2 p_{n,t} + \sum_{m \neq n} \zeta_{n,t} \zeta_{m,t} p_{n,t} p_{m,t} \right)$. The value of $cons$ mainly depends on $p_{n,t}$ and $\zeta_{n,t}$, so $cons$ is independent of the variables and not relevant for the minimization of the objective function. We can see this is a quadratic programming problem. In order to prove the convexity of the objective function, we define $\mathbf{Q}_t$ as its Hessian matrix, whose elements are given by:

$$
\begin{aligned}
[\mathbf{Q}_t]_{n,n} &= k_q(p_{n,t} + \beta) \\
[\mathbf{Q}_t]_{m,n} &= k_q(p_{m,t} p_{n,t} + \beta), \ n \neq m \\
[\mathbf{q}_t]_n &= -2k_q \left(\zeta_{n,t} p_{n,t} + \sum_{m \neq n} \zeta_{m,t} p_{n,t} p_{m,t} \right)
\end{aligned} \tag{A2}
$$

Proof: suppose that $[\tilde{\mathbf{Q}}_t]_{n,n} = p_{n,t}$, $[\tilde{\mathbf{Q}}_t]_{m,n} = p_{m,t} p_{n,t}$ ($n \neq m$ and $n,m \in \{1,2,\ldots,N\}$), then:

$$
\tilde{\mathbf{Q}}_t = \mathbf{P}_t^T \breve{\mathbf{Q}}_t \mathbf{P}_t \tag{A3}
$$

where, $\mathbf{P}_t = \mathrm{diag}\{p_{1,t}, \ldots, p_{N,t}\}$, $\left[\breve{\mathbf{Q}}_t \right]_{nn} = \frac{1}{p_{n,t+1}}$, $\left[\breve{\mathbf{Q}}_t \right]_{nm} = 1$. Let us set vector $\mathbf{b} = \left[\sqrt{\beta} \ \ \sqrt{\beta} \ \ \cdots \ \ \sqrt{\beta} \right]^T$, then we have $\hat{\mathbf{Q}}_t = \tilde{\mathbf{Q}}_t + \mathbf{b}\mathbf{b}^T$, and:

$$
\mathbf{Q}_t = k_q \hat{\mathbf{Q}}_t \tag{A4}
$$

Therefore whether $\mathbf{Q}_t$ is a positive definite matrix can be determined by the nature of $\hat{\mathbf{Q}}_t$. First, $\tilde{\mathbf{Q}}_t$ can be proved to be a positive definite matrix. Here g_n is defined as the n-order principal minor determinant of $\tilde{\mathbf{Q}}_t$, $n \in \{1, 2, \ldots, N\}$, i.e.,

$$
g_n = \begin{vmatrix} \alpha_1 & 1 & \cdots & 1 \\ 1 & \alpha_2 & & \\ \vdots & & \ddots & \\ 1 & & & \alpha_n \end{vmatrix}
\tag{A5}
$$

where $\alpha_n = \frac{1}{p_{n,t+1}} > 1$, and then:

$$
g_n = \left(\alpha_1 + \sum_{k=2}^{n} \frac{1 - \alpha_1}{1 - \alpha_k} \right) \prod_{k=2}^{n} (\alpha_k - 1)
\tag{A6}
$$

We have $g_n > 0, \forall n$, i.e., all principal minor determinants of $\tilde{\mathbf{Q}}_t$ are positive, thereby $\tilde{\mathbf{Q}}_t$ is a positive definite matrix, meaning that $\tilde{\mathbf{Q}}_t$ is also positive definite. According to Sylvester's theorem:

$$
\det(\mathbf{X} + \mathbf{cr}) = \det(\mathbf{X})(1 + \mathbf{r}\mathbf{X}^{-1}\mathbf{c}) = \det(\mathbf{X}) + r\,adj(\mathbf{X})\mathbf{c}
\tag{A7}
$$

we can write:

$$
\left| \hat{\mathbf{Q}}_t \right| = \left| \tilde{\mathbf{Q}}_t + \mathbf{b}\mathbf{b}^T \right| = \left| \tilde{\mathbf{Q}}_t \right| \left| 1 + \mathbf{b}^T \tilde{\mathbf{Q}}_t^{-1} \mathbf{b} \right|
\tag{A8}
$$

Because $\tilde{\mathbf{Q}}_t$ is positive definite as shown above, we can get $\left| \hat{\mathbf{Q}}_t \right| > 0$, therefore it can be concluded that the objective function's Hessian matrix $\mathbf{Q}_t$ is a positive definite matrix, which ends our proof that the optimization problem in Equation (A1) is a convex quadratic programming problem.

References

1. Cisco Visual Networking Index: Global Mobile Data Traffic Forecast Update, 2016–2021. Available online: https://www.cisco.com/c/en/us/solutions/collateral/service-provider/visual-networking-index-vni/mobile-white-paper-c11-520862.html (accessed on 23 January 2018).
2. Lee, D.; Zhou, S.; Zhong, X.; Niu, Z.; Zhou, X.; Zhang, H. Spatial modeling of the traffic density in cellular networks. *IEEE Wirel. Commun.* **2014**, *21*, 80–88. [CrossRef]
3. Zhao, Z.; Li, M.; Li, R.; Zhou, Y. Temporal-spatial distribution nature of traffic and base stations in cellular networks. *IET Commun.* **2017**, *11*, 2410–2416. [CrossRef]
4. Leland, W.E.; Taqqu, M.S.; Willinger, W.; Wilson, D.V. On the self-similar nature of Ethernet traffic (extended version). *IEEE/ACM Trans. Netw.* **1995**, *2*, 1–15. [CrossRef]
5. Park, K.; Willinger, W. Self-similar network traffic: An overview. In *Self-Similar Network Traffic and Performance Evaluation*; Park, K., Willinger, W., Eds.; John Wiley and Sons: New York, NY, USA, 2000; pp. 1–38, ISBN 978-0-471-31974-0.
6. Zhang, Y.; Lu, H.; Wang, H.; Hong, X. Cognitive cellular content delivery networks: Cross-layer design and analysis. In Proceedings of the IEEE Vehicular Technology Conference (VTC spring), Nanjing, China, 15–18 May 2016; pp. 1–6.
7. Wang, B.; Wu, Y.; Liu, K.J.R.; Clancy, T.C. An anti-jamming stochastic game for cognitive radio networks. *IEEE J. Sel. Areas Commun.* **2011**, *29*, 877–889. [CrossRef]
8. Han, C.; Harrold, T.; Armour, S.; Krikidis, I.; Videv, S.; Grant, P.M.; Haas, H.; Thompson, J.S.; Ku, I.; Wang, C.; et al. Green radio: Radio techniques to enable energy-efficient wireless networks. *IEEE Commun. Mag.* **2011**, *49*, 46–54. [CrossRef]
9. Ismail, M.; Zhuang, W. Green radio communications in a heterogeneous wireless medium. *IEEE Wirel. Commun.* **2014**, *21*, 128–135. [CrossRef]
10. Kangasharju, J.; Roberts, J.; Ross, K.W. Object replication strategies in content distribution networks. *Comput. Commun.* **2002**, *25*, 376–383. [CrossRef]

11. Vakali, A.; Pallis, G. Content delivery networks: Status and trends. *IEEE Internet Comput.* **2003**, *7*, 68–74. [CrossRef]

12. Pallis, G.; Vakali, A. Insight and perspectives for content delivery networks. *Commum. ACM* **2006**, *49*, 101–106. [CrossRef]

13. Ahlehagh, H.; Dey, S. Video-aware scheduling and caching in the radio access network. *IEEE/ACM Trans. Netw.* **2014**, *22*, 1444–1462. [CrossRef]

14. Ahlehagh, H.; Dey, S. Video caching in radio access network: Impact on delay and capacity. In Proceedings of the IEEE Wireless Communications and Network Conference (WCNC), Paris, France, 1–4 April 2012; pp. 2276–2281.

15. Xu, Y.; Li, Y.; Wang, Z.; Lin, T. Coordinated caching model for minimizing energy consumption in radio access network. In Proceedings of the IEEE International Conference on Communications (ICC), Sydney, Australia, 10–14 June 2014; pp. 2406–2411.

16. Shoukry, O.; Elmohsen, M.A.; Tadrous, J.; Gamal, H.E.; Elbatt, T.; Wanas, N.; Elnakieb, Y.; Khairy, M. Proactive scheduling for content pre-fetching in mobile networks. In Proceedings of the IEEE International Conference on Communications (ICC), Sydney, Australia, 10–14 June 2014; pp. 2848–2854.

17. Shoukry, O.K.; Fayek, M.B. Evolutionary scheduler for content pre-fetching in mobile networks. In Proceedings of the 2013 AAAI Fall Symposium Series, Arlington, VA, USA, 15–17 November 2013; pp. 386–391.

18. Tadrous, J.; Eryilmaz, A.; Gamal, H.E. Joint smart pricing and proactive content caching for mobile services. *IEEE/ACM Trans. Netw.* **2016**, *24*, 2357–2371. [CrossRef]

19. Bottger, T.; Cuadrado, F.; Tyson, G.; Castro, I.; Uhlig, S. Open connect everywhere: A glimpse at the internet ecosystem through the lens of the Netflix CDN. *ACM SIGCOMM Comp. Commun. Rev.* **2018**, *48*, 28–34. [CrossRef]

20. Hasslinger, G.; Hartleb, F. Content delivery and caching from a network provider's perspective. *Comput. Netw.* **2011**, *55*, 3991–4006. [CrossRef]

21. Kimbler, K.; Taylor, M. Value added mobile broadband services innovation driven transformation of the 'smart pipe'. In Proceedings of the 2012 16th International Conference on Intelligence in Next Generation Networks, Berlin, Germany, 8–11 October 2012; pp. 30–34.

22. Yang, Z.; Ma, Z. Analysis of communication operators transformation on smart pipe. In Proceedings of the 2013 5th International Conference on Intelligent Human-Machine Systems and Cybernetics, Hangzhou, China, 26–27 August 2013; pp. 131–134.

23. Jiang, L.; Parekh, S.; Walrand, J. Time-dependent network pricing and bandwidth trading. In Proceedings of the NOWS Workshops 2008-IEEE Network Operations and Management Symposium Workshops, Salvador da Bahia, Brazil, 7–11 April 2008; pp. 193–200.

24. Joe-Wong, C.; Ha, S.; Chiang, M. Time-dependent broadband pricing: Feasibility and benefits. In Proceedings of the 31st International Conference on Distributed Computing Systems (ICDCS), Minneapolis, MN, USA, 20–24 June 2011; pp. 288–298.

25. Sen, S.; Joe-Wong, C.; Ha, S.; Chiang, M. Smart data pricing: Using economics to manage network congestion. *Commun. ACM* **2015**, *58*, 86–93. [CrossRef]

26. Zhang, L. Smart Data Pricing in Wireless Data Networks: An Economic Solution to Congestion. Ph.D. Thesis, Hong Kong Polytechnic University, Hong Kong, China, 2016.

27. Zhang, L.; Wu, W.J.; Wang, D. Time dependent pricing in wireless data networks: Flat-rate vs. Usage-based schemes. In Proceedings of the 33rd IEEE Annual Conference on Computer Communications (IEEE INFOCOM), Toronto, ON, Canada, 27 April–2 May 2014; pp. 700–708.

28. Kesidis, G.; Das, A.; de Veciana, G. On flat-rate and usage-based pricing for tiered commodity internet services. In Proceedings of the 42nd Annual Conference on Information Sciences and Systems, Princeton, NJ, USA, 19–21 March 2008; pp. 304–308.

29. Chau, C.K.; Wang, Q.; Chiu, D.M. On the Viability of Paris Metro Pricing for Communication and Service Networks. In Proceedings of the Conference on IEEE INFOCOM, San Diego, CA, USA, 15–19 March 2010; pp. 1–9.

30. Ma, R.T.B. Usage-Based Pricing and Competition in Congestible Network Service Markets. *IEEE/ACM Trans. Netw.* **2016**, *24*, 3084–3097. [CrossRef]

31. Zou, M.; Ma, R.T.B.; Wang, X.; Xu, Y. On optimal service differentiation in congested network markets. In Proceedings of the IEEE Conference on Computer Communications (INFOCOM), Atlanta, GA, USA, 1–4 May 2017; pp. 1–9.

32. Dai, W.; Jordan, S. ISP Service Tier Design. *IEEE/ACM Trans. Netw.* **2016**, *24*, 1434–1447. [CrossRef]

33. Nesse, P.J.; Gaivoronski, A.; Lonsethagen, H. Ecosystem, QoE and pricing of end to end differentiated services. In Proceedings of the 6th International Conference on Information, Intelligence, Systems and Applications (IISA), Corfu, Greece, 6–8 July 2015; pp. 1–7.

34. Gibbens, R.; Mason, R.; Steinberg, R. Internet service classes under competition. *IEEE J. Sel. Areas Commun.* **2000**, *18*, 2490–2498. [CrossRef]

35. Ma, R.T.B.; Misra, V. The public option: A nonregulatory alternative to network neutrality. *IEEE/ACM Trans. Netw.* **2013**, *21*, 1866–1879. [CrossRef]

36. Wang, S.; Xuan, D.; Bettati, R.; Zhao, W. Providing absolute differentiated services for real-time applications in static-priority scheduling networks. *IEEE/ACM Trans. Netw.* **2004**, *12*, 326–339. [CrossRef]

37. Nandy, B.; Ethridge, J.; Lakas, A.; Chapman, A. Aggregate flow control: Improving assurances for differentiated services network. In Proceedings of the 20th Annual Joint Conference of the IEEE-Computer-Society/IEEE-Communication-Society, Anchorage, AK, USA, 22–26 April 2001; pp. 1340–1349.

38. Bouyoucef, K.; Khorasani, K. A robust distributed congestion-control strategy for differentiated-services network. *IEEE Trans. Ind. Electron.* **2009**, *56*, 608–617. [CrossRef]

39. Farrahi, K.; Gatica-Perez, D. Discovering human routines from cell phone data with topic models. In Proceedings of the 12th IEEE International Symposium on Wearable Computers, Pittsburgh, PA, USA, 28 September–1 October 2008; pp. 29–32.

40. Song, C.; Barabási, A.L. Limits of predictability in human mobility. *Science* **2010**, *327*, 1018–1021. [CrossRef] [PubMed]

41. Fikir, O.B.; Yaz, I.O.; Ozyer, T. A movie Rating Prediction Algorithm with Collaborative Filtering. In Proceedings of the International Conference on Advances in Social Networks Analysis and Mining (ASONAM), Odense, Denmark, 9–11 August 2010; pp. 321–325.

42. Salter, J.; Antonopoulos, N. CinemaScreen Recommender Agent: Combining Collaborative and Content-Based Filtering. *IEEE Intell. Syst.* **2006**, *21*, 35–41. [CrossRef]

43. Feknous, M.; Houdoin, T.; Guyader, B.L.; Biasio, J.D.; Gravey, A.; Gijon, J.A.T. Internet traffic analysis: A case study from two major European operators. In Proceedings of the 2014 IEEE Symposium on Computers and Communication (ISCC), Funchal, Portugal, 23–26 June 2014; pp. 1–7.

44. Lewis, R.M.; Torczon, V. Pattern search methods for linearly constrained minimization. *SIAM J. Optim.* **2000**, *10*, 917–941. [CrossRef]

 *electronics*

Article

A Load Balancing Routing Mechanism Based on SDWSN in Smart City

Xin Cui [1,2], Xiaohong Huang [1], Yan Ma [1,*] and Qingke Meng [2]

[1]   Institute of Network Technology, Beijing University of Posts and Telecommunications, Beijing 100876, China; cxsd2007@163.com (X.C.); cxsd@bupt.edu.cn (X.H.)

[2]   College of Computer Science and Technology, Shandong University of Technology, Zibo 255000, China; cx@sdut.edu.cn

*   Correspondence: mayan@bupt.edu.cn

Received: 12 November 2018; Accepted: 15 February 2019; Published: 1 March 2019

Abstract: In the wireless sensor network infrastructure of smart cities, whether the network traffic is balanced will directly affect the service quality of the network. Because of the traditional WSN (wireless sensor network) architecture, load balancing technology is difficult to meet the requirements of adaptability and high flexibility. This paper proposes a load balancing mechanism based on SDWSN (software defined wireless sensor network). This mechanism utilizes the advantages of a centralized control SDN (software defined network) and flexible traffic scheduling. The OpenFlow protocol is used to monitor the running status and link load information of the network in real time. According to the bandwidth requirement of the data flow, the improved load balanced routing is obtained by an Elman neural network. The simulation results show that the improved SDSNLB (software-defined sensor network load balancing) routing algorithm has better performance than LEACH (Low Energy Adaptive Clustering Hierarchy) protocol in balancing node traffic and improving throughput.

Keywords: WSN; SDN; Elman neural network; load balancing

---

1. Introduction

With the rapid development of smart cities, the requirements for the resource allocation mechanism of wireless sensor networks are gradually increasing. In [1], wireless sensor networks are the infrastructure of many fields in smart cities, including automotive electronics, avionics, building automation and industrial automation. In [2], Over the past two decades, various sensing system environments have been designed and deployed in cities, towards the realization of so-called smart cities. Such systems are based on dedicated sensor nodes, as well as ubiquitous but not dedicated devices such as smart phones and vehicle sensors. Due to the dynamic changes of the sensor network structure, network resources (including the remaining energy of the nodes, available bandwidth, etc.) are also constantly changing, and the requirements for the adaptability of routing protocols are proposed. In particular, in wireless sensor networks, the routing protocol is not only the resource allocation of a single node, but also the resource balancing problem of the overall network. In [3], the architecture of a smart city can be divided into four layers, including sensing, networking, cloud computing and applications. In the future, smart cities and smart sensors will be built based on sensor technology, hybrid networks, cloud computing and storage, and big data analysis. By achieving the load balancing of resources, the QoS (quality of service) can be improved and the lifetime of the whole network can be prolonged. Therefore, it is an urgent problem to improve the routing optimization of the communication link, enhance the efficiency of network deployment, and realize network load balance in smart city sensor networks.

The problem of load balancing in WSN has been studied by a large number of scholars for a long time. In order to solve the problem of load imbalance in wireless sensor networks, researchers put forward many solutions. In [4], Based on LEACH, an improved LEACH protocol in WSNs is proposed. The LEACH protocol acts as a low-power adaptive hierarchical routing protocol, randomly selecting cluster heads in a cyclical manner to evenly distribute energy consumption in the network. In WSN, sensor nodes depend on each other when forwarding information packets from a source station to a base station by routing algorithm. Some routes may be better than others, which may result in an unbalanced contention for different routes, as one route may be exhausted more often or faster than others. In [5], they analyze this problem from the perspective of game theory and model the path selection problem in WSN as an evolutionary anti-coordination routing game. In order to prolong network lifetime, candidate forwarders should be selected so that load is balanced among nodes. In [6], they proposed an ORR, an opportunistic routing protocol. In [7], they proposed a simple and effective queue utilization based RPL (QU-RPL) that achieves load balancing and significantly improves the end-to-end packet delivery performance compared to the standard RPL. QU-RPL is designed for each node to select its parent node considering the queue utilization of its neighbor nodes as well as their hop distances to an LLN border router (LBR), owing to its load balancing capability. In [8], a framework is proposed for load balanced routing in WSN. In-network path tagging is used to monitor the network traffic load of nodes. Based on this, nodes are identified as being relatively overloaded, balanced or under loaded. A mitigation algorithm finds suitable new parents for switching from overloaded nodes. The routing engine of the child of the overloaded node is then instructed to switch its parent.

The above dynamic routing data forwarding mainly relies on the local node information, which easily falls into the local optimum, while the global improved routing algorithm is difficult to distribute and is not suitable for large-scale sensor networks.

SDN came into being, control and forwarding separation features provide effective way for WSN routing algorithms. As shown in Figure 1, SDN−based network architecture will be more flexible, and application upgrades will be more simplified.

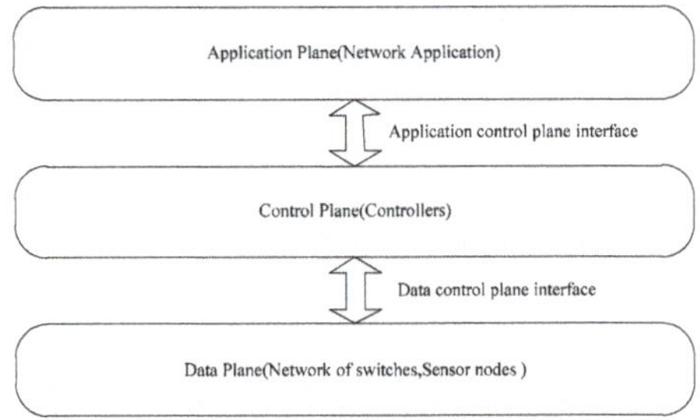

Figure 1. Software defined network (SDN) overall architecture.

This paper discusses the WSN architecture based on SDN. For the multi-path optimized SDWSN load balancing problem, a routing scheme based on an Elman neural network for improved solution is proposed. In order to minimize the maximum link utilization in the network, this paper establishes a mathematical model based on multi-path routing technology while satisfying the quality of service, and the model is simulated and verified. The results show that the load balancing strategy can minimize the maximum link utilization in the network, and fully utilize the network link resources to reduce intra-domain delay and extend network lifetime. This paper summarizes and analyzes the SDN technology, and designs the load balancing model of the data plane and control plane in the SDWSN, which provides a new solution for the load balancing problem. Our major contribution can be summarized as follows:

The algorithm model combines the hierarchical structure of an Elman neural network with the clustering structure of a wireless sensor network routing protocol, and designs an Elman neural network model in each cluster structure. By designing a neural network algorithm model, a little amount of data information reflecting the characteristics of the original data is obtained. The fused feature data is transmitted to the controller node for quickly performing load balancing of the sensor node link.

We analyze and derive the proposed traffic matrix clustering algorithm, which describes the dynamic adaptive adjustment process. The central controller performs a cluster analysis and adjustment according to the flow matrix of each controller, quickly combining the sensor node traffic data to determine the output of the improved path matrix.

In addition, because the fairness of the path selection strategy is very important to load balancing, we use the principle of max-min to measure the uniformity of traffic. The max-min means that when there are multiple routing schemes, the routing scheme with the smallest bandwidth utilization in the network is selected.

The rest of the paper is organized as follows: related work about routing protocol to resolve traffic load is summarized in Section 2. In Section 3, system framework and problem analysis are described. Section 4 formulates the traffic load allocation with end to end multipath, proposes the SDSNLB algorithm, and the improved solution. Section 5 shows the performance evaluation and simulation. In Section 6, a summary conclusion is derived.

2. Related Work

In [9], it is proposed that traditional sensor networks are inflexible due to over-reliance on proprietary services, so data and control separation modes are suitable for wireless sensor networks. They also point out the challenges of this wireless sensor network combined with software-defined networks, as well as the necessary basic design load balancing requirements. In [10], a new mobile network architecture based on OpenFlow to achieve centralized control of energy-aware on demand for load balancing is proposed. In [11], the research results of the software-defined wireless sensor network into actual hardware systems are translated. The OpenFlow switch built a software-defined wireless sensor network platform and runs a traffic-aware routing algorithm on it. The Open DayLight cluster can accurately analyze the data. The flow direction in the network proves that the traffic-aware routing algorithm can improve network utilization and reduce controller response time. Although these new WSN architectures can solve some of the problems of traditional WSN, we should also see that the resource allocation design of software defined wireless sensor networks is not perfect and the research on load balancing needs to be further improved.

In [12], they propose a QoS-based multi-path routing protocol in SDN. In order to meet the QoS requirements of network applications, this protocol designs a multi-path routing protocol based on SDN, which significantly improves the utilization rate of idle resources in the search space. In [13], they present a unified multi-layer architecture with multiple controllers and a dynamic orchestra plane for software defined multi-domain optical networks. In [14], a framework for multi-layer; multi-vendor optical network management using open standards-based SDN is proposed. In [15], a routing algorithm based on SDN technology is proposed, which is used for a routing calculation between AS (Autonomous Systems). The above documents, in the SDWSN network architecture, can solve some unsolved problems of traditional routing protocol, but cannot respond in real time and be dynamic in the aspect of load balancing of traffic.

In [16], a new control system based on the integration of SDN and IoT in smart city environments is proposed. This control system actuates when an emergency happens, modifies dynamically the routes of normal, emergency urban traffic in order to reduce the time that the emergency resources need to get to the emergency area. In [17], a novel routing protocol applied SDN in wireless multi-hop network is proposed. The routing protocol provide a shortest path, disjoint multipath routing for nodes, and its network lifetime is longer. In [18], they highlight the application challenges faced by wireless sensor networks for surveillance environments, those faced by the proposed approaches, as well as opportunities that can be realized on applications of SDWSN. In the SDWSN network architecture, the above literature focuses on the special functions that should not be ignored when trying to improve the network function, however, the load balancing design of the traffic is insufficient.

In summary, the research results of the routing protocols in the classic wireless sensor networks have been quite abundant. The software-defined routing protocols for new network architectures have also achieved preliminary research results. However, the software defined wireless sensor network technology is still immature and needs to be explored and studied in many aspects. It is of great significance to conduct in-depth research on its routing protocols.

3. System Framework and Problem Analysis

We propose a wireless sensor network model based on SDN, as shown in Figure 2. The core idea of this new architecture is to separate the logical control and network forwarding devices in the WSN. The control organization is responsible for abstracting the underlying network device and application logic. It also supports extended deployment through reserved interfaces to achieve flexible control of the entire network. The model adopts a hierarchical network structure, which mainly consists of a data plane, a control plane, and an application plane. The entire network can be divided into multiple sub-areas. Each sub-area may be a particular network formed by the same or different types of terminal sensor nodes. The sensing node is responsible for sensing the collection and forwarding of object information. One or more controllers aggregate, manage, and reconfigure information across multiple network topologies and node behaviors. The data center is mainly responsible for storing and managing the upload information data of each cluster, and providing the terminal application or user with an interface such as a query. The application provides monitoring and other services for different users such as mobile terminals, desktops, and the cloud to provide convenient feedback for each area's information and status.

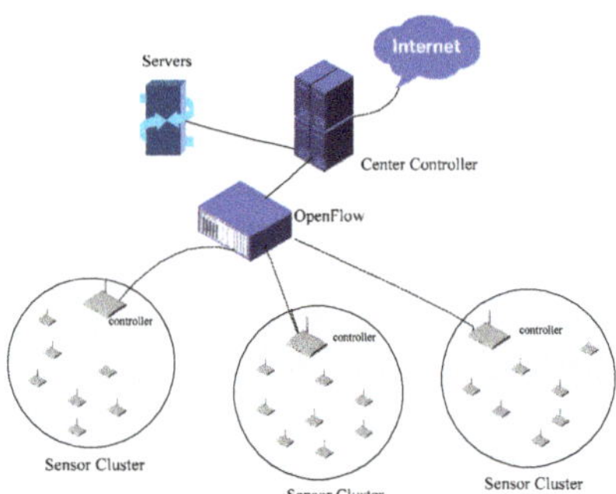

Figure 2. Software defined wireless sensor network architecture.

There are three basic roles in this model, namely the master node, the central node, and the normal node. The master node acts as a controller for the entire network structure. This is the central execution unit of programmable control, which controls the real-time status of the network, such as network topology, routing, and routing restrictions, and implements the management and control functions of the entire network. The center node is similar to the OpenFlow switch in SDN, the network device maintains a Flow Table and processes the data stream only through the Flow Table. The generation, maintenance, and delivery of the Flow Table are completely implemented by an external controller. As shown in Figure 3, it is responsible for the matching and forwarding of data streams in wireless sensor networks. A normal user node is only responsible for receiving and executing data streams.

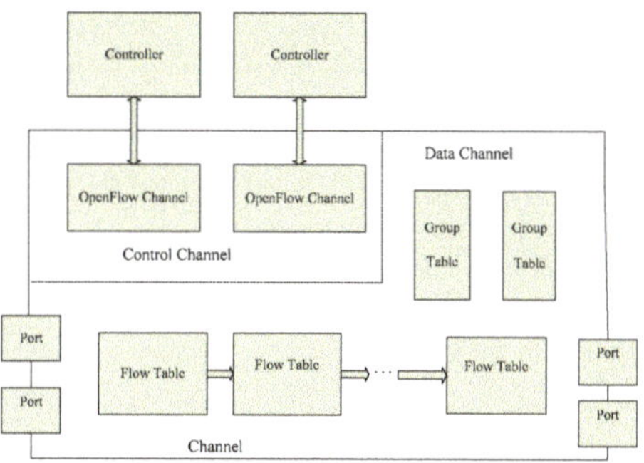

Figure 3. Key components of OpenFlow switches.

A major feature of SDN networks is the separation of the control layer and the data layer. The controller can obtain the topology of the entire network. At the same time, it can obtain real-time network status information from the switch, including link load, delay, etc. We can develop a load-balancing routing strategy for forwarding packets at the control layer.

4. SDSNLB Algorithm and Solution

In SDWSN, data traffic can be assigned to multiple paths to improve network utility. In this part, we propose end-to-end multipath bandwidth allocation as an optimization problem to achieve efficient use of network resources. In a smart city, load balancing is realized by a multipath transmission of information. Therefore, constraining this problem includes two aspects: multiple paths from source to destination and link bandwidth that makes up each path. The parameters used in our model are summarized in Table 1.

Table 1. List of notation.

Parameters	Meaning
V, E	The set of all devices and the set of links between them
$C_{(e)}$	The capacity of link e, e$\in$E
$l_{(e)}$	The load of link e, e$\in$E
$f_e^{(s,t)}$	The traffic of between the nodes s,t by link e
TM	The traffic matrix
$TM_{(s,t)}$	The traffic from the routing node s to node t
$U_{(s,t)}$	The utilization of link e
A	The set of all link utilization
m	The amount of utilization contained in A
$x_{i,j}$	The connection weight between the i-th hidden layer (or input layer) to the j-th output layer (or hidden layer)
β_j	The output value of the jth input layer (or hidden layer)
$\hat{y}_i$	The output value of the i-th output layer
y_i	The expected value of the i-th output layer
K	The number of expected cluster centers
θ_N	The minimum number of samples in each cluster domain
θ_S	The standard deviation of the sample distance distribution in a cluster domain
θ_C	The minimum distance between two cluster centers. If it is less than this number, the two clusters are merged
L	The maximum number of cluster centers that can be merged in one iteration
I	The number of iterations
S_j	The cluster domain of traffic matrix
N_j	The number of traffic matrices in S_j
n	Dimension of sample feature vector

Definition 1. *End-to-end path: A transmission line consisting of a series of store-and-forward nodes, transfer data information from the source to the destination.*

Definition 2. *Available link bandwidth: Assume that an end-to-end path contains n links, $C_{(e)}$ is the initial capacity of link e. The carried traffic is $l_{(e)}$, Define the available link bandwidth is $C_{(e)} - l_{(e)}$. The available link bandwidth reflects the link characteristics actually transmitted.*

Definition 3. *Link Bandwidth Utilization: For $\forall (s,t) \in E$, the bandwidth utilization of the link is $U_{(s,t)} = \frac{l_{(s,t)}}{C_{(s,t)}} \times 100\%$.*

Definition 4. *Average utilization of links: The average utilization of links in the network is the average of the bandwidth utilization of all links, defined as $\overline{U_{(s,t)}} = \frac{\sum_{U_{(s,t)} \in A} U_{(s,t)}}{k}$.*

Because the fairness of the path selection strategy is quite important to load balancing, we derive a load balancing objective function by using the fairness principle of Min-Max. Therefore, the objective function of link load balancing is as follows:

Objective function: minimize $y = \frac{\sum_{U(s,t) \in A} \left(U_{(s,t)} - \overline{U_{(s,t)}} \right)^2}{m}$

Subject to:

$$\sum_{i<j(i,j) \in E} \sum f_{(i,j)}^{(s,t)} - \sum_{k>j(j,k) \in E} f_{(j,k)}^{(s,t)} = \begin{cases} -TM_{(s,t)} j = s \\ TM_{(s,t)} j = t \\ 0 j \neq s,t \end{cases}$$

$$l_{(e)} = \sum_{(s,t) \in v*v} f_e^{(s,t)} \leq C_{(e)} e \in E$$

$$f_e^{(s,t)} \geq 0 e \in E; s,t \in v$$

The Elman neural network, which is a typical dynamic recurrent neural network, which adds a receiving layer to the hidden layer as a one-step delay operator to achieve the purpose of memory, thus enabling it. The system has the ability to adapt to time-varying characteristics and enhances the global stability of the network. It has more computing power than the feed forward neural network, and is very suitable for establishing prediction models for nonlinear data such as network traffic time series. However, the traditional Elman network uses the gradient descent method to train the network parameters, but the gradient descent method has the disadvantages of slow convergence and easily falls into local minimum values. Therefore, we use the cluster and parameter adjustment methods to train network parameters, and achieve the goal of rapid optimization.

During Elman's learning of the sample, the error is distributed among the neurons in each layer. According to the error, the least squares method is used to solve the error.

Then there exists $\sum_{j=1}^{n} x_{ij} \beta_j = y_i (i = 1, 2, 3, \ldots, m)$

$$X = \begin{pmatrix} x_{11} & \cdots & x_{1n} \\ \vdots & \ddots & \vdots \\ x_{m1} & \cdots & x_{mm} \end{pmatrix} \quad \beta = \begin{pmatrix} \beta_1 \\ \beta_2 \\ \vdots \\ \beta_3 \end{pmatrix} \quad y = \begin{pmatrix} y_1 \\ y_2 \\ \vdots \\ y_n \end{pmatrix}$$

Obviously, Equation $X\beta = y$ is generally unsolvable, but $X\beta = \hat{y}$ is known, so the parameters should be modified from the relationship between the predicted and expected values of the Elman neural network.

$$y_i = \hat{\beta}_0 + \hat{\beta}_1 \times \beta_1 + \hat{\beta}_2 \times \beta_2 + \cdots + \hat{\beta}_n \times \beta_n + e_i$$

$$e_i = y_i - \hat{\beta}_0 - \hat{\beta}_1 \times \beta_1 - \hat{\beta}_2 \times \beta_2 - \cdots - \hat{\beta}_n \times \beta_n$$

$$Q = \sum_{i=1}^{n} e^2 = \sum_{i=1}^{n} (y_i - \hat{y}_i)^2 = \sum_{i=1}^{n} (y_i - \hat{\beta}_0 - \hat{\beta}_1 \times \beta_1 - \hat{\beta}_2 \times \beta_2 - \cdots - \hat{\beta}_n \times \beta_n)^2$$

Solving the partial guide of $\hat{\beta}_0$, $\hat{\beta}_1$, $\hat{\beta}_2$, $\cdots$, $\hat{\beta}_n$,

$$\begin{cases} \frac{\partial q}{\partial \hat{\beta}_0} = 2 \times \sum_{i=1}^{n} (y_i - \hat{\beta}_0 - \hat{\beta}_1 \times \beta_1 - \hat{\beta}_2 \times \beta_2 - \cdots - \hat{\beta}_n \times \beta_n) \times (-1) = 0 \\ \frac{\partial q}{\partial \hat{\beta}_1} = 2 \times \sum_{i=1}^{n} (y_i - \hat{\beta}_0 - \hat{\beta}_1 \times \beta_1 - \hat{\beta}_2 \times \beta_2 - \cdots - \hat{\beta}_n \times \beta_n) \times (-\beta_1) = 0 \\ \vdots \\ \frac{\partial q}{\partial \hat{\beta}_n} = 2 \times \sum_{i=1}^{n} (y_i - \hat{\beta}_0 - \hat{\beta}_1 \times \beta_1 - \hat{\beta}_2 \times \beta_2 - \cdots - \hat{\beta}_n \times \beta_n) \times (-\beta_n) = 0 \end{cases}$$

Thus, $\hat{\beta}_0$, $\hat{\beta}_1$, $\hat{\beta}_2$, $\cdots$, $\hat{\beta}_n$ are solved, so

$$x_{ij} = \hat{\beta}_j + \frac{\beta_0}{n \times \beta_i} i = 1, 2, 3, \cdots m; \; j = 1, 2, 3, \cdots n$$

Constantly determines the predicted value and adjusts the parameter, until the difference between the predicted value and the expected value ends within the allowable interval.

4.1. Clustering and Parameter Adjustment

The traditional Elman network uses the gradient descent method to train network parameters, but the gradient descent method has the disadvantages of slow convergence and easy to fall into local minimum values. Therefore, we use clustering and parameter adjustment methods to train network data, and achieve the goal of rapid optimization. And the trained model, that is, the improved routing decision is stored in the SDN controller. When there are new requests, the path can be quickly predicted to achieve SDWSN network load balancing.

Firstly, the training samples are fuzzy clustered, and they are subordinate to each category. These memberships can classify the training samples and construct a neural network classifier. For new unknown samples, it is not necessary to repeatedly calculate the clustering process. The category of the sample can be identified directly by the classifier. The process of clustering is as follows:

1. Enter link matrices $\{TM_i, i = 1, 2, \ldots, N\}$, and select initial cluster centers $\{ TM_i, TM_2, \ldots, TM_{Nc}\}$, it may not be equal to the number of cluster centers required. The initial value can be arbitrarily selected from the sample.

2. The N traffic matrix is assigned to the type S_j, for the non-cluster center traffic matrix TM in the sample.

$$D_i = min\{\|TM - TM_i\|, i = 1, 2, \cdots, N_c\}$$

If $D_j = \|TM - TM_j\|$ is the minimum value, then $TM \in S_j$.

3. If $S_j < \theta_N$, cancel the sample subset, then subtract 1 from N_c.

4. Correcting Cluster Centers

$$Z_j = \frac{1}{N_j} \sum_{TM \in S_j} TM j = 1, 2, \cdots, N_c$$

5. Calculate the average distance between the traffic matrix and cluster centers in each clustering domain S_j

$$\overline{D_j} = \frac{1}{N_j} \sum_{TM \in S_j} \|TM - Z_j\| j = 1, 2, \cdots, N_c$$

6. Calculating the average of the distances between clusters of all link matrices and the corresponding clustering domain.

$$\overline{D} = \frac{1}{N}\sum_{j=1}^{N} TM_j \overline{D_j}$$

7. Splitting, merging and iterative operations

• If the number of iterations has reached I, that is, the last iteration, go to 11.

• If $N_c \le \frac{K}{2}$, that is, the number of cluster centers is less than or equal to half of the initial value, go to 8 and split the existing clustering domain.

• If the number of iterative operations is an even number, or $N_c \ge 2k$, do not split, go to 11; otherwise, go to 8.

8. Calculate the Standard Deviation Vector of Sample Distance in Each Cluster.

$$S_j = (S_{1j}, S_{2j}, \cdots, S_{nj})^T$$

The components of the vector are $S_{ij} = \sqrt{\frac{1}{N_j}\sum_{k=1}^{N_j} (TM_{ik} - Z_{ij})^2}$ i $= 1, 2, \ldots, n; j = 1, 2, \ldots, N_c$.

9. Find the maximum component of each standard deviation vector $\{\delta_{j\max}, j == 1, 2, \cdots, N_c\}$,

10. In any maximum component set $\{S_{j\max}, j == 1, 2, \cdots, N_c\}$, if $S_{j\max} > \theta_S$, and satisfies one of the following two conditions:

• $\overline{D_j} > \overline{D}$, and $N_j > 2(\theta_N + 1)$

• $N_c \le \frac{K}{2}$ Then Z_j is split into two new cluster centers, and N_c plus 1.

11. Calculate the distance of all cluster centers

$$D_{ij} = \|Z_i - Z_j\| i = 1, 2, \cdots N_c - 1; j = i + 1, \cdots, N_c$$

12. Compare the values of D_{ij} and θ_c, The value of $D_{ij} < \theta_c$ is arranged incrementally by the minimum distance.

13. Merge two cluster centers Z_{ik} and Z_{jk} with distance D_{ikjk} to get the new center.

$$Z_K^* = \frac{1}{N_{ik} + N_{jk}}\left[N_{ik}Z_{ik} + N_{jk}Z_{jk}\right] k = 1, 2, \cdots, L$$

14. If the last iterative operation (the L-th time), the algorithm ends.

4.2. Adjustment of Link Matrices

Through multiple Elman networks, the input of the link traffic Y, the output of the traffic matrix $\hat{X}$ does not necessarily satisfy the constraint of $Y = A \times \hat{X}$. Therefore, some adjustments must be made to $\hat{X}$ to obtain $\hat{X}_0$.

Definition 5. *K-L distance: Let the random variable x be in the two probability distributions $P_{(x)}$ and $q_{(x)}$. The K-L distance is defined as:*

$$I_{(Q\|P)} = \sum_{i=1}^{n} P_{(x)} \times \log \frac{P_{(x)}}{q_{(x)}}$$

where i represents the i − th value of x and p, q is the probability density function.

Definition 6. *I-Projection: Given a joint probability distribution set $Q_{(x)}$ and $P_{(x)}$, if $Q_{(x)} \in Q$, and satisfy*

$$I_{(Q\|P)} = I_{(Q\|P)}$$

$Q_{(x)}$ is I-Projection of $P_{(x)}$. For a joint probability distribution set, if the constraint condition $p_{(Y)}$ is satisfied, I-Projection of $p_{(Y)}$ on $R_{(Y)}$ as follows:

$$
Q_{(x)} = \begin{cases} 0 & P_{(Y)} = 0 \\ P_{(x)} \times \frac{R_{(Y)}}{P_{(Y)}} & P_{(Y)} \neq 0 \end{cases}
$$

By iterating the constraints, the probability of all elements is estimated by minimizing the $K-L$ distance. Through iterative calculations, adjustments are made while the constraints are met, so that the final result satisfies the maximum likelihood estimate.

4.3. Parameter Adjustment

The link traffic changes of the input layer of multiple Elman networks are random, and the parameters of multiple different Elman networks need to be adjusted. It is assumed that the validity periods T of a plurality of different Elmans are the same. When $t < T$, the flow matrix components for a short period of time when $t_1 - t_2 = \Delta t \rightarrow T$ is selected are input for re-clustering, prediction, and comparison with the current clustering result. The grouping of changes in classification indicates that the current multi-Elman network is not applicable and needs to be adjusted, otherwise no adjustments.

5. Performance Evaluation

In this paper, the SDSNLB algorithm was simulated and tested by Matlab. In the simulation test, the wireless sensor network model consists of one center controller and three controllers, each controller is connected to control 10 sensors. In the subsequent tests, the number of sensor nodes was increased from 10 to 26, and the messages in the topology were fed back. The controller was operating normally and was able to process and process each message. In practical applications, the node layout is more dispersed, the number of hops from the node to the controller is different, and the message that the node interacts with the controller is concentrated at the same time is extremely unlikely, so the controller can efficiently process the incoming message.

In order to better demonstrate the effectiveness of the improved algorithm, the SDSNLB algorithm, the LEACH and improved LEACH protocol algorithm were compared and simulated. The LEACH protocol is a classic clustering-based routing protocol proposed in the WSN. Despite the shortcomings, studying the basic clustering protocol LEACH can help to better understand other clustering protocols. In addition, the hierarchical organization of the LEACH protocol is suitable for the dynamic distribution of resources. The cluster head node in the cluster can be regarded as a controller, and the cluster member node can be regarded as a node user, thereby better performing simulation. The improved LEACH algorithm is designed to extend network lifetime and improve efficient data transmission through balanced elections. The main analysis and comparison of the three algorithms on the network node link bandwidth utilization, network throughput, and network jitter.

Figure 4 shows the experimental results of the data flow under three different algorithms. As can be seen from the figure, when the conventional LEACH protocol algorithm is used, in a period of 0 to 10 s, the data flow in the network is relatively simple. Therefore, the effective throughput of the data stream is close to the uplink rate. And after 10 s, as the data traffic increases, the effective throughput of the data stream is significantly reduced. For the improved LEACH algorithm, the effective throughput of the data stream is close to the uplink rate from 0 to 20 s, and after 20 s, the effective throughput decreases. When using the SDSNLB algorithm, the effective throughput of the data stream approaches the uplink rate in 0 to 100 s.

In Figure 5, it can be seen that when there are multiple data streams in the network, the load balancing algorithm proposed in this paper can reasonably schedule the data flow according to the load of the actual gateway egress node, and the final traffic does not exceed the uplink rate of the link. The average bandwidth utilization is maintained at around 1.

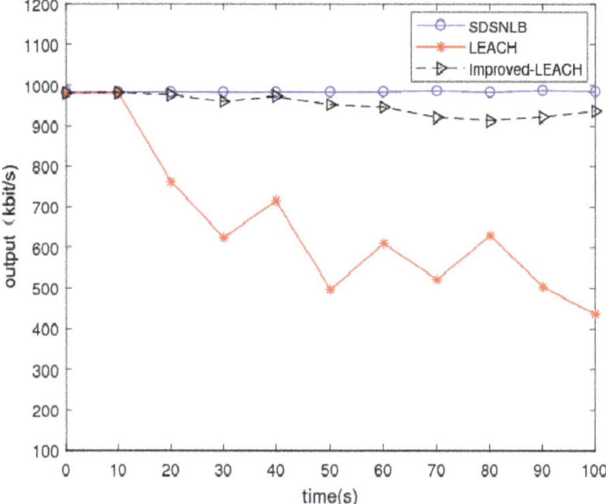

Figure 4. Data flow effective throughput.

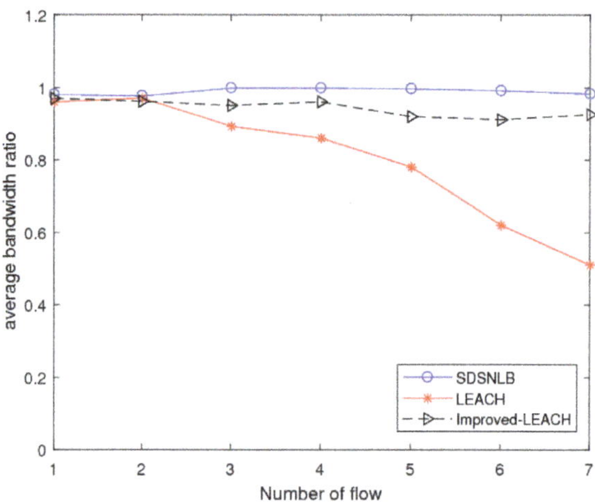

Figure 5. Average bandwidth utilization varies with the number of streams.

Figure 6 shows the performance of the link load jitter. When running LEACH protocol, the link load jitter is the highest. Compared with LEACH protocol, the standard deviation of link load in improved LEACH is smaller, but the link load jitter is still obvious. When the load balancing algorithm SDSNLB is running, the load standard deviation of all links in the network is minimum, the traffic load is more evenly distributed in the network link. Due to the load balancing algorithm proposed in this paper, it is possible to perform reasonable scheduling in real time according to the current distribution of traffic load in the network, so as to avoid premature traffic overload of individual transmission links in the network, thereby improving network performance.

From the above experimental results and analysis, the load balancing mechanism proposed in this paper can be verified. Comprehensive calculations were performed by an Elman neural network using software-defined features. The clustered feature data is transmitted to the controller node for fast load balancing of the sensor link, which can improve the average bandwidth utilization of the network and reduce the link load jitter of the network, thereby improving the overall performance of the network.

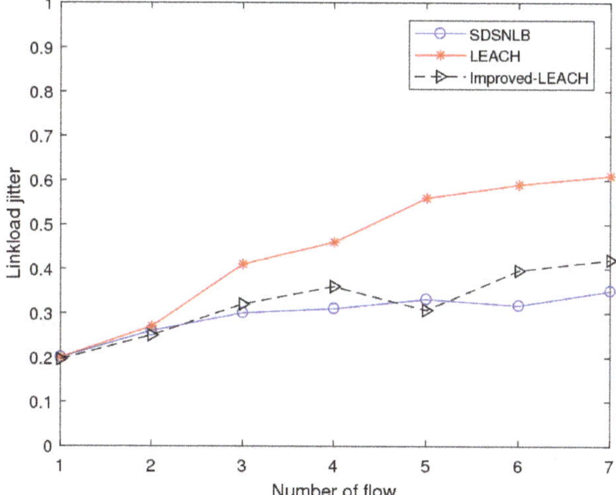

Figure 6. Link load jitter varies with the number of data streams.

6. Conclusions

The existence of a diversity set of paths for sensor nodes in SDWSN raises many technical issues related to data routing, where some routes become preferable for the nodes and lead to an imbalance. In order to improve the route optimization of the communication link and realize the load balancing of the network in the smart city sensor network, based on the characteristics of SDN centralized control and flexible traffic scheduling, the Elman neural network is used for the optimization calculation and the improved load balancing forwarding path is obtained. The simulation results show that the load balancing algorithm proposed in this paper can improve the average bandwidth utilization and reduce the link load jitter of the network, thus improving the performance of the entire network. It can also provide programmable data flow control method for software-defined sensor networks. The research in this paper has practical guidance and application significance for the smart city wireless infrastructure node link load balancing optimization problem.

Author Contributions: For this articles, individual contributions are as follows, conceptualization, X.H. and X.C.; methodology, X.C.; software, Q.M.; resources, Y.M.; writing—original draft preparation, X.C.; writing—review and editing, X.H., Y.M. and X.C.; funding acquisition, X.H. and X.C.

Funding: This research was funded by "Ministry of Education China Mobile Research Fund Project, grant number MCM20160304" and "National College Student Innovation Training Project, grant number 201810433023".

Conflicts of Interest: The authors declare no conflict of interest.

References

1. Park, P.; Ergen, S.C.; Fischione, C.; Lu, C.; Johansson, K.H. Wireless Network Design for Control Systems: A Survey. *IEEE Commun. Surv. Tutor.* **2018**, *20*, 978–1013. [CrossRef]
2. Du, R.; Santi, P.; Xiao, M.; Vasilakos, A.V.; Fischione, C. The sensable city: A survey on the deployment and management for smart city monitoring. *IEEE Commun. Surv. Tutor.* **2018**. [CrossRef]
3. Qiu, T.; Chen, N.; Li, K.; Atiquzzaman, M.; Zhao, W. How Can Heterogeneous Internet of Things Build Our Future: A Survey. *IEEE Commun. Surv. Tutor.* **2018**, *20*, 2011–2017. [CrossRef]
4. Ying, Z.; Peisong, L.; Lin, M. Research on Improved Low-Energy Adaptive Clustering Hierarchy Protocol in Wireless Sensor Networks. *Shanghai Jiao Tong Univ. Sci.* **2018**, *23*, 613–619.
5. Attiah, A.; Amjad, M.F.; Chatterjee, M.; Zou, C. An evolutionary routing game for energy balance in Wireless Sensor Networks. *Comput. Netw.* **2018**, *138*, 31–43. [CrossRef]

6. So, J.; Byun, H. Load-Balanced Opportunistic Routing for Duty-Cycled Wireless Sensor Networks. *IEEE Trans. Mob. Comput.* **2017**, *16*, 1940–1955. [CrossRef]
7. Kim, H.S.; Kim, H.; Paek, J.; Bahk, S. Load Balancing under Heavy Traffic in RPL Routing Protocol for Low Power and Lossy Networks. *IEEE Trans. Mob. Comput.* **2017**, *16*, 964–979. [CrossRef]
8. Kamal, A.R.M.; Hamid, A. Supervisory routing control for dynamic load balancing in low data rate wireless sensor networks. *Wirel. Netw.* **2017**, *23*, 1085–1099. [CrossRef]
9. Kobo, H.I.; Abu-Mahfouz, A.M.; Hancke, G.P. A Survey on Software-Defined Wireless Sensor Networks: Challenges and Design Requirements. *IEEE Access* **2017**, *5*, 186–197. [CrossRef]
10. Donato, C.; Serrano, P.; De La Oliva, A.; Banchs, A.; Bernardos, C.J. An openflow architecture for energy-aware traffic engineering in mobile networks. *Netw. IEEE* **2015**, *29*, 54–60. [CrossRef]
11. Ariman, M.; Secinti, G.; Erel, M.; Canberk, B. Software defined wireless network testbed using Raspberry Pi of switches with routing add-on. In Proceedings of the 2015 IEEE Conference on Network Function Virtualization and Software Defined Network (NFV-SDN), San Francisco, CA, USA, 18–21 November 2015.
12. Chemeritskiy, E.; Smeliansky, R. On QoS Management in SDN by Multipath Routing. In Proceedings of the 2014 International Science and Technology Conference (Modern Networking Technologies) (MoNeTeC), Moscow, Russia, 28–29 October 2014.
13. Yang, H.; Cui, Y.; Zhang, J. Unified Multi-Layer among Software Defined Multi-Domain Optical Networks. *Electronics* **2015**, *4*, 329–338. [CrossRef]
14. Cusatis, D. Reference Architecture for Multi-Layer Software Defined Optical Data Center Networks. *Electronics* **2015**, *4*, 633–650. [CrossRef]
15. Huang, L.; Zhang, Y. Research on Application of ONF OpenFlow-Based SDN Typical Architecture. *Appl. Mech. Mater.* **2014**, *543*, 3692–3695. [CrossRef]
16. Rego, A.; Garcia, L.; Sendra, S.; Lloret, J. Software Defined Network-based control system for an efficient traffic management for emergency situations in smart cities. *Future Gener. Comput. Syst.* **2018**, *88*, 243–253. [CrossRef]
17. Wang, J.; Miao, Y.; Zhou, P.; Hossain, M.S.; Rahman, S.M.M. A software defined network routing in wireless multihop network. *J. Netw. Comput. Appl.* **2017**, *85*, 76–83. [CrossRef]
18. Modieginyane, K.M.; Letswamotse, B.B.; Malekian, R.; Abu-Mahfouz, A.M. Software defined wireless sensor networks application opportunities for efficient network management: A survey. *Comput. Electr. Eng.* **2018**, *66*, 274–287. [CrossRef]

MDPI

St. Alban-Anlage 66

4052 Basel

Switzerland

Tel. +41 61 683 77 34

Fax +41 61 302 89 18

www.mdpi.com

Electronics Editorial Office

E-mail: electronics@mdpi.com

www.mdpi.com/journal/electronics